"An intriguing inter-disciplinary and cross-cultural exploration that seeks to develop a public, socially embodied, theology of God's Word drawing on both Western and East Asian traditions."

—Lois Malcolm
Associate Professor of Systematic Theology, Luther Seminary

"I enjoyed this book, especially the survey of recent major thinkers as they bear on the question of encounter between religious traditions."

—Andrew P. Porter
Graduate Theological Union, Berkeley

"Chung's book is at once an epistemological-hermeneutical essay and an essay on the reality of God as physically and socially embodied, with a *Theologia Crucis* at its center. It offers a creative alternative to 'christo-monism,' which undermines the Jewish identity of Jesus and conceals the identity of the God of Jesus Christ, not only as the God to whom Judaism, Christianity, and Islam bear witness, but also as the God to whom 'irregular' witnesses may be found in East Asian religions, and even in non- and anti-religious traditions."

—David J. Lull
Professor of New Testament, Wartburg Theological Seminary

"Paul Chung stands at the crossroads of East and West as a unique and provocative interpreter of philosophical and theological traditions for the sake of reconciliation in a world of difference. *The Cave and the Butterfly* brings wide-ranging philosophical knowledge to important questions of social and political engagement in a globalized world."

—Dwight Zscheile
Assistant Professor of Congregational Mission and Leadership,
Luther Seminary

The Cave and the Butterfly

The Cave and the Butterfly

*An Intercultural Theory of Interpretation
and Religion in the Public Sphere*

Paul S. Chung

CASCADE *Books* • Eugene, Oregon

THE CAVE AND THE BUTTERFLY
An Intercultural Theory of Interpretation and Religion in the Public Sphere

Copyright © 2011 Paul S. Chung. All rights reserved. Except for brief quotations in critical publications or reviews, no part of this book may be reproduced in any manner without prior written permission from the publisher. Write: Permissions, Wipf and Stock Publishers, 199 W. 8th Ave., Suite 3, Eugene, OR 97401.

Cascade Books
An Imprint of Wipf and Stock Publishers
199 W. 8th Ave., Suite 3
Eugene, OR 97401

www.wipfandstock.com

ISBN 13: 978-1-60608-530-1

Cataloging-in-Publication data:

Chung, Paul S., 1958–

The cave and the butterfly : an intercultural theory of interpretation and religion in the public sphere / Paul S. Chung.

xx + 298 p. ; cm. 23. — Includes bibliographical references and index.

ISBN 13: 978-1-60608-530-1

1. Hermeneutics — Religious aspects — Christianity. 2. Religious pluralism — Christianity. 3. Christianity and other religions. I. Title.

BL410 .C49 2011

Manufactured in the U.S.A.

Contents

Acknowledgments / ix

Introduction: Engaging Cave and Butterfly / xi

1. Cave of Soul and Mimetic Creativity / 1
2. Cave of Soul and Embodiment in the Christian Tradition / 15
3. Christian Theology and the Public Sphere / 21
4. *Theologia Crucis* and a Socially Embodied Life / 48
5. The Iron Cage and Emancipation of the Lifeworld / 67
6. A Postmodern View of Power and Knowledge in Interplay / 103
7. The History of Effect and the Conflict of Interpretation / 133
8. A Postmodern Ethics of the Other and the Hermeneutics of Saying / 183
9. Interpretation of Scripture and Analogical Hermeneutics / 212
10. Christian Mission and the Interpretation of the Gospel in the Presence of the Other / 238

EXCURSUS: Wang Yangming and the Investigation of Things in an Ontological Context / 266

Conclusion: Odyssey, Abraham, and Laozi / 275

Bibliography / 287

Index / 295

Acknowledgments

ABRAHAM HESCHEL CONTENDS THAT human life is characterized by existence on the way—striving, waiting, and hoping in a quest for the truth. This idea finds application here in an intellectual journey that investigates tension between the Enlightenment concept of Western civilization (using the Platonic-Christian analogy of a cave) and East Asian philosophy (using the dream metaphor of the butterfly).

In examining an interdisciplinary reframing of religion and an interpretive theory in reference to the public sphere, it becomes important to discuss the Western form of rationality in view of the art of interpretation through the eyes of the Other. A cross-cultural project involving such topics follows my own intellectual trajectory, which is connected to the context of my life.

During my studies of Theology, Social Critical Theory, Postmodern Theory, and Philosophical Hermeneutics, I was privileged to learn and to deepen my interest areas under the guidance of excellent teachers in South Korea, Europe, and the U.S. I remain grateful for their instruction and pedagogy. In terms of academic teaching, my intellectual development owes a great debt of gratitude to colleagues and students at Luther Seminary, Minneapolis.

My exploration of the Theology of Embodiment, of a dialectic of the Enlightenment, and of post-foundational hermeneutics is an attempt to construct a theological-philosophical hermeneutic of God's speaking-in-action within a cross-cultural and religious context, paying attention to postmodern genealogy and to an Ethics of the Other. Interpretation is an endless task, constantly returning to the root and source to the extent that the subject matter of divine speech transcends human mimetic imagination—imagination that understands God as the *topos* of the world. In revisiting the root (*radix*) of the text and in contextualizing and reinterpreting it within the social location of human life, any interpretive theory is of a radical character and horizon.

Acknowledgments

The conviction that equates *different* understanding with *better* understanding belongs to a hermeneutic of the Other that one sees attempted and explored in the interdisciplinary investigation of religion, the public sphere, and human discourse. Insofar as interpretive conflict belongs to the primordial human constitution, I do not intend to conclude my study in a systematic way. Rather, I will leave the conclusion open by way of narrating three different figures of importance for our shared global civilization: Odysseus, Abraham, and Laozi. I extend my special thanks to colleagues and friends who encourage my faith journey by accompanying this text with their excellent blurbs. The Bible quotations and references are based on New Revised Standard Version.

Easter 2010
St. Paul, Minneapolis

Introduction

Engaging Cave and Butterfly

It will be helpful to begin this interdisciplinary and cross-cultural journey with Plato's analogy of the cave and with Zhuangzi's story about the butterfly dream. Plato, a pupil of Socrates, uses the analogy of a cave to illustrate his well-known and powerful image of the human condition in his book *Republic*.[1] He likens the ordinary human to a prisoner in a cave, forced to gaze at shadows. The human being strives to see the light that brings illumination to the truth. According to Plato, there is a spiritual movement, which turns away from the shadows of the cave toward the light of the illuminating sun. This story venerates the human soul with its journey toward the sun and devalues the human body. This articulates an understanding of the truth through the idea of the soul's immortality without connection to the socially embodied life.

Around Plato's time, there lived a philosopher in China called Zhuangzi. He was a pupil of Laozi. Zhuangzi spoke of his dream about a butterfly:

> I once dreamed that I was a butterfly, fluttering here and there. I was so pleased that I forgot that I was Zhuangzi. When I suddenly woke up, I was astonished to find that I was, as a matter of fact, Zhuangzi. Did Zhuangzi dream of the butterfly or did the butterfly dream of Zhuangzi? Between Zhuangzi and the butterfly there must be some distinctions. This is called the transformation of things.[2]

Zhuangzi advocates for human life to return to the nature in which transformation of things can occur. By his account, human rationality is

---

1. Plato *Republic* 514a–519a.
2. *Zhuangzi* I, 39–41.

not sufficient to understand the truth that comes to us as the "transformation of things."

These cave and butterfly metaphors echo throughout my intercultural study of religion, interpretive theory, sociological configuration of the public sphere, and Christian and philosophical hermeneutics. *Dialectic of Enlightenment* (Horkheimer and Adorno), which might be traced back to Plato, finds its place in a sociological analysis of Western civilization in the process of disenchantment with the world. Postmodern discussion of human rationality and discourse in terms of the interplay between power and knowledge challenges such a dialectical understanding of Western civilization. Taking issue with the Enlightenment dialectic, the postmodern desire to transcend takes on a radical form in Foucault's resistance in the name of the Other, or in Levinas' project of Infinity and ethics in the face of the Other.

In the East Asian context, the concept of enlightenment (from a philosophical Daoist perspective) does not dissolve into sameness or immanence. A dialectic of enlightenment in this context neither invades nor violates "God" as freedom and transcendence of Dao or Heaven. The Western idea of civilization as a grand narrative coupled with universal totalization meets resistance when it encounters East Asian logic, which presupposes mutual co-existence of human life and nature. This East Asian logic implies a life of Dao that recognizes the unworthy, the deviant, and the feminine.

Cross-cultural investigations of interpretation and the public sphere (in contrast with Girard[3]) do not necessarily censure mimetic desire, since desire belongs indispensably to human life. Mimetic desire within the field of social philosophy finds its classical formulation in view of the struggle for recognition between master and slave in Hegel's *Phenomenology of Mind*.[4] According to Hegel, a dialectic of desire and fulfillment at a social level becomes an important factor in the development of human society, moving toward freedom and emancipation. At the literary level, Auerbach also contributes to a deciphering of social reality in Western literature through mimetic desire.[5]

The central issue in this book is the interdisciplinary exploration of religion, hermeneutics, social public relation, and an ethical theory of

3. Girard, *Things Hidden*.
4. Kojève, *Introduction*.
5. Auerbach, *Mimesis*.

the Other in relation to intercultural fertilization and enrichment. The Latin term "*relegare*" means "to assemble" and has to do with transmitting worship or with the cultic veneration of the gods. "*Religare*" means "to bind together" in reference to a set of doctrines and practices that form and constitute a human's relationship with the divine. According to Augustine, the knowledge of God and the worship of God are inseparably connected in religion.[6]

How one defines religion depends upon a person's beliefs, perspectives and academic disciplines. The term *Homo religious* implies that all societies have order and belief systems that justify transcendental signs, gestures and orientations, although all social orders and cultures do not necessarily imply belief in a supernatural reality. At an existential level, religion involves something unconditional and serious—something for which a person is ready to risk his/her life.

The word *theologia* first appears in Plato,[7] *tupoi peri theologias*, which means "viewpoints concerning the representation of the divine." *Theologia* is for Plato the true goal and the heart of philosophical and theological thinking. For Aristotle, theology is the *prima philosophia*—the knowledge of the highest principles, which implies the heart of goal of metaphysics.

Here Aristotle mentions theology as the question about God—the question about the ultimate, all-determining reality.[8] Aristotle defines philosophy as the science of truth (*episteme tis tes aletheias*) which simultaneously characterizes the science of being, namely with regard to their Being. If truth has a primordial connection with being, Heidegger argues that the phenomenon of truth moves into the scope of fundamental ontology.[9] When one views and discusses the problem of God in terms of truth and being in an ontological-hermeneutical sense, an existential understanding of being-in-the-world replaces the priority and the freedom of God through human interpretation.

On the other hand, the definition of theology, in the Greek metaphysical sense, transposes and transforms into Christian thinking and into discourse about God, humanity, the church and the world. Christian theology is a form of bearing witness to the mystery, grace, and presence

---

6. Pannenberg, *Systematic Theology* 1, 121.
7. *Republic* II, 379, a 5.
8. Gollwitzer, *Introduction*, 17.
9. Heidegger, *Being and Time*, 197.

of God as attested to in the Bible and mediated through ecclesial tradition and confessional language. The reality of God's mystery transcends human witness. Therefore, the human witness, when it comes to the subject matter of divine reality, must be questioned and interpreted anew in different places and times. In this task, the search for a new interpretive model constitutes an effort to understand, actualize, and deepen the word of God in an ever-changing context. This interpretive strategy moves beyond every kind of dogmatism, and moves the ecclesial community to be more relevant for and accountable to non-Christian communities in the public sphere.

At this juncture, a theological deliberation on God's Word in mystery, love, and freedom can be juxtaposed with an attitude of *homo religious* in pursuit of Ultimate Reality. A theology exploring God's Word analogically correlates with the religious interpretation of the truth of supernatural reality to the degree that God comes to us as the Word of Truth rather than being captive to human epistemological and scientific method.

In the theological realm, John's Prolog articulates physical embodiment: The Word became flesh. Without Philip's interpretation of this embodied Word, the Ethiopian eunuch would not be capable of accepting it for his life (Acts 8:26). Interpretation, as an important dimension of the Christian gospel (*kerygma*), connects with the embodied Word, which became one of us. Mimetic creativity in interpretation of the Word of God takes shape in the public sphere, acculturating a bodily dimension of the Christian gospel and projecting its resistance to the reality of "lordless powers" (Karl Barth).

Biblical insight into public relevance comes from the statement that God reconciles the world in Christ. In light of God's reconciliation, the Christian church is primed and called to undertake discipleship in conformity with the gospel of Jesus Christ. The gospel becomes reality in the embrace of those whom Christ names as his brothers and sisters: the stranger, the hungry, the thirsty, the naked, the sick, and the captive—in short, the lowest of the low (Matt 25:35–45), God's *massa perditionis*.

In an era marked by the clash of civilizations, a theology of public engagement immerses itself into the socio-political and religious-cultural spheres in order to become more ethically and inter-religiously responsible.[10] A theology of the public sphere creates a new way of in-

10. Huntington, *Clash of Civilizations*.

terpretation by engaging with social critical theory, with postmodern philosophy, and with hermeneutics. It takes a stand for the lives of those who find themselves marginalized and deviated—the *massa perditionis*, God's minority people.

Against Heidegger, who criticized the "public-ness" in which the masses uphold the status quo of domination,[11] I argue that the authenticity of human life must be founded in the real life world of the public sphere. For a theology of public-ness in association with the *massa perditionis*, I will not hesitate to adopt an interpretation that engages with God's act of speaking through the face of the Other in the public realm, as well as one that draws on the wisdom of non-Christian religions. In this project, a post-foundational and analogical standpoint implies a philosophical-theological way of thinking that steers between the totalizing universalism of modernity and the nihilistic-deconstructive relativism of postmodernity. The term post-foundational is hermeneutically relevant to a socio-cultural and linguistic episteme in reference to God's "irregular" speech event. Moreover, the irregular side of the divine speech act does not necessarily contradict the regular side of God's Word in the form of physicality and incarnation.

A speech-act hermeneutic from a post-foundational, analogical, and ethical perspective (such as this book explores) tours through an analysis of a Western Enlightenment dialectic on a sociological-postmodern level, ending up at Levinas's hermeneutic of the Saying over and against the Said. This book will undertake an interdisciplinary investigation of the relationship between a theology of God's Saying and a hermeneutic of the Other in an intercultural study of interpretation theory in the East Asian context.

At a sociological level there are significant efforts to salvage "colonized lifeworld" (*Lebenswelt*, or life as lived prior to interpretation) from the political, economic system. Additionally, a genealogical project of freedom and emancipation in a non-fascist fashion (Foucault) finds its voice in a sociological, hermeneutical, and postmodern field. In this light, an interdisciplinary discussion from a post-foundational perspective must explore the incomplete project of modernity in reference to the postmodern ethical passion for the marginalized, the deviated, and the Other.

11. Heidegger, *Being and Time*, 119.

To speak or to interpret is one thing; to do is quite another. Nonetheless, the doing depends on one's definition and interpretation of reality in the sociological setting. Mediating interpretation with praxis calls for deliberately analyzing the public sphere of human life where human speech and act intersect. Gadamer contends that the conception of knowledge and of truth corresponds to the whole of a hermeneutical experience. Insofar as truth comes to speech in our investigation of the object of knowledge, it goes beyond a methodological, scientific self-consciousness.

In the philosophical tradition, Husserl's phenomenology begins its return to the thing itself by challenging scientific mathematization of the world, whereby the world becomes a kind of technology. Phenomenology implies a rehabilitation of the lifeworld, which has been positivistically and empirically grounded and idealized. Along this line, Heidegger and Gadamer represent a philosophical hermeneutic that takes issue with the methodical spirit of science—a spirit that underlines the growing rationalization of society and scientific techniques in its administration.

Gadamer proposes a hermeneutical, ontological alternative to what sociological analysis views as a reality of an iron cage. Interpretation, as seen in light of a history of effect, inheres in human life in the public sphere because of the use of language in daily communication. Being historical implies that one's knowledge can never be complete.[12] A fusion of the horizon between the past and the present within human life is dialectically structured and dynamically oriented in openness toward the future. The dynamism of this fusion of horizon challenges narrowness in any given society and pushes for expansion of new horizons. All the while, this happens in conversation with tradition and in engagement with others in the world.

The public sphere, the sociological setting in which we live, is not fixed; rather it is malleable and in flux. Kant's newspaper article "What is Enlightenment?" stands as a classic example of critique of the public sphere. The Enlightenment legacy of critique holds validity in terms of judging and developing the public issue. A dialectic of Enlightenment (as promised by the project of modernity), however, stands under the suspicion of postmodern theory, which calls for recognition of and respect for the Other. The openness to dissonance, ambiguity, and recognition of the different must be articulated and integrated into a cross-cultural

---

12. Gadamer, *Truth and Method*, 302.

investigation of religion, interpretation, and the public sphere. Such an approach intends to coordinate interpretive action with emancipating praxis in a way that is both responsible and ethical.

The system of global empire, which expands international politics and the global economy through the extension of capital, informative knowledge of mass media, and political power, has saturated the infrastructure of the lifeworld—shaping and generating social, cultural, and religious life according to the image of global capital. In the process of colonizing the lifeworld, we are aware of crisis, disorder and the loss of meaning, as well as of the dynamics of protest and the utopian desire for a better life.

Habermas proposes a communicative theory of the public sphere set against the colonization of the lifeworld, which is taking place within the global empirical system. The communicative praxis of the lifeworld offers insight for a new contour of deliberate democracy. Thus, the communicative interest in emancipation advocates for the process of social modernization to turn in other non-capitalist directions. If an emancipation project is to change the structures that oppress and alienate human life, a hermeneutic allied with an interest in emancipation must be discussed in presence with the Other. Thus, a public theory in light of the interpretation that this book undertakes takes on four basic contours.

1. Construction of an embodied theology will be undertaken in critical conversation with the theology of the soul in the Platonic and Augustinian traditions. A reflection on bodily resurrection takes priority over the contemplation of the soul's immortality. Thus, a necessity for grounding theology within a socially embodies sphere is of special significance to our discussion. In this light, Christian spirituality, *theologia crucis*, and God's transcendence will be discussed in reference to the public dimension of human life. Foucault once argued that a critique of governmentalization began with Luther's interpretation of Scripture.

A positive side of critique associated with the Enlightenment is connected with Luther's critique of economic injustice. Given this fact, it is crucial to explore the Reformer's combination of theology and economy as an example for promoting a social material dimension of Christian theology against "the ideological weapon of death."[13] Furthermore, a theology of God's Saying that retains an "irregular" character will be dis-

---

13. Hinkelammert, *Ideological Weapons*.

cussed in the context of embodiment and inculturation (from chapters 1 through 4).

2. In addition to the Platonic cave imagery, Max Weber diagnosed Western civilization as instrumentalized, finally leading to an iron cage through the process of disenchantment with the world. Weber's study of Protestantism and the ethos of Capitalism proposed that there is a selective affinity between Protestant Christianity and the Western development of human rationality in an instrumentalized sense. Weber's legacy is critically appreciated, integrated, and enhanced in the theory of reification (Lukacs) and by the representatives of social critical theory of the Frankfurt school (Horkheimer, Adorno, and Habermas). This sociological debate about a dialectic of Enlightenment also finds its place in the postmodern, genealogical strategy of the power–knowledge interplay (Foucault).

Given the sociological, postmodern debate of the iron cage and the emancipation of the lifeworld, theological engagement with the public sphere must examine and analyze the project of emancipation of human rationality from the colonized lifeworld for the sake of Christian theology's relevance to political, economic, and cultural issues in society. When the Christian church engages in the public sphere and articulates its message and religious discourse opting for life against death, it is an indispensable task for Christian theology to learn from the sociological–postmodern theory of the public sphere and to integrate it into its framework (chapter 5 and 6).

3. A conversation with hermeneutical theory helps to construct a theology of God's speech act, of the history of effect, and of the importance of social location. The dispute surrounding language and ideology between Gadamer and Habermas offers an important insight for reframing hermeneutical theory to be more relevant to the social public sphere through a hermeneutic of suspicion (Paul Ricoeur). The conflict of interpretation is such that the art of interpretation becomes more pluralistic and interdisciplinary in its search for meaning and critique. A hermeneutic of suspicion can assume an ethical configuration, as seen in light of a hermeneutic of Saying through the face of the Other (Levinas). Given the hermeneutical debate and its significance for the religious public sphere, it is instructive to discuss the hermeneutical dimensions of Rudolf Bultmann and Karl Barth in view of Gerhard Ebeling's Word-

event theology, David Tracy's analogical imagination, and the post-liberal theology of George Lindbeck (chapters 7–9).

4. The metaphors of "cave" and "iron cage" might be associated with the logic of exclusion, which has been visible in the Holocaust, in other genocides, and in various religious conflicts around the globe. In view of the Western form of rationality, a cross-cultural exploration of the dialectic of enlightenment from an East Asian perspective is a necessary project for the promotion of intercultural exchange and peace in an increasingly global civilization. In the cross–cultural configuration, one sees in the wisdom of the butterfly (or the freedom from self-confinement) an appreciation for and integration into a discussion of inter-religious encounter, inculturation, and interpretation. One can view the Christian mission in this regard as a Christian interpretation of the gospel in the presence of the Other. The history of Christian mission work in ancient China in the seventh century Dang dynasty (as expressed in the Inscription text in the so-called "Nestorian" tablet in Xi'an) and Matteo Ricci's mission in the sixteenth century are important examples indicating the inter-cultural reality of the gospel in recognition of the ethics, wisdom, and worldviews of people of other faiths.

Regarding Christian mission in Chinese history, it is meaningful to retrieve the art of interpretation in philosophical Daoism and Zhu Xi's and Wang Yangming's Neo-Confucian theory of interpretation (in chapter 10 and excursus). These two thinkers (Zhu and Wang) can contribute to an interpretive theory that regards the Dao's dynamic action in encounters with human life in different contexts. These theories are more ontologically, methodologically, and socially engaged than Western theories of interpretation. In conclusion, three figures—Odysseus, Abraham, and Laozi—will be used to symbolize our global civilization, and then will undergo cross-cultural comparison and examination within their own particular contexts. This comparison will remain only a torso—a fragment of potential, open to further discussions of human rationality and interpretation of the truth for our civilization.

1

Cave of the Soul and Mimetic Creativity

LANGUAGE AND REPRESENTATION IN GREEK METAPHYSICS

According to Greek tradition, there are three useful models for understanding relational language: likeness, representation, and reflection. *Likeness* implies a relationship involving similarity or symmetry between an original object and a re-presentation of that object. *Representation* is a relationship of imitation, which embraces the symmetrical, and yet transcends it. In this imitative relationship, the original is not truly present in the image, but is only represented in it, and so the product is not dependent upon its source or upon the artist who produced it. *Reflection* corrects the representative model: it seeks a relationship between the original and the image, advocating that the original is truly present in the image, insofar as it stands in dependence upon and in continuity with the original. The reflective model articulates the significant role that language plays.

In Book X of the *Republic*, Plato talks about the *idea* of a bed, about an *actual* bed built by a carpenter, and about a *painting* of a bed. He argues that the original concept of the bed in the artisan's mind is the only real Form, and that the other subsequent representations are merely derivatives of that real object.[1] Here one sees that ordinary, sensible objects like beds depend upon the Forms from which they receive their names. However, the Forms themselves do not depend upon the names they receive or upon the realization of the objects.

In Book VII (514a—519a), Plato likens ordinary human beings to prisoners chained in a cave, unable to turn their heads. Behind them

1. Plato *Republic* 596e–7a.

rages an illuminating fire, whose light casts shadows of puppets onto the wall in front of the prisoners. Since the prisoners can only see what lies before them, they mistake the shadows for reality. Here, the language of illumination articulates the continuity between sensible objects and an illuminating Form. The imagery of emanation expresses the relationship of dependence between the source and the product.

Using Plato's two examples, we see that language is a tool—a copy that is constructed and appreciated in terms of the original. We may use language to discuss the One who is truly ineffable. However, language is not fully capable of disclosing the One. It is one thing to say something *about* the One; the Saying *of* the One is something else entirely. Discussion about the One in an intransitive sense is available, while disclosing of the One in a transitive sense is not. No truth can be attained in language. The pure thought of ideas (*dianoia*) is silent because it is a dialogue between the soul and itself.[2]

The root for the word "hermeneutic" is the Greek verb *hermeneuein*, usually translated "to interpret." The Greek word *hermeios* refers to the priest at the Delphic oracle. The Greek messenger-god Hermes is associated with the function of transmitting, conveying, and interpreting divine oracles for human understanding. Hermes brings the message of destiny from God. Thus, the function is the laying-open of something. This becomes a "laying out" that explains something from a divine oracle. The etymology of the term hermeneutic implies a multiplicity of meanings. Hermeneutic has to do with the process of bringing out an understanding involved in language.[3]

Language is appreciated as a way of speaking about God, insofar as we are aware of the limitation of speech. The interpretation of language through language becomes a possible methodology in dealing with God's speaking to us. For Plato, writing the language down leads to an alienation of language. The specific weakness of writing lies in the fact that no one could come to the aid of the written word in case of misunderstanding, whether intentional or unintentional.[4]

In the Western theological tradition, a theology of the Word of God is a dominant and compelling motif. When Augustine reflects language he concludes that it does not measure up to the heart. Because of hu-

---

2. Gadamer, *Truth and Method*, 407.
3. Palmer, *Hermeneutics*, 13.
4. Gadamer, *Truth and Method*, 392–93.

man estrangement from God, human language falls short of what the speaker wants to express. Augustine's concept of language is close to the Platonic idea of language which only inadequately represents the subject matter.[5]

In Reformation theology, God's speech event is not confined to Scripture *per se*, but is understood in connection with it. A fundamentally Christian notion of biblical inerrancy is not tenable in this view. *Deus absconditus* remains an abstract idea for human contemplation when dissociated from *Deus revelatus*. Nonetheless, *Deus revelatus*, as attested and witnessed to in Scripture, does not mean the dissolution of divinity into humanity, or the reduction of divinity to humanization, leading to captivity in human interpretation. The act of interpretation does not *exhaust* its text, but moves rather in a direction of approximation to the subject matter of the text.[6]

When one says that Justice is beautiful, Beauty is transparent to Justice and vice versa. Human interpretation can never exhaust its speech about Justice or Beauty. According to Heraclitus, "the god whose oracle is in Delphi neither says, nor conceals, but gives a sign [*semainei*]."[7] A sign comes as the gift of God. God comes as a sign-language to us. In view of a Greek metaphysical understanding of language, Gadamer contends that Greek thought and ontology was not able to properly develop the issue of the real being of language because it is replete with the sense of the factualness of language. Thus, it conceives of the essence of language in terms of statements.[8]

TRUTH AS REPRESENTATION OR SELF-REVELATION

In light of the Greek understanding of truth and language, it is important to pay attention to Heidegger's critical conversation with the Platonic tradition. Heidegger critically addresses Plato's basic assumptions about truth as a representation. According to Plato, the world of sensory experience contains an image of the Form of the Good. This representation can be understood as correspondence or imitation (mimesis or adequation). The word is correct if it brings the thing to presentation: in other

---

5. Rist, *Augustine*, 38.
6. Ebeling, *Luther*, 93–109.
7. Schroeder, "Plotinus and Language," 351.
8. Gadamer, *Truth and Method*, 446.

words, a representation (mimesis). The mimesis represents something different from what the word itself contains. The word provides a point of departure for considering the ontological gap between the imitation and the original. The *logos* (discourse and speech) and the manifestation of things taking place in it are different from the act of intending the meanings to be contained in words.

However, Heidegger argues that truth is not a representation of something existing outside thinking, nor does it correspond to the concept of reality. Likewise, truth cannot be appreciated in terms of adequation between the concept and the reality.

According to Plato, the world that appears to our senses is in some way defective and filled with error. Apart from this there is a more real and perfect realm populated by entities (called "forms" or "ideas") that are eternal and changeless. Plato makes a distinction between the many observable objects that appear beautiful (good, just, unified, equal, big) and the one object that is what beauty really is (Goodness, Justice, Unity). From the latter, those many beautiful (good, just, unified, equal, big) things receive their names and their corresponding characteristics. The soul is a different object from the body. It is not dependent on the existence of the body for its functioning. The soul always retains the ability to recollect what it once grasped of the forms. Thus, the lives we lead are to some degree a punishment or reward for choices that we made in a previous existence.

According to Aristotle, the experience of the soul and the representation (the *noemata*) are correspondence to things. This assertion became the occasion for the later formulation of truth as *adaequatio intellectus et rei*. Aristotle equated the *aletheia* with *pragma* and *phainomena*, which signify things themselves. Here *aletheia* belongs to the *logos*.[9]

Against this tradition, Heidegger argues that the Greek-Platonic concept of mimesis or imitation does not represent the truth. It is wrong for us to apply a notion of mimesis unilaterally to naturalistic or primitive copying and reproducing.[10] Heidegger defines truth as revelation. "As unhiddenness truth is a fundamental trait of beings themselves."[11] In Greek, unhiddeness is called *aletheia* (translated as truth). Truth is conceptualized as a form of revealing. Truth as *aletheia* stands in con-

---

9. Heidegger, *Being and Time*, 202.
10. Heidegger, *Nietzsche* I, 185.
11. Heidegger, *Pathmarks*, 177.

trast to truth as the correctness of the gaze (*opthotes*) which is based on the correctness in apprehending and asserting.[12] Truth as a correctness of the gaze is the representational form of truth. Truth as a correctness of representation recurs as *adaequatio*. However, Heidegger strives to retrieve the truth as *aletheia* in order to overcome the limitation of the mimetic–representational model of truth. *Aletheia* as unhiddenness pertains to things themselves and is thus non-representational.

For Heidegger, what is true is a discovering of ontological truth and thus truth ontologically becomes possible by analysis of human being-in-the-world (*Dasein*). *Dasein* is the foundation of the primordial phenomenon of truth. Truth is not encountered as something objectively present. Truth is relative to the being of *Dasein* so that "being and truth are equiprimordial."[13] At any rate, Heidegger finds a clue in Platonic tradition to overcome limitation of Platonism, clearing of Platonism. For Heidegger, twisting free of Platonism implies the need to discard a mimetic-representational notion of truth in favor of truth as *aletheia*.

Furthermore, his notion of truth as unhiddenness allows for consideration of all the activities of humankind in an all-encompassing manner. A traditional separation of metaphysics in terms of logic, ethics, and aesthetics does not hold in Heidegger's view. Heidegger locates art between *techne* and *poiesis*. The former refers to an ability in the sense of a thoroughgoing and masterful know-how, while the latter signifies "what is brought forward in a process of bringing-forth."[14] Thus, aesthetics is not merely restricted to a representational action of mimesis or reproduction, but goes beyond and above it.

In view of Greek metaphysics, Gadamer—unlike Heidegger—contends that in the theory of anamnesis, Plato combined the idea of remembrance with his dialectic of seeking truth in the *logoi*—i.e., the ideality of language (*Phaedo*, 73ff.). Here, a joy of recognition of the original state is that of knowing more than is already familiar. The knowledge comes into its true being, manifesting itself as what it is only when it is recognized. In light of recognition, imitation and representation transcend a repetition, a copy, but imply knowledge of the essence. There is a "bringing forth" of the original through the recognition of the ideality of language. Plato's theory of recognition, which is all knowledge

12. Ibid.
13. Heidegger, *Being and Time*, 211.
14. Heidegger, *Nietzsche* I, 165.

of essence, offers a basis for Aristotle's concept of poetry, which is understood more philosophically than historically.[15]

When we consider a dimension of truth as *aletheia* in the Neoplatonic tradition, Plotinus' model of reflection can be a corrective to the Platonic idea of mimesis by pointing to the horizon of *aletheia*. Art is endowed with the power to bring forth truth in the form of Reason-Principles. Thus, it is more than mere craftsmanship or nature. The natural objects are themselves imitations; then, they give no bare reproduction of the thing seen. Rather they go back to the Reason-Principles from which Nature itself derives. Furthermore, that much of their work are holders of beauty and add where nature is lacking.[16] Aesthetics can be conceived of as the vehicle for truth in a broader manner, in reference to truth. Here, mimesis can be deepened in light of *aletheia* rather than discarded.

AESTHETIC LIFE AND INTERPRETATION IN THE SOUL'S JOURNEY

An aesthetic is an expression of beauty experienced in the world, or one's experience engaged in it. Thus, an experience of beauty is dialectical with the physical world rather than merely spiritual. The experience of beauty is also a trace of a higher beauty, being open to what comes from the source of beauty as such. Here, it is important to consider Plato's idea of the Good, which allows one to see the beauty of all beautiful things. Aesthetics is interrelated with the ethical and the true. Those who seek beauty also pursue the Good. What is called beautiful is inspired by the Good. The Good is above Beauty.

Although the Good itself does not need Beauty, it is not devoid of Beauty. Thus Platonic philosophy demonstrates a close connection between the idea of the Good and the idea of Beauty, recognizing the difference, which involves "the special advantages of the beautiful."[17] Both ideas of the Good and the Beautiful transcend everything that is conditional and multiform. The order of being in the orientation toward the good is in agreement with the order of the beautiful. According to Plato,

---

15. Gadamer, *Truth and Method*, 115.
16. Plotinus *Enneads*, 411.
17. Gadamer, *Truth and Method*, 480.

the Good takes flight into the Beautiful, which, in turn, reveals itself in the search for the Good.[18]

Thus when we call God good, it means that God is also beautiful. The Good is the flower bud of Beauty, so that the expression of Beauty can be an intelligible manifestation of the transcendent Good. Here, we conceptualize an aesthetic in terms of the purification of the soul. The soul's contemplation of Beauty culminates in the concept of grace as an affinity to divinity, a state of perfect happiness and sufficiency. Aesthetics can be a theology of grace, which is to be traced in God's Beauty. Thus, through the aesthetic God's goodness shows itself through grace. Ethics (the Good) is a presupposition for aesthetics (the Beautiful) which, in turn, characterizes a dimension of grace in the good and spiritual life of the soul.

Plato underlies the connection between the realm of Forms (or the Ideas) and the re-existence (or the immortality) of the soul (as described in *Phaedo* and Book X of the *Republic*). Whenever one applies a name to many different things there is a Form corresponding to the name (*Republic* 596a). True knowledge is a recollection of what the soul once knew. Because of the kinship between Ideas and souls, the soul's search for knowledge of the Form is its homecoming. This is done in the act of contemplation (*theoria*) of Being, Truth, Beauty, and Goodness. This act of *theoria* is a participation in and a pursuit of union with the Form. Plato's concern lies with the soul's search for the true reality.

Anyone who wants to attain the knowledge of the Forms or Ideas can really live only beyond death. Therefore, philosophy implies a preparation for death. Pure knowledge is impossible, because the body is with us: We can acquire it only when we are dead. While we live, we shall be nearest to knowledge when we avoid, as far as possible, intercourse and communion with the body. We should keep ourselves pure from the bodily life until God sets us free.[19]

Inheriting Plato's spiritual legacy, Plotinus articulates the human desire to return to heaven at the most effable level. His position deepens and radicalizes Plato's philosophy instead of creating a new departure (in the sense of Neo-Platonism) within the Platonic tradition. This continuity is visible in Plotinus' concept of a soul's ascent to the One.[20]

18. Ibid., 481.
19. Plato *Phaedo* 66 E–7 A.
20. Gatti, "Plotinus," 27. See Louth, *Origins*, 37.

Plotinus expresses an ontological hierarchy in terms of three principles or gods (*hypostases*). At the highest, there is the One or the Good, Intelligence (*nous*), and then Soul (*psyche*). If the Soul refers to the level of life in the realm of sense-perception, Intelligence is the more unified realm which corresponds to Plato's realm of the Forms or the Ideas. If, for Plato, the realm of Forms is the ultimate reality, the One for Plotinus is absolutely simple and the source of all. "Generative of all, the Unity is none of all . . . ; it is the self-defined, unique in form, or better, formless."[21]

The three *hypostases*, the One, Intelligence (*Nous*), and Soul, are related by the process of emanation and return. Intelligence emanates from the One, and the Soul from Intelligence. The process of emanation is a process of overflowing, so that the One overflows into Intelligence, and then Intelligence into the Soul. Emanation is also met by return, which is the One's drawing everything to Oneself. Everything desires the One and longs to return to it.

Plotinus's teaching of emanation and return does not mean escape or flight from the world. Rather, his teaching indicates that everything— all animated life—was generated through the One, thus calling human beings to contemplation, vision, and illumination of the One. The embodied soul strives to free the Soul from the body, and then the Soul strives to *Nous*, and *Nous* to the One. The process of return is a movement of desire or longing as nourished in the act of contemplation.

For Plotinus, the notion of the image is important in his understanding of the movement of procession and return. Intelligence is an image of the One while the Soul is an image of Intelligence. The image longs for its archetype. In virtue of the likeness between image and archetype, the image can know the archetype. An epistemology is established: like is known by like.

Plotinus' philosophy results in *unio mystica*. Plotinus's primacy of genuine and deep contemplation, in which action is regarded as a form of weak contemplation, underlines the soul's desire for return to the One—in other words, *mystica unio*. The emanation from and return to the One, in terms of Intelligence and Soul, is also internally structured. The higher is the more inward and the more introverting.

Plotinus speaks of the soul's ascent to the One by using the image of the Fatherland. The soul has come from the Fatherland, but it has forgot-

21. Plotinus *Ennead* VI.9.3.

ten the Fatherland. Purification (*katharsis*) is the way to achieve a union with the Fatherland. Suddenly the soul is swept out of itself into union: "the vision floods the eyes with light."[22] The *mystica unio* comes upon the soul: it is not implying something the soul can achieve. In the union with the One, a genuine ecstasy takes place in the sense of pouring out of a human self. Ecstasy happens when the soul is overwhelmed and captured by the One in union with the soul. This experience is ineffable, thus the soul has finally arrived at the Fatherland, the real homecoming.

According to Plotinus, the aesthetic begins with the soul's ascent to the One, perfecting it. The One who is the source of the beauty is the soul's ultimate fulfillment. The aesthetic discovery is connected with the soul's ultimate fulfillment in the Beauty of the One. The Intellect emanates to the Soul. The hypostatic Soul includes the world's soul, human, animal, and plant souls, including souls of various species. The world's soul and individual human, animal, and plant souls are all species of the eternal, hypostatic Soul.

The soul is the source of all external beauty. The soul in its ascent to the One discovers its true internal beauty. External aesthetic begins with the ascent of the soul while the internal aesthetic perfects and completes it. In the visible world a beautiful thing is perfect and complete in its form. The One is beautiful in its ultimate, self-sufficient completion and perfection. This beauty is without form. Form is beautiful to the degree that it mirrors the Beauty of the One.

The beautiful soul turns inward, withdrawing from a desire for external things. It purifies itself: independent and pure from the body. The soul can exist and thrive without the body. Detached from the body, the soul's inward turn becomes intellect, and by turning it inward, the soul becomes like the divine Intellect. The beautiful soul imitates the divine Intellect in a self-sufficient contemplation. The divine Intellect rests in an eternal and perfect contemplation. It finds the truth within itself and the truth beautifies the soul. In this self-knowledge, it achieves happiness and freedom. The light from the One beautifies the soul.

The One is the ultimate source of the Soul and the Intellect. The One is beyond all sensible and intellectual images. Direct knowledge of the One is possible because the One is transcendent and immanent in a human soul. The soul comes to complete rest in its center, becoming like the One and joining the One in an unmeasured love. The true beauty of

22. Plotinus *Ennead* VI.7.36.

the soul is the beauty of the One, which the soul discovers at its own core. Unlike Plato, Plotinus puts the beauty of art on a level with the beauty of nature, which is a path to the intelligible beauty. Nature is divinized through its participation in the divine Beauty. The divinity makes the universe beautiful and harmonious. The soul is the image of intelligence (*Nous*) and intelligence is the image of the One. The aesthetic ascent of the soul is a participation in divine beauty through its assimilation to it.

MIMETIC CREATIVITY AND POETIC IMAGINATION

What and how can mimetic representation articulate social reality in the Greek tradition? In the Platonic-Plotinian tradition, ascetic life in the soul's journey is disengaged from a socially embodied life in the public sphere. If social reality is an indispensable part of mimetic creativity in the interpretation of human life with reference to the ultimate thing, interpretation becomes a general method for comprehending reality. The representation of daily life becomes a real basis of interpretation.

Likewise, in Aristotle's theory of interpretation, we notice interpretation as a method of comprehending human reality. In *Peri hermeneias* (*On Interpretation*), the second treatise in the *Organon*, Aristotle defines interpretation as enunciation. For him, meaningful discourse is *hermeneias*—interpretation of reality.

In *Nicomachean Ethics* Aristotle contends that a human being is sociable by nature.[23] His concept culminates in the definition of a human being as a political animal in his *Politics*.[24] Interpretation has a *vox significativa*, a meaningful voice. Interpretation is the signification of the sentence which Aristotle calls *logos*. Interpretation in the sense of textual exegesis is the enunciation of the truth or falsity about a statement. Therefore, "to say something of something" interests Aristotle only insofar as it is the locus of true or false.[25]

For Aristotle, interpretation is related to the issue of justice in the public sphere. Aristotle's understanding of human life in a socio–political context is connected with the power of human speech. Speech serves to indicate what is useful or harmful, and also what is just or unjust.

---

23. Aristotle, *New Aristotle Reader*, 370.
24. Ibid., 509.
25. Ibid., 14.

Equipped with the ability of speech, a human being participates in political association and the public sphere.

Aristotle appreciates the social reality, critically integrating Plato's idea of Form into his concept of the actuality (*entelecheia* or *energeia*). This implies that essence is underlined in the material element. Plato's idea of *anamnesis*, the inborn ability of the human soul to recollect its previous existence, depreciates the social and public place of human life. The doctrine of recollection (*anamnesis*) is an exclusive orientation of the *gnosis* for what has existed. Plato explains the Idea, or the Form as the Original, which is the heavenly place. Truth and knowledge are illumined by the sun, the idea of the Good. A human being is capable of building a house based on such an Idea. In this sense, the material thing takes part in the Idea, that is, *methesis*.

This participation (*methesis*) corresponds to the side of the Idea, in other words, the presence of the Idea in the material thing. A material sphere participates in the world of the Idea while presence of the Idea in the material phenomena is not related to a dimension of the sociomaterial reality of becoming in the public sphere. Against Plato, Aristotle replaces the world of Ideas or the Form with the concept of the Pure Act. Thus, he reinterprets a Platonic concept of non-being, an irrational reality (material thing) through the concept of potentiality (or tendency toward new perfection).

Now that the Pure Act is the efficient and final cause of the potentiality, the tendency of potency is directed toward the Pure Act. In this light, Aristotle establishes the concept of Form, or *entelechy* in a different way. For Aristotle, *entelechy* is the form immanent in matter. The *entelechy* develops and moves itself according to its own nature. Therefore, the concept of *entelechy* is a principle that limits and determines the possibilities of matter.[26]

By the actuality of a thing, Aristotle means that to be something is always to be at work in a certain way. The material thing determines a potentiality for activity in which the corresponding activity has the character of an end (*telos*). For Aristotle the act is an end and the being-at-work is the act. Now that *energeia* is named from the *ergon* it also extends to the being-at-an-end (*entelecheia*).[27] Aristotle's concept of

26. He uses the word *energeia* as a synonym for *entelecheia*. The word *energeia* is translated as actuality.

27. Aristotle *Metaphysics* 1050a 21–3.

becoming or developing differentiates him from Plato. Pathos of movement or becoming appears to be a new concept in Aristotle. The material element and the Form are integrated into the relationship with becoming and development. In reference to a dynamism of a material element, his definition of a human being as a political animal paves the way of understanding the importance of human life in the public sphere. Justice, and more specifically social economic justice, is fundamental in society according to Aristotle.[28]

Aristotle divides the philosophical categories into logic, physic, and ethic. Logic is preparation for thinking or ontology of a general category of being. Physic is a philosophy of nature, and ethic is a philosophy of history and society. In Rom 11:36, St. Paul states: "For from him and through him and to him are all things. To him be the glory forever. Amen." Thomas Aquinas interprets St. Paul's theology of God's relationship with the world in an Aristotelian sense: the logic as the thought of God ("about God"), the physic as the philosophy of the world ("through God"), and finally the ethic as the doctrine of salvation ("to God"). Hegel later accepts this division: Logic, philosophy of nature, and philosophy of the Spirit.

What is interesting in Aristotle's theory of categorization is that in the four principles (matter, Form, cause, and *telos*) the Form swallows up the cause as well as the *telos*. This movement is open and actuality remains incomplete. The relationship between the material element and the Form is central. The material element is not discarded as in Plato, but is a being (*ein Seiendes*) *par excellence*, different from the Form. The Form is the actuality, which is shaped in the growth of the material element. The material element has a motherly character, producing material things.

If we formulate this relation between matter and Form in terms of the public sphere, the economy and society are high actuality, but the formation of the infrastructure is dependent on material things. The material thing can again become the form for the higher Form. Human life as a political animal cannot escape a life context of the public sphere. The material thing is what exists in possibility as the womb of birth, or potentiality in view of the Form, or *entelechy*.

Coming back to our discussion of mimetic action, Aristotle contends in his notion of mimesis that it is not a copy, nor the duplication of

---

28. Duchrow, *Alternatives*, 21–9.

reality. But it is *poesis*, construction or creation. These are the differentiae of poetic mimesis. Here, Aristotle completely differs from Plato's view. Aristotle contends that tragedy is a mimesis of a high, complete action, as enhanced in speech. A tragedy is a mimesis of an action, which implies people engaged in it. The plot, the mimesis of the action, which Aristotle defines as "the ordering of the particular actions," is the principle—the principle of life. This emplotment (*muthos*) is the organization of the event. A primacy of narrative understanding comes into relation with a sociological or structural explanation of human life in society and history.[29]

As far as a tragedy is a mimesis of an action, and a mimesis of the people engaged in it,[30] Aristotle's definition of mimesis entails another indication to effect "through pity and fear [what we call] the catharsis of such emotions."[31] Reversal, recognition, and suffering are characteristics of the complex plot. Here, *pathos* (suffering) is an important component in representing the praxis. Poetic understanding of human action is not separated from suffering or passion which ethic articulates.

Thus, tragedy is an imitation of human actions that makes them appear better, higher, and nobler than they are in reality. It also presents a mimesis of things involving people's action in it by arousing fear and pity. To the degree that mimesis endows the plot with a referential relation to the real world of action, mimesis of tragedy presents the reality in a more creative light, making it appear higher and nobler than a copy of reality. Mimesis and *poesis* in the Aristotelian sense imply the disclosure of a world. Therefore, mimesis–interpretation for Aristotle represents an ontological projection—human activity in social reality higher than the *status quo*.

In an ontological-hermeneutical context, Gadamer takes up Aristotle's theory of tragedy, situation in the context of poetics, to support his concept of play and representation. The theory of the tragic play, i.e. the poetics of tragedy, is consulted in order to arrive at the essence of the tragic. What Aristotle contributed to the problem of the aesthetic in definition of tragedy is his inclusion of its effect on the spectator. Here,

---

29. Ricoeur, *Time and Narrative*, I, 33, 36.
30. Aristotle, *New Aristotle Reader*, 545.
31. Ricoeur, *Time and Narrative*, I, 42.

the spectator belongs to the playing of the play. The representation of tragic action has a specific effect on the spectator.[32]

Given the tragedy's effect on the spectator, Gadamer understands mimesis as having ontological import of representation in reference to Plato's theory of recognition. Here, unfortunately, a dynamic concept of *telos* in Aristotle's framework is relegated to the presentation of essence. Ontological openness for projecting the future is based on that which imposes itself on every interpreter.[33]

For Aristotle, unlike Gadamer's view, the act of interpretation is engaged in the material text, or language as used in the public sphere. Interpretation thus holds the possibility of transforming the world of the Idea in the service of human public interest. Implicitly, it indicates an investigation of human mimetic activity in all aspects of human life. Interpretation becomes an indispensable part of investigating, shaping, and renewing human life in the public sphere.

---

32. Gadamer, *Truth and Method*, 130.
33. Ibid., 119.

2

Cave of Soul and Embodiment in the Christian Tradition

AUGUSTINE'S AMBIVALENCE: SOUL OR BODY

IN THE PREVIOUS CHAPTER, we dealt with a Platonic interpretation of language and truth and the soul's journey toward God. In this tradition, Aristotle marks an exceptional direction in speaking of relationships between interpretation and human life in the public sphere. Moreover, the Neo-Platonic tradition has made a considerable impact on Western Christian development through Augustine, while Aristotle did the same thing through Thomas Aquinas. Here, our investigation is to trace and analyze the Platonic (or Neo-Platonic) influence on Augustine's theology of soul.

Augustine began his interest in philosophy by reading Cicero's *Hortensius*. Augustine found in it an overwhelming sense of divinity and felt "an incredible burning desire" for God and Wisdom (*Conf*. 3.4.7).[1] In Milan, Bishop Ambrose had some knowledge of Greek Neo-Platonism and through him, Augustine met a Platonizing interpretation of Christianity. Augustine was introduced to a number of Platonic books (*Conf*. 8.2.3), some of which were by Plotinus. Through Plotinus, Augustine came to the view that there is much in common between Platonism and Christianity.[2]

In *Confessions* 7, 9, and 14 Augustine explains the Trinity through Platonic teachings about God and the eternal Word. A human being

---

1. Augustine, *Confessions*. This book is abbreviated as *Conf*. in the main text.

2. Augustine would read a smallish portion of the *Enneads* in Victorinus's translation. For instance, "On beauty" (*Enneads*, I.6), "On the Three Divine Hypotheses" (*Enneads*, 5.1), "On the Descent of the Soul into the Body" (*Enneads*, 4.8).

must return to oneself, looking within for God, toward one's own soul. The truth is something incorporeal (*Conf.* 7.20.26). In the *Retractationes*, however, Augustine reproaches himself for having assimilated the kingdom of Heaven to the Platonic Intelligible World (I.3.2).

In the beginning of the *Confessions*, Augustine's spiritual theology is expressed in the following sentence: "Thou hast made us for thyself and our hearts are restless till they rest in thee." The soul has a longing for God, a restless longing. Plato expresses this longing as a way of escaping the shadows of the cave to the pure light of the sun in the intelligible world. In Plotinus, such longing is for the Fatherland, from which we have come: "The fatherland to us is There whence we have come, and There is the Father."[3] Augustine underlines and transforms Platonic longing into the restless longing for God through the incarnation of the Word and the presence of the Spirit.

In one of his first writings, *De vita beata*, Augustine shows Plotinus' influence on his theology. Augustine describes his spiritual journey as a pathway of going beyond the reflection of reason toward the vision of the unchangeable light. This is not the light of reason, but the light over all possibilities of reason. Nonetheless, Augustine's spiritual journey has less to do with Plotinus' methodical, technological manipulation. For Augustine, *visio Dei* comes all of a sudden. It needs love because *amor* knows the light. The vision of the eternal light is the most profound and ultimate meaning of life in Augustine's spiritual theology.

In *Confessions*, we read of his Ostia experience on the Tiber (*Conf.* 9.10.23–25). This experience grows out of his conversation with his mother in which there is a dimension of the interpersonal nature of the final beatitude. The vision is experienced in companionship with others rather than in a solitary experience. For instance, Augustine strives to touch the pleasure of the eternal light, which God feeds to Israel forever with the food of truth. The ecstasy, a transitory experience of rapture is sudden and fleeting in the thrust, or the blow of a trembling glance (*Conf.* 7.17.23). The experience of ecstasy or rapture is absorbed and wrapped in an inward joy, a foretaste of the joys of heaven.

Ecstasy and the beatific vision have a common place between Plotinus and Augustine to the extent that ecstasy in a fleeting sense brings the beatific vision. Despite his indebtedness to Plotinus, an eschatological interpretation of ecstasy as a foretaste of heaven makes

---

3. Plotinus *Enneads* I.6.8.

Cave of Soul and Embodiment in the Christian Tradition

Augustine distinct from Plotinus. Understanding God and the soul in an intimate relationship lies at the heart of Augustine's theology. His understanding of the soul is essentially connected with the Platonic claim for the superiority of the soul over the body. In accordance with this Platonic claim, Augustine is convinced that the soul is not spatially limited, having nothing to do with a material substance, nor any kind of epiphenomenon.[4] The soul is created in the image of God.

In a later stage, however, we discern that Augustine's view of the body changed in light of the grace of God and the resurrection of the body. Thus, he does not follow a Neo-Platonic spiritualizing way that takes place apart from the body. In the *City of God* (13.24.2) "the soul (like the body) is not the whole man; it is the better part of him. It is the conjunction of the two parts which is entitled to the name 'man.'" In the unity of the soul and body, the body subsists as a body does by the soul. The soul enables the body to be a body, although the soul and the body form a unity. Here Augustine stands against both a spiritual reductionism and a material reductionism.[5]

The body, according to Augustine (who follows St. Paul), is the dwelling place of the Holy Spirit. In heaven, men and women will enjoy the beauty of their body without being troubled by lust.[6] Ephesians 5:29—"No one ever hates his own body"—plays an important role in Augustine's changed view of the body in reference to the doctrine of the resurrection of the body. Commenting on the story of the resurrection in John's gospel, Augustine contends that "the whole preaching and dispensation given through Christ [is] . . . the Resurrection—Resurrection not only of soul but of body."[7]

Augustine rejects Platonist concept of the soul's escape from the body for the sake of the Christian idea of resurrection of the body. Commenting on the Pauline text (1 Cor 15:26), "The last enemy to be destroyed is death," Augustine adds: "my flesh shall be my friend throughout eternity."[8] In the *Confessions*, Augustine believes that the soul falls into the body and temporality from above rather than existing together with body and time. Nonetheless, in his theological development the

4. Augustine *Immortality* 10.17.
5. Rist, *Augustine*, 101.
6. Augustine *City of God* 22.24.
7. Rist, *Augustine*, 110.
8. Ibid., 111.

Christian idea of the resurrection of the body keeps Augustine distinct from a Platonist soul reductionism.

Memory encompasses the whole mind, conscious and unconscious. Memory touches God, although it cannot contain God. God remains unchangeable over all, while all other things suffer change. Yet God designed to dwell in our memory (*Conf.* 10.15.36). "Thou didst call and cry to me and break open my deafness . . . Thou didst breathe fragrance upon me . . . : Thou didst touch me, and I have burned for Thy peace" (*Conf.* 10.17). Truth, like a light, shines in our mind. Truth, like the eternal Thou, calls and cries, breaking our deafness. The Truth, like the fountain of life, breathes fragrance upon us. This is because we dimly apprehend, hunger, and thirst for the Truth. Memory, driven by the desire for God, recognizes God as the One who reveals and discloses Oneself in the soul. Plotinus's One is immutable and insensible, and cares nothing for the soul, while Augustine's God is passionate for calling, crying, and breaking open our deafness.

Augustine's concept of grace refers to God's coming to us through Christ, which is foundational for his theology of the soul's ascent to the triune God. The image of God is the human rational soul. Since God is the triune God, so the image of God in the human soul also has a Trinitarian implication. Unlike Plotinus who sees the soul's experience of the One as the culmination point, Augustine takes the soul's flash vision as the beginning of the way in longing for the truth. The soul loves and longs for God in an eschatological openness. It discovers within itself the realm of eternal reality because the higher is the more inward.

As the true image of God, the soul returns to its archetype, God. The soul's ascent to God is an event as well as a progress. In its memory, understanding, and will the soul learns how to pass beyond the image to God in contemplation of God through withdrawal and introversion. By virtue of the image of the Trinity imprinted on the soul, the soul is capable of remembering, knowing, and loving the God who created it. In cleaving to God through remembering, understanding, and loving, the soul can be reformed by God. The reformation or renewal by God begins at the moment of baptism, but the perfection is the result of a long process, taking effect by a gradual progress.

The soul returns to God in a long process of renewal in which the triune God gradually reveals Godself in the heart of the Christian soul. The end of Christian life is the contemplation of the Trinity who is present in the soul through the Holy Spirit, the bond of love, which unites soul and God. God's humility in incarnation and the pouring out of the Holy Spirit in the hearts of Christians shapes and characterizes Augustine's life journey.

AUGUSTINE AND DISENGAGEMENT FROM LIFE-CONNECTION

In Augustine's theology of God's grace, however, there is a lack of consideration for the socially embodied life in a social-historical connection. Although Augustine integrates the body in conjunction with the soul at a later stage, the interplay between the bodily life and this historical condition remains a problem. This division can be challenged and overcome by the connection between historical relativity and social interest. If the human quest for the truth is influenced by historical relativity and shaped by social interest in a particular life context, the public sphere inevitably occupies a significant place in Christian discourse on God, humanity, and the world.

As we already have seen, from a philosophical perspective Heidegger challenges Augustine's alliance with Neo-Platonism. In *Augustinus und der Neuplatonismus*, Heidegger critically analyzed Augustine's Christianity (especially its orientation for the enjoyment of God as the *summum bonum*, or *fruitio Dei*) in light of the ontological facticity of lived experience. Augustine's famous expression—"Our hearts are restless till they find rest in Thee"—implies that "I" must be pressed out of the flux of factual-historical life. "I" am merely on-hand to contemplate and to enjoy being disengaged from "my" life-connections.

In this regard, God becomes an eternal Being outside and above time, place, and history, which finally amounts to Thomas's concept of God as the unmoved mover.[9] Augustine's concept of *fruitio Dei* (enjoyment of God) removes God out of the flux of daily life–connections. Consequently, this subjectivism makes God into a projection of human experience (in the case of Feuerbach) and the object of a human feeling of dependence (in the case of Schleiermacher).

At a theological level, an attempt at transcending an Augustinian model of God and soul becomes obvious in Troeltsch's concept of historical relativity and critical history. Additionally, Troeltsch's study of

---

9. Palmer, *Hermeneutics*, 143.

historical relativity and interconnection demonstrates a bifurcation of the historical study of Christian religion from dogmatic–ethical Christianity. This relates Christianity to non-Christian religions. Before dealing with Troeltsch, however, it is instructive to discuss Moltmann's critique of Augustine in light of his public theology.

3

Christian Theology and the Public Sphere

THEOLOGIA PUBLICA AND AN EMBODIED DIMENSION OF LIFE

To retrieve the place of the body against the Augustinian tradition, Moltmann proposes an embodied theology in his contribution for *theologia publica*. Moltmann critically focuses on Augustine's theology of God and the soul because of his excessive emphasis on the inner self, the soul. In his *Confessions*, Augustine depreciates the importance of the body and nature, preferring an inward, direct self-experiential path to God.

In Augustine and the subsequent mystic tradition, Moltmann recognizes that the human soul attains the divine essence at its apex. The soul is mystically wedded to God, which implies a mutual knowing between God and the soul. Moltmann contends that Western soul mysticism, as seen in Augustine, has repressed the body and fixated on the human mind over against nature, thus generating Western individualism. In the name of the body and sociality, Moltmann advocates for a public theology and public spirituality.

From this standpoint, Moltmann takes issue with Augustine's prayer in his *Confessions* (10.6.8). Augustine's prayer reads: "But what do I love when I love you? Not the beauty of any body or the rhythm of time in its movement; . . . not the sweet melodies in the world of manifold sounds; not the perfume of flowers . . . not the limbs so delightful to the body's embrace."[1]

In contrast to Augustine's prayer, Moltmann contends that God-experience is the social experience of the self and the personal experi-

---

1. Moltmann, *God for a Secular Society*, 98.

ence of sociality. The Spirit of God is the Spirit of Christ and the Spirit of the resurrection of the dead. Christian hope of the transfiguration of the body shapes and directs Christian spirituality toward the liberation of the body from the soul's repression imposed on it. God's Spirit, the *fons vitae* (well of life), is a foundation for a Christian spirituality of life. Thus, life in God's Spirit is life against death, proposing a prophetic struggle against life's negation.[2]

Moltmann's offers a counter prayer to Augustine: "When I love God I love the beauty of bodies, the rhythm of movements . . . the sounds of all this protean creation . . . But you were outside—outside myself—and enticed me out of the narrowness of my heart into the broad place of love for life."[3]

The theological focus of the broad place of love for life and for others leads Moltmann to develop a public theology in reference to mystical experience. For Moltmann, "mystical" does not necessarily mean a special supernatural experience. Rather it means the intensity of the experience of God in faith. The *sapientia experimentalis* has an ethical and a mystical character.

Moltmann's theology of public spirituality attempts to inspire a journey filled with the vitality of life in the midst of the world. The Hebrew word *Yada* (knowledge) implies that knowledge is an act of love rather than an act of domination. In this regard, Moltmann integrates meditation and contemplation in a direction for a theology of the cross. Mediation is the loving, suffering, and participating knowledge of something, while contemplation is the reflective awareness of one's own self in this meditation.[4] Christian meditation is on the passion and death of Christ.

A narrative of Christ *extra nos* is inseparable from the presence of the risen Christ *in nobis*. A historical narrative of Christ's passion for us forms a single whole together with an experiential dimension of Christ's dwelling in us through the presence of the Spirit. "It is no longer I who live, but Christ who lives in me" (Gal 2:20). The open history of Christ through resurrection for us continues in history and society with us and in us.

---

2. Ibid., 93–4, 98.
3. Ibid., 98.
4. Ibid., 203.

Mysticism—in the narrow sense of the *unio mystica*—implies that human love for God is withdrawn from the world and the self. God is enjoyed for God's own sake in Augustine's phrase, *fruitio Dei*. Here Moltmann's interest in Meister Eckhart is striking. Eckhart's concept of detachment argues that God continues to withdraw from God's role as Creator of all things. The soul in its attachment to God comes to resemble the detachment of God. The love of God attains perfection when it lets God go for God's sake.

Moltmann characterizes this detachment as a mystical atheism, that is, an atheism for God's sake. Meditation on the history of Christ outside and for us, associated with contemplation on the presence of the Spirit in us, is directed toward the mystical element in the abolition of human likeness to God for God's sake, and finally the abolition of God for God's sake.

Here, the soul finds its home and passion ends in infinite enjoyment. Then, the ineffable deification (*theosis*) begins. Moltmann interprets the real-life situation of mysticism as political rather than religious. The place of mystical experience is the prison cell, a place of *conformitas crucis*. This refers to the political mysticism of the martyr as witness to the truth which we perceive in liberation theology, Asian *minjung* theology, and others suffering on the downside of history.

The *unio mystica* finds its political dimension in the human rights movement, social activism, and movements of social and prophetic witness to God's justice for the poor. Moltmann appropriates mysticism as a preparation for public discipleship. The dark night of the soul is understood as a Golgotha experience, so that mysticism and discipleship belong together.

Moltmann's strategy becomes obvious in reading Christian mysticism for the sake of a panentheistic vision of the world in God and God in the world. Mystic expressions of the vision of the world in God such as a homecoming, entering in, sinking into, and dissolving are the Neo-Platonic language of the emanation of all things from the All-One, and their coming back to the All-One.

At this juncture, Moltmann seeks to integrate Neo-Platonic soul-mysticism within a pneumatological framework. The Holy Spirit is poured out on all flesh (Joel 2:28ff.; Acts 2:16ff.) and into our hearts (Rom 5:5). The end of this is that God will be all in all (1 Cor 15:28). Human experience of the Spirit's indwelling embraces a different divine presence among others. Moltmann's panentheistic project of God's Spirit and *theologia crucis* offers a public dimension of Christian spirituality that embraces the experience of persecuted people and the martyrs who are aware of God's presence in the midst of their imprisonment.

However, one notices that Moltmann runs the risk of sacrificing God's freedom for the sake of the Spirit's full immanence in the world. A public dimension of mysticism is accepted as a path to God-experience as in Augustine or Plotinus. To what extent is our loving the beauty of bodies connected and mediated to a theology of new life without running into a panentheistic dissolution of God into the world? Does not St. Paul's theology of God's freedom lead in a different direction than Moltmann? "How unsearchable are his judgments and how inscrutable his ways! . . . For who has known the mind of the Lord?" (Rom 11:33–34) "When all things are subjected to him, then the Son himself will also be subjected to the one who put all things in subjection under him, so that God may be all in all" (1 Cor 15: 28).

RELIGIOUS LIFE AND HISTORICAL RELATIVITY

If Moltmann begins with Trinitarian theology and a panentheistic vision of eschatology concerning a public theology, Troeltsch takes a different direction in considering the historical connection as an indispensable factor, which shapes and conditions the Christian understanding of God, humanity, and the world. Prior to Moltmann, Troeltsch (1865–1923) underscored significance of mysticism and historical life setting for understanding Christian religion. His work has the ramification of evaluating a place of Christianity in the world of religions.

At the end of the century, Troeltsch brought extreme suspicion to the harmonious interconnection between faith, history, and ethics through his critical, historical method. The triad of history, relativity, and pluralism set the agenda for Troeltsch. He argues that the essence of Christianity must be defined through religio-historical investigation and deliberation. For Troeltsch, dogmatic work must be conditioned historically. It must be set in terms of the historical development of Christianity.[5]

Troeltsch conceptualizes God as the Transcendent One, who is also immanent within the unfolding of history. In other words, God is coter-

---

5. Troeltsch, *Protestantism and Progress*, v–vi.

minous with human history, which is, in turn, a march of God through the world. He also argues for the human spirit or self-experience in bearing testimony to the immanence of God within human individual souls. Schleiermacher defines a feeling of dependence on God as the locus of religion. Troeltsch calls this feeling a religious *a priori* built within the human spirit.

The idea of a religious *a priori* in consciousness grounds religious ideas in human reason. For example, mysticism may be seen as the actualization of religious *a priori*. Thus, it is the primary and basic phenomenon of all religions.[6] However, historicism remains at the center of his approach to religious and cultural spheres rather than remaining merely a defender of religious *a priori*. Religious history is not separable from cultural history. Troeltsch insists that the significance of historicism generally is a fundamental way of historicizing all human thought about humanity, culture, and values.

In no sense can Christianity be exempted from historical investigation and examination. Indeed, Troeltsch appears to be the father of historical relativism. He characterizes three basic principles of historical critical method in terms of criticism, analogy, and correlation, which are regarded as the backbone of historical method. The historian, who has independence and autonomy from the traditional data, must critically examine all traditions. In the realm of history, judgments of probability work.

Criticism of history is possible on the basis of the principle of analogy, in which the historian is capable of discerning analogies between events in the past and in the present. The importance of the analogy lies in comprehending cultural, historical, and religious differences; it also makes empathy possible. The method of analogy assumes a basic consistency of the human spirit in its historical manifestations.

The form of criticism also assumes similarity in human historical activities. Historians acknowledge and recognize the interaction and interplay of all events in an historical life setting in terms of the principle of correlation. As the principle of historical knowledge, correlation in favor of historical relativity places limitations on all absolute claims of human knowledge by articulating that events and individuals in history are anchored in interrelationship with one another, neighbors, and events. For Troeltsch all historical happening is knit together in a perma-

---

6. Troeltsch, *Social Teaching*, II, 734–38.

nent relationship of correlation. The concept of correlation constitutes a current in which everything is interconnected. Thus each single event is related to all others.[7]

In his early stage, Troeltsch did not deny the superiority of Christianity. For him, Christianity is not the absolute religion. Rather, the Christian religion is a purely historical phenomenon, subject to all the limitations, just like the other religions.[8]

Given this fact, historical relativity is understood without reference to absoluteness. Thus, the absolute cannot be articulated in an absolute way. At this point, Troeltsch affirmed that the future would bring complete deliverance, perfect knowledge, because Jesus relegated the absolute religion to the world to come.[9] Nevertheless, in the first edition of *The Absoluteness of Christianity and the History of Religions*, Troeltsch understands Christianity not only as the culmination, but also as the convergence point of all religions.[10]

But in the second edition of *The Absoluteness* (1912), Troeltsch distances himself from his former position. In his lecture, "The Place of Christianity among the World Religions" at the University of Oxford, Troeltsch argues against the superiority of Christianity and its place as the convergence or culmination point for all other religions. Being aware of a form of cultural imperialism, he identifies Christianity as the best—or the absolute—religion only for Westerners. Buddhism and Brahmanism are really humane and spiritual religions; they are capable of appealing to the inner certitude and devotion of their followers as Christianity does in the same way.[11] Troeltsch paved the way for religious pluralism in our century. However, a public dimension of Christianity, its social political dimension, is left behind for the sake of religious individualism.

How does an experience of God transcend religious individualism and a panentheistic dissolution of God into the world, in configuration of a more prophetic imagination of Christian narrative about God, humanity, and the world? This question turns us to a theological project proposed by Friedrich -W. Marquardt.

---

7. Ibid.
8. Troeltsch, *Absoluteness of Christianity*, 71, 85.
9. Ibid., 123.
10. Ibid., 114.
11. Hick and Hebblethwaite *Christianity and Other Religions*, 23.

EXPERIENCE OF GOD AS THE PLACE OF THE WORD

F.-W. Marquardt became Helmut Gollwitzer's successor at the Free University of Berlin and paved the way for Jewish–Christian renewal with his lifelong commitment to political radicalism and Israel. Through his writings on Karl Barth and Israel, and "Theology and Socialism: Example of Karl Barth,"[12] Marquardt, together with his teacher and friend, Gollwitzer, was known as an important representative of the radical-prophetic side of Martin Luther and Karl Barth in the German Protestant context.

Throughout his life Marquardt was devoted to rediscovering and acknowledging the essential roots of Christian identity within Judaism. Marquardt, through his seven volumes of dogmatics, made the first attempt to reformulate and renew a Christian understanding of the God of Israel in a Trinitarian-eschatological perspective, examining Christology and eschatology in conversation with theological aspects of postbiblical Judaism. Auschwitz, for him, is a judgment against Christianity and demands a call for repentance involving ethical action as well as theological changes.

In his concept of a theological utopia,[13] Marquardt hermeneutically retrieves a Jewish category of the *topos* (*Makom*) for the sake of a theology of eschatological utopia. God, as *Makom*, awakens and inspires God's people to long for the coming world. Postbiblical Jewish thought in rabbinic Judaism developed a new way to express God's transcendence from creation and God's presence within it. The most important rabbinic designation for God's presence in the world is *Shekhinah*, a biblical expression that God dwells (*shekken*) in the midst of God's people, in the Tabernacle during the wilderness wanderings, and in the House on Mount Zion. How can God, who fills heaven and earth, confine God's presence to a small Tabernacle?

In rabbinic Judaism, the concept of the *Shekhinah* is used to designate God's nearness to a human being in various moments of holiness. In addition, *Makom* (the place) is used in the tannaitic period as a complement to Heaven. The God of Heaven or the kingdom of Heaven articulates a certain distance between God and the human being. In the

---

12. Marquardt, *Theologie und Sozialismus*.
13. Marquardt, *Eia*.

context of Deuteronomy, the usage of *Makom* for God is associated with the Temple ("the place where the Lord your God shall choose").

By the third century CE, however, it received the opposite meaning of divine transcendence. The world is contained in God, but not God in the world. From Ps 90:1 ("Lord, Thou hast been our dwelling-place"), it follows that God is the dwelling-place of the world, but the world is not God's dwelling-place. For instance, the rider is not subsidiary to the horse.

Biblical language expressing the closeness between God and human beings is related to the concept of the place, articulating essentially a social relation. In 1 Sam 20:23, 42, we perceive an existential-social definition of God's place. "As for the matter about which you and I have spoken, the Lord is witness between you and me forever." When it comes to a biblical concept of God and *topos* we should recall the encounter between God and Moses in Exod 33:21: "See, there is a place by me where you shall stand on the rock." Here is a *topos* (*Makom*) in God's closeness to Moses in which Moses can become close to God without endangering his life. "I will cover you with my hand until I have passed by; then ... you shall see my back" (Exod 33:22–23).

From this encounter, the basic conviction comes: God is the place of the world, rather than the world as the place of God. Which one is originally real, God or the world? Does God stand before the forum of the world, or does the reality of the world stand before the forum of God? In the Jewish rabbinic tradition, we are aware of God as *Makom* of the world, without limiting and obscuring God's presence in the world. Furthermore, we read in John 14:2–3 that "in my Father's house there are many dwelling places."

In exegesis of a biblical concept of the *topos*, Marquardt interprets Abraham's life of calling in reference to God's place. Abraham's vocation demonstrates his journey out of his father's household toward the place that God promised. Faith, in Abraham's sense, is thinking on the way to a better insight into the revelation of God. This refers to Abraham's wandering in his faithfulness to God's place (Gen 20:13). This wandering involves mistakes, confusion, and deception as seen in Abraham's interaction with Abimelech of Gerar when it comes to Abraham's relationship with his Sara.

For Marquardt, Abraham is an example of public vocation in reference to life's relation with the Jewish people, the poor, and the humanity of the suffering in a collective sense.[14] Transcendence comes from the transformation of this world toward God's place, which is to awake a utopian desire for a better society. A theology that aims at the place of God can become a theology of socially embodied life in pursuit of life in solidarity with those who suffer. A crisis of utopian praxis for the realm of freedom is to be integrated into a praxis of God's place in faith's journey, which takes a stand for life against the death of fetishism.

God has determined not only a certain place (for instance, the temple) where God is known, but God is also the place of self-acknowledgement. Thus, God is called the Place. A place *extra nos*, the place of encountering with God, is the place of life. Abraham can see God in the place where God sees Abraham. A theology is defined by and depends on the place that shapes its theological direction. A public theology, as seen in light of a theology of place, advocates for a non-sacrificial theology of the cross.

GOD'S *TOPOS* AND *AQUEDAH*

Abraham's theology can be a model for a contextual theology in search of the place of God's life. In the story of Abraham's calling and "binding" of Isaac, the same verb *lech lecha* (go for yourself) is used in connection with God's test. Calling and testing are embedded within a faith journey.

Biblical law clearly indicates that child sacrifice is abhorrent to Israel (Deut 12:29–31). YHWH disliked the ritual slaughter of children which was practiced among neighboring pagan people as well as those Israelites who imitated this pagan rite of child sacrifice (2 Kgs 3:27, 16:2–4, 21:6). In the context of Leviticus giving the children to Molech is regarded as profaning God's holy name (Lev 18:21, 20:2–3). God's provision of a ram for sacrifice in Isaac's place and Abraham's unswerving trust in God's command constitutes a foundation for God's non-terminated covenant with Israel according to St. Paul (Romans 11).

In a different context, we are aware of a law which asks about giving God their first-born (Exod 22:29; cf. Ezek 20:26). Nevertheless, prophetic literatures are vehement in their opposition to child sacrifice (Jer 19:5–6). How then do we understand Abraham's life journey in relationship with God alongside his willingness to sacrifice his son?

---

14. Marquardt, *Von Elend und Heimsuchung*, 263.

The story of *aquedah* in Abraham's binding of Isaac is often associated with the story of the military hero Jephthah's vow to sacrifice (Judg 11:29–40). Although the *aquedah* is intended as an etiology of animal (over and against human) sacrifice, in the religious life of Israel we can discern, implicitly, that the sacrifice of the first-born son is not completely rejected as an abomination to God. The *aquedah* as a foundational narrative might be integrated and rewritten in the Passover sacrifice. Finally, an Abraham-Isaac typology is inserted without reservation into the theological understanding of Job's suffering and Jesus' death in reference to God's willingness and abandonment.

"You are my Son, the Beloved; with you I am well pleased" (Mark 1:11; cf. Matt 3:17; Luke 3:22; 2 Pet 1:17). This wording recalls the designation of Isaac in the *aquedah*. The passion of Jesus has been seen in light of a suffering servant of God as prophesized in Isa 53:7. The Lamb of God (John 1:29) has a parallel with a sheep substitute for the first born son for sacrifice (Exod 34:20) which is crucial to the binding of Isaac and the Exodus from Egypt (Exod 13:11–16).

The Lamb of God in John 1:29 and the crucifixion of Jesus in the Johannine account stand in reference to God's law: "None of his bones shall be broken" (cf. John 19:36). Matthew argues that Jesus does not come to abolish the law and the prophets, but to fulfill them (Matt 5:17). Jesus's faithfulness to the Torah is affirmed in the context of the synoptic gospels (Matt 22:34–40; Mark 12:28–34; Luke 10:25–28). St Paul, in 1 Cor 5:7, affirms this continuity: "our paschal lamb, Christ, has been sacrificed."

St. Paul projects the life of Jesus Christ into the story of Abraham (Gal 3:13–16; cf. Deut 21:23). In this regard, unfortunately, a theological supercessionism occurs among Christian theologians who interpret Jesus through the displacement of Abraham and Isaac.[15] A sacrificial interpretation of the Christian gospel easily becomes a supercessionism of Israel.

When Israel's "No" to Jesus Christ becomes apprehended only in a negative sense as a rejection of the central teaching of the Church, a dangerous consequence is that the Jews are written off as God-killers. Consequently, Paul's theology becomes spiritualized, interiorized, and supercessionist, cutting off his physical connection with Israel.[16] Against

---

15. Levenson, *Death and Resurrection*, 213.
16. Stendahl, *Paul among Jews*, 8.

this trend, the Christian truth claim of Jesus Christ calls for a deep conversation with the Jews, whose "No" to the Christian church in light of their covenant with God, signified a rejection of Jesus Christ as their Messiah.

Against a supercessionist interpretation, Paul defends Israel's right as the chosen people of God; furthermore, he retains an eschatological reservation about the Christian finality over Israel (1 Cor 15). For him, God's covenant with Israel is not terminated. God has not rejected God's people. Paul related his interpretation of the Jews to Ps 94:14 ("For the Lord will not forsake his people; he will not abandon his heritage.") Gentile Christianity as a wild olive shoot was grafted alongside Israel to share the rich root of the olive tree. Israel becomes the enemy of God for our sake as regards the gospel. But regarding election, Israel is beloved for the sake of the ancestors. Therefore, the gifts and the calling of God are irrevocable (Rom 11:28–29).

In this light, Israel has salvific-historical significance and priority, which cannot be eradicated. If Israel were rejected, God's faithfulness to Gentile Christians would also be precarious. "The Jew in Romans" becomes a christological theme for St. Paul, speaking of the Jew in a horizon of the universality of the gospel for the Gentile. The relationship between the Jew and the Gentile Christians is articulated in his specific proclamation of the gospel in dialectical correlation with the people of the world. The social structure of Paul's teaching of the gospel becomes decisive in this regard. Paul understands Jesus Christ and his world-historical movement as *diakonia* for the Jews, as well as for people of the world.[17]

The biblical writers in ancient Judaism tend to take the side of the victim on moral–ethical grounds, standing for the defense of victims. In rabbinic interpretive tradition, God's word is interpreted according to a given context rather than finally established. "You shall not add to the word which I commend you, nor shall you take anything from it" (Deut 4:2). However, during the time in the desert, Moses and the Israelites established a judicial system with a supreme court to resolve legal problems. As Deut 17:8–12 states, "If there arises a matter too hard for thee in judgment . . . then you shall come to the priests and the Levites and to the judges who shall be in those days." A living interpretation of the law is engaged in the text of the law, in search of guidance for new situations.

---

17. Marquardt, *Die Juden*, 45.

There are no pre-existent final truths in doctrine or law. The truth calls for on-going conversation with interpreters in a different context and generation.[18]

Moses set the Torah out before the Jewish people for life or death (Deut 30:15ff.), but he intended for the people to use the Torah for life and not for death. It is absurd and foolish to use the commandments to bring someone into life-threatening circumstances.

Given this fact, it is of special significance to examine the sacrificial language of Jesus's death in light of God as the source of life. Jesus as the sacrifice in the context of 1 Cor 11:23–25 and Isaiah 53 is a brutal fact. A theological concept of God as one who demands such a sacrifice has been saturated into the death of Jesus in such a way that God—as the source of life—becomes disfigured into an image of Moloch, the one who devours human life. The concept of the sacrifice of a human being is underlined in the mechanism of war, violence, and death in our society. In the story of Isaac, however, the God of Israel is a marked contradiction to the God Moloch who demands children's lives in Kidron (Jer 7:31–32, 19:5–6).

God does not take pleasure in the death of the godless (Ezek 33:11), not to mention the righteous. Death is a contradiction to the living God. A theology of God's abandonment, which envisions a brutal sacrifice of humanity, is unacceptable in this regard. The Hebrews (Heb 9:19–20) know a sacrificial side of the covenant in Exod 24:4–8, comparing it to Jesus's death. St. Paul also is in agreement, saying that Jesus's words—"This cup is the new covenant in my blood" (1 Cor 11:25). Mark (14:24) affirms that Jesus' death is not the sacrifice of atonement, but the establishment of communion with God. Thus, St. Paul calls the cup communion with the blood of Christ and the bread communion with the body of Christ (1 Cor 10:16). Here Jesus's death is conceived of in a social-ethical and covenantal sense rather than in a sacrificial cult.

A Christian theology of the cross must be conceptualized as a theology of protest against the social and cultural mechanism that justifies human sacrifice, violence, or scapegoating as a penalty and juridical system. *Theologia crucis* provides a basis and a criterion for configuring and concretizing God as the place of the world standing for the marginalized, the voiceless, and the nameless who are victimized and scapegoated by the social and cultural mechanism. A theology of God as the *Makom*

---

18. Bokser *Talmud*, 11.

contradicts and challenges *theologia providentia* built on the sacrifice of the innocent, pointing to a God of compassion in *theologia crucis*. Christian theology challenges the concept of presupposing God's image as demanding of human sacrifice. An understanding of Jesus as a priest, therefore, comes from Melchizedek (Heb 5:6; 7:11): king of peace and righteousness.

This considered, Girard convincingly argues for a human scapegoat against the idea of sacrificial language of divine violence or *aquedah*, as he compares it to the life and death of Jesus Christ. In Jesus's interpretation of the Old Testament his gospel message is directed against the idea of sacrifice or violence. A sacrificial interpretation of God and the Passion should be criticized in light of the gospel of reconciliation and the kingdom of God. According to Girard, in view of the rejection of violence, the gospel fulfills the work of the Old Testament (Matt 5:43–45).

According to Girard, desiring things through mimesis produces our emotion of rivalry and envy and becomes an internal basis for external behavior of violence. The external violence is the tip of the iceberg, namely mimetic desire. A victim called "the substitute victim" is chosen to represent the whole community and bring about catharsis through the ritualized violence. The scapegoat is identical with the substitute victim whose function is to pacify the society and control violence and mimetic desire.

The prophetic message that Jesus quotes—"I desire mercy, not sacrifice" (Matt 9:13)—demonstrates an immanent critique of the scapegoating mechanism of his time. Jesus challenges the chain of violence which was burdened by the innocent victim in the history since Cain and Abel (Matt 23:34–36). Revealing "what has been hidden since the foundation of the world" (Matt 13: 35), Jesus proclaims the God of Israel as a non-sacrificial God who demonstrates a counter-proposal to cultural religious mechanism of violence, by becoming himself scapegoating of cultural religious violence.

Jesus's message of the kingdom of God puts an end to the mimetic desire and crisis of humanity, resulting in terms of universal renunciation of every form of violence, sacrifice, and vengeance in human relationships (Matt 5:38–40).[19] A sacrificial interpretation of the Passion and the redemption entails a persecutory character, resulting in the scapegoating of the Jews.

19. Girard, *Things Hidden*, 183.

A Christian reading that finds a structural analogy between the Passion and the sacrifices of the Torah (especially in Epistle to the Hebrews) fails to understand what Jesus's death actually manifests and reveals: "the founding death of the scapegoat."[20] "Go and learn what this means, 'I desire mercy, not sacrifice'" (Matt 9:13). "First be reconciled to your brother or sister, and then come and offer your gift" (Matt 5:23–24).

It is essential to propose a non-sacrificial interpretation of the Passion in confrontation with a sacrificial interpretation of God and the Passion that tends to justify divine permission of violence and Holocaust inflicted on the innocent victim.

God as the place of the world can be defined as the place which denounces human violence against God and fellow people. A theology of God's *topos* affirms a God of the living against a concept of a God of violence. Here, the gospel of *theologia crucis* can be understood as a non-sacrificial language of counter-critique regarding the sacrificial violence, scapegoating, and *skandalon* in a society.

A THEOLOGY OF GOD'S *TOPOS* AND THE PUBLIC SPHERE

In the rabbinic tradition, David reduced the Torah given to Moses to the eleven commandments found in Psalm 15. Isaiah reduced them to six or two as seen in Isa 33:15 and 56:1. Micah reduced them to three (Micah 6:6–8). Amos reduced them to one (Amos 5:6). Habakkuk reduced them to one, "The Righteous shall live by his faith" (Hab 2:4).

A Christian theology of the Word of God gives full credit to human life and other creatures' in light of God's grace of justification and justice, promoting the meaning of Torah in option of the culture of life: doing justice, loving goodness, and walking modestly with the God who calls for reconciliation and forgiveness.

In Luke 6:20 and Matt 25:40 we come to see Jesus as one who is with and behind the poor. In John 3:16, God loves the world, the people of all nations. God accepts the humanity of all humans and takes it up in unity with the eternal Son of God. The dogmatic term, *assumptio carnis*, fundamentally refers to biblical universalism (Rom 5:21–21). This biblical universalism does not eliminate biblical particularity as seen in

---

20. Ibid., 225. Girard seems to ignore Jesus's message of reconciliation grounded in the message of Torah as God's invitation to life against death.

Abraham's journey in search of God's place. A theology of God as the place of the world takes into account three realms: Israel, option for the innocent victim, and solidarity with the human suffering and marginalized in the world.

God is the place of Abraham's life in a profound sense. Jesus leaves the world to prepare a place for his disciples. The issue of God's *topos* is not only structured with respect to God's covenant with Israel in the Hebrew Bible, but is also christologically and soteriologically oriented and structured in the Greek Bible. God is constitutive for *topos*. The world is not the place of God, but God is the *topos* of the world. In this regard, God is to be construed in a geographical-social-historical relation and in the public sphere. As the *topos* of the world, God transforms the reality of the world in a direction for God's shalom and kingdom. The public sphere is to be shaped and renewed in accordance with God's *topos*.

Biblical promise and hope are rooted in and oriented toward the kingdom of God as God's *topos*. God's word to Moses entails God's self-definition: God will be what will be. God is ahead of the world. In John 1:1, "The Word was with God." Jesus Christ as the Son of God is in the most intimate closeness to God. God has the place and grants it to us in our relationship to God. Jesus comes to us in, with, and through the kingdom of God. A theology of God's *topos* radicalizes Christian eschatology in light of God's world transformation and shalom.

An attempt at defining the eternal life in light of God's *topos* protects against the possibility of the identification between God and humanity by juxtaposing God with the creature and the creature with God. God is more than humanity and the world. When God is conceived of as the *topos* of the world, God is always the living God, calling for our interpretative imagination of the word of God speaking to us in a completely different manner. In Sam 20:42 God's existence in-between belongs to a biblical definition of place. God's being is in becoming by sharing God's life with us historically, socially, and publicly.

"Seek the Lord and his strength, seek his presence continually" (1 Chr 16:11). A biblical person seeks the face of God, longing for the encounter with God, face to face. "My soul thirsts for God, for the living God. When shall I come and behold the face of God?" (Ps 42: 2). This question is constitutive for an eschatological source of hope about beatific vision. Biblical people strive to find comfort in God's face. God shines God's light or faces toward them. Human existence before God expresses the relationship between God and humanity, which is an indispensable part of the Reformation teaching of justification.

Luther's concept of justification *extra nos* in a forensic sense circumscribes a concept of the place or forum in which God and human beings encounter. The teaching of justification which presupposes God's place *extra nos* is characteristic of a meeting place for the public life. Luther's way of speaking of God retains a tendency toward all-inclusive comprehensiveness. From Luther's jargon "righteous and a sinner at the same time" the term "at the same time" characterizes and underscores an all-embracing comprehensiveness of the *particula exclusiva* in Luther's thought.[21]

At issue here is God's universal grace for all. In such a way, justification is connected with God's justice in the public sphere in the world. Thus according to Luther, *Deum justificare* means giving God justice, which actually expresses the justification of God. As God is truth, justice, and life, so God will be truth, justice, and life outside of God's self. This takes place when the Word of God stands in the Word made flesh. According to Hans J. Iwand, "this truth–becoming–God in us is what Luther calls *Deum Justificare*."[22] Through human openness toward the public sphere we participate in a forum for witnessing to the gospel, which means the justification and justice of God, pursuing what is noble in the sight of all, and living in peace with all (Rom 12:17–18).

Dietrich Bonhoeffer, in 1932, asserted that loving the earth and God are one in the same.

> Wanderers love the earth that carries them, yet love it only because in it they meet the foreign land that they love above all things, since otherwise they would not be wanderers. Only those who wander thus, who love earth and God in one, can believe in the kingdom of God.[23]

The biblical people experience God as the essence of place, fortress, rock, shield, horn, and stronghold (Ps 18:2, 31, 91:2; Ps 42:9; 62:7), or place of escape, abode, and refuge (Deut 33:28; 2 Sam 22:3; Joel 3:16). To the degree that we attempt to bring the biblical language of God as a

---

21. Ebeling, *Luther*, 246–47.
22. Iwand, *Righteousness of Faith*, 21.
23. Bonhoeffer, *Gesammelte Schriften*, 3:270.

place in connection to the Word of life (1 John 1:1) for the sake of social relationship and the public sphere, a Christian theology of the public sphere has a character of utopian longing for the city that is to come (Heb 13:14), as exemplified by Abraham's journey toward God's place (Heb 11:8).

Jesus's table fellowship with *massa perditionis* (the public lost: *ochlos, minjung*) introduces and articulates Jesus as the partisan of the *ochlos* who does not contradict his identity as "a light for revelation to the Gentiles and for glory to your people Israel" (Luke 2:32). The writer of Mark's Gospel affirms the Hebrew Scriptures, and he converses with scribes, Pharisees, and Sadducees over issues in interpretation of Torah while challenging the pharisaic code of the tradition of the elders and attacking the corruption of the temple, which economically dominated Jerusalem.[24]

In Mark 7:1–8 (cf. Matt 15:3) we perceive that Jesus's answer to the Pharisees and Torah-teachers stands in line of Isaiah. "This people honors me with their lips, but their hearts are far from me; in vain do they worship me, teaching human precepts as doctrines" (Mark 7:6–7). The commandments of the Torah take precedence over the traditions of the elders. Jesus's confession of Israel's *shema* (Mark 12:29–30; cf. Deut 6:4–5) is striking as far as it is the foremost commandment of all. It is important to perceive that Jesus proclaims the kingdom of God to the scribe ("You are not far from the kingdom of God,") when Jesus finds the scribe's answer wise. The Asian *minjung* hermeneutic of Jesus's socio-biography with *ochlos-minjung* in the context of Galilee finds its expansion in Luke's theology of the poor and Israel with emphasis on Jerusalem. Thus, Jesus who "bring[s] good news to the poor," "proclaim[s] release to the captives, recovery of the blind, and let the oppressed go free" (Luke 4:18–19) is the One who is "a light for revelation to the Gentiles and for glory to your people Israel" (Luke 2: 32).

Thus, in his proclamation of the kingdom of God (Luke 4:43), Jesus, as the partisan of those historically and socially on the margin, stands in continuity with the spirit of the prophet Isaiah (61:1–2). Jesus represents and actualizes the hope for Israel, the promise of the liberating and reconciling future of God. The promise of healing, reconciliation, and liberation break into our relations and conditions in the public sphere.

---

24. Meyers, *Binding the Strong Man*, 41.

A theological deliberation of God as the coming Place embraces not only human cities but also the animal kingdom in its hope for an eschatological reign of peace: "The wolf shall live with the lamb, the leopard shall lie down with the kid, the calf and the lion and the fatling together . . ." (Isa 11:6–7). God's holy mountain is the place of eternal peace in which all living beings find reconciliation, rest, and beatific life.

In Rom 8:19–23, St. Paul expresses this prophetic vision with emphasis on the solidarity of the children of God with creation. Creation eagerly longs for the revealing of the children of God because creation has been subjected to futility. A theology of God's *topos* awakens us to long for God's healing, forgiveness, and reconciliation in the public sphere in accompaniment with all sentient creatures, which are also blessed to share with humanity the hope for liberation from bondage to decay and to obtain the freedom of the glory of the children of God.

A BODILY DIMENSION OF FUTURE LIFE: PUBLIC SPIRITUALITY

Our future life is not the life of the immortal soul. The Platonic concept of the immortality of the soul is different from the biblical concept of the future life. In the Greek tradition, death is understood as the soul's liberation from the imprisonment of the body and flesh. Thus, death is greeted and celebrated as an entrance to eternal freedom. However, according to Paul, death is the enemy of God (1 Cor 15:26). Jesus' struggle on Gethsemane (Mark 14:33–34) is different from Socrates' attitude toward death.

In a biblical context, God creates a human being as a united and whole body and soul. A human body is a body animated by the soul, and the soul is the soul of body. "You shall love the Lord your God with all your heart, and with all your soul, and with all your might" (Deut 6:5). From Jesus's charge to his disciples, the proclamation of the Kingdom of heaven includes curing the sick, raising the dead, cleansing the lepers, and casting out demons (Matt 10:7–8).

In Matt 10:28 we know that the unity in the biblical understanding of a human being has to do with an understanding of God as affecting the whole of body and soul. Against the immortality of the soul where the soul is separated from the body, the Bible speaks of the resurrection of the body where soul and body remain united.

When it comes to new life, the wholeness of body and soul is maintained. The soul can be called the spiritual principle, and the new life can, as bodily life, correspond to God's closeness with a human being. In the biblical idea of resurrection, the body has primacy. The resurrection has a bodily and material character. Jesus' risen body retains the wounds and the scars. The previous body is transformed into a body without the decay of death (Acts 13:34).

The corruptible body will be clothed with incorruptibility, the mortal body with immortality: the heavenly body and the earthly body (1 Cor 15: 40). God will give us a body when God wakes us from the dead. In this way, the heavenly body relates to the new life. A spiritual body (1 Cor 15: 44) can be conceived of as the body which God's Spirit permeates and reinvigorates in the new life. The body has eternal life in the Spirit. The body is oriented through the Spirit toward life. The Spirit who raised Jesus from the dead dwells in us. God will bring our mortal bodies to life also, through the Spirit dwelling in us (Rom 8:11–12).

Paul sees in Christ's resurrection the resurrection of all human beings. The first man, Adam, became a living being while the last Adam became a life-giving spirit (1 Cor 15:45). It is not the spiritual that is first. But the physical, and then the spiritual. The new life will be a bodily life. As we have borne the image of the person of dust, we will also bear the image of the person of heaven (1 Cor 15:48).

In 2 Cor 5:1 we learn that we have a house from God, eternal in the heavens. God prepares us for a new life for God has given us the Spirit as a guarantee for the new life. The soul is not resurrected, but the body is resurrected and transformed into the immortal body. The body of life is a definition of social relationship. Sexuality belongs to sociality. The body is meant for the Lord, and the Lord for the body (1 Cor 6:13).

In the body, we are physically and socially bound to others in the public sphere. This is the fundamental, social, and public dimension in the life of the body. The body is, ontologically speaking, the structure of being for others. Glorifying God in our body (1 Cor 6: 20) is crucial in the context of 1 Cor 6:13. God is related to our body. The mutual relationship between God and body is articulated in a way that our bodies are members of Christ (1 Cor 6:15). The body of Christ is for Paul an expression for the Christian community: an understanding of Church as a social body. God is for our bodies to the extent that Christ is the collective person (Bonhoeffer). Christian spirituality grounded in the Spirit as the life-giver must be understood and implemented as public spirituality engaged in material dimension of human life.

In a concept of Church, the relationship between God and the body is conceived of in the sense of interpersonal and social relationship. In the biblical notion of reality, social relationship is actually bodily relationship. Our body is "a temple of the Holy Spirit" (1 Cor 6:19). In 1 Cor 11:23–24 St. Paul advocates for the bodily and communal dimension of the Lord's Supper. Jesus has lived his bodily life in the structure of being for and in accompaniment with others, identifying his physicality through the bread and wine. In the drinking and eating of bread and wine we have a physical, communal meaning of the body in a social life relationship.

Eucharistic participation calls for our resistance in solidarity with the innocent victims against the world. Our eucharistic participation in the body of Christ brings us to engage in the public sphere of socially embodied life in company with *massa perditionis*. Thus, the bodily life is a possible site of communication with the living reality of Jesus Christ and in interaction with our fellow-neighbors for the sake of engagement and solidarity with the underprivileged and through spiritual–communal togetherness and material distribution. The struggle for the emancipation of the body in confrontation with social, political, and juridical forces of oppression and destruction stands in continuity with a biblical understanding of the body.

In this regard, Foucault's provocative thesis of deployment of sexuality is closer to a biblical concept of the human body than a repressive hypothesis of sexuality; Western "man" is an animal of confession.[25] The Christian practice of spiritual direction, confession, and examination of conscience, which has become transformed into discourse of power and knowledge, must be reexamined in light of a biblical understanding of bodily life and public spirituality.

The biblical view of the body as social also encompasses an understanding of the body as historical. The body is the place and domain of the struggle for liberation from domination over human beings. The body is a site of the struggle for liberation and freedom from imposition and dominion. The interplay between power and knowledge is inscribed in the human body. In 2 Cor 3:17 we find that the Lord is in relationship with us in the Spirit. This relationship is not one of dominion, but

---

25. Foucault, *History of Sexuality* I, 59.

of freedom in agreement, consensus, communion, and emancipation. Therefore, we are "members of the household of God" (Eph 2:19), "heirs of God," and "joint heirs with Christ" (Rom 8:17).

A dominion-free reality of our body in a socially open relationship has to do with our future life, which is a life of communion intimately related to the public political sphere. The resurrection of the body from death means the possibility for life as communion. This is the life of the future and the condition necessary for public engagement and the adoption of a culture of life rather than one of death.

THE KINGDOM OF GOD AND A REALITY OF LORDLESS POWERS

Two different understandings of God's kingdom have to be avoided: an individualistic-separatist vision of God's kingdom in which otherworldliness comes to the fore, and a secularist-humanitarian vision of God's kingdom in which the earthly kingdom is identified with the heavenly kingdom. Regarding the first vision, Marx's critique of religion has validity: "religion is the sign of the oppressed creature, the heart of a heartless world, and the soul of soulless conditions." In short, "it is the opium of the people."[26]

Regarding the second vision, Marx, unlike his followers, gives credit to the socio-critical dimension of religion. "Religious suffering is at the same time an expression of real suffering and a protest against real suffering."[27] However, protest atheism, which followed Marx's vision of the elimination of religion, fell into a seedbed of anthropological malnutrition and Procrustean reductionism in the name of human liberation.

In Jesus's prayer, "Thy Kingdom Come," God's kingdom as the place of the world has to do with the proclamation of the gospel for those who suffer in the predicaments of our society. The heart of the gospel is the message of the kingdom of God. In Hebrew, *malkuth* YHWH (kingdom of God) means God's rule in a verbal sense. In the New Testament God's reign in the full sense is only present where the last enemy, death, is overcome (1 Cor 15:26; Rev 21:4). In a biblical eschatology transcendence is directed toward the future while, as a critique, it is breaking into the present condition of the world under contradiction and alienation.

26. Marx, *Early Writings*, 43.
27. Ibid., 44.

For this reason, God's transcendence, which can be articulated in light of God's future, begins with a criticism of the *status quo* in a given society, which is built on the cost of the other's life. Society is the product of humanity, which is captive to its rule. Self-preservation and self-profit in social life ruins our relationship with creation, transforming the stewardship mandate (Genesis 2) into a ruthless exploitation. God's will is in creation's favor, becoming the ground for promise and the hope of all creatures.

Through the story of Jesus Christ, God's reign is already present, while at the same time belonging to the future. The *metanoia*, which centers on the kingdom of God, begins with Jesus' message and the apostolic exhortations (*paranesis*) which articulate the life of community in the midst of a society in which the kingdom of God is anticipated. Thus, the kingdom of God is embedded within a new social, public life.

Martin Buber once wrote of the life of Jesus in reference to God's kingdom. For Buber, the kingdom of God that Jesus calls is the perfect life of people together. It refers to the perfect fellowship, which implies the immediate reign of God, his *basileia*, God's earthly kingdom.[28]

God's kingdom is a coming as well as a becoming. The time is qualified as *kairos*, the opportune hour, the space as a sanctified sign of God's place in light of God's kingdom. We must be involved and react as God's co-workers against the reality of "the lordless powers" rather than waiting for the kingdom of God as idle spectators. We should make the most of time (Eph 5:16, Col 4:5), not letting it pass by idly, but engaging and filling it with prayer and action.

Barth circumscribes principalities and powers in Ephesians in terms of the lordless powers. There is parallel to the history of human emancipation from God. There runs that of the emancipation of human own possibilities from God. This indicates history of overpowering human desires, aspirations, and will by the power, the superpower, of human ability.[29]

Barth refers to the myth of the state, to its absolutizing power, which makes blind government and oppression an apparatus of the instrument of human order. He thinks of the destructive power of mammon—the rule and sway of the profit motive, to which countless people, especially at the bottom but also at the top of the social ladder, fall victim. He also

---

28. Gollwitzer, *Introduction*, 151.
29. Barth, *Christian Life*, 214.

mentions the perverting rule of ideology, which so often tries to put those who fashion it on the Procrustean bed of its dictates, and in this way deforms them. He critically surveys the chthonic powers, including technology. These are at first a liberating force, but soon become threatening and controlling forces, which increasingly destroy the environment. They also include less harmful powers such as sport and fashion.

Barth's critique of the lordless powers can be understood as a theological critique of fetishism. In the process of rationalization or disenchantment of the world (Max Weber), Barth keenly discerns an unreconciled reality of lordless powers in the public sphere of political absolutism, economic mammon, ideology of idol-producing, and chthonic powers. Barth's theological critique of fetishism is related to an analysis of the human condition in estrangement and alienation from God. Furthermore, his critique of fetishism takes issue with reification (commodity fetishism) and the dominion of mammon (money fetishism).

Barth analyzes the reality of lordless powers in comprehensive spheres in light of his ethics of reconciliation and God's kingdom. Barth's language of lordless powers can be in parallel with Hinkelammert's critical analysis of the capitalist order in terms of the principle of fetishism. The liberation theology in Latin America is a critical reflection of Christian praxis in light of the liberating Word of God.

Through the analysis of the ideological weapon of death in a capitalist society, Hinkelammert proposes a critique of the idols of oppression. This constitutes his core message of liberation theology as an option for the theology of life, which is physically oriented toward the hope of God's kingdom. Marx's analysis of fetishism of civil society, which accumulates capital and, in turn, capital shapes, explicates the structure of political economy as well as human consciousness and thought form.

A consequence of the fetishism of society is the legitimation of the death of the poor. The myth of justifying the treatment of a victim, connected with the Oedipus tragedy, is strictly rejected. If a scientific rationality justifies victimization, however it might bring heaven on earth, it is wrong. A theory is scientifically valid if it does not demand a victim through history, but unearths the mechanism generating the victim. The victim must be the criteria on which the truth of a theory is judged.

The political responsibility of the Christian community is directed toward a better communal life, and movement toward a concrete utopia that is an ever-changing self-renewal in deconstruction of the rule of privilege, dominion, and violence.[30] A movement toward life, which comes from God's reign, finds its active fulfillment in the second petition of Lord's Prayer: "Thy will be done on earth as it is in heaven." Against the lordless powers, "the coming world" of God, in which many from east and west sit at table with Abraham, Isaac, and Jacob (Matt 8:11–12), breaks into our midst here and now, moving into the future.

A THEOLOGY OF LIFE AND ECONOMY

God and the sharing of a meal belong together: "Give us this day our daily bread." When it comes to theology and economic life, Luther can become an illuminating example. For Luther, theology is deeply connected with economic life. Alternatives such as "God versus mammon" creates a driving force in shaping and characterizing Luther's teaching of justification and prophetic *diakonia* on behalf of those who are alienated, maltreated, and economically weaker. Luther opposed the expanding money system and credit economy. He felt that manipulation of prices in one's own interest was contrary to God's word, reason, and every sense of justice.

Luther's critique of mammon is based on God's commandment: "You shall not steal." This became the vehicle for Luther's struggle with the reality of early capitalism at his time. Economic issues became an integral part of Luther's theological reflection on God. Therefore, Luther described the problem of capital expansion in terms of the metaphor of "devouring capital."[31] Luther's theological view of economic justice has a face looking forward while his political theology is relegated to a face looking backward.

In view of progressive side of Luther's theology of economic justice, even Karl Marx was not hesitant to quote Luther in his analysis of the conversion of surplus-value into capital. For Marx, Luther appeares to be the prophetic denouncer of capital accumulation associated with usury. Luther argues that the heathen were able to conclude that a usurer is a double-dyed thief and murderer. However, Christians hold them in such honor. Even Christians worship them for the sake of their money. Little thieves are put in the stocks, while great thieves go

---

30. Gollwitzer, *Introduction*, 153.

31. Luther, "An die Pfarrherren," 331–424 (=WA). See Marquardt, "Gott oder Mammon," 189.

flaunting in gold and silk. Therefore there is, on this earth, no greater enemy of people (after the devil) than a gripe-money, and usurer. They want to be God over all.[32]

Hence, Luther's teaching of justification cannot be understood properly without regarding his critique of capital monopoly. In exposition of the first commandment in *The Large Catechism*, Luther contrasts God with Mammon. Idolatry, for Luther, is primarily "a matter of the heart." There are those who think that they can trust in money and property. They have a god: mammon, that is, money and property. Luther argues that money and property are the most common idol on earth.[33]

According to Luther, we should not view God as an invisible hand regulating the market exchange and bringing a profit-making accumulation of capital for the rich. Luther's denouncement of "devouring capital" in early capitalism demonstrates that God is present with suffering humanity and encourages us to follow God's reign in presence with the economically victimized.

The theology of economic justice includes a critical analysis of reified thinking and the fetish character of the world economic system. Thus, a critical analysis of the enforcement of the neo-liberal world economy guides Christian theology in the context of the downside of universal history of globalization to take a postcolonial character.[34] By bringing a prophetic-ethical challenge to the "Capitalist revolution" in light of the gospel of Jesus Christ, the Christian Church must start with a conversion from the previous model of an alliance with the "haves," toward God's reign which is revealed in Jesus Christ as the companionship with those historically and socially on the margin.

A theology of economic justice articulates our *metanoia* from destruction toward a constructive project of a more democratically, economically, and ecologically viable and sustainable human society. Polluted ground water also runs in the village of high society. A critical analysis of society and the economic system is an indispensable part of a Christian theology of the public sphere. Where growth is the characteristic mark of Capitalistic development, the drive to growth overcomes all obstructions and ethical protests through the expansion of capital for the sake of profit gain.

32. Marx, *Capital*, 1:649–50.
33. Luther, "The Large Catechism (1529)," 387.
34. Hinkelammert, *Ideological Weapons*, 5–42.

In the past, exploitation, division, and penetration by European colonialism destroyed the condition of development for dependent and periphery nations to the benefit of the central nations. Today's economic reality of globalization and "hyper-capitalism"[35] have similar destructive economic, social, and ecological consequences through the rich nations' international institutions (for instance, the G7/G8 world economic summits, the IMF, the World Bank, the Organization for Economic Cooperation and Development, and the World Trade Organization). These institutions are misused as political means for capital accumulation and profit-making in service of the rich nations. In the framework of the world economic system, the global empire prevents governments from regulating social and environmental obligations and responsibilities on invested capital.[36]

Luther's alternative of God versus idol is not merely a question of Christian morality, but a question of the necessity of confessional renewal. For Luther, a confession of God, who emancipates Israel out of Egypt and justifies us through Christ, cannot be properly understood and implemented apart from a critical deliberation of the socioeconomic consequences of idolatry, which was a reality of the early capitalist system in Luther's time. Luther's "theological" critique of Roman Catholicism was embedded within his "socioeconomic" critique of its structure and system. Charles V was dependent on the Fuggers. Thus, Luther ironically characterized his Catholic opponent, John Eck as a "plutologian," rather than a theologian.[37] In the Roman Church "the whole spiritual governance is nothing but money, money, money. Everything is geared to money-making."[38]

Sharply seeing the "devouring" system and the process of capital concentration and accumulation, Luther denounced the Christian character of early capitalism in reference to colonialism. As a matter of fact, Luther dealt with mammon as a totality and a system of reality which conditions and dominates socioeconomic life in the public sphere.

Luther's view of economic relations underlines the consequence of the greed of the rich under which the poor suffer. The concept of greed assumes a central meaning in Luther's theological thought, when the

---

35. Rifkin, *Age of Access*, 89.
36. Duchrow and Hinkelammert, *Property for People*, 99.
37. Marquardt, "Gott oder Mammon," 193.
38. Duchrow, *Alternatives*, 220.

greed is seen as contradiction to faith in God. Understanding the greed in terms of biblical prophetic realism, Luther felt it difficult to create directly the kingdom of God in the economic and social historical realm.

Therefore, Luther demands the accountability of the faithful believers in the Church of Christ for the worldly and economic realm. In the demand for the kingdom of God, which is included in the gospel, Luther perceives this accountability as orientation and indication for the promotion of positive change in the economic realm.[39]

Given the relationship of justification to economic justice, the Reformer's theology of justification implies a notion that God's righteousness is also established through the discipleship of the justified in the service of God's kingdom. At this juncture, Luther's teaching of justification articulates justification of God. *Deum justificare*, which means giving God justice, actually, expresses the justification of God. The Reformer's teaching of justification embraces the justification of human being before God, as well as the justification of God in social and public life.[40] In this light Luther's model of two kingdoms is rendered more amenable to life arrangements in the public economic sphere.

Justification, which has a protological-forensic moment, is to bring God's justice in the world in an eschatological openness. Thus, the Reformer's theology of justification is connected with ethical praxis of *paranesis* and evangelical delight in doing the law.[41] Justification embraces justification of humanity before God *extra nos* and also promotes God's righteousness in human life. Once we are justified, we, as coworkers with God, proceed to an active life of discipleship.[42]

Following Luther's theological relationship between justification and discipleship, Bonhoeffer also offers a model of ethical concretization of dogmatic and confessional theology. Bonhoeffer helps us to see the reality of the world from the angle of those from below. From the start, Bonhoeffer was aware of the prophetic line and direction coming out of the gospel of Jesus Christ which stands for ethics, co-humanity, serving church, discipleship, social justice, and peace movement: all in all, political commitment.[43]

39. Rieth, *Habsucht*, 220–21.
40. Iwand, *Righteousness of Faith*, 21.
41. Luther, "Prefaces (1545, 1523)," "How Christian," 118–34, 135–48.
42. Chung, *Christian Mission*, 41–43, 56–57.
43. Rumscheidt, *Fragments*, 119.

4

Theologia Crucis and a Socially Embodied Life

THEOLOGIA CRUCIS AND THEOLOGIA VITAE

St. Paul's theology of the Word of the Cross (1 Cor 1:18) structures his *theologia crucis* to the degree that he sees all life under the sign of death. *Theologia crucis* affirms St. John's theology of life. The Word of the cross includes the proclamation of the *Logos* as the light of the life for all. Here we see an inseparable connection between *theologia crucis* and *theologia vitae*.

God lives and is known as the living God. The new life is the life coming out of God. From a Biblical perspective, an invocation of God is not based on a human projection of an experience with God, for God can meet us in a different way from what we expect. Here we ascribe freedom as a definition of God. God is free of us, independent of us, ahead of us, rather than being captive to human projection. The freedom of God also has another positive meaning: liberation. This implies setting us free. Liberation is the reality that proclaims freedom by setting us free. "So if the Son makes you free, you will be free indeed" (John 8:36). Christ has set us free for freedom (Gal 5:1). Freedom without liberation results in an irresponsible self-indulgence while liberation without freedom results in an experiment of a society of barbarianism in the disguise of liberation.

Those who experience God in Jesus Christ experience this freedom. This experience characterizes human existence like Israel, which experiences God in Exodus. Freedom and the life of liberation belong together. In freedom, we know of true and genuine life. This is the law of the Spirit of life in Jesus Christ, who set us free from the law of sin and death (Rom 8:2).

From this perspective, we hear in John 5:26. God has life in God's self, so God has granted the Son also to have life in himself. God's life in God's self refers to the inner life of God, which says that God is the living God. St. John witnesses that in the beginning was the Word that was with God, and the Word was God. The life was the light for all humanity. This is confirmation of the freedom of God, in which God shares God's inner life with the Son. God let God's fundamental action of sharing life shine in the darkness of the world. The new life is the inner life of God, which proves that God is free, living, and liberating.

Given this fact, a theological concept of the immanent Trinity denotes God's internal life through freedom and communion *(perichoresis)* within God's self. A theology of Trinity is christologically and covenantly articulated in the sense of Jesus's prayer (John 17:21), which implies the Biblical concept of God's covenant with Israel and the world. A Biblical concept of God's transcendence is secured in the concept of God *in se* as the one who loves in freedom, communion, and liberation. God's transcendence in the innertrinitarian life points to the God of Abraham, Isaac, Jacob, and the Father of Jesus Christ.

The God of Israel should not be superseded by the name of Jesus Christ. Rather, the name of Jesus Christ enters into the mystery of the name of the God of Israel. A Trinitarian history of God in sending the Son in the presence and promise of the Spirit expresses three modes of God's historical action in Trinitarian relationality. God *for us* (the economic Trinity) is grounded in God *in se* as the source of eternal life. The triune God is the God of promise in a historical horizon from Abraham until Jesus Christ who retains a new creation of the world in a utopian sense (Revelation 21).

Transcendence and the future of God in the Trinitarian action are not dissolved into a prolepsis or anticipation of God's eternal life here and now. A Trinitarian confession to the God of Israel is connected with God's eschatological dynamism to the extent that God's name, YHWH "God will be that will be," finds its locus in St. Paul's theology of eschatology which states that "God may be all in all" (1 Cor 15:28). Thus, self-communication and revelation of God's name, YHWH, is structured and framed in a Trinitarian-eschatological manner.

God's internal dynamism becomes a basis for bringing us to the love and liberation of God *for us* in God's sending the Son through the Holy Spirit. Doxology is an indispensable dimension of the Christian confession of the triune God for and with us. God, seen in Trinitarian perspective, gives an account of the Father's communal event with the Son in the movement of the Holy Spirit for and with us.

Opera trinitatis ad intra (the work of the Trinity toward God's self) is secured for the sake of God's transcendence, freedom, and future. *Opera trinitatis ad extra* or the economic Trinity bears witness to God's internal dynamic social life within God's self, that is the *topos* of the world. This economic Trinity inspires our utopian longing for a better life and a new sphere and embraces the Israelite hope of God's coming unity in an eschatological direction.

This Trinitarian theology in an eschatological contour makes us into cooperators with God for God's sake in the public sphere, and has a primary meaning of a theology of eternal life: *vita aeterna*. The eternal life implies that God constantly shares God's life with us. This is the basis for a theology of Christian hope. This hope is oriented for the new world and the new humanity in expectation of the new heaven and earth. This hope is not merely limited to a mystical concentration on God and soul or an individualistic pietism.

A theology of hope is a meditation on the new life in view of God's action of sharing God's life with us in a personal, social, historical, and eschatological manner. God is in becoming by sharing God's life with us in expectation of the coming world of God. This hope stands as the sign of the transformation of reality of life and the world. Eschatology stands prior to the doctrine of creation, so that the history of creation must be interpreted in light of God's history of liberation with Israel from Egypt and God's eschatological creation in Jesus Christ.

In 2 Cor 5:17, we read, "If anyone is in Christ, there is a new creation. Everything old has passed away. Everything has become new." A Christian theology of hope in expectation of new life is based on God's act of reconciliation in Christ with the world. All that was historical in Jesus is integrated to God's transforming action of the world. In Jesus Christ, the old reality has become the new one and Jesus himself stands in the midst of the breakthrough of the new reality. Through the glory of the Father who awakens Jesus from the dead, everything is changed into the new life.

In his farewell sermon Jesus promises a completely new event: the coming of the Spirit of truth. The future is connected with the coming. The Spirit of truth will declare the things that are to come (John 16:13).

To the degree that God shares God's internal life with Jesus and brings us into the life of a fundamentally new eon through the resurrection of Jesus, God liberates us from the law of sin and death and bestows on us a new life as liberated ones from the root of death. God is the One who causes breath to enter the dry bones and makes them alive (Ezek 37:5–6).

Eternal life is not the infinite postponement of death, or a bliss experienced by an immortal soul, as imagined in Neo-Platonic philosophy. Such philosophy has no biblical connection to God's transforming action that brings the new life to the new world here and now through Jesus Christ in the presence of the Spirit. The cosmological hymns of Christ in Col 1:15–20 and Eph 1:4–10 state that the Christian proclamation is interested not only in the redemption of the soul, but in that of the world.

In Christ, as the first-born of all creation, all things in heaven and on earth were created through him and for him. Through Christ, God was pleased to reconcile God's self to all things (Col 1:20). Cosmological assertions have limiting and critical implications. Promise, hope, and expectation of the coming world have already become actual in Christ because these are God's gifts, presented to Christians.

As for Christian eschatology, genuine hope comes from the Word of God, which is a flower bud of Christian hope. We are not in a position to anticipate something of the *eschaton*. We are not capable of knowing or anticipating what is to come in the future of God. Rather, Christian hope resides in clarifying and actualizing what we receive as a gift of God in light of God's promise. A theology of Christian hope, seen in light of God's promise, is connected with the pre-sign of the coming world of God. God gives a sign of the eternal life to our present life, which is not yet redeemed.

For this eschatological project, it is hard to ground a theology of hope or prolepsis only in the Christian message of future resurrection. When Christian hope is connected with the natural hope of humanity (*spes naturalis*) a principle of *spes quaerens intellectum* (hope in search of understanding) becomes *docta spes* of Christian theology rather than *fides quaerrens intellectum* (faith in search of understanding). Consequently, a Christian message of hope is made into the genitive theology, which absolutizes an aspect (hope) of the Christian message as the theological grounding principle by integrating an extra-theological pre-understanding of hope. This tendency of genitive theology can be found also in the universal-historical project of God's prolepsis, which should be played off against God's past (in covenant or election) and present (through the grace of justification in Christ through the Word and sacrament).

In the universal-historical framework, theological knowledge rests on God's indirect revelation in history and positivistic anticipation that repeat the prolepsis of the *eschaton* in the history of Jesus Christ. This universal-historical project is based on a metaphysical concept of God as the reality that determines all and is powerful over all. God, as the prolepsis of the world, rules universally, without recognizing God's special history of covenant with Israel.

A project of revelation as history is depicted as universal history as revelation. The revelation of the God of Israel is understood as a universal historical event, which is fulfilled in the anticipation of the end in the resurrection of Jesus Christ. A program of revelation as history eliminates the special place of Israel and substitutes the implication of Israel for the Church in light of God's universal history. This perspective contradicts a biblical understanding of God's specific covenant history with Israel.

Given this fact, it is wise to consider Christian eschatology not by beginning with the hope or prolepsis of God, but with the Word of God in an eschatological dimension through the established covenant with Israel and the grace of justification through Christ for all. Covenant is a presupposition of reconciliation so that Christ's reconciliation does not discard God's covenant with Israel, but fulfills it in embrace of Torah. A Biblical argument with the Jewish religion is not critical of the Torah as such. Rather it takes issue with the Jewish cult and rituals in context of Levitical sacrifice in light of the sacrifice of Jesus Christ. Christian eschatology is the Christian hope, which is grounded in God's grace of justification through the reconciliation of Jesus Christ with the world.

The eschatological theology of the Word of God based on the word of justification and reconciliation is interconnected with *theologia crucis* and *theologia vitae*. In light of this, we separate ourselves from a pan-eschatological project of totalizing and dissolving everything temporal and particular into the future. The biblical witness of the existential-presentative eschatology of God in Jesus Christ retains its reality from the eschatological coming of God. Conversely, our language of eschatology can be actualized and concretized in the framework of existential-presentative eschatology, which has begun in Christ. The two forms of biblical eschatology are mutually attested. Nonetheless, Christ's eschatology does not replace God's eschatology because the former is not in competition with the latter (1 Cor 15:28).

The cross, as St. Paul understands it, is not simply an historical event of the past; rather, it entails a self-explicating future in itself. In other words, it is an eschatological event. The character of the future in Paul's concept of the Word of the cross comes from the event of the Spirit, which is already an event in the Word of the cross. God has revealed it to us through the Spirit. The Spirit that is from God searches even the depths of God (1 Cor 2:10-16), bestowing God's life on us.

Theologia crucis is not simply a narrative of the Golgotha-event, but it speaks of the crucified Jesus whom God had made into the power of God (1 Cor 1:18) who has raised him from the dead. *Theologia crucis* as *theologia vitae* is cautious to accept fully a concept of the godforsakeness of Jesus on the cross. For instance, a Trinitarian framework of the resurrection of the crucified one places God into humiliation and abandonment. Consequently, God is no more powerful than in the state of contradiction of self-abandonment. As a result, the doctrine of *kenosis*, the self-emptying of God, surfaces. Based on abandonment and surrender, Jesus's death is understood as death in God.[1]

For a Trinitarian theology of the cross, Moltmann unfortunately retrieves a sacrificial interpretation of Jesus's death in light of God's abandonment. He rejects a Jewish non-sacrificial interpretation as seen in Luke 23:46 in connection with Ps 31:6. ("Father, into thy hands I commit my spirit.") In the context of Luke and John, the non-sacrificial language of Jesus's death is replaced by Moltmann's model of the abandonment of the divine Son. In it "Jesus died with the signs and expressions of a profound abandonment by God."[2]

St. Paul's theology of the cross (1 Cor 1:18), as witness to God's reconciliation with humanity and the world, implies an exchange of money, a ransom. Luther's recognition of the exchange of trade and the market as a conflict between the worship of God and the worship of mammon comes as no surprise. Luther calls God a glowing oven full of love,[3] while

---

1. Moltmann *Crucified God*, 207.
2. Ibid., 147.
3. WA 10, III, 56.

relating his struggle and resistance to economic injustice and the love of God in the gospel.

In this regard, the Word of the cross is the Word of new life in which God's future has already begun. Our existence in this Word shifts to the sphere of God's future. In glory we will see Christ. For Paul a vision of God is connected with love. Now we see in a mirror, dimly, but then we will see face to face (1 Cor 13:12). Here is a parallel to the exchange between God and Moses as seen in Exod 33:18, 20. God creates a way for Moses to see God's glory without endangering his life (Exod 33:21–22). In Num 12:8 God is a dialogue partner with Moses: With Moses God speaks face to face—clearly, not in riddles; and he beholds the form of the Lord.

In Jesus's farewell sermon as recorded by John (14:7), Jesus claims that his disciples have seen God. Therefore, we can conclude that the eschatological expansion of God-humanity-vision has already begun in Jesus. St. Paul sees that it begins in the operation of the Spirit. The Lord is the Spirit. Where the Spirit of the Lord is, there is freedom. In this specific freedom of the Spirit Paul actualizes a dimension of God's future (2 Cor 3:17–18). The freedom that the Spirit brings enables a pre-mirroring of the future vision.

A BODILY-ESCHATOLOGICAL DIMENSION IN A VISION OF ETERNAL LIFE

First John mentions the participation of the human being in God's life, explaining that in the last revelation we will become the children of God. When God is revealed, we will be like God, for we will see God as God is (1 John 3:2). This is a biblical concept of grace as a gift of God's future. The Gospel of Matthew speaks of it in a similar way: "Blessed are the pure in heart, for they will see God" (Matt 5:8). God as the wholly other is known by God as the *topos* of the world. The Greek term for knowledge in a Biblical context has its origin in the Hebrew term, *Yada*, which implies sexual, spiritual, and bodily knowledge.

Knowledge is defined in the sense of personal–social wholeness: the I-Thou event between God and human beings is embedded within public sphere. Explaining the completion of this event, Paul uses thinking and reasoning (1 Cor 13:11): vision implies engaged thinking and eschatological vision points to an existential, intellectual event of the knowledge of God. There is no adequate concept in the description of the reality of the biblical God except for the word of love. Anyone who loves God is known by God (1 Cor 8:3). An acknowledging relationship is a living relationship. To see and love God is a whole and complete relationship.

In a similar fashion, Augustine explains his Christian identity in light of love. In *armor Dei*, he sees the recollection of all previous love relationships sublated. The love of God and the reflection of world reality become one (*Conf.* 10). Unlike Augustine, however, Paul is convinced that all previous loves were only a part of previous knowledge (1 Cor 13:9). When the complete comes, the partial will come to an end. Paul expects something radical from love.

God comes to Job in the eschatological time where he sees God: in his flesh Job shall see God (Job 19:27). Seeing becomes reflective of what is seen. This corresponds to the unity between knowing and being known in St. Paul. Job sees God as the savior, friend, and helper, not as the enemy.

Paul, in Rom 1:20, affirms that God is revealed in God's works, but also identifies God's self as God in God's work. A participation in God's history implies the new creation. We remain in faith, which is not the same as seeing: We walk by faith, not by sight (2 Cor 5:7). But in faith we experience a future vision promised to faith. A longing or desire for God's future awakens. "The eyes of all look to you, and you give them their food in due season" (Ps 145:15; 42:2).

The ancient Church taught a vision of eternal life as an experience of the highest beatitude: *vita aeterna*. In the beatific vision, the mutual glorification between God and the human being occurs in our body, in the desire and longing to move toward the better, heavenly place in the communion of saints and in communion with God. Here, a body-soul wholeness in the biblical understanding of human being plays a role so that an appreciation of the spiritual does not rise above that of the bodily. In the God-vision, there is a bodily dimension in the enjoyment of heavenly place or the communion experience between God and the saints.

The experience of eternal life is a feast of life, which one could call a fest of physicality. In Luke 14 Jesus is invited to eat a meal on the Sabbath in the house of a leader of the Pharisees. Here Jesus speaks to the guests about a wedding banquet as a parable for the coming kingdom of God. One of the dinner guests replies: "Blessed is anyone who will eat bread in the kingdom of God!" (Luke 14:15). This is the expanded hope of Israel: a feast meal in the coming new world. The apocalyptic Jesus, in the congregation of Laodicea, shares the meal with people from all nations (Rev 3:20).

In Luke 22:29–30 Jesus makes a meal table for his disciples in the new aeon: They may eat and drink at my table in his kingdom. This expectation of the guest meal in the future world plays an important role in the life of Jesus. Jesus lives as a new human being, a being of the future. For him, the meal is open to the future. The miracle of feeding five thousand people with five loaves and two fishes belongs to this story (Matt 14:13–21). The story of the wedding in Cana of Galilee according to John is the beginning of the signs pointing to an eschatological transparence of the feast and the beginning of Jesus's glory (John 2:1–11).

In Isa 25:6, we read of a vision of "a feast of rich food, a feast of well-aged wines, of rich food filled with marrow, of well-aged wines strained clear." Here, table fellowship among people anticipated a fellowship of peace of the world. Exodus 24: 9–11 speaks of a vision of God and a covenant meal as a wholeness in which God participates: "They beheld God, and they ate and drank."

The Church as *sanctorum communio* can be characterized in light of existence in a double dimension, *simul peccator et justus* in Luther's sense. As an assembly of sinners, the Church lives in a sinful reality, but as a justified body, it lives in hope (Rom 4:7). In understanding Luther's theology of *simul peccator et justus*, the issue is a proclamation of new existence, so that God's grace integrates human existence into the future of God.[4] Luther's theology of justification should be understood as a theology of God's future in an eschatological sense. For Luther the Kingdom of God is what the Church expects and prays for. The Christian church serves the Kingdom of God rather than being occupied with an interest of self-apotheosis.

According to Rev 21:22, God and the Lamb are the temple in the midst of the new city. In the Revelation God opens God's self in an Old Testament-Trinitarian sense: in the name of the Lord (*adonai*), in the name of God (*elohim*), and in the name of pantocrator (*zebaoth*). The Lamb of God, who takes away the sin of the world, stands next to God. Eternal life in the Kingdom of God is the life of communion for all rather than the life of the soul.

---

4. Iwand, *Luthers Theologie*, 74.

Everything separated finds itself whole again in the vision of God. God is the place of the world and God opens the world anew. God is the essence of the public sphere and openness in relationship with the world, which does not encapsulate or dissolve God into itself. In the beatific vision, we do not strive for our soul's sake, but for God's sake and the world's sake. God's Spirit anointed Jesus "to bring good news to the poor," "to proclaim release to the captives and recovery of sight to the blind, to let the oppressed go free, to proclaim the year of the Lord's favor" (Luke 4:18–19).

A theology of beatific vision is a theology of the life-promoting Spirit which becomes foundational for *theologia crucis*, proclaiming God's grace of liberation to all, especially in companionship with those who are "the outcast, the suspects, the maltreated, the powerless, the oppressed, the reviled, in short . . . those who suffer."[5] The theology of the cross does not negate God's universal reign, but makes it more explicit and sober in matters of limitation and corruption in human life. Furthermore, Jesus "will proclaim justice to the Gentiles . . . He will not break a bruised reed or quench a smoldering wick . . . And in his name the Gentiles will hope" (Matt 12:18–21).

Theologia crucis from below, which originates from the physical life of Jesus in companionship with the *ochlos-minjung*, finds its first articulation in God's passionate solidarity with God's people in the history of Israel and propels a political hermeneutic of *anthropologia crucis* which articulates beneath what is said and written to decipher hidden interest and repressed life. *Theologia crucis* mobilizes a counter-memory for salvaging life from the exclusive encapsulation of dogmatic truth, revealing an interplay of domination and theological knowledge that completely denies the bodily dimension of the gospel. Given this fact, it is important to discuss a theology of the Word of God culturally embodied in the process of inculturation.

GOD'S WORD AS EMBODIED IN INCULTURATION

Theologia crucis, which is embedded with *theologia vitae,* is of Trinitarian, eschatological, and hermeneutical character. *Theologia crucis* is Christian interpretation of God's Word incarnated and embodied in life, death, and resurrection of Jesus Christ, a born Jew, in the presence of the Holy

---

5. Bonhoeffer, *Letters and Papers*, 17.

Spirit. When *theologia crucis* is seen in light of the dynamism of God's speech event, it underscores an aspect of God's act of speech in recognition of the margin and voiceless in the world of religions. Thus, it implies an eschatological dimension as *theologia viatoroum*. *Theologia crucis* is an interpretation of God's self-communication in Christ and God's involvement in the world through the Word and the Spirit. It presupposes a theology of Word of God embodied in other cultures and religions. This perspective leads to a theological and hermeneutical deliberation of inculturation and emancipation in the context of religious pluralism.

In a context of the Global South or East, an endeavor for theologizing in one's own particular life setting becomes necessary and inevitable. We perceive that there is an attempt to propose the indigenous discovery of Christianity.[6] The indigenous discovery of Christianity is in contrast to the Christian discovery of indigenous culture and religious belief system. In a postmodern context, suspicion of the universal narrative of human reason—or "incredulity toward metanarratives"[7]—functions as a synchronic hermeneutic of doubt and refusal, revealing a nexus between power and knowledge in politics, institutions, and social sciences. Recognition of the Other and the Different becomes a main issue in postmodern challenge, as well as in the circle of theology of religions.[8]

Inculturation is necessary for co-existence, for living and working in peace with non–Christian religious communities. However, the Christian message of the gospel must not merely be accommodated to the *status quo* of indigenous culture and religion. An intercultural issue of translation and interpretation of the Christian mission into non-Christian life setting does not remain satisfied with recognizing the conservative and backward-looking elements as such. Every religion can be patterned and structured in sacramental-ritual, prophetic-ethical-social, and personal-experiential-mystical components. The Christian idea of incarnation, the divine assumption of human flesh, basically refers to the fact that the gospel calls for being embodied and acculturated in an on-going way as it encounters human life and religious orientation in a particular place and time. The subject matter of the gospel is looking ahead rather than looking backwards, because God is ahead of us.

---

6. Sanneh, *Whose Religion*, 10.
7. Lyotard, *Postmodern Condition*, xxiv.
8. Knitter, *No Other Name?*

Human interpretation remains an approximation of the subject matter of the Scripture. This perspective also helps Western Christianity also free itself from a Babylonian captivity to Christendom or Eurocentrism.[9] It also helps indigenous Christianity to take seriously the subject matter of the Scripture through its interpretative imagination and appropriation. The Hellenization of Christianity, as well as the indigenous domestication of the gospel, does not indicate a promise in dealing with inculturation and emancipation.

When the Church engages in dialogue with people of other cultures and faiths, mission and evangelization assume the form of witnessing to God's gracious embrace of the world, justice for human life, and peace among religions in light of God's reconciliation with the world through Jesus Christ in the presence of the Holy Spirit.

For the task of theological inculturation, it is significant to articulate a theology of the Word of God from an irregular and postfoundational perspective. Here, the speech act of God is not simply reduced to the ecclesial sphere. For example, in Heb 1:1, "God spoke to our ancestors in many and various ways by the prophets." The Word of God in Jesus Christ cannot be understood apart from God's speech in action throughout all the ages in plural horizons of effect.

God's Word is happening to the extent that it is an illuminating word involving continually human social existence (Matt 18:20; 1 Sam 23:42). The God who speaks shapes the life of humanity as dialogue. What is essential in the creatures' experience of God is a message of the Word of God to all. This word-event takes place in the gospel, which is the living voice of God. If understanding becomes possible through language in a hermeneutical sense,[10] the Word of God in the presence of the Holy Spirit poses the problem of understanding, opening up and bringing human existence to an encounter with the reality of divine speech in action toward the world. Thus, a theology of dialogue draws special attention to the dialogical mode of the presence of God in Christ.[11]

The theology in dialogue, which is of universal openness, protects ecclesial theology from the dangers of dogmatization, encapsulation, and parochialism. *Theologia crucis* is essentially structured in the sense

---

9. Bosch, *Transforming Mission*, 447–54.
10. Ebeling, *Word and Faith*, 318.
11. Marquardt, *Von Elend und Heimsuchung*, 162.

of theology of dialogue which implies "the mutual conversation and consolation of brothers and sisters"[12] in Luther's thought.

God, as one who speaks in promise, reconciliation, and freedom, moves and challenges the Christian Church to embrace an understanding of Scripture in light of subject matter of the Scripture, namely God as the infinite horizon of the Scripture. This horizon of God's Word can be likened to the source of a stream, which is a critique of the Church's errors in its successive historical development and its painful tragedy in the history of mission.[13]

Thus, it is important for the readers of the Scripture to concern themselves with and reflect upon the source's claim on its stream. God, as the origin and source of the Scripture, is here seen as a contemporary reality in the life of the Church through the Word and sacraments. This brings into sharper profile the task of emancipation and inculturation in light of the event of divine speech. A hermeneutic of God's act of speech is grounded in the universal grace of God in Christ for all. Consequently, this leads to the critique of the Church's parochialism and collaboration with the *status quo,* which is deaf to God's reign in the world.

In this regard it is essential to heed God's speech event coming outside of the walls of the Christian Church. An irregular, postecclesial configuration of God's act of speech deals with unmethodical, chaotic, unexpected, and provocative dimensions of divine speech. In this irregular, postecclesial approach, a more productive result would be expected and gained than what regular and systematic methodology achieves. This irregular and postfoundational hermeneutic (in the sense of God's dynamic saying beyond the ecclesial-foundational sphere) is no less scientific than the regular systematic deliberation of the word of God.

Deliberation on God's mystery, which is unsearchable and inscrutable (Romans 11), is associated with God's irregular, postecclesial act of speech, offering a possibility of thinking about God's way for people outside the ecclesial sphere. St. Paul's theology of God's irrevocable covenant with Israel must be a primary influence for the theological task of inculturation. Thus, God may speak to the Christian Church not only through Old Testament Israelites, but also through postbiblical rabbinic Judaism. Israel and Christianity stand in solidarity under God's covenant, which shapes and characterizes a common hope for God's future.

---

12. Luther, "The Smalcald Articles," 319.
13. Las Casas, *Devastation*.

Furthermore, God's universal covenant with the Gentiles through Noah implies God's "No" to ecclesial triumphalism.

A Christian theology of inculturation in light of God's act of speech challenges anti-Jewish tendencies as visible in a theology of religions, and lifts up the image of "God with us" as God who is the indwelling place with all. If we acknowledge Israel's faithfulness to God through Torah (in the Jewish "No" to Christian triumphalism), it is important to acknowledge every serious atheism and people of other cultures and religions in light of God's universal covenant through the reconciliation of Jesus Christ. *Theologia crucis*, which can be seen as a *topos* of God, presupposes basically *theologia vitae* for all in light of the dynamism of God's act of speech.

CHRISTIAN THEOLOGY AND RELIGIOUS OUTSIDERS

We perceive that there is one way of approaching the irregular speech of God as seen through the natural knowledge of God in the New Testament. Paul was confronted with such a problem in his missional setting. Paul did not want people to persist in paganism, so he invited them to faith in the gospel message of Christ. According to Rom 1:20–22 and 2:12–16, the pagans have knowledge of the existence of God even apart from any special or historical revelation. Moreover, in the Lucan account, Paul recognizes in Athens a religious concern, a reverence, and an awe in the presence of the gods, especially in their veneration of "the unknown God."

Although this presentation of God is misguided and distorted in temple worship or in the cult of images, the pagans, without Christian revelation were not godless or Godforsaken (Acts 17:22–28). As St. Paul argues, in God "we live and move and have our being." This idea is also affirmed by the Greek poets who have said, "For we too are God's offspring" (Acts 17:28). In the biblical context, none of the biblical writers wants to limit God's freedom and mystery in relation to non-biblical people. God's universal lordship of love and reconciliation is able to reach out to all. Herein, God's loving power is not limited to Israel, but remains awe-inspiring, and praise comes forth from all nations.

Prior to the covenant with Abraham, God established a universal covenant with Noah. God is pleased to have Abraham blessed by Melchizedek. In today's biblical study, Melchizedek could be understood as the non-Jewish leader of a religious community, different from the

Levitical or Aaronic order. We perceive that God is pleased to help and bless God's people Israel through religious outsiders.

In our general climate of religious tolerance and indifference, God speaks to us through symbolic figures like Melchizedek on behalf of righteousness and universal peace. God has used Cyrus, a pagan king, to help Israel. God changes Balaam's intended curse by speaking through a donkey. From the mouth of Balaam, God's speech is not to be neglected regardless of its sinister message (Num 22:22–35). All nations will call upon the name of the Lord with one voice in order to serve God with one accord (Zeph 3:9).

Given this biblical orientation, Genesis 12 contains a comprehensive blessing story for the descendents of Abraham. Ishmael, the first circumcised, enters into Abraham's blessing. Besides Isaac, Ishmael is also a participant in God's blessing of Abraham's descendents (Gen 17:20, 23). Ishmael and his descendents are granted God's irregular grace and blessing.

Furthermore, the dimension of the promise of blessing is valid for all the people of the world. We are aware of God's sympathy in Genesis for Hagar and Ishmael. The God of Abraham hears the outcry of the oppressed Hagar, a cry that echoes today in the form of suffering Muslim women in Palestine. The God who elects Israel is also the advocate for Ishmael and Hagar. In this regard, a theology of divine act of speech can be articulated in cultural, political service for Lazarus-*minjung*, the innocent victim who is burdened by the unrighteousness of the powerful in our global world.

In the synoptic gospels we are aware that Jesus's openness to religious outsiders is striking. "Whoever is not against us is for us" (Mark 9:40). "In my Father's house there are many dwelling places" (John 14:2). "For the children of this age are more shrewd in dealing with their own generation than are the children of light" (Luke 16:8ff.). In missional settings we see also God's plan of mission for Gentiles ahead of apostles in the life of Cornelius (Acts 10:34). In the case of Cornelius, Peter affirms God's universal covenant through Noah for all nations. It is important to take into account more positively God's universal covenant with Noah from an evangelical point of view.

To the Athenians in front of the Areopagus, St. Paul bears witness to *solus Christus* in a conviction that everybody lives, moves and has his/her being in the universal reign of God (Acts 17:22, 27b, 28).

We perceive that a universal dimension of the Old Testament plays an important role in Paul's understanding of God's reconciliation with the world. Eph 1:10 says, ". . . to unite all things in Christ, things in heaven and things on earth." There are Biblical passages in support of Christological universalism in light of God's reconciliation with the world (Col 1:20; Phil 2:10ff.; 1 Cor 15:22, 25, 28; Rom 5:18, 11:32; Rev 21:5, etc.). Paul's theology of justification refers not to the selfish private encapsulation of God's salvation in Jesus Christ in the interest of excluding and condemning religious outsiders. Rather it needs to be seen in a universal dimension of the Spirit in favor of them. "The wind blows wherever it pleases" (John 3:8).

In fact, a model of God's universal reign in the threefold life arrangements articulates God's twofold dynamic way of breaking into each life arrangement for the sake of justice, peace, and transformative recognition of the Other. God speaks to us through the religious outsiders in an unexpected, provocative, and postecclesial manner. Non-biblical religions or languages may serve as extraordinary ways of God's communication in a hermeneutical-analogical sense for giving an account of the mystery of God's reign.

In today's global context it is an indispensable task for non-Western Christians to read and interpret the Scriptures in their own life context in engagement with their tradition of interpretation and commentary in their religious classics. For instance, in an East Asian religious lifeworld, we perceive that there are scholarship, spirituality, and interpretation of their own classics, which have shaped and influenced their life in pursuit of the mystery of the truth and human dignity.

A Christian religion should learn primarily and wisely a prophetic-ethical aspect inherent in other cultures and religions. For instance, Christian prophetic-ethical orientation can be complemented with Buddhist ethic of compassion in socially engaged sense. Most religions have and appeal to sacred scriptures foundational for their beliefs, wisdom, spirituality, social justice, and ethical practices. These religious texts stand in a special relationship to the truth of ultimate reality as they express their religious experience, ethical life, and belief system.

A Christian approach to inculturation and emancipation in the reality of multi-religious life context needs to take seriously presence and dynamism of God's speech act through reconciliation and freedom in the world of non-Christian cultures and religions. A fusion, expansion, and new emergent form of multiple horizons occurring in the conversation between the gospel and other cultures (and religions) is directed and approximated toward the subject matter of Christian narrative: God's *novum* in continuous creation. Approach to the subject matter of God's *novum* can be seen in a hermeneutical-analogical process through appropriation of meaning from other religious discourse while at the same time adopting a critical distance from incommensurate elements.

Thus a dynamism of God's speech through the face of religious Others constitutes an infinite life horizon for inviting Christian Church toward a prophetic discipleship of *diakonia* of reconciliation, enriching and renewing the Christian Church toward a new form of inculturation and emancipation in accompaniment with those who are marginalized, deproblematized, and voiceless in the world of religion. "Inculturation as prophetic dialogue"[14] is hard to maintain and develop without a Christian attitude of repentance and *diakonia* in humble attitude, spiritual poverty, and radical openness toward the mysterious dynamism of God's speech through the face of religious outsiders.

Inculturation and emancipation belong to an indispensable dimension of Christian mission which is embodied in the life of people in different time and place by attending the dynamism of God's speech ahead of missionary agency. God's grace does not destroy language, wisdom, and religious experience in the world of religions. God's grace socially and materially institutes, renews, and transforms non-Christian language as a witness to God's universal, irregular grace for all, in which God's partisanship of those historically and socially on the margin is highlighted as one of the important gospel messages.

The world of religions and religious classics are also a locus where God's act of speech takes place. Human language and interpretation may correspond to the speech event of God because God comes to us through language by making it into analogical medium for articulating and expressing God's grace.

This considered, a theology of inculturation is a critical and constructive reflection on the dynamic aspect of God's act of Speaking, taking into account an embodied dimension of the Word of God and its aspect of freedom and emancipation in extraecclesial sphere; in other words, an aspect of God's act of speech takes place in every way and all directions. God who takes up the world of plurality through Christ's

---

14. Bevans and Schroeder, *Constants*, 385–89.

reconciliation is the One who speaks in promise, reconciliation, and freedom to the Christian Church through religious outsiders.

As far as God's Word seeks understanding and dialogue with the Church through non-Christian classics, wisdom, and other religious experiences of ultimate reality, Christian faith which seeks understanding is "on the way" and stands under eschatological reserve; it presupposes and characterizes Christian theology as *theologia viatorom* which attentively listens to, is challenged and surprised by dynamic, unexpected, and postecclesial irruption of God's speech event through the religious Others.

God as the subject of speech event encourages the Christian Church to discern the signs of the times and to recognize people of other faiths as the children of God to promote peace, justice, and ecological sustainability together with other religious communities.

An emancipation in the process of inculturation becomes visible in its orientation toward the mystery of God's speech event which prevents the Christian Church from Babylonia captivity to colonial expansionism, racism, and assumption of Western cultural and religious superiority.

God, who is coming and becoming, is the One who is ahead of us, working in a lifeworld of non-Christian religions and cultures. Christians renew and expand horizons of ecclesial discourse and doctrinal belief systems in encounters with and in recognition of religious outsiders. Christian mission, which includes inculturation as an important aspect of Christian relations with other religious communities, is characterized by surprise, delight, and discipleship in *diakonia*. A concept of God's mission adopts a willingness to audaciously risk its ecclesial position in service of God, who speaks continually through Israel, Christ's reconciliation, and religious symbolic figures of Melchizedek and Cornelius through the power of the Spirit.

Christian mission and inculturation, as seen in light of *theologia crucis*, becomes an embodied theology of the Word of God. It retains and sharpens a *metanoia* in retrospect to painful history of mission in the past and proposes a hope of sharing the good news of God with people of other faith communities in the reconciled world. Here, Christian faith is deepened in openness toward the dynamism of God's speech event in a completely different manner than the Christian Church would expect. At this juncture, *Fides quaerens intellectum* paves the way to *Verbum Dei quaerens intellectum et dialogum* which, in turn, characterizes and sharpens Christian faith in search of understanding of God's Word in the context of inculturation and emancipation.[15]

---

15. Chung, *Constructing Irregular Theology*, 1–3.

5

The Iron Cage and Emancipation of the Lifeworld

IN THE PREVIOUS CHAPTERS we dealt with a spiritual theology and socially embodied theology in view of the Greek metaphysical and Christian traditions. Here an attempt was made to configure and reframe Christian theology in engagement with human life in the public sphere. In discussing the bodily dimension of Christian theology in the public sphere, we looked at an analysis of Luther's view of theology and economy and attempted to reframe a model of God's universal reign in view of three life arrangements. We discussed the task of inculturation as an indispensable part of a prophetic dialogue with people of other faiths in light of God's communication with the world.

Contrary to my evaluation of the Reformer's view on economic justice, Max Weber (1864–1920) raised an important yet controversial thesis arguing that there is an affinity between Protestantism and the spirit of capitalism. In his sociological analysis, a Western form of rationality finds its echo in Protestant inner-worldly asceticism. A consequence of Western civilization is disenchantment with the world where a Protestant ethic juxtaposes with a purpose-driven form of rationality, an instrumental reason, and results in a cul de sac of lost meaning, and an iron cage of nihilism.

In this chapter, it is crucial to deal with Weber's sociological analysis of the Protestant ethic and the spirit of capitalism for the discussion of the relationship between religion and the public sphere from a sociological perspective. Furthermore, we shall map and configure Weber's influence on socio-critical thinkers such as Lukacs, Horkheimer, and Habermas in order to advance their arguments with Weber.

PROTESTANT CHRISTIANITY AND INNER-WORLDLY ASCETICISM

Max Weber defines sociology as meaningful social action. Unlike Karl Marx, Weber argues that ideas can and sometimes do have an independent and decisive influence on the course of events. Weber introduces social action in a fourfold way: 1) social action is rational in the sense that it employs appropriate means to a given end (purpose–rational); 2) it is rational in the sense that it attempts to realize some absolute value purely for its own sake, regardless of consequences (value–rational); 3) it is affectively—and in particular emotionally—determined (affection–rational); 4) it is traditional behavior, the expression of settled customs and religious ideas (tradition–rational).

Distinguishing between formal and substantive rationality, Weber characterizes formal rationality as purpose rationality. Purpose rationality is Weber's core concept in explaining the Western process of modernization. According to Weber, the rise of purpose rationality leads to the disenchantment of the world and of religious worldviews. This process of disenchantment has gradually led Western people to experience a loss of meaning. Weber states that a progressive rational bureaucratization of society, particularly in the economy and the state, forces society into an iron cage.

Weber's analysis centers on the relationship between religious beliefs and the status and power structure of the groups composing a society. His specific objective is to analyze the social conditions under which the charismatic inspiration of the few (the Puritan divines, the Confucian scholars, the Hindu Brahmins, and the Jewish Levites and Prophets) became first a style of life and eventually the dominant orientation of a whole civilization. Weber uses the word "ethos" in order to emphasize that each individual's participation in society involves a personal commitment both to the behavior patterns and to material and ideal interests of a particular status group.

In other words, Weber focuses on understanding the influence of certain religious ideas on the development of an economic spirit, or the ethos of an economic system. Weber's famous study, *The Protestant Ethic and the Spirit of Capitalism*, demonstrates the connection of the spirit of modern economic life with the rational ethics of Protestantism.

Much has been written and discussed about Weber's use of the term ideal type, a key term in his methodological discussion. The conception

The Iron Cage and Emancipation of the Lifeworld

of ideal type is linked with the comparative method. Weber relates ideas and interests in terms of the concept of selective affinity. There is no pre-established correspondence between the content of an idea and the interests of those who follow. By a selective process of elements, Weber finds their relevance in an affinity between the autonomous role of ideas and the origin of modern capitalism. His interpretive strategy reads: "it is not necessary to be Caesar in order to understand Caesar."[1] An ideal type enables a sociologist to understand the real action.

Weber's focus is not on religion, but rather on the relationship between religious ideas and commitments and other aspects of human conduct. In *The Protestant Ethics and the Spirit of Capitalism*, Weber identifies capitalism with the pursuit of profit. Profit constantly renews itself means of a continuous, rational, and capitalistic enterprise. Benjamin Franklin is portrayed as a typical representative of the spirit of capitalism. Weber argues that the development of the Capitalist spirit is best understood as part of the development of rationalism.[2]

For Weber, Luther's concept of calling is not consistent with the spirit of capitalism. Luther's concept of calling is traditional, and makes it difficult to establish a fundamental connection between worldly activity and religious principle. However, Weber overlooks Luther's theology of integrating economic life into a theological discussion of the gospel. As we discussed earlier, Luther prophetically criticized the Christian character of capital accumulation at his time, clearly seeing the political–economic alliance between the Catholic Church, Charles V, and the Fuggers.

Weber takes issue with the Calvinist doctrine of predestination that God predestined some to blessing, others to damnation, and that even Christ died only for the elect. The influence of the doctrine of predestination is obvious in the elementary forms of conduct and attitudes toward life among Calvinist communities. The elected Christian is in the world only to increase the glory of God by fulfilling God's commandments to the best of his/her ability. The doctrine of predestination becomes foundational for the idea that it is necessary to prove one's faith in worldly activity. The Calvinist doctrine of double predestination led to the ascetic action of Puritan morality in the sense of methodically rationalized economic-ethical conduct.

1. Runciman, *Weber Selections*, 8.
2. Weber, *The Protestant Ethic*, 17–19.

According to Weber, Calvinists are the seedbed of Capitalist economy. In the Calvinist view, the attainment of riches as a fruit of labor in a calling signals God's election and blessing. This argument becomes obvious in the way that Weber deals with the relationship between asceticism and the spirit of capitalism. The religious valuation of restless, continuous, systematic work in a worldly calling is regarded as the highest means of asceticism, and at the same time, the surest and most evident proof of rebirth and genuine faith. This faith attitude has a selective affinity to the spirit of capitalism. According to Baxter, the care for external goods should only lie on the shoulders of the saint like a light cloak. This cloak can be thrown aside at any moment. However, according to Weber, this cloak will become an iron cage.[3]

SOCIAL INTEREST AND EMANCIPATION IN THE PUBLIC SPHERE

Weber's analysis of rationality finds its echo in Georges Lukacs (1885–1971) and representatives of the Frankfurt school: Max Horkheimer and Theodor Adorno. Lukacs's work becomes a field of controversy in the history of Western Marxism. In 1913 Lukacs studied at Heidelberg and made the acquaintance of Max Weber. In 1923 Lukacs published a number of essays in book form as *History and Class Consciousness* (English trans. 1971), his *magnum opus*. With emphasis on the Hegelian source of Marx's philosophy, he presents the category of totality as the essence of Marxist dialectics. This interpretation leads him to disparage Engel's concept of the dialectics of nature and dispute Lenin's principle of reflection.

With Lukacs's self-criticism of *History and Class Consciousness*, the work disappeared. However, after Stalin's death, it began to have an impact on Western non-communist intellectuals. In his later stage, Lukacs's contends that "social being determines consciousness" has little to do with economic reductionism: instead, this Marxist principle relates to the whole of social being. Human existence and the reality of life in social location is a determinant factor of human consciousness. The basic dependence in social life rests on the relationship between the whole of social being and particular elements of the whole (culture, politics,

---

3. Ibid., 180–82.

The Iron Cage and Emancipation of the Lifeworld

economic, and ideology) rather than an unqualified, casual link between the base and the superstructure.[4]

Lukacs incorporates Weber's sociology into a Hegelized reading of Karl Marx. Through Lukacs and later representatives of the Frankfurt school, Weber's analysis of rationalization and disenchantment with the world aligns with Marx's analysis of the commodity form. This theoretical, heuristic combination of Weber's sociology and Marx's critique of political economy is constitutive for Habermas' theory and the practice of communicative rationality for civil society and lifeworld.

RATIONALIZATION AND THE REALITY OF REIFICATION

In *History and Class Consciousness* Lukacs defines reification as a typical feature of the mystified consciousness of capitalist society. The term reification, although Marx himself did not use it, is related to Marx's analysis of commodity fetishism in volume I of *Capital*. In that work, Marx analyzes the reified consciousness in terms of commodity fetishism, which he defines as the universal structure principle of bourgeois-capitalist society.

According to Marx, "the existence of the things *qua* commodities," and "the value relation between the products of labor which stamps them as commodities" "assumes the fantastic form of a relation between things." By way of religious illustration, Marx defines fetishism as "attach[ing] itself to the producers of labor, as soon as they are produced as commodities, and which is therefore inseparable from the production of commodities." Therefore, the fetishism of commodities originates "in the peculiar social character of the labor that produces them."[5]

In his treatment of the fetish character of commodity and its mystery, Marx understands Capitalist production in terms of commodity production. In capitalist production, all products of labor are related to each other in the exchange of the commodity. As labor products assume the form of commodity, the exchange value of labor products appears on the market. Exchange of the commodity in the market forms and shapes the social character of labor products.

According to Marx, under the imperative of exchange law, the societal relation of humans becomes a relationship between things. In this

---

4. Lukacs, *Zur Ontologie*, 39.
5. McLellan *Marx Selected Wirings*, 436.

regard, Hinkelammert defines the fetish as "the personification of commodities (and money and capital) and the reification or commodization of persons."[6] In Marx's logic, commodity fetishism is mediated by money and capital, and the personification of both assumes a fetish character.

Starting from Marx's theory of commodity fetishism, Lukacs insists that the labor process, the political order of society, the bourgeois–modern science, philosophy, and art are subject to the principle of reification.[7] Herein Lukacs interprets Weber's analysis of rationalization in terms of the anonymous process of capital reification. In Lukacs' view, in this case the structure of the commodity–relations can be made to produce a model of all the objective forms of bourgeois society coupled with all the subjective forms that correspond to them.[8]

The interaction of human beings with their environment in a Capitalistic society determines a specific form, which prejudices the world–relation and interpersonal relation by relating to them as things in the social and interpersonal world, namely, the reified objectivity of their inner and outer lives. This prejudice is called reification, wherein subjective experiences and social relationships are coordinated and manipulated as things. To use Habermas' phrase, the lifeworld is colonized and reified.[9]

By extracting a basic reification model from Marx's theory of commodity fetishism, Lukacs diagnoses the cause of this deformation in a capitalist mode of production, which necessitates "this transformation of a human function into a commodity."[10] In the production process, the human as the subject loses regulation over the product. Conversely, the product gains power over the producer. There arises a world full of ready-made things and relationships between things. Humans are subordinate to the independent law of the commoditized world. The reification of persons and interpersonal relations is the reifying effect upon the commodity form, and the other side of the rationalization.

Lukacs' analysis of reification is connected with the self-alienation of humans. He takes the laborer's self-alienation not to be the bringer of the labor process, but to be inserted, as a mechanical part, into a

6. Hinkelammert, *Ideological Weapons*, xv.
7. Lukacs, *History and Class Consciousness*, 84.
8. Ibid., 83.
9. Habermas, *Theory of Communicative Action* I. 356.
10. Lukacs, *History and Class Consciousness*, 92.

mechanical system. A human being is no longer a specific individual, but rather becomes a mere unit of labor force—a part of a huge system of production and exchange. However, the self-alienation of the non-worker (the employer) is highlighted in the phenomena of bureaucracy.

The bureaucrat becomes the executive organ for the regulatory system of right and administration, while the laborer becomes the instrument of strange objectivity. The commodity affixes its structure to the society of capitalism. The attributes of humans are not connected any longer with the organic unity of the person, but they appear as things that other humans possess and dispose.

Lukacs views rationalization and reification as two aspects of the same process under the commodity form, taking on a universal character and becoming the form of reified objectivity of the Capitalist society. Max Weber uses the term "formal rationality of economic action under the instrumental aspects" to designate the extent of calculation that is technically possible and actually applied. He measures the concept of substantive rationality against the results of economic action with respect to value rationality or substantive purpose rationality.[11]

Unlike Marx, who sees the rationalization of society in the development of productive forces, Weber sees the institutional framework of the capitalist economy as a subsystem of purpose–rational action rather than as relations of production fettering the potential for rationalization. Weber sees cultural rationalization in modern science and technology generating a universal-historical processes of disenchantment with the world, and in so doing, modern science is the fateful power of rationalized society. This bureaucratization leads to the reification of social relationships.

Alongside Weber, Lukacs discerns that the principle of rationalization is based on what is and *can be calculated*. According to Weber, the modern capitalist concern is based inwardly above all on *calculation*. Specific to modern capitalism is the strictly rational *organization of work* on the basis of *rational technology*. "This rationality did not come into being *anywhere* within such irrationally constituted political systems nor could it have done so."[12]

However, at this juncture, Lukacs criticizes Weber because Weber detaches the phenomena of reification from the economic basis of their

11. Weber, *Economy and Society*. I, 85.
12. Lukacs, *History and Class Consciousness*, 88, 96.

existence and eternalizes them as "a timeless type of possible human relationship."[13] In following Marx's analysis of commodity, Lukacs reveals the effects of reification to the extent that the labor power of producers becomes a commodity. Furthermore, the bureaucratic intensification of a one-sided specialization exhibits a violation of humanity. Marx's comment—the individual is transformed into the automatic mechanism of a partial labor and thus alienated and crippled to the point of abnormality[14]—is relevant and meaningful for Lukacs' argument.

The same phenomenon repeats itself in the split between the worker's labor power and his personality; as its metamorphosis is split into a thing, labor becomes an object that he/she sells on the market.[15] Under the sign of reification and rationalization, Lukacs views the basic phenomenon of societal rationalization in terms of Capitalist commodity exchange. Reification is, according to Marx, "the condition of their [the producers'] standing as independent private persons in a social context."[16]

In critically viewing Weber's discussion of the encompassing dimension of Occidental rationalism, Lukacs argues that the commodity form becomes the dominant form of objectivity in a Capitalist society. The unified structure of Capitalism is expressed in that problems of consciousness arise from wage labor and are reiterated in the ruling class in a refined, spiritualized, and intensified form.

According to Lukacs, the transformation of the commodity relation into a thing of "ghostly objectivity" does not reduce all objects for the gratification of human needs to commodities. Rather, it stamps its imprint upon the whole consciousness of human beings, their qualities and abilities. They are things that can be disposed of like the various objects of the external world.[17] The physical and psychic qualities of the human cannot come into play without subjection to the form of objectivity. As the commodity form is transferred to the form of objectivity, the rationalization of the world appears to be complete. It seems to penetrate to the very depths of human physical and psychic nature.[18]

13. Habermas, *Theory of Communicative Action*, I, 356.
14. Lukacs, *History and Class Consciousness*, 99.
15. Ibid.
16. Habermas, *Theory of Communicative Action*, I, 359.
17. Lukacs, *History and Class Consciousness*, 100.
18. Ibid., 101.

RATIONALIZATION AND THE EMERGENCE OF POLYTHEISM

However, Weber saw the paradox of societal rationalization in the development and institutional embodiment of formal rationality, which is in no sense irrational. Against Marx's analysis of capitalist society, Weber's critique consists of the idea of value judgment. It is impossible to make a value judgment in the name of scientific analysis because it is the exclusive responsibility of the individual to make any decision about values.

From Scholasticism to Marxism, the idea of an objectively valid value—namely, an ethical imperative—was amalgamated with the empirical process of price formation.[19] When it comes to an ethical imperative, Weber argues, "an empirical cannot tell anyone what he *should do*–but rather what he *can* do—and under certain circumstances—what he wishes to do."[20] Economics is the sphere in which real life is reproduced for Marx, while for Weber it is the sphere for calculability. Economic action can be spoken of only where the satisfaction of a need depends on relatively scarce resources and where there is a limited number of possible actions. This state evokes a specific reaction.

Weber's circumscription of economics to calculability implies that any activity may become economic if it involves specific reactions coming from the relationship between preferences and scarce means. In the hands of Weber, the calculation of subjective preference in respect to scarce means is called formal rationality, which is the only possible objective of social science. Economic rationality lies in the calculability of means and ends. All economic phenomena such as impoverishment, unemployment, underdevelopment, and the destruction of nature are irrelevant to economics and the sphere of economic rationality.[21]

Social reality is an immense chaotic stream of events and the analysis of infinite reality becomes possible on the assumption that only a finite portion of reality constitutes the object of scientific investigation. Before "the stream of immeasurable events," which "flows unendingly towards eternity," and constitutes "the eternally inexhaustible flow of life,"[22] human beings can discover and choose gods rather than search for the

---

19. Weber, *Methodology*, 95.
20. Ibid., 54.
21. Hinkelammart, *Ideological Weapons*, 66–67.
22. Gerth and Mills, *From Max Weber*, 147.

one God directing the flow. Weber finds meaning in the voice of the elder Mill who said: "If one proceeds from pure experience, one arrives at polytheism. This is shallow in formulation and sounds paradoxical, and yet there is truth in it."[23]

The gods of the various orders and values are engaged in a struggle. The world of the ancient was not yet disenchanted of its gods and demons, and we are likewise enthralled nowadays, albeit in a different sense. "Only the bearing of man has been disenchanted and denuded of its mystical but inwardly genuine plasticity."[24]

As Weber further argues, the grandiose rationalism of an ethical and methodical conduct of life has dethroned this polytheism in favor of the "one thing that is needful." However, "many old gods ascend from their graves; they are disenchanted and hence take the form of impersonal forces."[25] They strive to gain power over human life, resuming their eternal struggle with one another.

These old gods, ascending from their graves and seeking to rule us, are what Marx calls the fetish, Lukacs calls reification, and what Karl Barth refers to as "lordless powers." Rebellion against these gods would amount to Christianity's deconstruction of polytheism in favor of the one thing that is needful. Gods and demons hold sway over the world and the gods are equal. Rebellion against them makes things worse. From traditions of grandiose rationalism such as Christianity, the Enlightenment, and Marxism, we have seen great effort and good intention in this direction, but they have not been enough to ameliorate subsequent bad results.

In the return of a new polytheism, in which the struggle among the gods assumes the depersonalized and objectified form of antagonism, Weber sees the sign of the age. Over these gods and their struggles among irreducible orders of value and life, fate—not science—holds sway. Weber's formulation of a new polytheism accounts for the loss of meaning associated with Nietzsche's experience with nihilism. The practical rationality, which binds purposive–rational action orientation in a value–rational manner, can find its place only in the personality of the solitary individual. Out of the loss of the substantial unity of reason comes an inevitable struggle with the polytheism of gods and demons.

23. Ibid.
24. Ibid., 148.
25. Ibid., 148–49.

The Iron Cage and Emancipation of the Lifeworld

An attempt to send the old gods back to their graves would be like making heaven on earth. This millennial, socialist attempt will fail because it amounts to transforming earth into hell. For Weber, good can produce evil just as evil can produce good. In other words, there is an unbridgeable gap between "be" and "ought to be" in which a teleological idea of historical progress is rejected. When the old, disenchanted gods reappear in the form of impersonal powers locked in conflict with one another, Weber sees a clash, not only between classes, but also between worldviews.

Disenchantment with religious-metaphysical worldviews coupled with the emergence of modern structures of consciousness has brought liberation as well as the inevitable bondage of the iron cage. We don't know who will live in this cage in the future. No one knows whether at the end of this tremendous development entirely new prophecies will arise, or whether there will be a powerful rebirth of old ideas and ideals. Otherwise, we do not know if mechanized petrification, embellished with a sort of convulsive self-importance.[26] Weber has expectations for the last men of this cultural development: "Specialists without spirit, sensualists without heart; this nullity imagines that it has attained a level of civilization never before achieved."[27]

Weber highlights autonomy, freedom, and parliamentarian charismatic leaders as a way of prescribing and averting the negative and oppressed aspect of the process of rationalization. For this he proposes an ethics of responsibility in relation to the ethics of conviction (or the ultimate ends), both of which call for politics.[28] The former demands purposive rational reflection on intention, means, and results in action on behalf of consciousness of responsibility. The latter chooses subjectively ultimate value rationality and seeks its realization. The ethic of conviction, which is committed to one's own ideology, is exposed to a chiliastic prophet who attempts to change the world in accordance to his/her own conviction.

For Weber, two different ethics are not mutually exclusive, but can be complementary. An ethic of conviction is not necessarily identical with irresponsibility while an ethic of responsibility is not always iden-

---

26. Weber, *Protestant Ethic*, 182.
27. Ibid.
28. Gerth and Mills, *From Max Weber*, 127.

tical with responsibility.[29] Nevertheless, this complementarity of ethics remains subordinate to the power and principalities of the idols. The production of commodity is inevitable, and a system of bureaucratic rule is inescapable. To those who have the option of a Socialist society of the future, Weber predicts that bureaucratic tendencies will increase still higher in a centralized planning society. The bureaucratic (rather than the proletariat) dictatorship will come to the surface.[30]

However, Weber's attempt at recognizing and worshiping the impersonal powers of the old gods meets a profound challenge in Lukacs' theory of reification. Against Weber's legitimation of formal rationality, Lukacs supplements his theory of reification with a theory of the proletariat's class–consciousness. The proletariat becomes the identical subject-object of history in light of which Lukacs interprets Hegel's *Phenomenology of Mind* finding its authentic realization in the existence and the consciousness of the proletariat. Lukacs argues that political praxis can break through the alienation and reification, which dominate in the capitalist society of the commodity.

Adorno, an important representative of the critical theory at Frankfurt School develops Lukacs' conception of alienation and reification in Capitalistic society into a theory of the administered world. Unlike Lukacs, for Adorno a direct political fight against the administered world becomes questionable—and even impossible—because such a fight could serve inhumane methods.[31] How do the representatives of critical theory integrate and discuss a reality of reification and an iron cage of instrumental rationality in their engagement with the public sphere?

CRITICAL THEORY AND TRADITIONAL THEORY

It is important to begin with Max Horkheimer (1895–1973). His interest lies in highlighting the constant connection to real life. For him critical theory attends to social genesis, function, and change of human knowledge. This insistence on the real life contexts and social consequences of every science marks Horkheimer's critical thinking and remains a hallmark of his critical theory. Horkheimer's aim was to overcome

29. Ibid., 120.
30. Bendix, *Max Weber*, 459.
31. Adorno, *Negative Dialectics*, 14–20.

traditional theory with its destructive combination of epistemological empiricism and bourgeois atomistic individualism.

Horkheimer paid special attention to the historical and social embeddedness of reason, knowledge, truth, and the process of historical dialectic. For him, Marx's theory of materialism does not reject human thinking. Rather materialism, unlike Hegel's idealism, understands human thinking to be the thinking of particular people within a particular period of time and place.[32]

Against Hegel's view, which holds that knowledge and ideas lead to progress in history, Horkheimer, along with Marx, contends that the fundamental historical role lies in economic relations. The critical theory of society is, in its totality, the unfolding of a single existential judgment regarding the Capitalist society and its commodity economy because this society drives humanity into a new barbarism.[33]

However, unlike Marx (who discusses the humanization of nature and the naturalization of humanity) and Lukacs (with his concept of the complete unity between the subject and object as realized in proletarian consciousness), Horkheimer rejects a harmonious unity between human life and society. He does advocate for critical theory in favor of proletarian liberation, but theory, as far as it is critical, should remain independent and autonomous from the existing form of social consciousness. Critical theory, which conceives of itself as an aspect of praxis, is in service of human emancipation and the creation of a better society.

On the other hand, Adorno—in his critique of Kant and Hegel—articulates his suspicion of a philosophical project dominated by a quest for an absolute starting point or in search of identity. This philosophical project reduces all other particulars to the primordial being of identity or sameness. This trend is visible in German idealism and positivism. The goal is to identify oneness of the universe from which all others are derivatives. This trend strengthens a totalitarian system that sacrifices other particulars in favor of a single principle of identity or sameness.

Sharing an anti-totalitarian direction with Horkheimer, Adorno opposes all ideas of totalization that reduce the human subject to the reified form for the sake of the perpetuation of dominion. Practice does not illuminate its theoretical implication. He advocates for a praxis-

---

32. O'Connell et al. *Critical Theory*, 233–43.
33. Ibid., 227.

connected theory against the unqualified primacy of practice, which denies any notion of the autonomy of theory.

Adorno's negative dialectic is a way to refuse faith in the ultimate identity or sameness that explains everything. Thus the dialectic is an act of opposition to all methods that pretend to be universal. Inverting Hegel's thesis that the whole is the true, Adorno argues that the whole is the false.[34] Adorno (in similarity with Nietzsche) calls the negative dialectic an anti-system. However, Adorno shares Marx's critique of society, in which individuals and things are reduced to a common level under the domination of the exchange value. The identity or sameness principle implies an acceptance of society dominated by exchange-value, being ignorant of qualitative differences. The dialectic seeks negation of the identity principle or totalization, which casts off human beings into the status of thing-ness.

DIALECTIC OF ENLIGHTENMENT AND IMMANENT CRITIQUE

Horkheimer employs the concept of ideology and undertakes a critique of it. His understanding refers to this as an immanent critique. He witnesses that large segments of the proletariat in Germany enthusiastically embraced fascism and anti-Semitism. This situation led Horkheimer in a different direction from Marxism, which—in its Soviet form—moved problematically toward accelerated bureaucratization and eventually to Stalin's bloody and coercive Socialist organization and to the Soviet Communist Party.

In fascism, the bourgeoisie and the proletariat collaborated together to justify anti-Semitism, which was expressed as the repressed desires of working people and the paranoia of the bourgeoisie. Bourgeois anti-Semitism conceals domination in economic production.[35] For Horkheimer, the merchant of the Jew presents the workers with the bill which they have signed away to the manufacturer. The merchant becomes the bailiff of the whole system and takes the hatred of others upon him/herself.[36]

Throughout the ages in Europe, Jews found access to social economic life through trade and commerce. Here, economic business ap-

---

34. Adorno, *Minima Moralia*, 50.
35. Horkheimer and Adorno, *Dialectic of Enlightenment*, 173.
36. Ibid., 174.

peared unproductive compared to manufacturing because it disturbed the process of creating social wealth in the national interest. Jews were blamed for non-productivity and for the failures in the economic system. They were called usurpers, thieves, or parasites. As a result, they became easy targets of persecution and victims of accusations.

Horkheimer borrows an insight from Max Weber's sociology of rationalization in connection with Lukacs' analysis of capitalism. Based on these two insights, Horkheimer reconceptualizes critical social theory as a critique of instrumental rationality. Horkheimer believed that a rational potential resides within Western capitalist society. This latent and powerful seed of reason exists in the great bourgeois ideals of freedom, justice, and brotherhood.

However, the overwhelming poverty and immense suffering of the proletariat within the capitalist society provided the evidence for Horkheimer that these ideals exist merely as rational potentiality. This conviction led him to the notion of an immanent critique, according to which normative rational ideals are present (immanent) within the capitalist social system itself. Immanent critique summons the existent society with the claim of its conceptual principles, so that it criticizes the relation between the two and thus transcends them.[37]

In *Dialectic of Enlightenment*, Horkheimer and Adorno are concerned to discover what has brought humankind into a new kind of barbarism.[38] At issue here is the analysis and addressing of the rise and domination of instrumental reason. For example, Adorno and Horkheimer hold Christianity, idealism, and materialism accountable for the barbaric acts perpetrated in their names. As representatives of power, they played a bloody role in the history of the instruments of organization.[39]

It was Kant who discussed the Enlightenment's concept of reason. The human individual organizes him or herself as the transcendental, universal self, representing the idea of universality and constituting the judgment of calculation. This adjusts the world for the reasons of self-preservation and prepares the object to serve material subjugation.[40]

---

37. Horkheimer, *Eclipse of Reason*, 182.
38. Horkheimer and Adorno, *Dialectic of Enlightenment*, xi.
39. Ibid., 224.
40. Ibid., 83–84.

Here reason appears to be universal, common to every individual, while it is domination of the external, particular.

Hegel, in his *Phenomenology of Mind*, notices an internal relationship between Enlightenment, an ethic of utility, and terror (the terror of the French Revolution). For Hegel, a human being is self-consciousness—being conscious of self, human reality and dignity. Furthermore, he/she is a conscious desire that transforms being and nature. Born of desire, human action tends to seek satisfaction by negation, or transformation. Human desire is directed toward social desire that produces a free and historical individual.[41] However, this Enlightenment consciousness objectifies the world. Nature is disenchanted. According to Francis Bacon, scientific knowledge is the instrument for mastering nature. Science provides the key to the controlling nature and human beings.

In *Dialectic of Enlightenment* Horkheimer and Adorno argue that the dominance of nature is the basis of the philosophy of Enlightenment. "For the Enlightenment, whatever does not conform to the rule of computation and utility is suspect."[42] They perceive the domination of nature in the Judaeo-Christian tradition. The Renaissance and Reformation propelled the idea that nature is a tool to be dominated in service to human purposes. Nature becomes instrumental rather than essential.

According to the authors of *Dialectic of Enlightenment* Nietzsche was a philosopher after Hegel, who clearly recognized limitation of dialectic of Enlightenment. Nietzsche discerned a nihilistic anti-life force in the Enlightenment.[43] For Nietzsche, knowledge works as a tool of power. The utility of preservation stands as the motive behind the development of the organs of knowledge. The measure of the desire for knowledge depends upon the measure to which the will to power grows. A species grasps a certain amount of reality in order to master it, pressing it into service.[44]

Scientific–technical progress in the nineteenth century undermined religious and metaphysical worldviews. Thus, the course of the Enlightenment is of nihilistic character. Science distances itself progressively from nature, disenchanting and instrumentalizing it. The external world is reduced to object of manipulation. Through enlightened rea-

41. Kojève, *Introduction*, 6.
42. Ibid., 6.
43. Ibid., 44.
44. Nietzsche, *Will to Power*, 266–67.

The Iron Cage and Emancipation of the Lifeworld

son's control and domination, nature has turned against itself. Technical advancement and scientific progress does not bring liberation to society. A development of enlightened rationality signals the eclipse of reason.

In *Eclipse of Reason*, Horkheimer changed his conceptual orientation. He begins to be suspicious of an immanent rationality existing in Western society that could serve as the normative standard for critique and reconstruction. According to Horkheimer, advance in technical facilities for enlightenment gives rise to a process of dehumanization. Progress threatens to nullify the very goal it is supposed to realize and implement. In our civilization, progressive rationalization tends to obliterate the essence of reason in the name of which this progress promised.[45]

This paradigm shift led Horkheimer to adopt more of Max Weber's analysis of the Western type of reason. Horkheimer finds a similarity in Weber's distinction between purposive rationality and substantive rationality as compared with his own distinction between subjective reason and objective reason.[46] In basic agreement with Weber, Horkheimer insists that the eighteenth-century Enlightenment unleashed a different type of reason, which Weber calls purposive rationality. Horkheimer calls this rationality an instrumental reason. This instrumental type of reason underlies our contemporary industrial culture and dominates it in a radical, total, and destructive way.[47] The rationality of instrumental reason refers only to the efficiency and effectiveness of a selected means.

Whatever meaning remains in life becomes tethered to self-preservation and thus to self-interest. In a society in bondage to instrumental reason, a loss of freedom accompanies the loss of meaning. Horkheimer contends that the increase in instrumental rationality ushers in a change in the character of freedom.[48] Freedom is no longer conceived of in terms beyond self-preservation and self-interest. Horkheimer sharpens his diagnosis of the modern loss of freedom and meaning. According to Lukacs, reification becomes so dominant that it determines how individuals interpret everything. Determining the interpretation of nature, of interpersonal relations, reification means "thingification."

---

45. Horkheimer, *Eclipse of Reason*, v–vi.
46. Ibid., 6.
47. Habermas, *Theory of Communicative Action*, 1:v.
48. Horkheimer, *Eclipse of Reason*, 98.

In Horkheimer's view, the domination of nature involves the domination of the human being.[49] Every relationship becomes an "it," so that reification converts every human reality into an object to be scanned, manipulated, and controlled. Under Capitalism, the potential of every "thing" dwells in its potential as a commodity. Therefore, reification means commodification. For Horkheimer, reification is typical of instrumental rationality.[50]

Reification, arising from the structure of society, extends not only to the natural world (ecological crisis) and to social relationships, but also to the core of human subjectivity. Reason, once instrumentalized, has become assimilated to power—that is, domination in the service of self-preservation. It has given up its critical power. The dark writers of the bourgeoisie have "trumpeted far and wide the impossibility of deriving from reason any fundamental argument against murder."[51]

Horkheimer thus made the turn to a totalistic critique of instrumental reason. His suspicion of human reason leads him to negative theology, "a longing for the wholly Other."[52] Without the thought of God, there is no absolute meaning or truth so that morality becomes a matter of taste. If God dies, eternal truth dies. In agreement with Marx, Horkheimer contends that religion is the sigh of the oppressed creature and the protest against real misery.

Still, unlike Marx, there remains "the longing for the wholly Other." Theology, to which morality returns in the final analysis, contains the hope that the injustice in the world is neither permanent nor the last world. The murderer will not triumph over the innocent victim. Religious longing for God as the wholly Other finds its indispensable part in Horkheimer's critique of human reason. Here Habermas argues that Horkheimer was not capable of perceiving a space for communicative reason and action in the world.[53]

---

49. Ibid., 93.
50. Ibid., 40.
51. Horkheimer and Adorno, *Dialectic of Enlightenment*, 118.
52. Horkheimer, *Die Sehnsucht*.
53. Habermas, *Justification and Application*, 144.

INTEREST IN EMANCIPATION AND THE PUBLIC SPHERE

Horkheimer and Adorno's social critical concern finds its inspiration and a new direction in Jürgen Habermas (born in 1929), a German sociologist at the University of Frankfurt. Habermas, in his *Structural Transformation of Public Sphere*, refers to the public sphere as a realm of social life in which something approaching public opinion can be formed. It is a realm in which the human being, as a political animal, can discuss political life openly, in accordance with critical reason and rationality. In a historical study of the process of structural transformation of the public sphere, Habermas demonstrates that the public sphere has replaced the rule of tradition with the rule of reason.

Here he raises important issues regarding the spread and expansion of instrumental reason to many areas of social life; a new constellation of economics, and politics in view of the growth of large-scale economic and commercial organizations, advancement of science, technology and industry, and the commercialization of the media. Technical issues threaten essential aspects of human life. In this changing structure of the public sphere, ideology assumes a technocratic justification of the social order. Technocratic consciousness justifies a particular class interest in dominion, as well as affecting the structure of human interests.

The structure of communication is changed. The structural transformation of the public sphere embeds itself in the transformation of the state and economy. State and society integrate into the structural change of the public sphere. The principle of publicness in the process of a structural change in the public sphere can be clarified and improved in terms of critical analysis of human knowledge and social interest, equipped with ideology-critical orientation, while proposing and refining communicative rationality and action in view of the rationalization of the lifeworld.[54]

Habermas's lifelong sociological and philosophical concern is characterized by the raising up of deliberate democracy and civil society in light of a communicative rationality against the systems' (money, administrative power of the state, and mass media) medicating and colonizing actions on the public sphere of the lifeworld.

In his work, *Knowledge and Human Interests*, Habermas proposes that knowledge is historically conditioned and interest-bound. This re-

---

54. Habermas, *Structural Transformation*, 40–45.

fers to his thesis of knowledge-constitutive interests. All knowledge is mediated by social historical interest and experience. The human species organizes and develops its existence and knowledge in light of *a priori* interests or knowledge-guiding and constitutive interests.

Furthermore, there is another interest in the reflective appropriation of human life: an interest in reason, in the human capacity to be self-reflective, and to act rationally. This is, in fact, an interest in emancipation that Habermas proposes and actualizes regarding the public sphere. Habermas categorizes human interests into technical, practical, and emancipatory. These give rise to the conditions which make possible three sciences: the empirical-analytic (technical or instrumental knowledge in natural science), the historical-hermeneutic (practical interest in *Geisteswissenschaften*), and the critical-social (emancipation and autonomy in critical social sciences). The critical theory, which Habermas represents, contends that all speech is oriented to the idea of a genuine, rational consensus, which is the ultimate criterion of the truth. The structure of speech is involved in the public sphere of life in which truth, freedom, and justice become possible.

In every communicative situation, Habermas is suspicious of a consensus established under coercion or dominion. Habermas criticizes this kind of consensus as systematically distorted communication, and thus it is fundamentally ideological. This implies an ideology-critical aspect in Habermas's theory. The process of emancipation calls for revealing and transcending the system of distorted communication. This process, in turn, entails engagement in critical reflection of unmasking dominion and power in a given society.

Habermas analyzes praxis as a complexity consisting of two key components: work (instrumental action) and interaction (communicative interaction). Language as a human capacity for communication plays a significant role in the structural change of the public sphere regarding the responsibility to act for emancipation.

In Habermas's interpretation of Hegel, he attends to the theme of labor and interaction in Hegel's *Jena Philosophy of Mind*. In this philosophy, Hegel proposes the three categories (language, tools, and family) in order to designate symbolic representation, the labor process, and interaction based on reciprocity. The concept of the Mind is determined

The Iron Cage and Emancipation of the Lifeworld

by dialectical interconnections between linguistic symbolization, labor, and interaction.[55]

As part of a project for recognition between master and slave, Hegel constructs a dialectical history of suppression and reconstitution. Hegel conceives of self-consciousness as the result of a struggle for recognition. He develops language and labor as media for the self-formative process. Thus, we may expect Hegel to "introduce communicative action as the medium for the formative process of the self-conscious spirit."[56] Language and labor are categories of mediation through which the self-conscious human attains existence.

According to Hegel, language is something universal, resounding in the consciousness of all. Within language, every speaking consciousness becomes another consciousness. Language comes into communicative action. Hegel establishes the interrelation of labor and language within his dialectical configuration of the struggle for reciprocal recognition between master and servant.

From Hegel's dialectics, Marx came to realize that there is an interconnection between labor and interaction in the forces of production and the relations of production. Reviewing Hegel's *Phenomenology of Mind*, Marx appreciates Hegel as a philosopher who has comprehended labor as the essence of the human being. Hegel understands the self-generation of the human being as a process. Thus, this process is the essence of labor in terms of a dialectic of externalization and sublation of this externalization.[57]

In Habermas's view, Marx attempts to reconstruct the world–historical process in terms of the reproduction of social life. However, Marx explicates the interconnection between labor and interaction only under the rubric of social praxis.[58] Thus, Marx reduces communicative action to instrumental action so that everything is resolved into the self-movement of production. Although he was aware of an interrelationship or interaction between the sphere of the superstructure and the economic base, Habermas chides Marx as being responsible for a mechanist interpretation of Marxist economic determinism. However, we must also

---

55. Habermas, *Theory and Practice*, 142–43.
56. Ibid., 152.
57. Ibid., 168.
58. Ibid.

point out that Marx attempted to uncover the embodiment of unreason in the sphere of political and economic life.

In contrast to Habermas's diagnosis of Hegel, however, Hegel conceptualizes the human being as a social being in interaction with the other. Hegel's concept of desire in his dialectic of struggle for recognition can be grounded in social reality and the public sphere because both adversaries must remain alive after the struggle for recognition. The slave must recognize the master without being recognized by the master. The reality of dialectic of recognition and unrecognition is not merely a fixed labor process, but is relevant in the cultural-linguistic-material life complex of externalization.

Human history is the history of interaction and struggle between master and slave for mutual recognition. The interaction of master and slave must finally end in the dialectical overcoming of both master and slave. Human desire in the Hegelian sense presupposes the reality of the public sphere in which there is an emphasis of the other's action of negativity in the service of the master. Such negativity for mutual recognition, an important form of social praxis, has potential in Hegel's thought to contribute to freedom and liberation in the public sphere.

Furthermore, Marx defends himself against a materialistic reductionism. After analyzing the social condition of the genesis of the Homeric epoch, he argues that there is no difficulty in understanding a connection between Greek art and epics with a definite social form of development. Rather there is difficulty underlying in the fact that Greek art and epics still prove to be enjoyable of art for us and are valid as the norm and unsurpassable criterion.[59]

For Marx, art and language have autonomous spheres so that these domains can be a practical consciousness in interaction with the other. Language and consciousness are similar in that both arise from the need of social intercourse with others.[60] Individuals express their life not only through material production, but also through cultural-communicative interaction.

Marx does not ignore the social-public character of language, but rather he critically appropriates it in his anatomy of civil society, which is to be found in the sphere of political economy. His social critical method articulates a way of seeking a corresponding relation between the eco-

59. Lukacs, *Der Junge Hegel*, 788.
60. McLellan, *Marx Selected Writings*, 167.

nomic structure of society, definite forms of social consciousness and interaction, and a legal, political, religious, aesthetic—in short, ideological infrastructure. Marxian social ontology in which social being shapes and determines human consciousness is critical method, revealing and explicating the complex structure of civil society in light of a dialectical circulation of integrating material life into socio–cultural episteme.

At any rate, to overcome the limitations of Hegel and Marx for the sake of communicative reason, Habermas reconstructs historical materialism by challenging and correcting its economic reductionism as visible in Marx's later work. Like Marx's, Habermas's approach is guided by the intention of recovering a potential for liberating reason that is encapsulated in the forms of social reproduction.[61]

The theory of base and superstructure is not adequate to comprehend many different forms of society and culture. Habermas contends that the normative structure of culture, morality, and collective identity evolve according to their own logic rather than simply following economic law and imperatives. Here, Habermas wants to analyze culture, knowledge, and reason as forms of "meaningful social action" in accordance with Weber's definition of sociology.[62]

For the sake of the theory of communicative rationality, Habermas takes up and renews Weber's sociology of rationalization, disenchantment, and practical rationality. Weber's unilateral analysis of purposive or instrumental rationality, as seen in the progress of Western civilization, treats all other forms of rationality (value, affectual, and traditional) as derivations or degradation of the instrumental rationality. Retrieving value-rational action against purposive-rational action, Habermas reconstructs meaningful social action in a theory of speech acts. This marks the linguistic turn of Habermas's later work on communicative reason and action.

Weber despairs because the process of rationalization, at the end of his *Protestant Ethic and the Spirit of Capitalism*, leads only to the iron cage of late capitalism. The iron cage becomes the symbol of modernity, of late capitalism, and also of a rationalization that Weber conceived in a completely negative way.[63]

---

61. Thompson and Held, *Habermas*, 221.
62. Weber, *Economy and Society*, I, 4–24.
63. Habermas, *Theory of Communicative Action*, 1:351.

For Habermas's reconstruction, Marx and Weber need to be read in a complementary way. Habermas argues that interests and ideas are of equal importance in shaping the course of history and rationalization. Habermas's own central position is communicative rationality, that is, a normative standard obscured behind Weber's despairing denunciation of the iron cage of modern capitalism. Habermas wants to oppose Weber's ethical skepticism, and thus provides—within a modification of Weber's own framework—an ethic of responsibility based on the intersubjectivity of communicative action and ethics.

COMMUNICATIVE RATIONALITY AND THE LIFEWORLD

Communicative competence implies the establishment of an ideal speech situation, leading to the capacity for consensus between communication partners. Language then, as a universal means of communication is capable of creating and sustaining social-cultural relationships. The universal aspect of speech articulates a dialogical character in which participants in communication are oriented to mutual understanding. At this point, Habermas speaks of conversation for which argumentation is perhaps the most important special case.[64]

For his concept of universal pragmatics, Habermas utilizes the insight of the post-Wittgensteinian ordinary language philosophy especially represented by Austin and Searl. In this line, the formal semantics of sentences extends to speech acts. According to Wittgenstein, truth claims take place in language games, which are embedded in the forms of life. They have a social context and horizon.

In his *Philosophical Investigation* (1959), Wittgenstein discovers a mode of living, a way of living in the grammar of every language, in a language game. He calls it a form of life. This later view is different from his earlier view on the representational function of language as explored in *Tractatus Logico-philosophicus* (1922). Here, true statements represent fact and thus correspond to it. Fact is verifiable through empirical scientific method. However, in his later stage, Wittgenstein notices the connection between a language game and a form of life (social practice). Thus, the social use or active character of language comes to the fore against a representational function.[65]

---

64. Ibid., 327.
65. Habermas, *On the Logic*, 125.

Wittgenstein's insight into the speech–act theory is further developed in John Austin and John Searle. Habermas utilizes this theory for the sake of his proposal of communicative theory. A theory of speech-acts offers a possibility of the synthesis of language and action. The speech act is open to an analysis of the multiplicity of illocutionary forces rather than confined to the representational function of language.[66]

According to Austin, when people speak to others they actually do things by saying something. The theory of speech–acts focuses on action. There is the double structure of all speech as communication. Austin makes a distinction between locutionary ("the speaker" says something) and illocutionary speech acts (the speech does something). For instance, in the sentence, "It snows a lot during the winter in Dubuque," the formal structures of speech reflect a validity claim in the formal structures of speech. However, the propositional content of "it snows a lot during the winter in Dubuque" leaves the performative action of speech neglected or even repressed. Beyond this locutionary statement, the illocutionary force of the speech act generates a legitimate or illegitimate interpersonal relation between the participants.

Through the illocutionary or performative dimension of a speech-act, the speaker performs an action in saying something. It contains another element: a promise or a command. "[I hereby assure (command or confess to) you that] it snows a lot during the winter in Dubuque." The interactive use of language (warnings, guarantees, admonitions, cautions, recommendation, promise, assurance, and the like) orient participants in communicative interaction to inter-subjectively recognized norms of social action.

Habermas presents the illocutionary or performative dimension of the speech–act as the universal pragmatic features of speech-actions and of communicative competence. The illocutionary-performative capacity of speech is built as universally into the structure of speech as the representational–propositional function.[67] Because the illocutionary dimension is interpersonally and socially oriented, Habermas takes it to be the most important dimension of speech for a critical theory of communication. Thus Habermas calls the type of interaction—in which "*all* participants harmonize their individual plans of action with one

---

66. Habermas, *Theory of Communicative Action*, 1:277–78.
67. Ibid., 54, 289.

another and thus pursue their illocutionary aims *without reservation*"—communicative action.[68]

All speech acts are oriented toward reaching an understanding; thus in the context of communicative action, speech acts are measured against the aspect of rightness, truthfulness, and truth.[69] Speech actors cannot eschew their speech acts embedded in the three world-relations (the world of social order, the world of exiting states of affairs, and the subjective world) and yet claim validity for their speech acts.[70] The goal of reaching understanding is to bring about an agreement in the intersubjective mutuality of: 1) reciprocal understanding, 2) shared knowledge, 3) mutual trust, and 4) accord with one another.

The illocutionary component of speech steers the pursuit of mutual understanding, constituting the knots in the network of communicative association. The social infrastructure of language is in flux, changing itself and its dependence on institutions and forms of life.[71] In this structure of communicative interaction, which is the very structure of speech communication, we perceive the original mode of communication, the archetypal form of communication. Communicative action is oriented toward reaching an understanding because "Reaching understanding is the inherent *telos* of human speech."[72]

Whatever we share and discuss in communicative action, we draw up from our shared lifeworld. "Communicative action takes place within a lifeworld that remains at the backs of participants in communication."[73] It points to the context-forming horizon of the lifeworld in which participants in communication come to an understanding with each other. Communicative action offers the medium for the reproduction of lifeworlds so that the concept of society is linked to a concept of the lifeworld "that is complementary to the concept of communicative action."[74]

68. Ibid., 294.
69. Ibid., 307.
70. Ibid., 307–8.
71. Ibid., 321.
72. Ibid., 287.
73. Ibid., 335.
74. Ibid., 337.

SYSTEM AND LIFEWORLD

Habermas develops his theory of communicative rationality and lifeworld to reveal a structure of systematically distorted communication. In other words, such distorted communication means colonization of the lifeworld by the ideology of the system. In light of the communicative-theoretic concept of the lifeworld, he improves and renews the concept of the lifeworld normally employed in the hermeneutic idealism of interpretive sociology.[75] His theory of communicative action as a critical theory of society is the key methodological term in Habermas' later work. Rather than identifying society with the lifeworld, he proposes to conceive of society in a twofold sense: a system as well as a lifeworld.

Habermas calls the social sphere, which is reproduced by communicative interaction a lifeworld, while calling a public (political, economic) sphere reproduced by power and money a *system*. A lifeworld embraces personality, culture, and society. In the process of social differentiation in modern society a political function of power and economic reproduction is separate from the lifeworld that embraces person, culture, and society. In the period of late capitalism, lifeworld comprises person, culture, and civil society while system comprises politics, economics, and mass media.

According to Habermas, the lifeworld is always present, forming the background for participants in communication who, in fact, belong to it. In the lifeworld, social, cultural, and economic structures interpenetrate with action and consciousness. Worldviews share the same relation to the lifeworld that the conscious does to the unconscious, according to Freud. We cannot step out of our lifeworld. The lifeworld sets the context-forming horizon of social action and consciousness.

Habermas asserts that language and cultural tradition assume a transcendental status, constitutive for the lifeworld itself. Participants in communication cannot take up an extramundane or privileged position in reference to their lifeworld or language in which every new situation appears. Lifeworld is a composer of a cultural stock of knowledge that is "always already" familiar. Thus, they continue understanding in drawing upon a cultural tradition.[76]

---

75. Habermas, *Theory of Communicative Action*, 2:119.
76. Ibid., 125.

In other words, participants in communication are always moving with and being shaped by the horizon of their lifeworld whose structure forms the intersubjectivity of possible understanding. Thus, Habermas grants a transcendental site to the lifeworld where actors in communication raise claims mutually, criticize, confirm the validity of their claims, settle disagreements, and arrive at agreements.

Unlike the philosophy of consciousness, the communicative-theoretic concept of the lifeworld is developed from the participant's perspective and suits the everyday concept of the lifeworld, locating the utterances and discourses of the actors in communication in social spaces and historical times. Narrative presentations that actors in communication give take place in the context of their lifeworld, describing socio-cultural events and objects.

Participants in communicative interaction stand in a cultural tradition which communicative action serves to transmit and renew under the functional aspect of mutual understanding. It also serves social integration and the establishment of solidarity (under the aspect of co-ordinating action). Finally, it serves the formation of personal identities (under the aspect of socialization).[77] Three interrelated dimensions are foundational for Habermas's strategy of communicative framework and structure of lifeworld: culture (cultural reproduction), society (social integration), and person (socialization).[78]

Communicative action presents itself as an interpretive mechanism through which the reproduction of the lifeworld consists in a continuation and renewal of cultural tradition. Habermas contends that communicative sociology takes into account the process of social integration and socialization. In these two dimensions "the lifeworld is 'tested' and measured . . . against standards for the solidarity of members and for the identity of socialized individuals" rather than against claims or standards of rationality.[79]

Within the expanding horizons of a lifeworld, Habermas reworks the very idea of socialization in terms of mutual learning. The concept of lifeworld helps clarify the reconstruction of Weber's process of rationalization.[80] Habermas supports explanations from the interplay

77. Ibid., 137.
78. Ibid., 138.
79. Ibid., 139.
80. Ibid., 113–52.

between the standpoints of the cultural sphere and the political, economic sphere.

In the first place, we must enter social reality from above through interpretations of the worldviews of those people we seek to understand. This interpretation of worldviews succeeds when it is adequate at the level of meaning. Furthermore, every explanation from the cultural sphere must be supplemented with an explanation from the political, economic sphere. This dialectical model refers to Habermas's concern for establishing a connection with the problematic of reification in a Marxist framework and his reception of the Weberian rationalization thesis.[81]

In connection to Durkheim and Mead, Habermas sees communicative rationalization in the process of the linguistification of the sacred. The disenchantment and disempowering of the domain of the sacred takes place in terms of linguistification. According to Habermas, sacred knowledge is superseded by a knowledge that is specialized according to validity claims and based on reason and rationality. As legality and morality get separated from one another, law and morality are universalized. In the final analysis "individualism spreads along with its heightened claims to autonomy and self realization."[82]

Cultural reproduction, social integration, and socialization from sacred foundations to linguistic communication and action are oriented toward mutual understanding. Habermas regards increasing differentiation as a hallmark of the development of the West into a modern society. The most fundamental differentiation in modern society is located between the lifeworld and the system of the market economy and the administrative state. He acknowledges a more pluralistically differentiated public use of reason. He discerns this pluralism of the public sphere and rationality in religious public, civil, social and human rights movements, Feminism, working class movements, institutions, and NGO's.

As we have already expounded, lifeworld has become differentiated into three components: culture (cultural reproduction), society (social integration), and personality (socialization making up personal identity). The lifeworld in which these different tasks and components are complicatedly intertwined exists as a life story, a highly integrated narrative.

---

81. Ibid., 113.
82. Ibid., 107.

Communicative action serves to transmit and renew cultural knowledge and serves social integration and the establishment of solidarity.

Under socialization, communicative action serves the formation of personal identities. The cultural reproduction of the lifeworld secures a continuity of tradition and coherence of knowledge, which are measured by the rationality of valid knowledge. The social integration of the lifeworld ensures the coordination of action and the stabilization of group identities, which are measured by solidarity among its members. This disturbs a social integration as manifested in anomy and corresponding conflicts. The socialization of the members of a lifeworld secures individual life histories in harmony with collective forms of life, which are measured by the responsibility of persons. This disturbs the socialization process as manifested in psychopathologies and phenomena of alienation accordingly.[83]

From the third perspective of socialization, participants in communication encounter one another in a horizon of unrestricted mutual understanding, which represents, at a methodological level, a hermeneutical claim to universality. For Habermas, this aspect of communicative mutual understanding offers an immanent critique of the hermeneutic idealism of interpretive sociology.[84] We shall have an opportunity to explore his argumentation against H.-G. Gadamer's concept of a hermeneutical claim to universality in the next chapter.

In a modern society, the lifeworld does not remain in the background, but is implicitly subject to testing. Communicative testing of the lifeworld can confirm cultural traditions and furthermore correct, expand, and renew it, even withdrawing meaning from traditions. A problem can be summarized with the following formula: rationalization as the loss of meaning plus rationalization as the loss of freedom is reification, which is the increasing penetration of exchange values and power into society, culture, and the lifeworld.

The pathologies of bourgeois society as well as post-traditional society (i. e., loss of meaning, anomie, and alienation) can be traced back to the rationalization of the lifeworld itself. The rationalization of the lifeworld enables a subsystem to emerge and grow whose influence can become destructive upon the lifeworld itself. Systemic constraints instrumentalize a communicatively structured lifeworld toward a charac-

83. Ibid., 140–41.
84. Ibid., 151.

ter of deception and objectively false consciousness. Structural violence can be done against the communication structure of the lifeworld in terms of systematic restriction. In this case, "the mediatization of the lifeworld assumes the form of a colonization."[85] According to Habermas, the communicative rationality, which reflects in the self-understanding of modernity, offers an immanent critical logic for resistance against the colonization of the lifeworld.

LEGITIMATION AND CRISIS

A Marxian approach focuses on the analysis of the commodity form from the double perspective of a crisis-ridden process of capital as well as from a conflict-ridden interaction between social classes. The capitalist mode of production is based on the exchange relation between labor power and variable capital. In other words, the productive forces of base and superstructure in productive interaction, deciphers the accumulation process of production in view of the process of exploitation. Marx is concerned to reveal a character of fetishism embodied in the labor power and commodity, calling the monetarized labor power (as a commodity estranged from the life context of producers) "abstract labor."

The Marxian approach to the double character of the commodity labor power provides an analysis of the exchange relations between the economic system and the lifeworld. The crisis-ridden model of capital accumulation (problems of system integration) can be reflected at the level of social integration (connected with the dynamics of class conflict). Thus, Marx brings together systems and action theory through the analysis of the bilingual character of labor, commodity, and capital.

However, in Habermas's view, Marx did not presuppose the separation of the system and the lifeworld even though he arrives at the two analytical levels of system and lifeworld.[86] To the extent that Marx conceptualizes a Capitalist society as a dialectical totality, he fails to grasp an intrinsic dimension of the medial-steered subsystem. For Marx, system and lifeworld surface in the metaphor of the "realm of necessity" and the "realm of freedom," so the Socialist revolution is meant to free the latter (lifeworld) from the former (the dictates of the system).

---

85. Ibid., 196.
86. Ibid., 338.

Against Marx's diagnosis, Habermas credits Weber's prediction: the abolition of private capitalism would not imply the destruction of the iron cage of modern industrial labor and bureaucratization.[87] Marx was not capable of distinguishing between the aspect of economic reification and that of structural differentiation of the lifeworld.[88] According to Habermas, in the reality of late capitalism the Marxian approach remains inadequate in explanation and clarification of multiple phenomena of reification: the bureaucratization and monetarization of public and private areas of life.[89] An economically narrowed interpretation is challenged to clarify between state and economy in favor of government interventionism, mass democracy, and social welfare state.

In the *Legitimation Crisis*, Habermas attempts to analyze crisis of the late Capitalism. Economic subsystem (capital) and political administrative system (the state) assume steering performances in which the state provides steering performance over the economic subsystem to legitimatize the crisis of late capitalism. To maintain popular assent and mass loyalty, the state has to use the fiscal revenues to provide social, educational, and welfare services and to justify the ideology that legitimates the whole system.

At the economic level, crisis occurs. At the political administrative level, a rationality crisis occurs. All the while, a legitimation and motivation crisis occurs on the socio-cultural level.[90] Ideology serves to hide or legitimate the underlying structure of a social organization. The state carries the burdens of social integration, assuming social welfare performances at the socio-cultural level. The crisis-ridden course of economic growth can be balanced through governmental intervention into the market world. Thus, economic progress is controlled through the medium of state power. Economy is steered via the money medium.[91]

Starting from a model with two steering media—money and power—the institutionalization of power is more compelling than that of money; consequently, a legitimation of political power is needed. Public opinion becomes pluralistic, gaining different meanings and perspectives in the public sphere. A pluralistic expression of general interest mani-

---

87. Ibid., 340.
88. Ibid., 340–41.
89. Ibid., 343.
90. Habermas, *Legitimation Crisis*, 45.
91. Habermas, *Theory of Communicative Action*, 2:344.

fests in mass democracy. The social welfare system becomes the political content of mass democracy. Reform politics in the social welfare state has created a pacification of class conflict. In fact, "late capitalism makes use its own way of the relative uncoupling of system and lifeworld."[92]

Against Marxian economic reductionism, Habermas contends that the economy depends on being supplemented by an administrative system that is differentiated out through the medium of political power. It is necessary to approach the genesis of reification in terms of interplay between system and interaction in the phase of late capitalism. Modernity's two great media, money and power, lead the economy and administrative power of the state to instrumental-strategic action, which does structural violence, colonizing the lifeworld's communicative moral reasoning and action.

At this juncture, Habermas pays attention to the mass media and mass culture in which the communication steered via mass media replaces the communication structure made possible by citizens and private individuals. The mass media presents itself as an apparatus completely permeating and dominating the language of everyday communication. Habermas distinguishes steering media (differentiated out of the lifeworld) from generalized forms of communication (remaining tied to lifeworld contexts). The public media make the efficacy of social control hierarchical and strengthened. Instead of false consciousness, we have a fragmented consciousness surrounded by the mechanism of reification. This forms a condition for a colonization of the lifeworld.[93]

Against the colonizing impact of instrumental-strategic logic and action, Habermas argues that the logic of everyday communicative practice establishes defenses against the direct manipulative intervention of the mass media.[94] It is important to transpose communicative action to media–steered interaction and the deformation of the structures of a damaged intersubjectivity. For this task, analysis of lifeworld pathologies calls for an investigation of tendencies and contradictions, consequently calling for a protest, which is potential for the lifeworld against internal colonization.[95] Habermas proposes deliberate democracy and civil society. As he argues, "the goal is . . . to erect a democratic dam

92. Ibid., 348.
93. Ibid., 355.
94. Ibid., 389–91.
95. Ibid., 391.

against the colonizing *encroachment* of system imperatives on areas of the lifeworld."[96]

Through the communicative action and strategy of erecting a democratic dam, deliberative democracy is growing. In addition to a critical analysis of money and administrative power, Habermas advocates for the political public sphere, civil society, and their medium of solidarity. The socially integrating force of solidarity has to develop through public spheres and procedures of democratic opinion and will-formation, which is institutionalized within a constitutional framework.[97]

In protest of the colonizing process of the system on the lifeworld, Habermas supports waves of social movements such as ethnic movements for civil rights, feminism, ecological movements, and peace movements. Social movements and new politics in which "quality of life, equal rights, individual self-realization, participation, and human rights"[98] are highlighted, can be understood as a potential for protest against the reality of system.

In the communicative social theory of lifeworld, the political public sphere presents itself "as a communication structure rooted in the lifeworld through the associational network of civil society."[99] The political public sphere entails open, permeable, and shifting horizons and can be defined as a network for communicating information and diverse opinions, expressed in both positive and negative ways. Like the lifeworld, the political public sphere as the social space reproduces and generates in and through communicative action.

RELIGION AND THE PUBLIC SPHERE

As for the connection between the political sphere and the lifeworld, Habermas credits religions with an important role. In the process of the reunification of Germany, the role of the Christian Church in former eastern Germany cannot be ignored. Civil society entails the plurality of institutions, associations, movements that more or less spontaneously emerge out of the lifeworld. The core of civil society comprises a network of associations. This network institutionalizes problem-solving

---

96. Calhoun, *Habermas and the Public Sphere*, 444.
97. Habermas, *Between Facts and Norms*, 299.
98. Habermas, *Theory of Communicative Action*, 2:392.
99. Habermas, *Between Facts and Norms*, 359.

discourses on questions of general interest as set within the framework of organized public sphere.[100]

Religion, speech, and association are necessary conditions for the operation of civil society. For Habermas, the political public sphere can be defined as a network for communication structure and information, positive or negative, in the coalescence of public opinions grounded in the lifeworld through the associational network of civil society.

Habermas offers an important insight for religion. Religious community is asked whether it is on the side of lifeworld or the system. The unfortunate alliance between the altar and the crown in the Christian tradition or Confucianism and Buddhism as the state religions in the East Asian tradition has undermined or blocked the prophetic, ethical, critical factor of the religious belief system against those who suffer under the ideologically distorted system of politics, economy, and culture.

Metanoia, in a Christian sense, implies a return from the previous wrong way toward the lifeworld of the gospel, forgiveness of sin, reconciliation, and embrace of the forsaken and the marginalized. The Christian Church is located within the civil community. The lifeworld of the gospel is engaged in the public sphere; that is discipleship in service of God's reign. Discipleship in service of God's reign of reconciliation and the lifeworld of the gospel do not ignore the reality of lordless powers in the area of economic constraints and bureaucratization of administrative power, and subsystem of media commercialized. Christian public theology considers the political sphere, the economic sphere, and the cultural sphere in light of the gospel in which God's righteousness stands in favor of those who are alienated, marginalized, and victimized in the process of the system's colonization of civil society.

According to Habermas, religious community and ethical norms are to be seen in the social space of communication through public process of interpretation. Religious statements find public relevance by taking into account public discourse, which calls for mutual recognition without coercion and institutional authority. Religious discourse is asked to be free of all forms of coercion and ideology, pursuing for truth or righteousness in a cooperative search with communicative reason and action in the public sphere.

As the reflective form of communicative action, Habermas refers to a form of argumentation in the strict sense. "The ideas of justice and soli-

---

100. Ibid., 367.

darity are already *implicit* in the idealizing presuppositions of communicative action."[101] Thus, the communication-theoretical interpretation of morality and discursive ethics has merit to discuss an ethical issue from the public sphere of socially organized communal life. Here, the moral point of view is implicit in the structure of reciprocal recognition among communicatively acting subjects.

Nonetheless, Habermas's assumption of the justification of the principle of universalization as a rule of argumentation is limited in its approach to the discourses of those who are marginalized, deviated, and unfit in the public sphere. Solidarity and justice are not the privilege of communicative reason; rather, they belong to the ethics of compassion in religious discourse. To what extent does a communicative idealization articulate its justice and solidarity regarding the community of the forsaken and involve its self-critique in the dynamic process of a power–knowledge interplay?

Reason does not replace the narrative of the gospel. Rather, the gospel exists in inseparable solidarity with the lowest of the low in the public sphere. It awakens a communicatively oriented rationality to be more sensitive to the complex of knowledge and power, which shapes and influences human life, including a communicative reason. The strategy of reading the community of the forsaken in this regard is not Habermas's task, but Foucault's.

---

101. Habermas, *Justification and Application*, 50.

6

A Postmodern View of Power and Knowledge in Interplay

AN ANALYSIS OF KNOWLEDGE-POWER in the public sphere begins more radically with Foucault. Born in Poitiers, France, in 1926, Paul-Michel Foucault was raised as a Roman Catholic and educated by Jesuits. In 1970, Foucault was elected to the Collège de France, occupying a chair in the history of the system of thought. Covering themes ranging from madness via the science of "the man," to discipline and punishment in prisons and sexuality, his writings are rich and comprehensive in variety and provocative in their challenges to truth, power, and the human subject. His works reject the limitation of humanism and the autonomous subject, preferring to explore the processes and structures that produce a human subject. His analysis of insanity, human sciences, sexuality, health, and confinement are only retrospectively identified in methodological terms of archaeology and genealogy, which are reminiscent of Nietzsche.[1] Although his works oppose a tradition of hermeneutics, his lectures at the Collège de France (1981–1982) are ironically entitled the *Hermeneutics of the Subject*.[2]

Foucault's early work in *Madness and Civilization* (1961) begins to describe the exclusion and confinement of lepers and demonstrates what reason excludes: madness, chance, and discontinuity. Foucault describes how madness, along with poverty and unemployment, was perceived as a social problem in the seventeenth century. The mad were allowed to wander in the open countryside during the Renaissance. The Ship of Fools, a strange "drunken boat" glides along the rivers of the Rhineland and Flemish canals. This was a common method for dealing with the

---

1. For the introduction to Foucault's work, see Dreyfus and Rabinow, *Michel Foucault*.

2. Foucault, *Hermeneutics*.

mad: put them to sail down Europe's rivers in search of their sanity, entrusting them to mariners, because folly, water, and the sea had an affinity for each other.[3]

From a theological perspective, the medieval church not only cast Abraham's sacrifice in light of Christ's passion, but also it interpreted the passion in excessive and unreasonable ways, integrating dreams and madness into its meaning.[4] A symbol of the knowledge tree as forbidden in paradise prefigures the Mast of Bosch's Ship of Fools.[5] "Madness is no longer the familiar foreignness of the world; it is merely a commonplace spectacle for the foreign spectator."[6]

However, within the space of a hundred years, the mad-ship was replaced by the mad-house. Enormous houses of confinement (sometimes called houses of correction) were created throughout Europe in the seventeenth century. The mad, together with the poor, the unemployed, the sick, and the criminals were sent to these places. Here they had to accept physical and moral constraint.[7] Labor in the house of confinement took on an ethical meaning: sloth was condemned as an absolute form of rebellion. Idleness was seen as the supreme pride of the human being, that is, the absurd pride of poverty.

During the Renaissance, people viewed madness in light of the idea of imaginary transcendence. During the classical age, they condemned madness as a form of idleness in transgression of a labor-based social community. Madness was understood on the social horizon of poverty and the incapacity for work.[8]

In the nineteenth century, the dialogue between reason and unreason was broken. Reason that gained mastery over unreason inscribed the latter. In an encounter between reason and unreason, the madness of unreason was mastered.[9] Confinement, prison, the dungeon and even torture disengaged dialogue between reason and unreason, because

---

3. Foucault, *Madness and Civilization*, 7.
4. Ibid., 19.
5. Ibid., 22.
6. Ibid., 28.
7. Ibid., 48.
8. Ibid., 64.
9. Ibid., 252.

there was no longer a common language. "The language of delirium can be answered only by an absence of language."[10]

With the dawn of the medical professional, the meaning of confinement dissolves. Medical certification becomes necessary in order to confine the mad person. The physician's power derives from his/her authority to cure madness. People view doctor as quasi-divine nearly omnipotent, holding power to cure the patient. Such positivism began to impose its myth of scientific objectivity.[11]

Most of Foucault's books are analyses of modernization process, like Weber. Early on, Foucault was interested in language and the constitution of the subject in the process of discourse. In it, the individual subject was understood as an intersection of the discourses. Foucault traced the structure of the human sciences, language, and labor in terms of discursive systems. His concern was to analyze how the human sciences historically came to be and what the historical condition of their existence is.[12]

In his later work, Foucault articulates more emphatically that individuals are constituted by power relations, in which power is the ultimate principle of social reality. How does Foucault's analysis of rationality and knowledge-power in the public sphere relate to his strategy of interpretation? For this task, let us first deal with his account of rationalization.

FOUCAULT AND RATIONALIZATION IN CUL-DE-SAC

For Foucault, one cannot speak of rationalization without placing an absolute value inherent on reason. Foucault examines and analyzes how forms of rationality inscribed themselves in practices or in systems of practices. However, he avoids Weber's ideal type, which forms a category of historical interpretation in terms of selective affinity.

For Foucault, it is important to avoid recourse to an ideal signification or to general types. He is concerned to "see how forms of rationalization become embodied in practices, or a system of practices."[13] Foucault attempts to demonstrate rationality as envisaged and embedded in penal imprisonment. This arose out of a whole technology of human training

10. Ibid., 262.
11. Ibid., 276–77.
12. Gordon, *Power/Knowledge*, 230–31.
13. Dreyfus and Rabinow, *Michel Foucault*, 133.

and surveillance of behavior. Therefore, discipline is not the expression of an ideal type.[14]

Weber saw that rationality, in the form of bureaucratization and calculative thinking, was becoming the dominant way of understanding reality in our time. Through scientific, sociological analysis, he saw that calculative, technical thinking brings about the disenchantment with the world that had an enormous impact on and cost in Western life. Horkheimer and Adorno analyzed the Capitalist economy as merely one form of the autonomous dynamic of a means–end rationality. Technical or instrumental rationality represents a more profound threat to human freedom than class oppression.

Sharing the view of Weber and the representatives of the Frankfurt school, Foucault takes into account Heidegger's ontology of being-in-the-world, according to which one is always already situated in a particular historical context. Hence, one's account of the significance of one's cultural practices can never be value-free, but always involves an interpretation. The historical study of the background of practices cannot be done by context-free, value-free, objective theory.[15] For the analysis of society, the individual, and language, Foucault contends that such an analysis is an inquiry which aims to discover the basis on which knowledge and theory became possible. On what basis could historical ideas appear, science be established, and rationalities be formed?[16] Here, Foucault's concept of episteme deserves consideration.

At a given period, episteme implies the total set of relations that unite the discursive practices. In turn, the discursive practices give rise to epistemological sciences and a formalized system. The episteme is the totality of relations to be deciphered and unearthed between the sciences in a given period. It is rather a type of rationality in which the sovereign unity of a subject crosses over the boundaries of the most varied sciences.[17] Foucault's inquiry into the epistemological field (the episteme) aims to rediscover on what basis, within what space of order, and what historical *a priori* knowledge was constituted where ideas would appear, sciences were established, and rationalities were formed. Thus his attempt to bring to light the episteme is not concerned with describing

---

14. Rabinow and Rose, *Essential Foucault*, 253.
15. Dreyfus and Rabinow, *Michel Foucault*, 165–66.
16. Foucault, *Order of Things*, xxi–xxii.
17. Foucault, *Archaeology of Knowledge*, 191.

the progress of knowledge, but rather with demonstrating a history that conditions the possibility of knowledge. Such a methodological enterprise is archaeological than historical in its traditional meaning.[18]

Foucault categorizes different episteme with respect to the Renaissance, the Classical Age, and Modernity. Modernity is characterized as the Age of "man." "Man" becomes a subject among objects. "Man's" finitude is heralded in the positivity of knowledge. The analysis of "Man's" mode of being does not reside within a theory of representation. From Kant onward, modernity begins with the idea of a being whose finitude allows the human being to take the place of God. The analytic of finitude is "an analytic . . . in which Man's being will be able to provide a foundation in their own positivity for all those forms that indicate to him that he is not infinite."[19] The threshold of modernity "is situated by the constitution of an empirico-transcendental doublet which was called Man."[20]

In a distinction between the empirical and the transcendental, Kant attempts to rescue the pure form of knowing from history or life-factuality. Furthermore, a human being discovers (in Heidegger's terms) that he/she is always already cast in the world, in language, and in history. "Man is cut off from the origin that would make him contemporaneous with his own existence."[21] Using language, "the men enter into communication and find themselves in the already constructed network of comprehension."[22] However, this communicative knowledge is circumscribed, diagonal, and incomplete to the degree that it is surrounded and conditioned by labor, life, and language.

If one reduces "Man" to his empirical side, one cannot account for the possibility of knowledge. But, if one overemphasizes the transcendental side, one cannot claim scientific objectivity nor account for the contingency of "Man's" empirical nature. For Foucault, a discourse free of the doubles would offer a new hope for understanding human beings. This refers to an interpretive aspect of Foucault's ontology of historico-critical investigation in the analysis of humanity as an empirico-transcendental doublet at the level of archaeological configuration. According to Foucault, Western "Man" is a quite recent invention and creature who

18. Foucault, *Order of Things*, xxii.
19. Ibid., 315.
20. Ibid., 319.
21. Ibid., 332.
22. Ibid., 331.

is not yet two centuries old. Before the end of the eighteenth century, "Man" did not exist. However, he has grown old so quickly. He is shaped and ruled by labor, life, and language through which is it possible to have access to him. One's body fundamentally gives his/her life the mode of being. Human finitude is marked by the spatiality of the body, the desire, and the time of language within which the content of knowledge has finite forms. Insofar as modern thought concerning life, labor, and language holds value as analytics of finitude, modern thought expresses the end of metaphysics. This event announces the appearance of "Man. The philosophy of life denounces metaphysics as a veil of illusion, while the philosophy of labor denounces it as an alienated form of thought and an ideology. The philosophy of language does it as a cultural episode.[23]

Foucault does not put his trust in reason as our hope or mimesis, continuing a critical argument in the public arena. For Foucault, the relationship between rationalization and excesses of political power is evident. To recognize such a relationship, we do not need to wait for bureaucracy or for the concentration camp. Here, it is meaningless to regard reason as the contrary entry to nonreason. "Such a trial would trap us into playing the arbitrary and boring part of either the irrationalist or the rationalist."[24] Similar to Weber, Horkheimer, and Adorno, Foucault grants a central role to reason, its historical effects, its limitation, and danger in the process of increasing rationalization and technological development.

Foucault argues that knowledge is power over others—the power to define others. Knowledge ceases to be liberation and becomes a mode of surveillance, regulation, and discipline. Foucault's hypothesis is that the prison was linked from its beginning to a project for the transformation of individuals. The prison did not reform but on the contrary, it manufactured criminals and criminality. The transformation of Western societies from monarchical power to disciplinary power is epitomized in Foucault's description of the Panopticon, an architectural device advocated by Jeremy Bentham toward the end of the eighteenth century. Foucault picks out Bentham's plan for the Panopticon (1791) as the paradigmatic example of a disciplinary technology.

In this circular building of cells, no prisoner could be certain of not being observed from the central watchtower. In this tower, the director

23. Ibid., 317.
24. Dreyfus and Rabinow, *Michel Foucault*, 208.

was able to spy on all the employees under his or her authority, altering their behavior, imposing new methods upon them, and even was able to observe the director him/herself. As a marvelous machine, the Panopticon produced homogeneous effects of power, functioning as a laboratory of power. "Knowledge follows the advances of power, discovering new objects of knowledge over all the surfaces on which power is exercised."[25]

As a generalized model of defining power relations in terms of every day human life, the Panopticon presented itself as a political technology, "a cruel, ingenious cage."[26] The Panopticon held the connection between bodies, space, power, and knowledge. It provided the mechanism for the insertion and activation of a new form of continuous administration and control of everyday life. This new mode of power was used in schools, barracks, and hospitals. "Its aim is to strengthen the social forces—to increase production, to develop the economy, spread education, raise the level of public morality; to increase and multiply."[27]

New techniques of power were needed to undertake its administration and control because of newly arising problems of public health, hygiene, housing conditions, fertility, and sex. Panopticism as the discipline–mechanism, whose object and end was the relations of discipline, is the general principle of a new "political anatomy." Sex was and is politically significant because it is located at the point of intersection of the discipline of the body and the control of the population. Thus discipline can be defined as a tactic of power, in short, to increase both the docility and the utility of political, economic, and social elements of the system.[28]

The Panopticon becomes the model for all forms of domination and discipline. The Panopticon is a machine, invested by its effects of power, like an iron cage, in which everyone is caught, since we are all parts of the mechanism.[29] The technologies of bio-power are in a perfect position to supervise and administer the anomalies. Prisons resemble factories, schools, barracks, and hospitals. The Panopticon arrangement, which provides the formula for this generalization, penetrates the ba-

25. Foucault, *Discipline & Punish*, 204.
26. Ibid., 205.
27. Ibid., 208.
28. Ibid., 221.
29. Ibid., 217.

sic functioning of a society thoroughly with disciplinary mechanisms.[30] Ironically, the "Enlightenment" invented discipline while discovering liberty.

ENLIGHTENMENT AND CRITIQUE

Foucault's view on Enlightenment ties in with Weber's critique of technical rationality. In "What is Enlightenment?" Foucault deals with Kant's philosophical characterization of the Enlightenment as the "way out" (*Ausgang*), of immaturity. In Kant's view, the Enlightenment is both a task and an obligation because human beings are responsible for their own immature status.

For Kant, the Enlightenment has a motto, an instruction, and a heraldic device: dare to know (*Aude sapere*), have the courage, and the audacity to know. Kant's word *räsonieren* refers to a use of reason, to reason for reasoning's sake. For instance, one pays one's taxes while arguing about the system of taxation. Enlightenment exists when the universal, the free, and the public uses of reason are superimposed on one another.

Since Kant, and because of him, the relationship between Enlightenment and critique has been raised in terms of knowledge. Kant engineered the gap between critique and Enlightenment and mobilized the procedure of analysis, that is, "an investigation into the legitimacy of historical modes of knowing."[31]

In a proposal to Frederick II, Kant argues that the public and free use of autonomous reason will be the best guarantee of obedience: "the contract of rational despotism with free reason."[32] On Kant's account, Enlightenment becomes possible when humanity puts its own reason to use without subjecting itself to any authority. Dogmatism and heteronomy are the illegitimate uses of reason. The Enlightenment heralds therefore the age of the critique. Foucault characterizes the Enlightenment project as the attitude of Modernity. In Foucault's view, the use of reason, which takes the public form, also must be obeyed in accordance with universal reason.

---

30. Ibid., 209.
31. Rabinow and Rose, *Essential Foucault*, 273.
32. Ibid., 46–47.

According to Foucault, the Kantian critique, which confronts ideology, marks the threshold of modernity by questioning representation on the basis of its rightful limits. Knowledge and thought are withdrawn from outside the space of representation.[33] Foucault characterizes the attitude of modernity in terms of consciousness of the discontinuity of time, a break with tradition, a feeling of novelty, and a will to idealize the present. What renders the painter a modern painter is that he/she transfigures the world by entailing a difficult interplay between the truth of what is real and the exercise of freedom rather than annulling it. The deliberate attitude of modernity is bound up with an indispensable asceticism.

According to Baudelaire, "modern man is not the man who goes off to discover himself, his secrets and his hidden truth; he is the man who tries to invent himself."[34] In agreement with Baudelaire, Foucault argues that the ironic heroization of the present, the transfiguring play of freedom with reality, and the ascetic elaboration of the self are related to a philosophical way of interrogation. For him this is true to the extent that it problematizes man's relation to the present, "man's" historical mode of being, and the constitution of the self as an autonomous subject which is rooted in the Enlightenment. Thus, Foucault designates the Enlightenment period as a formative stage for modern humanity.[35]

Negatively, Foucault calls this ethos the blackmail of the Enlightenment. The Enlightenment constitutes a privileged domain for analysis. However, this negative evaluation does not necessitate siding either for or against the Enlightenment. Instead, Foucault's interest is in the analysis of ourselves as beings who are historically conditioned and determined by the Enlightenment. Positively, Foucault takes this philosophical ethos of Enlightenment to be a limit-attitude.

His criticism of the Enlightenment is not transcendental, but rather genealogical in its design and archeological in its method. Foucault's genealogical criticism seeks to give new impetus to the undefined work of freedom rather than to make possible a metaphysic. His archeological critique attempts to treat the instances of discourse that articulate what we think, say, and do, rather than seeking to identify the universal structures of all knowledge. The historico-critical attitude of the Enlightenment re-

33. Foucault, *Order of Things*, 242.
34. Rabinow and Rose, *Essential Foucault*, 50.
35. Ibid., 272.

mains an experimental one, opening up a realm of historical inquiry on the one hand and putting itself to the test of contemporary reality on the other hand. Foucault is suspicious of all projects of the historical ontology of Western "man" which claim to be global, universal, or radical.

At this juncture, Foucault implicitly shares an ethos of the diachronic hermeneutic of the history of effect espoused by H.-G. Gadamer. Foucault argues that "the claim to escape from the system of contemporary reality so as to produce the overall programs of another society . . . another vision of the world, has led only to the return of the most dangerous traditions."[36]

From this point of view, which is the theoretical and practical experience of our limits, Foucault takes issue with the analysis of the axis of knowledge, the axis of power, and the axis of ethics. This analytic task belongs to Foucault's interpretive strategy of the historical ontology of Western "man." The historico-critical investigations of this historical ontology analyze the problem of the relationship between sanity and insanity, sickness and health, crime and the law, and the problem of the role of sexual relations.

Foucault's analysis of Enlightenment connects with his critique of governmentalization and confrontation of its authority. In governmentalization, "individuals are subjugated in the reality of a social practice through mechanisms of power that adheres to a truth."[37] Hence critique implies that the individual gives oneself the right to call into question both truth on its effects of power and power on its discourses of truth. A philosophical tradition of suspicion regarding something of rationalization and reason, which is accountable for an excess of power, has been established from the Hegelian Left via Max Weber to the Frankfurt School. In this tradition, we are aware of a complete critique of positivism, objectivism, and rationality. Furthermore, the first critical movement of not being governed comes from Luther's Reformation in connection with interpretation of the Scripture. Foucault argues that, "Critique is biblical, historically."[38] Reformation is a public issue engaging in critique of authority and tradition.

To promote his method of the nexus of knowledge-power, Foucault introduces the concept of eventalization. In the procedure of eventaliza-

---

36. Ibid., 54.
37. Rabinow and Rose, *Essential Foucault*, 266.
38. Ibid., 265.

tion, we consider the content of knowledge in terms of its diversity and heterogeneity, and we view them in the context of the effects of power they generate. In this context, the effects of power are validated by belonging to a system of knowledge.[39] Knowledge refers to all procedures and all effects of knowledge acceptable at a given point in time and in a specific domain; in a given episteme, power covers a whole series of a particular mechanism. In fact, "knowledge and power are only an analytical grid."[40]

Nothing can function as a mechanism of power without a coherent system of knowledge. An analysis of the nexus of knowledge and power aims at grasping that which constitutes the acceptability of a system, deciphering the connection between the mechanism of coercion and elements of knowledge. An analysis of the knowledge-power interplay brings out the conditions of a system's acceptability, following the breaking points that indicate its emergence at an archeological level.[41] Accepting a system at a given time and in a specific context cannot be dissociated from identifying knowledge and the violence of a system in terms of power.

GENEALOGY AND EFFECTIVE HISTORY

How does Foucault's genealogical analysis of the structure of knowledge–power in the public sphere relate to his strategy of interpretation? First of all, Foucault is opposed to any form of global theorizing. He draws on a vision of history that derives from Nietzsche's genealogy. Descartes's *cogito* is the ground of all certainty. Against this, Nietzsche argues that all previous foundations of human knowledge are undermined and seen as prejudices of faith. For Nietzsche, reason is only an instrument. Nietzsche argues that the questions of truth and knowledge have to be situated and assessed in the context of an appreciation of "the perspectival optics of life." The primary desire of a living being is to discharge and release its strength (life is will to power) and hence the drive to self-preservation. Nietzsche calls into question the will to truth. Nihilism is a historical necessity since the Enlightenment.

---

39. Ibid., 274.
40. Ibid.
41. Ibid., 275.

Sharing Nietzsche's diagnosis of Enlightenment and genealogy, Foucault contends that modernity's turn away from God toward "man" and its grounding of freedom in the unfettered rational human consciousness appear as new forms of hegemony. With expressions like discursive formation and episteme, he calls attention to the way objects, subjects, and truth are not the result of objective reflection. Rather, they are produced by the interrelation of language, social institutions, and power.

Genealogical analysis differs from traditional forms of historical analysis in several ways. Genealogical analysis attempts to establish and preserve the singularity of events, and turns away from the spectacular in favor of the discredited, the neglected, and a whole range of phenomena that have been denied in history. Genealogies focus on local, discontinuous, disqualified, and illegitimate knowledge against the claims of a unitary body of theory, which would filter, hierarchize, and order them in the name of some true knowledge.

Genealogy is a form of critique. It rejects the pursuit of the origin in favor of a conception of historical beginnings as lowly, complex, and contingent. In this view of history, there can be no constants, no essence, no uninterrupted continuities structuring the past. Interpretation for Foucault is not the uncovering of deep and hidden meaning, because interpretation is a never-ending task. Everything underneath is already interpretation. Genealogy records the history of these interpretations.

In his article, "Nietzsche, Genealogy, History" (1971), Foucault finds two terms useful: *Ursprung* ("cause" or "source") and *Entstehung* ("emergence") (or *Herkunft* ["descent"]). The latter is more exact than the former for a description of the true object of genealogy. Nietzsche's genealogy wants to find in history "something together different behind things."[42] In other words, according to Nietzsche, the original basis of morality is an invention. The concept of liberty is an invention of the ruling classes. Therefore, by opposing a search for an origin, genealogy "rejects the metahistorical deployment of ideal significations and indefinite teleologies."[43]

As we have already seen, Nietzsche was opposed to any theory that reduced the entire history and genesis to an exclusive concern for unity or eternal truth. A metaphysicist strives to seek the soul in the ideality of

42. Ibid., 353.
43. Ibid., 352

the origin. However, in a genealogist's view, what we find at the historical beginning of things is not the inviolable identity of their origin; rather it is the dissension of other things, disparity.[44] Therefore, the reason why the genealogist needs history is for dispelling the chimeras of the origin. The story of history is not the lofty development of truth.

Diachronic hermeneuticians articulate the belief that the past actively exists in the present. However, the genealogist does not share such belief. The genealogist, like Foucault, wants to discover that truth or being lies not at the root of what we know. Rather, he follows the complex course of descent. Such a search for descent is not interested in erecting foundations. Genealogy, as a critique and a critical analysis of descent, is meant to articulate the history of the body. It is to expose a body in critical view of the process of destruction of the body by history.[45]

When it comes to meaning and value, virtue, and goodness, Foucault looks for strategies of domination. *Entstehung* denotes emergence, or the moment of arising. Genealogy seeks to find the dangerous play of domination, rather than seeking the anticipatory power of meaning. The history of morals, ideals, and metaphysical concepts stand for the emergence of different interpretations.

Following Nietzsche's anti-progress conviction, Foucault argues that humanity does not gradually progress from combat to combat, but proceeds from domination to domination.[46] Hence, Foucault destroys the doctrine of development and progress by revealing the endlessly repeated play of dominations. This relationship of domination is not simply that of rulers and ruled and of dominators and dominated, but it is fixed throughout human history and present in meticulous rituals of power, which do not create subjects.

This concept of meticulous rituals of power is the conceptual basis, which is applied to the Panopticon of Bentham and the confessional in *Discipline and Punish* and *The History of Sexuality*. History is not the progress of universal reason, class struggle, or a patriarchal domination of women, but is a play of rituals of power such that humanity advances from one domination to another.

Genealogy as *wirkliche Historie,* or historical sense, questions the form of history, which reintroduces and assumes a suprahistorical per-

44. Ibid., 353.
45. Ibid., 357.
46. Ibid., 358.

spective. Such a perspective reduces "diversity of time into a totality fully closed upon itself."[47] This traditional history encourages a form of reconciliation (like Hegel) to all the displacements of the past. Against this traditional history, effective history or historical sense becomes a privileged instrument of genealogy by refusing the certainty of absolutes.

Introducing discontinuity into our very being and uprooting its traditional metaphysics and foundation, history becomes effective. As Foucault argues, "'effective' history leaves nothing around the self, deprives the self of reassuring stability of life and nature, and it will not permit itself to be transported by a voiceless obstinacy toward a millennial ending."[48] The genealogist, who writes effective history, seeks to put everything in historical motion, dissolving an illusion of identity, firmness, and solidity.

For Foucault, the effective history, in contrast to history of effect in Gadamer's sense, unearths decadence of traditional philosophy and metaphysical foundation, with an eye of suspicion.[49] This effective history affirms a perspectival knowledge rather than a fusion of horizons in the sense of dialogical dialectics. If hermeneutics in the sense of Heidegger and Gadamer is oriented to tradition, history, and language in a diachronic sense, Foucault's genealogy is a form of synchronic interpretation with an eye of strategic suspicion to the relation between power and knowledge in a form of discourse. Everything is potentially enmeshed in the networks of power, which is connected with the advance of knowledge. Knowledge is thoroughly enmeshed in the clash of domination. The body is directly involved in a political field. Power relations have an immediate hold upon it.

For Foucault, language is the medium through which the things of the world can be known. In becoming an object of knowledge, language began to fold in upon itself and deployed a history and laws of its own. Nietzsche was the philologist who connects the philosophical task with a radical reflection on language. For Nietzsche, the matter is to know who was speaking rather than knowing what good and evil were in themselves.[50] Language is given in the thread of which all the discourses of all times may be given. The origin does not give rise to historicity,

---

47. Ibid., 359.
48. Ibid., 360.
49. Ibid., 361.
50. Foucault, *Order of Things*, 305.

but historicity makes possible the necessity of an origin. One is never contemporaneous with the origin. When one defines one's essence as a speaking subject, all one finds is the previously unfolded possibility of language. For Heidegger, the ontological return is posited only in the extreme recession of the origin. Nonetheless, Foucault argues that the man in his infinite task of conceiving of the origin is not contemporaneous with the origin. Rather the person is within a power dispersing him/her by drawing him/her far away from his/her own origin. This power is origin of human own being.[51]

The strategy of genealogy is understood in a threefold sense. The first is parodic, directed against reality. The second is dissociative, directed against identity, opposing the history which is conceptualized as continuity or representative of a tradition. This refers to the systematic dissociation of our identity. Effective history in a genealogical sense contradicts a history of effect in a diachronic sense, in which history as a pre-given affects human understanding. Committing itself to the dissipation of our identity, it opposes "the homeland to which metaphysicians promise a return."[52]

Thus, a genealogy attempts to restore the conditions for the appearance of a singularity born out of multiple determining elements of the effect in which the singular effect can be accounted for in terms of relationships between individuals or groups. Foucault calls for an attempt at bringing out a whole form of analysis regarding the relationships of interactions strategy.[53]

The third strategy of genealogy is sacrificial, directed against truth, by constructing a counter memory—"a transformation of history into a totally different form of time."[54] It includes the sacrifice of the subject of knowledge because the various forms of scientific consciousness and transformations are aspects of the will to knowledge. The will to knowledge does not achieve a universal truth. Human being is not an exact and serene mastery of nature.[55] Following in the footsteps of Nietzsche, Foucault's strategy is to risk "the destruction of the subject who seeks

---

51. Ibid., 334–35.
52. Rabinow and Rose, *Essential Foucault*, 366.
53. Ibid., 277.
54. Ibid., 365.
55. Ibid., 366.

knowledge, in the endless deployment of the will to knowledge," by promoting "the affirmative and creative powers of life."[56]

For Foucault, archeology, strategy, and genealogy characterize three necessarily contemporaneous dimensions. This interplay of these three analyses accounts for eventualization. It is significant to approach the question in terms of power and eventualization rather than in terms of knowledge and legitimation. Power has to be considered in relation to a field of interactions connected with forms of knowledge rather than unilaterally as domination, mastery, or fundamentally given. In this regard, genealogy of knowledge and power entails an interpretive implication in a social, public location.[57]

GENEALOGY AND INTERPRETIVE STRATEGY

Genealogy proposes an interpretive strategy. In "What is an Author?" (1970), Foucault's subject matter, dealing with the meaning and function of the author, relates to the question of "what difference does it make who is speaking?" This question becomes a focus for Foucault rather than the question "what does it matter who is speaking." Foucault identifies writing with its own unfolded exteriority, that is, interplay of signs arranged according to the very nature of the signifier. Like a game, writing unfolds going beyond its own rules and limits. In writing, the point is not to pin a subject within language; rather, it is a question of creating a space into which the writing subject disappears.[58]

The task of literary criticism is to analyze the work through its structure, its intrinsic form, and the play of internal relationships. It questions the condition of the text; the space in which the text is dispersed, and the time in which it unfolds. Hence, the author in the text should not be transposed into a transcendental anonymity.[59] Foucault is aware of conflict between those locating today's discontinuity in the historico-transcendental tradition and those trying to free themselves from the tradition.

Navigating between these two poles, Foucault locates the space left empty by the disappearance of the author. However, he does not discard

---

56. Ibid., 367.
57. Ibid., 278.
58. Ibid., 378.
59. Ibid., 379.

the name of the author, but rather grants to it "a certain mode of being of discourse."[60] This indicates the status of the discourse within a society and a culture. According to Foucault, "the author function is therefore characteristic of the mode of existence, circulation, and functioning of certain discourses within a society."[61]

Discourses are objects of appropriation. We remain within the world of discourse. The authors are "founders of discursivity"[62] by establishing an endless possibility of discourse. For this example, Foucault mentions Freud and Marx. These two established and created an endless possibility of discourse about psychoanalysis or political economy. Reexamining Freud's texts modifies psychoanalysis itself while a reexamination of Marx's text modifies Marxism.

Foucault calls his approach to discourse a typology of discourse. Such a typology cannot be constructed from the grammatical features, formal structures, and objects of discourse. Rather, there exist relationships peculiar to discourse, which are not reducible to the rules of grammar and logic. The relationship with an author and different form of the relationship constitute one of the discursive properties. For instance, a historical analysis of discourses is performed according to their mode of existence. The modes of circulation, valorization, and appropriation of discourses vary with each culture and are modified with it. They are articulated according to social relationships and cultural locations.

In this light, the subject is analyzed as a variable and complex function of discourse. According to the traditional idea of the author, "the author is the principle of thrift in the proliferation of meaning."[63] Running counter to this traditional notion of the author, Foucault argues that text, discourse, and fiction are not limited by the figure of the author. The author is not an indefinite source of signification. At the heart of Foucault's synchronic hermeneutics is the quest to find the modes of existence of discourse in social locations and relationships.

---

60. Ibid., 382.
61. Ibid., 382.
62. Ibid., 387.
63. Ibid., 390.

POWER-KNOWLEDGE IN INTERDEPENDENCE

The interdependence of power and knowledge constitute the strategic fulcrum of Foucault's later work. Nietzsche specified the power relation as the general focus, while for Marx it was the production relation. Foucault replaced a judicial, negative conception of power with a technical and strategic one. This positive view, which is in contrast to his previous negative view of power, can be seen in *Discipline and Punish* and *The History of Sexuality*. Therefore, Foucault argues that rather than language and relations of meaning, relations of power should be the point of reference.[64]

On Foucault's account, power and knowledge directly imply one another. "There is no power relation without the correlative constitution of a field of knowledge."[65] These power-knowledge relations are to be analyzed according to their historical transformations. The process and the struggle based on the power-knowledge nexus both traverses and determines the forms, as well as the possible domains of knowledge.[66]

According to Foucault, relations of power do not emanate from a sovereign, a state, or a structure of patriarchic culture. Power in Western capitalism is denounced by socialists or post-colonialists as class domination or imperialistic dominion. Feminists denounce power as dominion and repression of patriarchy. However, in Foucault's view, the notion of repression or dominion is inadequate for capturing what is the productive aspect of power. This is critiqued as "a wholly negative, narrow, skeletal conception of power."[67] Instead, power is not simply a commodity to be acquired or seized. Rather, it has the character of a network; its threads extend everywhere.

Power is multidirectional, operating from the top down but also from the bottom up. We are all enmeshed in it. However, dominion is not the essence of power. Foucault's question is not: who has power? But his question is related to the processes by which subjects are constituted as effects of power. He rejects analyses that locate the source or origin of power within a structure or institution at a center.

---

64. Gordon, *Power/Knowledge*, 114.
65. Foucault, *Discipline & Punish*, 27.
66. Ibid., 28.
67. Gordon, *Power/Knowledge*, 119.

A Postmodern View of Power and Knowledge in Interplay 121

For Foucault, truth is not outside of power. Rather, it is of this world. Each society has its own regime of truth and its general politics of the truth. There is a central component in the historical transformation of various regimes of power and truth. Conceiving of power as repression, constraint, or prohibition is inadequate. Power produces reality. It produces domains of objects and rituals of truth. The exercise of power causes the emergence of new objects of knowledge. Conversely, knowledge induces effects of power. Foucault defines truth as "the ensemble of rules according to which the true and the false are separated and specific effects of power attached to the rule."[68]

Complex differential power relationships extend to every aspect of our social, cultural, and political lives. We should not view the subject as the knowing, willing, autonomous, self-critical, or transcendental subject in the sense of Kantian discourse. We should understand the subject as a locus of multiple, dispersed, or decentered discourse. At issue is "detaching the power of truth from the forms of hegemony, social, economic and cultural, within which it operates at the present time."[69]

Foucault is not trying to get meaning or the whole picture of a past. He is not reading present interests, institutions, and politics, by bringing them back into history. This would be called the well-catalogued error of presentism in a historical analysis. Foucault's genealogy writes the history of the present, by beginning with a diagnosis of the current situation and locating the manifestation of a particular meticulous ritual of power or political technology of the body.

For example, in *The History of Sexuality*, Foucault isolates the confession as an important ritual of power in which a specific technology of the body was forged. Confession is a vital component of modern power. Foucault writes the history of the confession in the seventeenth century for the purpose of writing a history of the present. Destroying the project of writing a true history of the past, Foucault concentrates his analysis on those cultural practices in which power and knowledge intersect, and in which our current understanding of the individual, the society, and the human sciences are fabricated.

For this task, he introduced another technical term: *dispositif* (apparatus; grid of intelligibility). *Dispositif* encompasses nondiscursive practices as well as the discursive, including "discourses, institutions,

---

68. Ibid., 132.
69. Ibid., 133.

architectural forms, regulatory decisions, laws, administrative measures, scientific statements, philosophical, moral and philanthrophic propositions—in short, the said as much as the unsaid."[70] This apparatus, having a strategic nature, brings together power and knowledge into a specific grid of analysis. The apparatus is inscribed in a play of power linked to certain coordinates of knowledge issuing from it while conditioning it. The episteme is a specifically discursive apparatus, whereas the apparatus in its general form is both discursive and non-discursive. The apparatus that "consists in strategies of relations of forces supporting, and supported, by types of knowledge" is a more general case of the episteme.[71]

Foucault starts with *dispositif* of sexuality, a fundamental historical given, for his discussion of sexuality. This *dispositif* Foucault calls decipherment, which revises and corrects the overemphasis on the actor's point of view ignoring the crucial importance of social practices. A strategy of *dispositif*, or decipherment, radicalizes a hermeneutic of suspicion toward another more important meaning rather than going into one deeper meaning.

Foucault's aim is to give a genealogy of knowledge of sex and power regarding how such a nexus has functioned and played in our society. Here, Foucault rejects the repressive hypothesis, which defines the relationship between sex and power in terms of repression. If sex is repressed and condemned to prohibition, the one who speaks about it, places oneself outside the reach of power to some extent.[72]

The power over life has evolved in a whole intermediary cluster of relations: the centering on the body as a machine and the focusing on the body imbued with the mechanics of life. The former is related to the discipline while the latter to regulatory controls, a bio-politics of the population. The organization of power over life was deployed around the two constitutive poles: the disciplines of the body and the regulations of the population.[73]

Social science came to be connected with technologies of bio-power. The administration of bodies and the calculated management of life have supplanted the old power of death and sovereign power, investing life through and through. The bio-power centered on the body is

70. Ibid., 194.
71. Ibid., 196.
72. Foucault, *History of Sexuality*, 1:6.
73. Ibid., 139.

an object to be manipulated. The basic goal of disciplinary power was to produce a human being who could be treated as a docile body. In workshops, barracks, prisons, and hospitals, the technology of discipline has its aim to increase the usefulness and docility of individuals and populations.

It is certain that numerous and diverse techniques are explored to achieve the subjugation of bodies and the control of populations. This marks the beginning of an era of "bio-power."[74] The disciplining of the body as a machine, the parallel increase of its usefulness and its docility, and its integration into systems of efficient and economic controls are ensured by the procedures of power characterizing the disciplines: "an anatomo-politics of the human body."[75] Disciplinary control and the creation of docile bodies are connected to the rise of Capitalism. The growth of disciplinary technologies became the technological preconditions for the success of Capitalism. This bio-power was an indispensable factor in developing Capitalistic social order, which would not be possible "without the controlled insertion of the bodies into the machinery of production and the adjustment of the phenomena of population to economic processes."[76]

BIO-POWER IN THE SPHERE OF SEXUALITY

The control of bio-power—control of the body and control of the species—came together in the nineteenth-century preoccupation with sex. Sex became the construction through which power linked the vitality of the body together with that of the species. One should not understand the discourse on sexuality in the Weberian manner as the rise of a secular asceticism. The deployment of sexuality led to an enormous explosion of discourse and concern about the vitality of the body rather than to decreased interest in sexuality. Sex became the object of a major investment of signification, of power, and of knowledge. Sexuality is a historical construct. We have had a concept of sexuality since the eighteenth century, and then the concept of sex since the nineteenth century. However, what we had before was a concept of the flesh.[77]

74. Ibid., 140
75. Ibid., 139.
76. Ibid., 141.
77. Gordon, *Power/Knowledge*, 211.

Foucault discredits the repressive hypothesis, which insists that sex became hidden and banished from everyday life as the West moved into the Victorian era. Repression is the effect of a relationship of domination between power and sex. Liberation from this domination comes from exploring sex and seeking pleasure without restraint. Open sexual speech and behavior belong to liberation, while silence and segregation to domination. This view of repression is easily linked with the rise of Capitalism. Sex was repressed because it was incompatible with the work ethic of Capitalism. Repression is the general form of domination under Capitalism. Thus it is argued that one adjusts repression to coincide with the development of Capitalism. The concept of repression becomes an integral part of the bourgeois order. The history of the modes of production transposes the chronicle of sex so that "its trifling aspect fades from view."[78]

Against the hypothesis of a power of repression, Foucault develops a strikingly different interpretation of the relationships between sex, truth, power, the body, and the individual. He calls this alternative synthesis a bio-technico-power or bio-power. Bio-power, or power over life, is a distinct regime of power whose objects and methods take shape with a particular type of rationality. Foucault contrasts rationality of bio-power to that of sovereign power. "On top of the older right of the sovereign to *take* life or to *let* live, was substituted the power to *foster* life or to *disallow* it to the point of death."[79] In the rationality of bio-politics, life, and its regulation come to fruition through the continuous regulation of its mechanism, technologies, and institutions. Life was understood as the basic needs, human concrete essence, and the realization of human potential.[80]

According to Foucault, sexuality is invented as an instrument effect in the spread of bio-power. Through the deployment of sexuality, bio-power spreads its net through the construction of a specific technology: the confession of the individual subject. Rather than seeing sex as repressed and hidden, Foucault sees a multiplication of sex and talk of sex. Furthermore, sex became linked to confession, be it to a priest, physician, or psychiatrist.

---

78. Foucault, *History of Sexuality*, 1:5.
79. Ibid., 137.
80. Ibid., 145.

Through confession, sex transforms speech so that sex becomes discourse. Consequently, the dissemination and reinforcement of heterogeneous sexualities link together with a religious ritual of the confession. "The confession is a ritual of discourse," unfolding within power relationships.[81] The revelation of confession was coupled with the decipherment of what is said. As far as sexuality is interpreted, it has a hermeneutic function operating within the regular formation of a scientific discourse.[82] The confession became a technique for producing truth about sex. "Western man has become a confessing animal."[83] The confession still remains the general standard, shaping and governing the way the true discourse on sex is generated.[84]

For the connection between procedures of confession and scientific discursivity, Foucault pays attention to a hermeneutic dimension regarding the decipherment of what is said. A discourse of truth on sex can be also constituted on the basis of its decipherment. Foucault claims that talk of sex multiplied as practices of confession moved from religious penance to judicial process, medical diagnosis, and psychiatric exploration of the corners of the psyche. In the study of sexuality, Foucault attempts to find a correspondence between the functional requirements of a discourse and the truth that is to be produced by the discourse. Thus, Foucault writes the history of sexuality from the standpoint of a history of discourse. Confession is integrated into a field of rationality, or functional requirements of discourse.

There have been two widespread methods for dealing with sex: erotic arts (*ars erotica*) and a science of sex (*scientia sexualis*). In non-Western civilization, sex is treated as an *ars erotica*, which has an end in pleasure. However, the West has followed the other path—that of the science of sexuality.[85] Here a Chinese formula of sexual behavior *plaisir–désir–[acte]* comes into view. Acts are bracketed because acts should be restrained in order to attain the maximum duration and intensity of pleasure. In the Greek formula of *acte–plaisir–[désir]* acts are underscored. Desire was condemned in the Stoic ethics. In the Christian

81. Ibid., 61.
82. Ibid., 66–67.
83. Ibid., 59.
84. Ibid., 63.
85. Ibid., 58.

formula of [*désire*]–*acte*–[*plaisir*], one acts only to produce children or to fulfill one's conjugal duty.[86]

In the life of the Greeks and Romans, a *techne tou biou*, the economy of pleasure played a dominant role. The Geeks from Socrates to Seneca or Pliny were concerned about the *techne* of life: how to live rather than the *techne* of the self. In Plato's *Alcibiades*, an issue of taking care of oneself is connected with the issue of how to rule the city. In this art of life, Greek ethics is centered on a problem of aesthetics of existence: which *techne* do I have to use for a living or for "I ought to live"? [87]

However, in the Christian hermeneutics of the self, flesh became devalued to the reality of sin. Some of the prohibitions in sexual life are much stricter and much more rigorous in Christianity than in the Greek period. The pivotal event occurred when *scientia sexualis* emerged as the merging of confessional practices with scientific discourse. More precisely, scientific discourse colonized or reconstituted the old practice of confession. Sex has become a key to the sciences of the human subject.

According to Foucault, *ars erotica* did not entirely disappear from Western civilization. In the Christian art of spiritual direction, in search for spiritual union with God, a whole series of methods exist that hold much in common with erotic art. Mystical experience of possession and ecstasy had effects outside the control of the erotic technique.[88] The most important elements of an erotic art lie in the multiplication and intensification of pleasures, which are connected to the production of the truth about sex.[89] The deployments of power and knowledge, of truth and pleasures oppose a thesis of repression. According to the thesis of repression in the study of history of sexuality, repression is fundamental and overarching.[90]

Foucault's basic conviction is that sexuality is the name given to a historical construct; it is "a great surface network" in which several complicated issues (such as the stimulation of bodies, the intensification of pleasures, the incitement to discourse, the formation of special

---

86. Rabinow, *Foucault Reader*, 359.
87. Ibid., 348.
88. Ibid., 70.
89. Ibid., 71.
90. Ibid., 73.

knowledge, and the strengthening of controls and resistances) are linked together, according to a strategy of knowledge and power.[91]

Unlike Weber's concept of inner-worldly asceticism associated with the disqualification of the flesh, Foucault advocates for an intensification of the body in which the deployment of sexuality can be seen as the self-affirmation of one class, which involves the cost of the different transformations "as a means of social control and political subjugation."[92] With this investment of the body and sex in terms of a technology of power and knowledge, "the bourgeoisie underscored the high political price of its body, sensations, and pleasures, its well-being and survival."[93] It ensures the strength, endurance, and secular proliferation of the body by organizing the deployment of sexuality.

The emphasis on the body is linked to the process of growth and the establishment of bourgeois hegemony, based on what the cultivation of its own body represented politically, economically, and historically for the present and the future of the bourgeois. Cultural dominance is dependent on the physical factor rather than simply on economic life or political ideology. A whole technology of control under surveillance and discipline safely imported the deployment of sexuality into the exploited class, which remains finally the instrument of the bourgeoisie's hegemony. The entire social body was provided with a sexual body, thus sexuality is originally, historically bourgeois, inducing specific class effects and class sexualities.[94]

Foucault's genealogy of sexuality assumes a form of a hermeneutics of desire. In order to understand how the modern individual experienced oneself as a subject of sexuality, it is necessary to recognize oneself as a subject of desire. A hermeneutics of the self in a genealogical framework is helpful to analyze the games of truth and error, which historically constituted the human subject. What kind of relationship is there between the games of truth and desiring individuals?[95] This question leads to issues defining the conditions in which human individuals problematize what they are and how they live in the world.

---

91. Ibid., 105–6.
92. Foucault, *History of Sexuality*, 1:123.
93. Ibid.
94. Ibid., 126–27.
95. Foucault, *History of Sexuality*, 2:6–7.

In the study of sexuality, sexual activity and sexual pleasures are problematized through practices of the self, taking into consideration the criteria of an aesthetic of existence.[96] An analysis of the desiring individual is located where an archeology of problematization intersects with a genealogy of practices of the self.

From the perspective of bio-power, Foucault is highly critical of those "universal" intellectuals like Sartre. This intellectual is taken "as the clear, individual figure of a universality whose obscure, collective form is embodied in the proletariat."[97] Foucault reveals that the benefit of the universal intellectuals is a component in the advance of bio-power. The intellectual, as spokesperson for conscience and consciousness, locates himself/herself in the privileged spot. He/she is regarded to be outside of power and within the truth.[98]

History is often used to describe a homogenizing approach to the past and is often associated with a master narrative. In contrast, Foucault adopts a genealogical perspective, which treats truth-claims as products of the ubiquitous will to power within language, discourse, or representation. Fascism and Stalinism, as a disease of power, used the ideas and the devices of our political rationality. Racism, as seen in light of the analytics of sexuality and the symbolic of blood, is accompanied by a long series of permanent interventions at the level of the body, conduct, health, color, and everybody life. Finally, it receives justification from the mythical interest in keeping the purity of the blood and ensuring the triumph of the race. "Nazism was doubtless the most cunning and the most naïve combination of the fantasies of blood and the paroxysms of a disciplinary power."[99]

A new economy of power relations consists of taking the forms of resistance against different forms of power as a starting point. This resistance functions as a chemical catalyst in order to bring to light power relations, locate their positions, and find out their point of application and the methods. Such resistance analyzes power relations through the antagonism of strategies rather than from the perspective of the internal rationality.[100]

96. Ibid., 12.
97. Gordon, *Power/Knowledge*, 126.
98. Ibid., 127–28.
99. Foucault, *History of Sexuality*, 1:49.
100. Dreyfus and Rabinow, *Michel Foucault*, 211.

RELIGIOUS DISCOURSE OF *PARRHĒSIA* AND THE PUBLIC SPHERE

Foucault's themes are of great interest for theological and religious studies. Religious discourse emerges in each period of history according to the epistemic structures that make its statements possible. Religious concepts and interpretive exegesis take shape according to the regimes of knowledge available at any given moment in time. Foucault's work provides an opportunity to examine the condition of religious knowledge and expose the hidden regimes of power behind religious discourse.

Given what Foucault has attempted regarding the relation of power and knowledge, several feminists find some affinities with him. Both identify the body as the site of power. This is the locus of domination, through which docility is accomplished and subjectivity constituted. Both draw attention to the local and intimate operations of power rather than focusing exclusively on the supreme power of the state. Both point to the crucial role of discourse in its capacity to produce and sustain hegemonic power and emphasize the resistance contained within marginalized or unrecognized discourses. Both share a critique that Western humanism has privileged the experience of the Western masculine elite as it proclaims universals about truth, freedom, and human nature. Both attempt to dismantle existing but unrecognized modes of domination. These convergences comprise some of the most powerful forms of resistance.[101]

For Foucault the deployment of sexuality is tied to recent devices of power. From the outset, sexuality is linked with an intensification of the body and its exploitation which was an object of knowledge and an important element in relation to power.[102] Foucault's challenge to society's will to knowledge and his assessment of the mechanism of power-knowledge are consonant with his ethics of genealogy. This is a social criticism on behalf of those who are marginalized, silenced, deviated, and suppressed in the public sphere. According to him, ethics is grounded in resistance to totalitarian power, whether it stems from religion, science, or political oppression. The very achievement of Western humanism has

---

101. Diamond and Quinby, *Feminism & Foucault*, x–xii.

102. Foucault, *History of Sexuality*, 1:107. According to Foucault, in the case of Herculine Barbin, who as a nineteenth-century hermaphrodite was forced to choose a sexual identity, bureaucracy formalized sexual essentialism. See Foucault, *Herculine Barbin*.

been built on the backs of women, people of color, and the marginal. For Foucault, rationalizing discourses suppress discourse of marginalized groups and such discourses are sites of resistance.[103]

Confession has long been central to religious traditions. Foucault claims that Western technologies of power have produced a uniquely modern subjectivity, sexual identity. Religious communities obsessed with the status of homosexuals are being normalized and disciplined by modern bio-power. According to Foucault, religion needs to be analyzed as a formation of discursive practices.

Foucault's critical methodology is a methodology for the silenced. Far from undermining religious discourse and practice, Foucault rather establishes a ground to develop new forms of negative theology and offers new perspectives for rethinking contemporary body theology, a theology of physicality and embodiment. His interpretive strategy in terms of an analysis of the power-knowledge relation is *parrhēsia*, "speaking frankly."

Parrhēsia, etymologically, is the act of telling all (frankness, openheartedness, plan speaking, speaking openly, speaking freely) which is generally translated as *libertas* in Latin. At issue in *parrhēsia* are frankness, freedom, and openness: the freedom of the person who speaks.[104] This form of speech is free from rhetoric, dismissing flattery. There can only be truth in *parrhēsia*, thus *parrhēsia* is the *kairos*, the occasion in which individuals choose to speak the truth with regard to each other.[105]

Truth-telling, as the obligation of confession, did not exist at all in Greek, Hellenistic, or Roman Antiquity.[106] Foucault sought to rehabilitate *parrhēsia* as a form of speech that is both resistant to the confessional-hierarchical mode and alert to the religious categories, which had come to be employed politically. Fascism cultivated a religious sensibility frequently described as a type of religion of nature, where the sanctification of biological life transforms into an adoration of national life. Foucault shows how the National Socialist religious mythology in Germany utilized categories from traditional Christian discourse to make Hitler a messianic figure, construct God as a symbol of vital forces, and articulate doctrines of human nature and redemption.

103. Foucault, *History of Sexuality*, I, xvii.
104. Foucault, *Hermeneutics*, 366.
105. Ibid., 384.
106. Ibid., 364.

In his Fall 1983 Berkeley course, Foucault retrieved *parrhēsia* as a personal frankness which is different from other forms of truth speaking (namely, those of prophet, sage or teacher-technician). *Parrhēsia* is a verbal activity in which a speaker expresses his/her personal relationship to truth, and risks his/her life. A speaker recognizes truth-telling as a duty to improve or help other people. The person who speaks *parrhēsia* articulates "criticism instead of flattery, and moral duty instead of self-interest and moral apathy."[107]

Foucault argues that there is a parrhesiastic pole, which represents the mystical tradition of Christianity. It involves human confidence in the overflowing love of God and the belief that God will answer the prayers of the Christian. At issue for Foucault's philosophy is to announce the imminence of the death of "man." "Man" may have killed God beneath the weight of all that he has said. With all "man" are saying, however, Foucault warns us not to imagine that we will make a man that will live longer than God.[108]

Foucault's thought of the death of "man" devalues the concept of the human subject as the transcendental subject. The project of modernity is a divinization of the human being. Against this project of modernity, Foucault proposes a new concept of God after the period of the death of God and the death of the human being. Foucault encourages Christian theology to take seriously mystical *parrhēsia*'s discourse flowing from God's love in Christ. Jesus appears in a synoptic framework to be one who speaks publicly and plainly.

Foucault argues, if genocide is the dream of modern powers, it is because power is situated and exercised at the level of life, related to the species, the race, and the large-scale phenomena of population.[109] Systematic exterminations of the population have continued into the midst of our present in the name of authoritarian discourse. It is necessary and compelling to propose and develop a strategic analysis, which calls into question the relationship of the administration of life and death. In this light, Foucault expressed his spirituality of resistance in the sense of Christian *parrhēsia*. Despair and hopelessness are one thing; suspicion is another. If we are suspicious, it is because we have a

---

107. Foucault, *Fearless Speech*, 19–20. See Bernauer and Carrete, *Michel Foucault and Theology*, 83.

108. Foucault, *Archaeology of Knowledge*, 211. See Foucault, *Order of Things*, 342.

109. Foucault, *History of Sexuality*, 1:137.

certain hope. The problem is to know which kind of hope we have, and which kind of hope it is reasonable to have for the sake of the things we want to avoid by these hopes.[110] Foucault possesses a non-ideological hope, a confidence that effective resistance could take place, even against the most entrenched systems of political or moral ideology. Foucault's suspicion of hermeneutics introduces the non-fascist life to religious discourse and the public sphere.

---

110. Bernauer and Carrette *Michel Foucault and Theology*, 93.

7

The History of Effect and the Conflict of Interpretation

IN THE PREVIOUS CHAPTERS, we discussed Weber's sociology and his influence on Lukacs, on representatives of the Frankfurt school such as Horkheimer and Habermas, and finally on Foucault. In developing the legacy of the critical social theory of the Frankfurt school, Habermas's effort to salvage the lifeworld from the colonization of a system steered by money, power, and mass media offers important insight to the discussion of the Church's responsibility in the public sphere. Moreover, in a different direction from Habermas, Foucault's postmodern, sociological analysis of power and knowledge proposes an interpretive strategy for the more subtle analysis of the network of power and knowledge which has penetrated into the whole of life. For an anti-Fascist life, Foucault advocates for a discourse of *parrhēsia*, truth-speaking against a grand narrative of universalizing and instrumentalizing rationality that totalizes the particular, the different, and the unfit into it. His genealogy entails a hermeneutics of subject in resistance to the totalizing system of the Panopticon.

In contrast Foucault's project of discourse and power related to the suspicious hermeneutics, Habermas promotes a communicative theory of the public sphere and is in a critical dialogue with philosophers of hermeneutics (such as Hans-Georg Gadamer) regarding tradition, language, and critique of ideology. Habermas finds a resource in the hermeneutical tradition of Wilhelm Dilthey against Heidegger and Gadamer's ontological hermeneutics. In the midst of the hermeneutic debate, Paul Ricoeur is engaged in mediating and integrating a hermeneutical project and ideology critique in light of a hermeneutic of suspicion. His work enlarges the horizon of ontological hermeneutics for the sake of configuration between truth and method in the area of the public sphere.

This chapter uses a hermeneutics of the history of effect in order to examine philosophical and sociological debate in terms of ideology critique and of the theory of the public sphere. In the midst of a hermeneutical-sociological debate, it is constructive to articulate a critical dimension of the hermeneutic engaging in conflict of interpretation.

HERMENEUTICAL EXPERIENCE AND LANGUAGE

Wilhelm Dilthey (1833–1911), a contemporary of Nietzsche, represents the watershed between Schleiermacher and philosophical hermeneutics, the methodological concern of the social and historical sciences. His program of hermeneutics is embedded into an analysis of human life, and his concept of historicity is set within the horizon of history. His concept of historicity provides Heidegger with an important impetus to develop his own existential hermeneutics in *Being and Time*.[1]

What is foundational to Dilthey is his turn to experience. He distinguishes the foundation of *Geisteswissenschaften* (human studies, or human sciences, the social and human sciences) from those of natural sciences (*Naturwissenschaften*). According to Dilthey, *Geisteswissenchaften* include all the humanities and social sciences aimed at interpreting expressions of human inner life. In the natural sciences, however, there is an absence of reference to human experience. Explanation is the cognitive task of the natural sciences, while the cultural sciences have a different cognitive goal—understanding. Dilthey's concern is to develop a method of objectively gaining a valid interpretation of expressions of the human inner life. Thus, concrete, historical, and lived experience must be the starting point for the *Geisteswissenschaften*. The natural sciences *explain* nature while human studies seek to *understand* the expression of life.

In 1883, Dilthey published his *Introduction to the Human Sciences*, with the subtitle: "Attempt at a foundation for the study of society and of history." This title runs counter to the positivism of natural science. For Dilthey, life is more important than reason. Dilthey is concerned with a critique of historical reason in confrontation with Kant's critique of pure reason. Kant elevates the mind to the center of the human knowing process (epistemology), contending that the human mind is active in the knowing process. The mind systematizes raw data, which the sense-

---

1. Heidegger, *Being and Time*, 363.

experience furnishes. Kant's elevation of the active mind in the process of knowing and in the life of morality and duty encouraged subsequent philosophers to focus their interest on the autonomous, individual self. The elevation of the autonomous self to the center of the philosophical agenda gives birth to the transcendental pretense of modernity.

In contrast to Kant's concept of a transcendental self, Dilthey contends that the structures of thought arise out of experience and derive their meaning from it. As Dilthey provocatively states, "in the veins of the 'knowing subject' constructed by Locke, Hume, and Kant, runs no real blood."[2] Human reason cannot be treated separated from the historical context of human life. A human person, as a mind-body unity, lives in interaction with the physical and social environment.

All experience and all thought arise out of this interaction. A critique of historical reason replaces a critique of pure, theoretical reason. Only through history do we come to know ourselves. Furthermore, life rooted in the reality of lived experience is seen in terms of meaning. As life is an historical reality, so history is an expression of life. Dilthey contributes the expansion of the individual self to the public sphere of historically and socially conditioned worldviews. The meaning in life and history is incomprehensible without reference to the context of the past and the horizon of future expectations.

For Dilthey there is affinity and universality of thought among people that forms a social historical world. When one person understands another, a real transposition can take place. Dilthey sees this transposition as a reconstruction and re-experiencing of the other person's inner world of experience. The real issue is not a psychological understanding as with Schleiermacher, but rather cultural understanding of a social historical world. Homogeneity intersubjectively binds together a group when its members communicate with each other using the same language. This homogeneity links the external life-expressions to the person who understands them. The individual experiences, thinks, and acts in the sphere of homogeneity.

Habermas interprets Dilthey's grasp on the homogeneity of life as the objective mind. He characterizes this idea at the horizontal level of communication through the relation of the totality of the language community to the individuals. And at the vertical level, Habermas does it through the relation of the totality of life to the individual's lived experi-

2. Palmer, *Hermeneutics*, 102.

ences and life connections. Thus, the cultural scientist must penetrate the object's language and the social context of the object. Only the establishment of intersubjective understanding can enhance knowledge. Individual life histories are constituted in the cumulative experience of individuals over time (the diachronic dimension) and in the intersubjectivity of communication common to different subjects (the synchronic dimension). The cultural sciences have to explicate these connections in the community of life unities.

Dilthey's contribution, according to Habermas, lies in offering an epistemological grounding of social and cultural praxis for the human sciences, which does not merely dissolve and reduce into the sphere of labor in a Marxist sense. Habermas describes this area as the interaction mediated through daily language.[3]

Dilthey proposes the historical aspect of understanding, in which interpretation of life expression can penetrate the human world instead of abandoning it to mere psychological introspection. Dilthey also influences Heidegger to overcome his teacher's (Edmund Husserl's) scientifically rigorous tendencies.[4] The spirit of the human being has objectified and externalized itself, thus this externalization belongs to the area of human studies. In the expression of lived experience, human inner experience comes to the fullest expression. Hermeneutics is relevant for understanding the socio–historical reality in which life is disclosed and externalized. "Understanding of other people and their life-expressions is developed on the basis of experience (*Erlebnis*) and self-understanding and the constant interaction between them."[5]

The human social sciences are grounded in the life-connection through expression, understanding, and interpretation. For instance, Luther's writings help us to understand the Reformation movement through the connection with the religious sphere, his historical setting, and his personality, etc. This process widens our horizon of the possibilities of human existence. The human being, as tied to and limited by life's realities, is liberated by historical understanding. "This effect of history ... is widened and deepened in the further of historical consciousness."[6] A human being, as a historical being, appears to be an interpreting

---

3. Habermas, *Erkenntnis und Interesse*, 200.
4. Heidegger, *Being and Time*, § 77. See Welton, *Essential Husserl*, 22–25.
5. Mueller-Vollmer, *The Hermeneutics Reader*, 152.
6. Ibid., 161.

animal relating to the fixed writings of the past and projecting oneself newly and creatively in the future. We may find a beginning of linguistically and socially oriented hermeneutics in Dilthey: language, history, and public sphere are inseparable in light of the hermeneutical circle.

BEING-IN-THE-WORLD AND INTERPRETATION

According to Heidegger, understanding is the way of being, of *Dasein* itself. This hermeneutics designates the basic movement of human existence, which is all-encompassing and universal. Sharing Heidegger's concept, in the foreword to the second edition of *Truth and Method*, Gadamer states that hermeneutics denotes the basic being-in-motion of *Dasein*. This concept constitutes its finitude and historicity, embracing the whole of its experience of the world. The nature of the thing itself makes the movement of understanding comprehensive, intellectual, and universal.[7]

For Gadamer, the experience of a work of art transcends every subjective horizon of interpretation, both the artist's and the perceiver's. Like Heidegger, Gadamer strongly criticizes the modern surrender to technological thinking, which is rooted in subjectivism. Gadamer's approach is closer to the dialectics of Greek thinking than to modern manipulative and technological thinking. Truth is reached in a dialectical way, not in a scientific, manipulative method.

In method, the inquiring subject leads, controls, and manipulates; in dialectic, the questioner finds him/herself as the being whom the subject matter interrogates. The interrogation of subject matter destroys the subject-object framework and conception. Self-consciousness lies at the core of Hegelian thought of dialectics, but Gadamer's dialectical hermeneutics does not follow the Hegelian concept of *Geist,* which finds its ultimate grounding in human subjectivity and consciousness. Gadamer's dialectic is not based on a dialectic of refining opposed theses between thesis and antithesis for the synthesis in a Hegelian sense, but rather a dialogical dialectic between one's own horizon and that of tradition. It is grounded in the linguisticality of human being-in-the-world.

If Dilthey sees hermeneutics in the horizon of a historically oriented theory of method regarding the *Geisteswissenschaften*, Heidegger uses the term hermeneutics in the context of his quest for a fundamen-

---

7. Gadamer, *Truth and Method*, xxx.

tal ontology. In *Being and Time*, Heidegger quotes Dilthey as saying that an understanding of life comes out of a life connection as such. Heidegger states that the problem of history grew out of his appropriation of Dilthey's work. In Dilthey's philosophical framework, Heidegger perceives that three moments of investigation, namely "investigations in scientific theory, the history of science, and hermeneutical psychology constantly interpenetrate and overlap each other."[8]

Dilthey establishes a hermeneutical foundation in terms of life in the historical context. In this context, hermeneutics is the self-clarification of the understanding of life, involving the methodology of historiography. Heidegger recognizes in Dilthey the importance of understanding historicity. If there is an interest in understanding historicity, it is an essential task to develop "the generic difference between the ontic and the historical."[9] For Heidegger the fundamental goal of the philosophy of life belongs to this task.

It is certain that Heidegger needs a more fundamental radicalization than Dilthey by bringing the ontological question and historicity into a more primordial unity: "The question of historicity is an *ontological* question about the constitution of being of historical beings."[10] From the beginning, Heidegger sought a method of going behind, getting to the root of Western conceptions of Being. He attempts to call the entire Western metaphysical tradition into question.

Heidegger learned from Edmund Husserl that phenomenology had opened up the realm of phenomena to pre-conceptual apprehension. The expression "phenomenology" signifies primarily a concept of method. This philosophy seems to express the maxim, that can be formulated as: "To the things themselves!" Husserl approached the realm of phenomena with the idea of illuminating how consciousness functions as transcendental subjectivity. But for Heidegger, Husserl's maxim is, after all, an expression of the principle of all scientific knowledge.

Heidegger sees in the field of phenomenology a historical being-in-the-world. In its historicity and temporality, Heidegger believes that being, as it discloses itself in lived experience, escapes the conceptualizing categories of idea-centered thinking. In the Western philosophical

---

8. Heidegger, *Being and Time*, 363.
9. Ibid., 368.
10. Ibid.

tradition, being is concealed and almost forgotten for the sake of critical reason or of human critical subjectivity in a Cartesian-Kantian sense.

Being-in-the-world belongs essentially to *Dasein*, which is inherently temporal. Time is explicated as the horizon of the understanding of being. In terms of temporality, the being of *Dasein* understands being.[11] Thus being-in-the-world includes the understanding of existence. "Understanding of being is itself a determination of being of *Dasein*."[12] Heidegger's fundamental ontology has to be sought in the existential analysis of *Dasein*.

In *Being and Time*, Heidegger develops what we call a hermeneutic of phenomenology. He defines his task as a philosopher as a hermeneutic one. He rethinks and reframes Husserl's concept of phenomenology in a radically different manner. According to Heidegger, the authentic dimensions of a phenomenological method make phenomenology necessarily hermeneutical. His project in *Being and Time* is a hermeneutic of *Dasein*.

In the section of *Being and Time* entitled "The Phenomenological Method of the Investigation," Heidegger refers to his method as a hermeneutic. For his new definition of phenomenology, he returns to the Greek root: *phainomenon* (or *phainesthai*) and logos. *Phainomenon*, according to Heidegger, means "what shows itself, the self–showing, the manifest."[13] The *phaino* belongs to the root *pha–*, like *phos*, meaning light or brightness, "that within which something can become manifest, visible in itself." Thus, phenomenology is the science of phenomena. Heidegger contends that "phenomenon is established as what shows itself in itself, what is manifest."[14] Phenomena are a collection of what can be brought to light. This is simply identified with the Greek *ta onta* (German, *das Seiende*; English beings or what is). This becoming manifest is a showing or a revelation of something as it is, in its manifestness. Every appearance depends upon phenomena, and this is only possible in a thing's self-revelation (which is phenomenon in the genuine and original sense).

The –ology suffix in phenomenology goes back to the Greek word *logos*. *Logos* is that which is conveyed in speaking. The basic meaning of *logos* is speech, but it also carries a deeper meaning that suggests self-

---

11. Ibid.,15.
12. Ibid., 10.
13. Ibid., 25.
14. Ibid.

manifestation. Heidegger suggests the *logos* as the speaking function, which makes both reason and ground possible rather than something like reason or ground. "*Logos* as speech really means *déloun*, to make manifest "what is being talked about?" in speech."[15]

Following Aristotle's explication of the function of speech (as *apophainesthai*), Heidegger argues that, "in speech (*apophansis*) . . . what is said should be derived *from* what is being talked about."[16] *Logos* has an apophantic ("as") function and structure—it points to phenomena. It lets something be seen as something. This function is a matter of disclosing, or bringing to manifestation, what a thing is. The mind does not project a meaning onto the phenomenon; rather, what appears is an ontological manifestation of the thing itself. *Logos* lets something be seen: as a result the truth of *logos* is understood in the concept of *alētheia*, which allows beings to be seen as something unconcealed. This concept of the truth stays clear of any concept of truth construed in the sense of correspondence or accordance.[17]

To understand phenomenology as a compound of *phainesthai* and *logos* is to allow things to manifest as their true selves—to not force our own categories on them. Things show themselves to us. This conception is Heidegger's expression of Husserl's intention to return "To the things themselves!"[18] Phenomenology neither designates the object of its researches nor describes its content. Starting with the breakthrough of Husserl's *Logical Investigations*, Heidegger understands philosophy as universal phenomenological ontology, taking its departure from the hermeneutic of *Dasein*, as an analysis of existence.[19]

For Heidegger, interpretation is grounded not in human consciousness and categories, but in the manifestation of the thing encountered. Being can be interrogated by an analysis of how appearing occurs. Now ontology becomes phenomenology. Ontology must turn to the processes of understanding and interpretation through which things appear. It must render visible the invisible structure of being-in-the-world. Ontology must, as a phenomenology of being, become a hermeneutics

15. Ibid., 28.
16. Ibid.
17. Ibid., 29.
18. Ibid., 30.
19. Ibid., 34.

of existence. Phenomenology is the science of the being of beings, that is, ontology.[20]

According to Heidegger, the methodological meaning of phenomenological description is interpretation (*Auslegung*, "laying open"). The *logos* of a *Dasein* phenomenology has an interpretive character in the original sense of the word. Hermeneutics now becomes the interpretation of the being of *Dasein*, an analysis of the extentiality of *Existenz*, that is, of the being's authentic possibilities for being. Hermeneutics as the theory of understanding defines the understanding in an ontological manner in contrast to the method.

According to Heidegger, the *logos* of the phenomenology of *Dasein* has the character of *hermēneuein*. Through it the proper meaning of being and the basic structures of the very being of *Dasein* are *made known*. Phenomenology of *Dasein* is *hermeneutics* designating the work of interpretation.[21]

FORE-STRUCTURE AND INTERPRETATION

Human being is thrown into and embedded with the world. Human being as being-there characterizes that human life is shaped and influenced within the life context. For Heidegger, *Dasein* is thrown in that it is the "there" as being-in-the-world. Beings in the character of *Dasein* find themselves in their thrownness. Attunement as one of the existential structures discloses *Dasein* in its throwness, and has its understanding. *Dasein* is "thrown possibility throughout" which is "the possibility of being free for its own most potentiality."[22]

Insofar as understanding is attuned, understanding as a fundamental existential can be conceived of as a fundamental mode of being of *Dasein*. Thus, "the mode of being of *Dasein* as a potentiality of being lies existentially in understanding."[23] Understanding, which is the being of such a potentiality of being, concerns the whole fundamental constitution of being-in-the-world and has the existential structure called the project. The project character of understanding implies that *Dasein* is thrown into the existential mode of being of projecting. As projecting,

---

20. Ibid., 33.
21. Ibid.
22. Ibid., 135.
23. Ibid., 134.

understanding is the mode of being of *Dasein* in which *Dasein* understands itself in terms of possibilities. Based on the existential of projecting, *Dasein* is more than it actually is. In this light, understanding of existence always refers to an understanding of world.[24]

Understanding as a projection of *Dasein* is the power to grasp one's own possibilities for being within the context of the lifeworld in which one exists. Heidegger defines the project of understanding in its own possibility of development as interpretation, so that interpretation is existentially based on understanding.[25] Understanding is the basis for all interpretation. Understanding is thus ontologically fundamental and prior to every act of existing. Besides, understanding always relates to the future, having a projective character. Understanding is also related to one's situation. The essence of understanding lies in the disclosure of concrete potentialities for being within the horizon of one's placement in the world. This aspect of understanding is called existentiality. Understanding always operates within a relational whole.

Dilthey has already asserted that meaningfulness is always a matter of reference to a context of relationship, an instance of principle, a hermeneutical circle. Going deeper, Heidegger explores the implications of the hermeneutical circle for the ontological structure of all human existential understanding and interpretation. A consideration of Heidegger's concept of the world will clarify this.

The term "world" for Heidegger does not mean our environment. Rather it points to our personal world. To conceive of the world as separate from the self would be antithetical to Heidegger's conception, because he opposes the scientific and methodological model of the subject-object relation. World is always already there prior to both subjectivity and objectivity. "World designates the ontological and existential concept of worldliness."[26] World and understanding are inseparable parts of the ontological constitution of *Dasein*'s existing and in its fundamental interpretation in the analytic of *Dasein*.[27]

For instance, Heidegger illustrates the hammer for clarifying the relationship between reference and sign. The sign is handy within the world in the context of useful things. As a useful thing, the sign as the pointer is

24. Ibid., 137.
25. Ibid., 139.
26. Ibid., 61.
27. Ibid., 54.

constituted by reference. The useful thing, hammer, is also characterized by serviceability. The referral serviceability, "for," is an ontological determination of the useful thing, hammer.[28] At the point of breakdown, we may observe a significant fact: the meaning of "a broken hammer" lies in its relation to a structural whole of interrelated meanings and intentions. A broken hammer at once shows what a hammer is.

Likewise, the being of something is disclosed in the moment in which it suddenly emerges from hiddenness in the context of the world. The phenomenon of breakdown lights up the being of a tool as tool, and points to its functional world. In the world, the temporality and historicity of being are radically present.

Herein, being is translated into meaningfulness, understanding, and interpretation. In the hermeneutical process, being becomes thematized as language. For Heidegger, meaningfulness designates the ontological ground for the structure of relationships. It is a basis for language. Meaningfulness is something deeper than the logical system of language. According to Heidegger, the logical system of language points beyond itself to a meaningfulness already resident in the relational whole of world. Understanding must be seen as embedded in this context. In understanding, things in the world are seen "as" this or "as" that.

Interpretation aims to render explicit the word "as." Under-standing becomes explicit as interpretation. Understanding and interpretation together are the basis for language and its meaningfulness. Language has its roots in the existential constitution of the disclosedness of *Dasein*. Discourse is the existential-ontological foundation of language.[29] In his later turn, Heidegger put the priority on language as "the house of being," because in language things first come into being.

The pre-structure of understanding raises grave questions about the basic validity of describing interpretation in terms of the subject-object relationship. According to Heidegger, interpretation does not throw a significance over what is objectively present. Rather what is encountered in the world is always already in a relevance which is disclosed in the understanding of world. This relevance is made explicit by interpretation.[30]

Interpretation is never a presuppositionless grasping of something given in advance. The hope of interpreting without prejudice and pre-

28. Ibid., 73.
29. Ibid., 150.
30. Ibid., 140.

supposition is an illusion. Presupposition rests in the context of world. Heidegger does not allow us to see the hermeneutical problem apart from human existing. Hermeneutics is a theory of how understanding emerges in human existence as grounded in the facticity of world and in the historicity of understanding.

In order to distinguish between an apophantic statement form of "as" and a hermeneutical form of "as," Heidegger gives again an illustration of the hammer: "The hammer is too heavy." In this assertion, the hammer has already been interpreted as a thing with properties. In the context of being ready-to-hand, the hammer disappears as object, appearing in the function of being a tool. We approach it as a tool, not as an object. The "as" which merely interprets the hammer as a tool or an object on hand before one's gaze is the "apophantic as."

In the statement which seeks to point out a fact, *logos* is apophansis.[31] This apophantic "as" no longer connects the hammer with the primordial totality of a lived, relational context. It cuts it off from the realm of meaningfulness in the ready-to-hand and puts the phenomenon as an instrumental tool. It becomes captive to a theory of judgments. As Heidegger contends, "the 'as' no longer reaches out into a totality of relevance in its function of appropriating what is understood."[32]

Heidegger calls for going deeper into the more original "as," the more primary "existential-hermeneutical as." It is to see the object in connection with the primordial totality of a lived, relational context. "We call primordial the 'as' of circumspect interpretation that understands (*hermēneia*), the existential-*hermeneutical* 'as' in distinction from the *apophantical* 'as' of the statement."[33] Things at hand are always already understood in terms of a totality of relevance based on a fore-having, a fore-sight, and fore-conception. The interpretation of something as something is at work in a totality of relevance as already understood and essentially grounded in fore-having, fore-sight, and fore-conception.

Given this fact, a presuppositionless grasping of something is nothing other than the self-evident, undisputed prejudice of the interpreter. Interpretation is pre-given with fore-having, fore-sight, and fore-conception. Something understood becomes revealed by an act of

---

31. Ibid., 144.
32. Ibid., 148.
33. Ibid.

appropriation in articulation of what is understood in disclosure, that is, the meaning.[34]

This fore-structure of understanding shows an existential-ontological connection with the phenomenon of project. In the projecting of understanding, beings are disclosed in their possibility. What is understood, strictly speaking, is not the meaning, but beings or being. The concept of meaning, structured by fore-having, fore-sight, and fore-conception, is to be understood as the formal, existential framework of the disclosedness belonging to understanding. "Meaning is an existential of *Dasein*, not a property which is attached to beings."[35] Therefore, interpretation occurs only within a given horizon of pre-understanding. The hermeneutical circle is the expression of the existential fore-structure of *Dasein* which only has meaning in the disclosure of being-in-the-world.

For Heidegger, the true foundation of language is the phenomenon of speaking in which something is brought to light. This is the hermeneutical function of language. In taking speaking as the starting point, one goes back to the living context of language. Interpretation becomes possible in the process of the appropriation of what is understood. According to Heidegger, the existential-ontological foundation of language is discourse. Discourse is existentially equi-primordial with attunement and understanding. He calls meaning that which can be articulated in interpretation.

What is articulated in discourse is called the totality of signification. Significations are always bound up with meaning. If discourse is primarily constituted by being-in-the-world, it also essentially has a specifically worldly mode of being. The attuned intelligibility of being-in-the-world is expressed as discourse. The way in which discourse gets expressed is language. Discourse is existential language, while being in thrownness to the world is essential to language. Hearing and keeping silent are possibilities belonging to discoursing speech which is constitutive for the existence of *Dasein*.[36]

Therefore, Heidegger understands the phenomenon of communication in an ontologically broad sense. In principle, communication is grasped existentially. Communication is not the conveying of experiences, opinions, and wishes, from the inside of one subject to the inside of

34. Ibid., 142.
35. Ibid.
36. Ibid., 151.

another. In communication, being-with-one-another is articulated and understandingly constituted. "*Mitda-sein* is essentially already manifest in attunement-with and understanding-with. Being-with is "explicitly" *shared* in discourse, that is, it already *is*, only unshared as something not grasped and appropriated."[37]

Hearing is constitutive for discourse. That is, existential being–open of *Dasein* as being-with for the other. *Dasein* has language. *Dasein* hears because it understands, and only the one who already understands is able to listen. Authentic silence is possible only in genuine discourse. Heidegger is concerned with reestablishing the linguistics more on an ontologically primordial foundation. Understanding is of a linguistic nature. However, in *Being and Time* Heidegger does not elaborate further on the linguisticality of understanding. This primary, hermeneutical function of language becomes a central factor in later Heidegger. Philosophically-hermeneutically it is left up to Gadamer to develop more fully the notion of the linguisticality of understanding which Heidegger had suggested.

HISTORY OF EFFECT AND LINGUISTIC DIMENSION

Gadamer's masterpiece, *Truth and Method*, marks a decisive event in the development of modern hermeneutical theory. Gadamer struggles with the philosophical problem of developing a new ontology in the event of understanding. Method is not the way to truth. Indeed, truth eludes the methodical person. What characterizes our age is the growing rationalization of society and the scientific techniques permeating everywhere in all corners of life. Against the methodical spirit of our time, Gadamer attempts to rehabilitate the universality of hermeneutics in light of the history of effect. Thus, "understanding belongs to the being of that which is understood."[38]

Hermeneutic experience resists the universal claim of scientific investigation, placing itself as a critique of philosophy of consciousness or a methodological self-consciousness. According to Gadamer, the truth speaks to us from tradition, coming as event effective in all understanding. To the extent that Gadamer universalizes the principle of effective

---

37. Ibid., 152.
38. Gadamer, *Truth and Method*, xxxi.

history in the structure of human understanding, "a hermeneutic consciousness exists only under specific historical conditions."[39]

Gadamer explicitly links his definition of hermeneutics to Heidegger. Hermeneutics can be used in Heidegger's sense of the mode of being of *Dasein* that constitutes its finitude and historicity, hence embracing the whole of its experience of the world. Heidegger describes the concept of understanding as the universal determinatedness of *Dasein* with respect to the future projectiveness of human understanding. Each encounter with language is an encounter with an unfinished event and is itself part of this event.[40] *Dasein* is radically temporal and understandable only in reference to its own time and future.

For Gadamer, the metaphor "play" refers to the way of being of the work of art itself. The concept of play is free from a concept of the subject's activity. Play, and not our participation in it, becomes the true subject of Gadamer's discussion. The play comes to stand, and it takes place in and through us. Play has its own essence, independent of the consciousness of the player. In play, movement happens by itself, without goal or purpose as well as without effort. Gadamer takes play as the starting point, rather than human subjectivity. Quoting Huizinga's concept of "holy play," Gadamer affirms the primacy of play over the consciousness of the player. The structure of play absorbs the player into itself setting him/her free from the burden of taking initiative.[41]

In fact, play has a self-presentation that masters the players. The classical theory of art, which grounds all art in the idea of mimesis, starts from play in the form of dancing. Thus, it is in fact a representation of the divine. An aesthetic consciousness is a part of the event of art taking place in presentation, because the being of art is not an object of an aesthetic consciousness. At this juncture, Gadamer compares the idea of mimesis to the play of art in the sense that the cognitive import of mimesis lies in recognition, which is the ontological import of representation. A definition of art as the beautiful representation of something (Kant) does not imply artistic technique. Our experience of a work of art depends on the extent to which we know and recognize something of it within ourselves. In other words, in recognition, what we know is grasped in its essence. In the phenomenon of recognition, "the 'known'

39. Ibid., xxxiii.
40. Ibid., 99.
41. Ibid., 105.

enters its true being and manifests itself as what it is only when it is recognized."[42]

Plato's theory of anamnesis refers to an issue of recognition in the ideality of language. Plato's consideration of all knowledge of essence as recognition became the ground for Aristotle's concept of mimesis and *poesis*. In this regard, Gadamer develops a concept of mimesis in the sense of the knowledge of the essence, a bringing forth. His basic thesis is that the aesthetic or epistemological attitude is "a part of the event of being that occurs in presentation, and belongs essentially to play as play."[43]

According to Gadamer, "the players are not the subjects of play; instead play merely reaches presentation (*Darstellung*) through the players."[44] The work of art, like a game, has its authentic being in transforming the one who experiences it. The work imposes itself on every interpreter in its own way, keeping him/her from simply imitating a model.[45] A dialectic of the recognition of the tradition and finitude of human historical existence moves in the ever-changing course of ages and circumstances. Here, a task of interpreting the work of art is to be undertaken in terms of time with which differences of ages and contexts are contemporaneous and immanent.[46]

With recourse to Heidegger, we understand a given text in terms of a pre-structure of understanding (pre-conception), not with an empty consciousness. We understand history only and always through a consciousness standing in the present. We see and understand the present only through pre-conceptions bequeathed from the past. For Gadamer, the past is a stream in which we move and participate in every act of understanding. At the point of hermeneutics, Gadamer credits Hegel's philosophy of history more than Schleiermacher's. Schleiermacher's concern in hermeneutics is to reconstruct the work as originally constituted. Thus, to the degree that historical knowledge restores the original occasion and circumstances, reconstructing tradition attempts to reproduce the writer's original process of production. However, Gadamer argues that Schleiermacher's endeavor of reconstruction turns out to

42. Ibid., 114.
43. Ibid., 116.
44. Ibid., 103.
45. Ibid., 119.
46. Ibid., 121.

The History of Effect and the Conflict of Interpretation

be a futile one with respect to the historicity of human existence. Thus, understanding in the sense of reconstruction would remain a practice of "handing on a dead meaning."[47]

Hegel disagrees with Schleiermacher, however, contending that restoration of original circumstances is still akin to fruit torn from the tree. Reconstruction, instead of providing us with a living relationship with the original, merely gives us an ideative representation. The historical self-penetration of the spirit carries out the hermeneutical task, which is the counter position to the self-forgetfulness of historical consciousness that Schleiermacher pointed to as inner feeling. The spirit's historical self-consciousness comprehends the truth of the text or art within itself in a higher way, culminating in a philosophy of absolute knowledge. A definite truth consists in thoughtful mediation with contemporary life rather than in the psychological restoration of the past.[48]

Gadamer integrates a Hegelian dimension of historical consciousness into Heidegger's project of a hermeneutic phenomenology. Under the banner of a hermeneutics of facticity, Heidegger advocates that phenomenology should be ontologically based on the facticity of *Dasein* in the world. It is certain that Heidegger's fundamental ontology project places the problem of history in the foreground. For Heidegger, "understanding is the *original form of realization of Dasein*, which is being-in-the-world."[49]

Following in the footsteps of Heidegger, Gadamer is concerned with expressing the existential structure of *Dasein* in understanding historical tradition. Already in his *Letter on Humanism*, Heidegger argues that language is the house of being, and that we live in and through language. Gadamer and Heidegger share the basic feature of language as reservoir and communicating medium of the tradition; tradition hides itself in language, and language is a medium like water. Thus, the linguisticality of being is at the same time its ontology—its coming into being—and the medium of its historicity.

---

47. Ibid., 167.

48. Ibid., 168–69. Gadamer evaluates Schleiermacher's contribution only in terms of psychological interpretation which, as a divinatory process, places oneself within the framework of the author. This interpretation is "an appreciation of the 'inner origin' of the composition of a work, re-creation of the creative act." Ibid., 187. However, Gadamer completely ignores a linguistic dimension of Schleiermacher's contribution to hermeneutics.

49. Ibid., 259.

This orientation of Gadamer contradicts Dilthey. Inheriting Schleiermacher's psychological concern, Dilthey expands it into an epistemology of the human sciences. For Dilthey, historical reality itself is a text to be understood. So, his hermeneutics is transposed to the study of historical life expression. Hermeneutics is the foundation for the study of history.[50] In Gadamer's view, Dilthey's hermeneutics contends that the experiencing and re-experiencing by the individual constitutes the point of departure for a theory of epistemology. Although there is a transition from a psychological to a hermeneutical grounding of the human sciences, Dilthey's project remains mere outline.

Against Gadamer's unfair evaluation of Dilthey, however, it is essential to heed Dilthey's insight into the history of effect and the sociohistorical construction of human inner life, and the linguistic dimension of daily communication in his hermeneutical project. For Dilthey, the expressions of life are really objectifications of life through which we can come to have objective knowledge. He held to the ideal of achieving objective knowledge in historical studies. Thus, the ideality of significance (Husserl) has to be understood as an expression of life rather than the result of logical investigation. Life, which is flowing temporality, is ordered and oriented toward the formation of enduring units of significance. Insofar as life constitutes the real ground of the human sciences, philosophy is grounded in life. Thus, Dilthey's hermeneutics of life retains the historical worldview.[51]

Nevertheless, at this point, Gadamer critiques Dilthey as entangled in the ideal of objectivity. Objective knowledge suggests a standpoint above and overlooking history. However, a finite, historical person always sees and understands from and within his/her standpoint in time and in space. In Gadamer's view, despite his critique of Hegel's intellectualism, Dilthey came closer to Hegel's spiritual concept of life in his later years.

As Dilthey contends, the reality of life as the point of departure has to be sought under a new concept of the objective mind, freed from the idealist construction based on universal reason. The objective mind "comprises language, customs, every form of life, as well as the family, civil society, state, and law. And what Hegel calls absolute spirit as distinct from objective—namely, art, religion, and philosophy—also come

---

50. Ibid., 199.
51. Ibid., 226.

under this concept."[52] Hegel's concept of art, religion, and philosophy has to be understood as objective forms of life self-expression. Rather than speculative conceptual knowledge, an expression of life is the basis for objectivity.

If Dilthey starts from life in a socio-historical connection or totality, should he not have paid attention to Hegel's dialectical, socio-critical dimension of self-consciousness engaged in the struggle for recognition between master and slave in the public sphere? Dilthey's hermeneutics of life is inclined to be idealistic, despite its emphasis on the concrete reality of life, when he sidesteps the economic reality of human labor and intersubjective recognition. When doing justice to the economic reality of labor and intersubjective recognition related to it, Dilthey's hermeneutics in an epistemological contour can arrive at the deciphering of the socio-historical experience of the reality of life.

Against Dilthey's project, Gadamer pays further special attention to Husserl's concept of the *Lebenswelt*. The *Lebenswelt* is the *lifeworld* that one can view and experience. Scientific limitations in mathematical formulas and chemical equations cannot comprehend the lifeworld. It is one thing to know that water is two hydrogen and one oxygen molecule, it is another to see, feel, and taste water. The lifeworld is pregiven and common to us all, "as persons within the horizon of our fellow [people]"; "in every actual connection with others."[53] Human beings live in the lifeworld whose own and constant ontic meaning is for the human beings. In the lifeworld, the subjective being is actually experienceable. The lifeworld is related to the objective-scientific world, which is grounded in the lifeworld's self-evidence. The lifeworld is pregiven to the scientific investigator or community. "Thus all of science is pulled, along with us, into the ▨merely "subjective-relative"—lifeworld."[54]

Required is the *epoché* with respect to all objective sciences, any critical position-taking, and all objective theoretical interests. Within this *epoché*, we are aware that there is a world-horizon of possible thing-experience. "To live is always to live-in-certainty-of-the-world,"[55] living in and conscious of the world. We are conscious of things, or objects within the world-horizon. We are constantly conscious of the world as a

52. Gadamer, *Truth and Method*, 228.
53. Welton, *Essential Husserl*, 363.
54. Ibid., 369.
55. Ibid., 375.

horizon. The life horizon as the universal field to which all our acts are directed functions like an intentional horizon-consciousness encompassing everything in advance. We are conscious of the objects within the horizon of lifeworld.

Husserl's concept of the lifeworld is the antithesis of objectivism. In a perfect *epoché*, where all positing of being by scientific knowledge is bracketed, the world still remains valid as that which is pregiven. This world that Husserl calls lifeworld represents the pregiven basis for all experience, existing, as the world horizon, in a constant movement of relative validity in a historical sense. Lifeworld as an ontology of the world implies a communal world including being with other people.[56] In Husserl's framework, the concreteness of life is based on the horizon of the lifeworld, nonetheless having no connection with Hegel's speculative idealism.

Gadamer's strategy is to retrieve the dialectical, structural correlation between life and self-consciousness as projected in Hegel's *Phenomenology of Mind*. According to Hegel, self-consciousness is dialectically derived from life, which is experienced only in the self-consciousness of one's own living. Gadamer notices Hegel's dialectics of desire in self-consciousness and appreciates that a metaphysical connection between life and self-consciousness in Hegel is superior to both Dilthey and Husserl. Nonetheless, Gadamer downplays a socio-critical dimension (negativity) of Hegel's concept of desire in relation to the Other in the context of dialectical interaction. Rather Gadamer navigates toward Heidegger's project of a hermeneutic phenomenology by integrating Husser's concept of lifeworld into Hegel's speculative idealism.[57]

Heidegger's hermeneutics of facticity offers Gadamer a basis to develop an ontological grounding of philosophical hermeneutics. Heidegger's project is to overcome the limitation of Dilthey's epistemological return to life as well as Husserl's transcendental reduction in light of the temporality and historicity of *Dasein*. In this project, Heidegger returns to the beginning of Western philosophy in order to revive the long-forgotten Greek metaphysics of being. For this task, Heidegger places the problem of history in the foreground. Being has to be determined from within the horizon of time: "Being itself is time."[58]

56. Ibid., 247.
57. Ibid., 254.
58. Ibid., 257.

The History of Effect and the Conflict of Interpretation

In distinguishing between being and beings, Nietzsche and Heidegger run parallel in their radical critique of Platonism. Understanding for Heidegger is the original form and characteristic of the realization of the being of human life—*Dasein* as being-in-the-world. Belonging to tradition (a condition of the original meaning of historical interest)—as opposed to homogeneity—points to the historical finitude of *Dasein* in reference to its projectedness toward future possibilities of itself.[59]

Thus, Heidegger explicates the fore-structure of understanding and derives the circular structure of understanding from the temporality of *Dasein*. The fore-structures (fore-having, fore-sight, and fore-conception) can be worked in terms of the things themselves.[60] Working out this fore-projection is an understanding of the temporality of *Dasein*, so that interpretation begins with fore-conceptions. Interpretation is the constant process of new projection, which constitutes the movement of understanding and interpretation.

In Heidegger's attempt to derive the fore-structures from the things themselves, Gadamer gains an insight into the new meaning of prejudices, which is relevant and important in the sphere of hermeneutics. For instance, in Enlightenment thinking, reason constitutes the ultimate source of authority. However, reason is shaped and influenced in an historical context, and dependent on the given circumstances. If prejudice inheres in the historical reality of human reason, then the Enlightenment's demand to subject all authority to reason is itself a prejudice.[61] Gadamer's basic thesis states that the abstract antithesis between tradition and historical research has to be discarded to the extent that "the effect of a living tradition and the effect of historical study must constitute a unity of effect."[62]

In this light, Gadamer contends that understanding is the participation of the event of a living tradition rather than a subjective act. The hermeneutical circle in this regard implies that the anticipatory movement of fore-understanding constantly determines textual understanding. Understanding is the interplay of the movement of tradition and the movement of the interpreter, which is in the play between the text's strangeness and familiarity to the interpreter. This hermeneutical

---

59. Ibid., 262.
60. Heidegger, *Being and Time*, 153.
61. Gadamer, *Truth and Method*, 276.
62. Ibid., 282.

"in-between" advocates for a co-determination in the understanding of the text by the interpreter's understanding of the text. If the text goes beyond its author, if understanding is always a productive activity, we understand the text in a different way.[63] The hermeneutical circle is called the "fore-conception of completeness" which guides all human understanding[64] in a different way through the interplay between belongingness and distance.

Here, a socio-critical dimension inherent in hermeneutical consciousness sharpens the methodological self-consciousness of human science. The critical distance, which performs the filtering process, is undergoing constant movement and extension, implying a critique of the text's strangeness to us. In all understanding, the efficacy of history is at work. Gadamer's concept of effective history, which is similar to Hegel's concept of absolute knowledge in the *Phenomenology of Mind*, historically affects the human consciousness.

This hermeneutical situation, for which the concept of horizon is essential, is framed within an ongoing movement from the narrowness of horizon via the possible expansion of the horizon toward an opening up of new horizons. This hermeneutical situation acquires the right horizon of inquiry for the questions critically raised by the encounter between one's own particular horizon and that of tradition. The horizon of the present is in the process of being formed and influenced in light of the history of effect, while at the same time, testing all our prejudices. Thus, "understanding is always the fusion of these horizons supposedly existing by themselves."[65]

If the principle of effective history plays a universal role in the structure of understanding, Gadamer's thesis becomes obvious to the extent that effective history affects all understandings of tradition and text. His ambiguous concept of the historically effected consciousness means that consciousness is effected in the course of history and is determined by history. This concept shapes Gadamer's understanding and interpretation in a hermeneutical and different sense from the text in light of the fusion of horizon.

Fundamental to Gadamer's conception of language is the emphasis on the character of living language and our participation in it. According

63. Ibid., 297.
64. Ibid., 293–94.
65. Ibid., 306.

to the sign theory of language, words are viewed as the tools of human beings for communicating their thought. Language is ultimately an instrument of subjectivity fully separated from what the word designates. However, for Gadamer, language is neither sign nor symbolic form created by human beings. Words do not belong to human beings, but to the situation. The ideality of the meaning lies in the word itself. Word is always already meaningful. When one says, "the tree is green," this sentence refers to the subject matter rather than to human subjectivity. The tree is being disclosed in a certain light. Experience, thinking, and understanding are thoroughly linguistic.

THE HORIZON OF LIFEWORLD AND INTERPRETATION

Even prior to Heidegger and Gadamer, Husserl was critical of objectivism on the basis of the intentionality of consciousness. All the beings given in one's world stand within the intentional horizon of consciousness, that is within the lifeworld. Consciousness is not an object but an essential coordination—which is a starting point for overcoming objectivism. This horizon or lifeworld is both personal and shared with other beings. The concept and phenomenon of the horizon is crucial for Husserl's phenomenological research. Everything that is given as existent is given in terms of a world and hence brings the world horizon with it.

Even in a perfect *epoché* (bracketing) the world still remains valid as something pregiven. Hence, epistemological self-questioning is not radical enough. As Gadamer rightly comments, "the all-embracing world horizon is constituted by a fundamentally *anonymous* intentionality."[66] Husserl calls this phenomenological concept of the world lifeworld

This phenomenological concept—lifeworld, as the antithesis of all objectivism, represents the pregiven basis of all experience. The lifeworld as an essentially historical concept refers to an ontology of the world. Lifeworld means the whole in which we live as historical creatures. In this light, Husserl illuminates the universal horizon of consciousness as the intersubjectivity of this world. Transcendental reflection must regard itself as included in the lifeworld, although it brackets the pre-giveness of anything else.

However, for Heidegger, lifeworld does not describe transcendental subjectivity, but points to an objectivity that takes the facticity of hu-

---

66. Ibid., 246.

man existence as its ultimate point of reference. In and through the lifeworld one makes judgments and reaches decisions. Heidegger calls his phenomenological method a hermeneutic of facticity, that underlines being-in-the-lifeworld. The human being belongs to the world, not vice versa. This belongingness occurs through the process of understanding. Human existence is a thrown project oriented to the past by being thrown into time and the world, and finally oriented to the future. Understanding always functions in three modes of temporality: past, present, and future. That is why understanding is called the historicity of understanding.

Heidegger attempts to explicate a hermeneutical circle of fore-structures in light of fore-having, fore-sight, and fore-conception. Working out this fore-projection, the constant process of new projection constitutes the movement of understanding and interpretation. Because of fore-grounding and the appropriation of one's own fore-meaning and prejudices, according to Gadamer the text can be present in all its otherness and thus can assert its own truth against one's own fore-meaning.[67]

For Gadamer, tradition is the ground of the validity of human reason. Understanding shares one fundamental condition with the life of tradition, letting itself be addressed by tradition. In Gadamer's hermeneutics, the effect of a living tradition and of historical study constitutes a unity of effect. A hermeneutical consciousness infuses research with a spirit of self-reflection.[68]

By criticizing the idea of an epistemological procedure or a method, Gadamer deepens Heidegger's idea of the hermeneutical circle and underscores hermeneutic work based on a polarity of familiarity (belongingness to tradition) and strangeness (distanciation from it). Temporal distance performs the filtering process, undergoing constant movement and extension. "Temporal distance can solve the question of critique in hermeneutics."[69]

Historically effected consciousness is not reduced into self-reflection or self-consciousness. Gadamer utilizes Hegel's dialectical model of recognition between master and slave, as expounded in his *Phenomenology of Mind*, for his hermeneutical consciousness, which is historically effected. At issue in Hegel's dialectical model of progress is the total fusion

67. Ibid., 269.
68. Ibid., 285.
69. Ibid., 298.

The History of Effect and the Conflict of Interpretation

of history with the present. However, Hegel's dialectical model of experience, which is attained and culminated in absolute knowledge, does not do justice to the hermeneutical consciousness of finitude.[70] As we already saw, in his reception of Hegel, however, Gadamer discards a dialectical moment of negativity in Hegel's socio-critical model of recognition, which implies the real transformation of the political economic reality.

In Gadamer's view, it is ridiculous to judge the achievements of a past age by the standards of today. We have no right to judge a literary work by today's standards. Hermeneutically speaking, there can be no "presupposionless" interpretation. We get our presuppositions from the tradition in which we stand. The tradition is the horizon within which we do our thinking. Besides, understanding is a dialectical process of interaction between the self-understanding (horizon) of the person and the horizon of the tradition.

Thus, tradition and authority no longer need to be seen as the enemies of reason and rational freedom as expressed in the Enlightenment. Reason always stands within tradition. Understanding the text means always applying it to the present rather than relating to the author or the text. For Gadamer, the historically effected consciousness is the term by which to describe openness to the Thou as tradition speaking.

For Gadamer, true experience is experience of one's own historicity, having to do with what one encounters as heritage. My belonging to the heritage comes to be experienced in the hermeneutical encounter. It is language, which is experienced. Thus, hermeneutical experience is linguistic experience. In the analysis of play, Gadamer demonstrates that play is more than the consciousness of the player. Likewise, language is more than the consciousness of the speaker.

Tradition expresses itself as language like a Thou. At this juncture, Gadamer transforms Hegel's dialectical model of mutual recognition based on desire and fulfillment in the public sphere into a linguistic model of the recognition of tradition or language as a Thou. Furthermore, a type of hermeneutical experience, which is higher than knowledge and recognition is "the openness to tradition characteristic of historically effected consciousness."[71]

According to Gadamer, the history of effect is at work in all our understanding. This refers to the power of history over the finite human

70. Ibid., 355.
71. Ibid., 361.

consciousness. We may compare Gadamer's concept of the history of effect to Husserl's concept of lifeworld or Hegel's concept of absolute knowledge. Gadamer's hermeneutics strives to highlight that consciousness of being affected by history is primarily consciousness of the hermeneutical situation grounded in horizon of past and present.[72]

Therefore, Gadamer speaks of the narrowness of horizon, of the possible expansion of horizon, and of the opening up of a new horizon.[73] The hermeneutical task acquires the right horizon of inquiry through the encounter with tradition. Gadamer refers to Greek tragedy and to the Aeschylean formula, *pathei mathos*: "learning through suffering."[74] Through suffering, one learns the boundaries of human existence itself. This is a religious insight, which gives birth to Greek tragedy.

Genuine experience is experience of one's own finitude or historicity. The hermeneutical experience of one's own historicity, in which we are neither master of time nor future, is of considerable importance to Gadamer's inquiry into the historically effected consciousness. This concept contradicts a theological concept of universal history in Pannenberg's fashion.

The task of hermeneutics is to bring the text out of a fixed and written form, and back into the living present of dialogue. Authentic interpretation relates itself to the question placed by the text. To understand the text means to understand this question. The horizon of meaning within which a text or historical act stands is approached from within one's own horizon. The horizon of the past is always in motion. The horizon of the present is in the process of being formed. One broadens one's horizon in order to fuse it with that of the text. The dialectic of question and answer results in a fusion of horizons, which takes place in a hermeneutical conversation. In the fusion of horizon, some shared thing is expressed: it is neither the reader's nor the author's.

What makes this possible is language. Language is the universal medium of hermeneutical experience, in which understanding takes place. The linguisticality of understanding that occurs in interpretation concretizes the historically effected consciousness.[75] Language precedes experience and is "a positive condition of, and guide to, experience

72. Ibid., 301.
73. Ibid., 302.
74. Ibid., 356.
75. Ibid., 388–89.

itself."[76] The fusion of horizons that takes place in understanding and that mediates between the text and its interpreter is what language actually achieves.

LANGUAGE AND THE UNIVERSAL CLAIM TO HERMENEUTICS

For Gadamer, understanding itself has an essential and fundamental connection with language. To interpret means to bring one's own preconceptions into play, making the text's subject matter speak for us. The language that has a universal function lives in speech. Gadamer contends that language and thinking about things are bound to one another. For this task Gadamer takes into account the Christian discourse of the Trinity and the incarnation.

The inner unity of thinking and speaking corresponds to the Trinitarian mystery of the incarnation. The Word was still Word even before it became flesh. The miracle of language lies in the fact that the Word is with God from all eternity. At this point, Gadamer supports the traditional doctrine of the eternal Word and God the Father as *homoousious* (of the same being) with God—over and against the concept of subordination.[77] The human relationship between thought and speech corresponds to the divine relationship within the Trinity. In a Christian discourse of incarnation, an event which achieves its full truth in the medium of language, there is a special ground of hermeneutical experience.[78]

In the case of language, its speaking power is the central and decisive fact. Language is the language of reason. Language comes to us historically. Language cannot be divorced from thought.[79] The language is living in speech. Language encompasses all understanding and all interpretation of texts, and so it is fused with the process of thought and interpretation. Language is like our unconsciousness.[80] Human being-in-the-world is primordially linguistic, having a world that differs from

---

76. Ibid., 350.
77. Ibid., 420.
78. Ibid., 428.
79. Ibid., 403.
80. Ibid., 405.

the environment. Language fashions the world orientation in which we live.[81]

Language discloses our lifeworld, not our environmental scientific world or universe. To have a world is to have language. Language is made to fit the world. World is the shared understanding between persons and the medium of this understanding. In language the world presents itself. Within the world horizon of language, language and world are bound and interconnected in a fundamental way. There is no point of view outside the experience of the world in language, because humans exist in the realm of shared understanding created by language as world.

To the extent that humans exist in language, the linguistic experience of the world has a priority over human consciousness. Every object of knowledge is encompassed within the world horizon of language. We may call this dimension the linguisticality of the human experience of the world. The world is linguistically created. The hermeneutical experience is an encounter between heritage in the form of a transmitted text and the horizon of the interpreter. "Every language has a direct relationship to the infinity of being."[82] Language is the medium in which and on which the tradition conceals itself and is transmitted to us.

A linguistic dimension permeates the life of the historical person's mode characterized by being-in-the-world. To the degree that we belong to language and history, we participate in them. This phenomenon of belonging is of great significance to the hermeneutical experience. Because of our belongingness to language and because of the belongingness of the text to language, a common horizon becomes possible. The historically effected consciousness is realized in language to the extent that language characterizes human experience of the world.[83]

A hermeneutical situation that characterizes the finitude of our historical experience implies that, in language, human experience is originally constituted and constantly changed. Thus, language is the record of finitude insofar as it expresses its experience of the world. The emergence of a common horizon is what Gadamer calls the fusion of horizons as it occurs for the historically operative consciousness. Gadamer's idea of belonging is based on the linguistically constituted experience of the world.

81. Ibid., 450.
82. Ibid., 453.
83. Ibid., 456.

The belongingness to (or participation in) language as the medium of our experience of the world and God is the real ground of hermeneutical experience. Through language, one gains access to the *logos*, to the word to which we belong. Language is always in process as an event of disclosure. Hearing is the basis for the hermeneutical phenomenon (Aristotle). The idea of belonging is dialectically connected with hearing because of the universality of *logos*. In hearing, language opens up a completely new dimension. In interpretation, the hearer relates the truth of the text to his/her own linguistic orientation to the world.[84]

In speaking, the speaker brings a relation to being into language. The interpretation of a text is not a passive openness, but a dialectical interaction with the text. It is a new creation and event in understanding. The hermeneutical experience depends on the character of language as event. Moreover, what constitutes the hermeneutical event proper "consists in the coming into language of what has been said in the tradition."[85] Here, event as appropriation of meaning from the past and interpretation of it for our contemporary life means the act of the thing itself rather than human action upon the thing. Following Hegel, Gadamer argues that the genuine method is an action of the thing itself.[86]

Human understanding is historical, linguistic, and dialectical. The human relation to the world is linguistic and thus understandable. Therefore, Gadamer sees a universal characteristic of being itself as the speculative conception of being which lies at the base of hermeneutics. This speculativity is the true ground of Gadamer's claims for its universality. The word "speculative" implies the mirror relation. When looking at the castle's reflection in the lake, the lake replicates the castle's image. Although it is like an appearance, it allows the thing to appear in terms of a mirror image. Hegel made a distinction between the speculative and the dialectical in which the dialectical is the expression of the speculative. However, Hegel superseded this distinction from the standpoint of absolute knowledge. Distancing himself from Hegel, Gadamer pursues a speculative dimension of language with respect to "the realization of meaning, the event of speech, of mediation, of coming to an understanding."[87] The speculative medium of language emerges as the

---

84. Ibid., 462–63.
85. Ibid., 463.
86. Ibid., 464.
87. Ibid., 469.

coming of the totality of meaning into language which refers to a universal ontological structure: "Being that can be understood is language."[88]

Language contains a distinction between its being and its presentation of itself, which is not a real distinction. Additionally, what comes into language is not something that is pre-given, prior to language. The speculative universality of language as a medium undermines an analogical image of a mirror, a notion of reflection in a mirror for the sake of universal aspect of hermeneutics. Understanding is always an historical, dialectical, linguistic event. Hermeneutics as ontology is the phenomenology of understanding. Here, Gadamer sidesteps an analogical power of language as well as linguistically distorted and manipulated form of language for the sake of speculative universalism of the language.

METHODOLOGICAL DIMENSION IN THE CONFLICT OF INTERPRETATION

In regard to language and ideology, a sensational debate took place between Gadamer's hermeneutics and Habermas's social critical theory. In contrast to the universal claim of hermeneutics, the social critical theory adopts a suspicious approach seeing tradition as a systematically distorted expression of communication under unacknowledged conditions of violence. This theory of ideology critique contradicts Gadamer's claim to the universality of hermeneutics. In this regard, Habermas integrates Marx's critique of ideology to his critical theory.

Marx's interest in emancipation becomes obvious; what is at issue for him is not interpretation, but praxis in the transformation of social reality. This direction has been unilaterally elevated as the antithesis of the tradition of interpretation. Before engaging with social transformation, however, Marx became a theoretician in the analysis and interpretation of the social mode of production and the institutional relation in an industrial capitalist society. His hermeneutics of suspicion challenged an interpretive tradition that ignored the socio-economic factor in previously shaping and influencing a human understanding and life of contact and ideological orientation. This notion secures the social locations as the social history of effect in a synchronic sense by challenging the history of effect in a diachronic sense.

---

88. Ibid., 474.

Thus, Marx's notion of interpretation, critique, and praxis poses a serious question to an interpretive theory that ignores social–economic factors as fore-structures in shaping human understanding. Marx takes into account productive labor in the socio-economic realm and human practical activity of interaction in the communicative, cultural, and institutional realms. He puts together an analysis of the forces of production and an analysis of the relation of production in a dialectical, reciprocal way. The latter entails forms of social interaction (domination) and social conflict (class struggle).

Regarding the conflict of interpretation between Habermas and Gadamer, Ricoeur makes a long detour to articulate his hermeneutics of self-reflection and suspicion by recourse to the masters of suspicion (Freud, Nietzsche, and Karl Marx). At this juncture, Dilthey is of special significance for Ricoeur to engage in the discussion of truth and method, or the dialectical movement between explanation and understanding. The question of how to understand a text is preceded by another question: how is an historical interconnection to be conceived? Before the text, history comes as the most fundamental expression of life. Dilthey is the interpreter of the pact between hermeneutics and history. Dilthey contends that every human science presupposes a primordial capacity to transpose oneself into the mental life of others. In the last analysis, the key to historical knowledge is to be found in the fundamental phenomena of interconnection, by which the life of others can be discerned and identified in its manifestation. Knowledge of others is possible because life produces and externalizes itself for deciphering.

After 1900, Dilthey relied upon Husserl to give consistency to the notion of interconnection between intentional consciousness and its correlates. During the same period, Husserl established that mental life is characterized by intentionality. His work was a break with the purely positivist orientation and understanding of the sciences. In *Logische Untersuchungen* (*Logical Investigations*; first edition, 1900–1901), Husserl distinguishes between the act of consciousness and the phenomena at which it is directed. Knowledge of essence would only be possible by bracketing all assumptions about the existence of an external world. This procedure is called *epoché*.[89]

---

89. This new concept prompted the publication of the *Ideen* (Ideas) in 1913 in which they were at first incorporated, and a plan for a second edition of the *Logische Untersuchungen*.

Epoché, the phenomenon of parenthesizing or excluding, is "a certain refraining from judgment which is compatible with the unshaken conviction of truth . . . or of evident truth."[90] All theories and sciences relating to this world, no matter how positvistically grounded, are under phenomenological *epoché*. Later, in *The Crisis of the European Sciences*, Husserl realized a necessity of phenomenological bracket to be placed onto scientific inquiry and its natural attitude, recognizing their increasingly, one-sidedly empirical and naturalistic orientation. In view of Galileo's mathematization of nature, nature is idealized and transformed into a kind of technique. "Through a calculating technique according to technical rules," "we measure the lifeworld for a well-fitting garb of ideas, that of the so-called objectively scientific truth." Now the scientists represent the lifeworld by "dress[ing] it up as 'objectively actual and true' nature."[91]

What remains in the *epoché* is the World as *Eidos* (Forms), although the world as matter of fact is excluded. Pure Ego, the consciousness in its absolute essence is untouched by the phenomenological exclusion. This remains phenomenological residuum as a region of being, which is a field of phenomenology. The essence abstracted via eidetic reduction is the intelligible structure of the phenomena found in consciousness.

For example, a chair might include the color, the materials used, and the shapes present in the structure. We apply basic, Platonic forms to all phenomena. Husserl proposed that the world of objects and ways in which we direct ourselves toward and perceive those objects is normally conceived of in what he called the "natural standpoint." Husserl proposed a radical new phenomenological way of looking at objects by examining how we, in our many ways of being intentionally directed toward them, actually "constitute" them; in the phenomenological standpoint, the object ceases to be something simply "external." In order to better understand the world of appearances and objects, phenomenology attempts to identify their general essential character with existing as the consciousness-of or appearance-of the specific things, thoughts, decisions, etc. Designating the basic character of being as consciousness, or as consciousness of something, is intentionality.[92] All subjective activities of consciousness need an ideal correlate, and objective logic (constituted

---

90. Welton, *Essential Husserl*, 64.
91. Ibid., 352, 355.
92. Ibid., 323.

noematically). The objective logic also needs a noetic correlate (the subjective activities of consciousness). For Husserl, *noema* are necessarily fused with noesis, which are the subjective activities of consciousness.

According to Husserl, through reduction, the phenomenological Ego can become an observer of itself, aware of itself, and self-conscious. Since we gain knowledge via this ego, we learn about the ego as we learn about the environment around us. We assume that other humans are self-aware, so that Husserl sought a "community of selves" in which all were aware of each other. "I experience the world not as my own private world, but as an intersubjective world."[93] This idea of intentionality and of the identical character of the intentional object would thus enable Dilthey to reinforce his concept of mental, psychological structure with the Husserlian notion of meaning. For Dilthey, life grasps life by the mediation of units of meaning. Our mental life finds its complete expression only through language. Thus, "explication finds completion and fullness only in the interpretation of the written testimonies of human life."[94]

In this statement, Ricoeur has restated Dilthey's idea of hermeneutic primacy of the written word and developed a model of textual interpretation as a foundation for a general hermeneutics of the human and social sciences.

In addition to Dilthey, Ricoeur takes issue with Heidegger's ontology. Heidegger attempts to dig beneath the epistemological enterprise itself, in order to uncover its proper ontological conditions. Heidegger's interest is to explicate the forgotten question of being. Heidegger places the emphasis on *Dasein*, the being-there. This *Dasein* is not a subject for which there is an object, but rather a being within being. This ontological explication will add nothing to the methodology of the human sciences; rather, it will dig beneath this methodology in order to lay bare its foundation. The question of understanding is wholly severed from the

---

93. Husserl conceptualizes the mediate intentionality of experiencing someone else as appresentation (analogical apperception), a kind of making co-present with the Other. An Other signifies an alter ego. The body of the Other in relation with my body can serve as the motivational basis for the analogizing apprehension of the Other's body. Ego and alter ego are given in an original pairing that Husserl designates as association appearing with mutual distinctness. My primordial ego constitutes the alter ego by an appresentative apperception. Thus community is produced by virtue of experiencing someone else. The community is the foundation for all other intersubjectively common things. In this light, Husserl overcomes the illusion of a solipsism. Welton, *Essential Husserl*, 148, 152, 159

94. Mueller-Vollmer, *Hermeneutics Reader*, 27.

problem of communication with others. There is indeed in Heidegger's *Being and Time* a chapter called *Mitda-sein*—"being-with."

However, Ricoeur argues that the question of understanding does not appear in this chapter as compared to Dilthey's position. The foundations of the ontological problem are sought in the relation of being with the personal lifeworld and not in the relation with another. Understanding, in its primordial sense, is implicated in the relation with "my" life-situation, in the fundamental understanding of "my" position within being. Therefore, the ontology of understanding may begin by a reflection on "being-in," (being in the world) rather than "being-with." The question of the world takes the place of the question of the other.

It is certain that Heidegger characterizes an encounter with others in orientation toward one's own *Dasein*.[95] The world of *Dasein* is with-world. *Dasein* in the world is essentially being with others. As being-with, *Dasein* is essentially for the sake of others. The other is initially disclosed in the taking care of concern.[96] Here Heidegger defines the other being as the same ontological level as *Dasein* in that the other is not understood as the objectively present thing. When one's own *Dasein* encounters the *Mit-dasein* of others in the public sphere, *Dasein* is subversive to the others. The "they," the great mass, unfolds its true dictatorship in which being-with-one-another creates averageness. "Everything gained by a struggle becomes something to be manipulated."[97]

What constitutes publicness are the ways of being of the "they," namely: distantiality, averageness, and leveling down. Heidegger's relationship between "being in" and "being with" needs to be read as his protest of the manipulation of publicness which is created by the great mass for the sake of averagness. The authentic self, *Dasein*, is different from the self of everyday. *Dasein* stands in communication based on language of discourse, hearing, and keeping silent against falling prey to the world. However, the inauthenticity of *Dasein* "means being absorbed in being-with-one-another as it is guided by idle talk, curiosity, and ambiguity."[98]

Against this trend, Ricoeur contends that in the human sciences, the subject and object retain mutual implications. The subject itself enters

---

95. Heidegger, *Being and Time*, 111.
96. Ibid., 116.
97. Ibid., 119.
98. Ibid., 164.

into the knowledge of the object in the sense of the hermeneutical circle. The hermeneutical circle is a background of this structure of anticipation. In *Being and Time*, Heidegger is less a philosopher of language than of ontology. Language remains a secondary articulation, the articulation of explication in assertions.[99] The language as pointing out, showing, and manifesting has its roots in the existential constitution of *Dasein*'s disclosedness. Discourse is the articulation of understanding. Discourse is the meaningful articulation of the understandable structure of being-in-the-world. At this point, saying (*reden*) appears superior to speaking (*sprechen*). Saying designates the existential constitution, whereas speaking indicates the mundane aspect, which lapses into the empirical. The first determination of saying is not speaking, but rather hearing/keeping silent. In Ricoeur's view, we, along with Heidegger, are always engaged in going back to the foundations, but we are left incapable of beginning the movement of return. We go astray from the epistemological question.[100]

With a critical view toward Heidegger, Ricoeur refers to Gadamer's *Truth and Method*. Here Gadamer takes up the debate about the human sciences in light of Heideggerian ontology. The methodology of social sciences implies a distancing, which, in turn, expresses the destruction of the primordial relation of belonging. Critical distanciation, alienating oneself from the lifeworld of language or the authority of tradition is the presupposition of the social sciences. Gadamer pursues the debate between critical distanciation and the experience of belonging in the sphere of aesthetics, history, and language. A theory of historical consciousness marks the summit of Gadamer's reflection on the foundation of the human sciences. This reflection is placed under the consciousness of history of effect. However, this category no longer pertains to methodology or to historical inquiry, but rather to the reflective consciousness of this methodology.

Given the direction of Heidegger and Gadamer, it is hard to introduce a critical instance into a consciousness of belonging. Nevertheless, the consciousness of effective history contains within itself an element of critical distance. It is efficacy at a distance. There is a tension between proximity and distance, which is essential to historical consciousness. Another index of the dialectic of participation and distanciation is provided by the concept of the fusion of horizons.

99. Heidegger, *Being and Time*, para. 33.
100. Thomson, *Hermeneutics & the Human Sciences*, 54–59.

This is the fruitful idea that communication at a distance between two differently situated consciousnesses occurs by means of the fusion of their horizons, that is, the intersection of their views on the distant and the open. This concept implies a tension between that which is one's own and that which is alien. Gadamer's concept of the universal linguisticality of human experience and mediation of language is directed against the reduction of the world of signs to instruments that we could manipulate as we want.

HERMENEUTICAL CONSCIOUSNESS AND INTEREST IN EMANCIPATION

Ricoeur becomes suspicious that Gadamer's concept of *Sprachlichkeit* does not become *Schriftlichkeit*. In other words, mediation by language does not become mediation by the text. Ricoeur calls into question whether Gadamer's book is really about *Truth or Method* rather than *Truth and Method*.[101]

In *Logik der Sozialwissenschaft*, Habermas attacks Gadamer's concept of historical consciousness and the provocative rehabilitation of the three connected concepts: prejudice, authority, and tradition. Habermas claims that it is upon these concepts that Gadamer raises his claim to universality. This reflects a struggle between Enlightenment and the spirit of Romanticism. The Enlightenment struggles against prejudices while Romanticism longs in nostalgia for the past. Prejudice must be put aside in order to think and reach the age of adulthood. Prejudice is a predominantly negative category for a critical philosophy of the Enlightenment. Romantic philosophy faced the challenge of the Enlightenment, which discredits prejudice.[102] The conflict between the social critique of ideology and the hermeneutics of Gadamer marks progress as hermeneutics is connected with human life in the public sphere regarding interpretation and critique.

Against Habermas Gadamer contends that Heidegger reconstituted the problematic of prejudice. The prejudice of the individual constitutes the historical reality of one's being. The rehabilitation of prejudice, authority, and tradition is directed against the reign of subjectivity and interiority over history, tradition, and the world. History precedes one's

---

101. Ibid, 60.
102. Gadamer, *Truth and Method,* 241–45.

life and reflection. One belongs to history before one belongs to oneself. The real sense of the fore-structure (or structure of anticipation) of understanding is the condition for any rehabilitation of prejudice. Thus, prejudice is a component of understanding, linked to the finite historical character of the human being. The concept of authority brings us to the heart of the debate with the critique of ideology.

Given this fact, authority is ultimately based on acceptance and recognition rather than on the subjection and abdication of reason. Authority in this sense has nothing to do with blind obedience to a command of tradition. The key concept of recognition retains a critical moment, offering the possibility of articulating the phenomenology of authority into the critique of ideology. It is certain that Heidegger offers an insight into the critique of publicly distorted inauthenticity of language in reference to the entanglement of *Dasein* with the world of idle talk, curiosity, and ambiguity.[103] This, however, is not Gadamer's concern, because he is more interested in linking authority to tradition, thus reconciling authority and reason. In contrast to Gadamer, Habermas's critique of language and prejudice belongs to Habermas's major concern of the critical sociology of communication rationality.

Gadamer borrows the concept of prejudice from philosophical Romanticism, reinterpreting it by means of the Heideggerian notion of pre-understanding. In contrast, Habermas develops a concept of interest, which stems from the Marxist tradition as reinterpreted by Lukacs and by representatives of the Frankfurt School such as Horkheimer and Adorno. Habermas makes recourse to the critical social sciences, directly aimed against institutional reification. It is important for him to critically introduce an interest in emancipation to the hermeneutical field. It is Habermas's assertion that the task of critical philosophy is to unmask the interests, which underlie the enterprise of knowledge, language, or interpretation.

According to Habermas, there is, first, the technical or instrumental interest, which governs the empirical-analytic sciences. The imminent possibility of ideology arises from the correlation between empirical knowledge and the technical interest. Habermas defines this interest more exactly as the cognitive interest in technical control over objectified processes.[104] There is a second sphere of interest, which is

---

103. Heidegger, *Being and Time*, 164.
104. Habermas, *Knowledge and Human Interests*, 309.

practical in the Kantian sense. The practical sphere is the sphere of intersubjective communication. Habermas correlates this sphere with the domain of the historical-hermeneutic science. This sphere is accomplished through the interpretation of messages exchanged in ordinary language, by means of the interpretation of texts transmitted by tradition. Finally, Habermas calls the third sphere of interest the interest in emancipation. He connects this interest with a third type of science, that is, the critical social science.

For Gadamer, however, the critical instance can be developed only as a moment that is subordinated to the consciousness of dependence upon the background of pre-understanding, which always precedes and envelops a critical element. The critical instance comes from the history of effect in its critical distance from the alien element of tradition.

However, the situation is quite different in Habermas's project of critical social science. The critical approach is governed by the interest in emancipation as such, which Habermas also calls self-reflection. Self-reflection is the interest in autonomy and independence. This critical instance is thus placed above the hermeneutical consciousness, putting critical self-reflection above tradition-related interpretation or institutional constraint. The concept of ideology plays the same role in a critical social science as the concept of prejudice plays in a hermeneutical tradition. In Habermas's terms, the phenomenon of domination takes place in the communicative sphere. Language is distorted in the personal-cultural lifeworld through power, economy, and mass media. The distortion of language comes from its relation to labor, political power, and social cultural system. This misrecognition is peculiar to the phenomenon of ideology that is called a systematically distorted communication.

Here, psychoanalysis provides a good model. Habermas adopts Alfred Lorenzer's interpretation of psychoanalysis as the analysis of language. Psychoanalysis remains in the sphere of understanding culminating in the awareness of the subject. Hence, Habermas calls it a depth hermeneutics. Regarding the three agencies (ego-id-superego), Habermas contends that they are connected to the sphere of communication by the dialogical process of analysis through which the patient is led to reflect upon him/herself. Thus, meta-psychology can be founded as meta-hermeneutics. Habermas constitutes the ideological phenomenon as a limit-experience of hermeneutics.

The interest in emancipation animates the critical social science, providing a frame of reference for all the meanings constituted in psychoanalysis and the critique of ideology. Self-reflection is the correlative concept of the interest in emancipation. In contrast to Habermas, Gadamer advocates for the dialogue "which we are" (*das Gespräch, das Wir sind*). Therefore, *Sprachlichkeit* is an ontological constitution. Even psychology as a meta-hermeneutics does not exist outside this sphere of *Sprachlichkeit*.

THE WORLD OF THE TEXT AND EMANCIPATION

Regarding a conflict of interpretation between self-reflection and hermeneutical tradition, Ricoeur's mediation between the critique of ideology and hermeneutics is heuristic. It is of special significance for Ricoeur to retrieve a dialectic between the experience of belonging and alienating distance. Dilthey located the specificity of interpretation in the phenomenon of fixation by writing and, more generally, of inscription. Writing is not simply a matter of the material fixation of discourse. There is a threefold autonomy: the intention of the author (implying a possibility that the matter of the text may escape from the author's intentional horizon), the cultural situation including all sociological conditions of the production of the text (implying the possibility that the sociological condition of production de-contextualizes the text itself); and the original addressee (transcending the original addressee).

What the text signifies no longer coincides with what the author meant. The text itself creates an audience, which potentially includes anyone who can read. The emancipation of the text constitutes the most fundamental condition for the recognition of a critical instance at the heart of interpretation, since the alienating distance now belongs to the mediation itself (self-reflection). This is one aspect of consciousness exposed to the efficacy of history, and thus *Schriftlichkeit* can be added to Gadamer's concept of *Sprachlichkeit*.

Beyond Dilthey's dichotomy between explanation and understanding, however, Ricoeur asserts that discourse takes hold in structure, calling for a description and an explanation that mediates understanding. This aspect is similar to Habermas's concept of reconstruction, which is the path of understanding. For Ricoeur, truth and method do not constitute a disjunction but rather a dialectical process. Gadamer's concept of the matter of the text can be called the referential moment by distinction between sense and reference. The sense of the text is its internal organization, whereas the reference is the mode of being unfolded in front of the text. What is sought is no longer an intention hidden behind the text, but a world unfolded in front of it.

According to Aristotle in his *Poetics*, the creation of a mythos is the path of mimesis, of creative imitation. The critical theme is present in the Heideggerian analysis of understanding. Heidegger conjoins understanding and the notion of the projection of one's own possibilities. The mode of being of the world opened up by the text is the mode of the possible. Therein resides the subversive force of the imaginary. This turns itself towards a critique of ideology. If the primary concern of hermeneutics is to unfold a world in front of it, the authentic self-understanding can be instructed by the matter of the text. The matter of the text gives the reader his/her dimension of subjectivity. For instance, if the tradition of Exodus in the biblical context is unfolded in front of the reader, it leads the reader to criticize what currently obscures and distorts the tradition of liberation as witnessed in the Scripture.

Thus, the critique of ideology can be assumed by a concept of self-understanding, which implies a critique of the illusions of the subject. The critique of false consciousness can thus become an integral part of hermeneutics. In this light, Ricoeur contends that hermeneutics and the critique of ideology are interpenetrating.

Habermas establishes a pact between interpretation and the social critical interest in emancipation. The historical-hermeneutic science inclines toward the recognition of the authority of traditions rather than endorsing a revolutionary action against oppression. However, revolutionary praxis creates a gulf between the interest in emancipation and the ethical interest. At the heart of communicative action, the institutionalization of human relations undergoes reification. Therefore, the interest in emancipation would be quite empty and abstract, were it not situated on the same plane as the historical-hermeneutic science. The task of the hermeneutics of tradition instructs that one can project one's emancipation only on the basis of the creative reinterpretation of one's cultural heritage. Thus, mimetic creativity in the interpretation of the text offers a basis for human praxis as embedded within an interest in emancipation.

Anyone who is unable to reinterpret his/her past may also be incapable of projecting concretely his/her interest in emancipation regarding the lifeworld of the public sphere. Therefore, a depth-hermeneutics is still a hermeneutic, even if it is called meta-hermeneutics in the sense of Habermas. Habermas centralizes self-reflection for arriving at unrestricted and unconstrained communication. However, it is an illusion if an appeal is made to the non-place of the transcendental intersubjective rationality without reference to emancipation in the tradition. For Ricoeur an interest in emancipation never effects a division capable of introducing a clean epistemological break at the level of knowledge. The critique of ideology never breaks its links to the basis of belonging. When this primordial tie is forgotten, a critical theory is elevated to the rank of absolute knowledge.

In theological thinking, the Exodus and the Resurrection belong to the emancipation and critique of tradition. There is no interest in emancipation and critique without reference to the tradition of emancipation. A task of philosophical-hermeneutical reflection entails an interest in emancipation regarding the futuristic projections of a liberated humanity by extending it to the interest in the reinterpretation of cultural heritage, which is received from the past.

For the reconstruction of reflective hermeneutics in matters of social science, Ricoeur defines hermeneutics as a way of concerning the rules required for the interpretation of the written documents of our culture. Based on this definition, Ricoeur remains faithful to the concept of *Auslegung* (exegesis, interpretation) in the sense of Dilthey. *Auslegung* covers a limited category of signs fixed by writing. *Auslegung* or text interpretation can become a methodology within the sphere of hermeneutics. Discourse is a language-event. It is the linguistics of the sentence, which supports the theory of speech as an event. Discourse is always realized temporally and implemented in the present.

Discourse is to be fixed because discourse disappears. Writing is given to a human being to rescue the weakness of discourse. This inscription, in spite of its perils, is discourse's destination. Not the event of speaking, but the "said" is fixed. The saying becomes *Aus-sage*—the enunciation, the enunciated. What we write is the *noema* of the speaking, the meaning of the speech, not the speech event as such. To understand a text is to light up our own situation or world. This opens up a world for us, a new dimension of our being-in-the-world.

For Gadamer, however, writing in relation to language has a secondary phenomenon. It is certain that writing has the methodological advantage of presenting the hermeneutical problem. Understanding is based on and driven by the subject matter. Within the hermeneutical horizon which creates understanding, the meaning of a text comes into force. The fusion of horizon, which acquires a horizon of interpretation, mediates between the horizon of the past or the text, and one's own horizon. By bringing one's own preconception into play, the meaning of the text can be made to speak for us.[105] Thus, Gadamer argues that the true method comes from an action of the thing itself.[106]

SOCIOLOGICAL METHOD AND HERMENEUTICAL CONCERN

Max Weber defines the object of human sciences as meaningfully oriented behavior. According to Ricoeur, action as meaningful becomes an object of science through a kind of objectification, which is similar to the fixation occurring in writing. Ricoeur calls it the noematic structure of action, which may be fixed, becoming an object for interpretation.

The meaning (*noema*) and the intention (*noesis*) coincide in the area of social science. Like a text, human action is an open work, the meaning of which is suspended. All significant events and deeds are opened to practical interpretation through the present praxis.

Similarly, in a later stage, Dilthey advocates that the expressions of life undergo a kind of objectification, which makes possible a scientific approach similar to natural science. Ricoeur transposes Dilthey's later question in terms of the dialectical character of the relation between explanation and understanding as it is displayed in reading a text. Ricoeur proposes the exchange and reciprocity between understanding and explanation for the interpretation of a text. The hermeneutic circle or circulation is a cumulative and holistic process. In social science, we proceed from naïve interpretations to critical interpretations and from surface interpretations to depth interpretations through structural analysis. The meaningful patterns, at which a depth interpretation wants to grasp, cannot be understood without personal and ethical commitment. This is similar to that of the reader who grasps the depth semantics of the text and makes it his/her own. Understanding is mediated by the whole of explanatory and analytical procedures, which precede it and accompany

---

105. Gadamer, *Truth and Method*, 397.
106. Ibid., 464.

it. The correlation between explanation and understanding, between understanding and explanation is processed in the hermeneutical circle.

However, Ricoeur's limitation is not to develop hermeneutical circulation in conversation with Marx's interpretation theory of historical materialism that aims to reveal a hidden and distorted interest of oppression and domination in a social, economic location. Marx's ontology of a human being in social location led to calling into question a social history in light of a dialectical interplay between economic, material life conditions, and the intellectual, cultural lifeworld. In this critical method, the economic factor is not the single determining moment upon the intellectual, religious, and cultural sphere. Diverse factors such as religion, ideology, and life arrangements of the public sphere are also influential in the process of a social, historical course.

Thus, an interpretation and a critical factor shape Marx's method in a hermeneutical manner. In reading the text, the social life condition of the author and its recipients cannot be ignored. Through socialization, human beings become "ensembles of social relation." This aspect becomes a corrective to a hermeneutics of ontology that ignores the social reality of the author, the text, and the reader. A critique of ideology is grounded in this critical method of questioning human life rooted in the social and material sphere.

As an activity and a capability, the Marxian method of analysis can become a form of hermeneutics in the endeavor to uncover the hidden meaning of power, knowledge, and legitimation in a given social context and episteme. An understanding of the ontology of social being can be developed in a dialectical interplay of part-totality that is a Marxian concept of totality in the sense of the social, hermeneutical circle. Interpretation and critique of ideology stand in reference to real, material historicity of human life and activity. From here a praxis is mobilized in an effort to change and renew the social reality which has distorted, invalidated, and colonized human life as a whole.

Losing sight of the connection between Marxian method and hermeneutics, however, Ricoeur is concerned to develop a hermeneutics of the text in terms of belonging and distanciation for the sake of an interest in emancipation. At this juncture, Ricouer deals with a relationship between ideology and utopia. Ricoeur's point of departure is based on the Weberian analysis of the concepts of social action and social relations rather than critically integrating a Marxian method of analysis into a hermeneutical circle.[107]

For Weber, social action occurs when human behavior is meaningful for individual agents and when the human behavior of one is oriented toward that of the Other. At this level of the meaningful, mutually oriented, and socially integrated character of action, the ideological phenomenon appears in all its originality. Ideology is par excellence the reign of the "isms": liberalism, Capitalism, Socialism, etc. In the function of ideology there is a conjunction between the general function of integration and the particular function of domination. What ideology interprets and justifies is the relation to the system of authority.

According to Weber, all authority seeks to legitimate itself, and political systems are distinguished according to their type of legitimation. Sharing Weber's conviction, Ricoeur contends that there is an irreducible phenomenon of surplus-value, if we understand the excess of the demand for legitimation in relation to a belief on the part of individuals in this legitimacy. Ideology asserts itself as the transmitter of surplus-value and, at the same time, as the justificatory system of domination. Ideology-dissimulation interacts with all the other features of ideology-integration.

For Weber, there is no fully transparent legitimation. Even without assimilating all authority to the charismatic form, there is an essential opacity to the phenomenon of authority. Every prince wants to be Caesar, every Caesar wants to be Alexander, and every Alexander wants to Hellenize an oriental despot. When the mediating role of ideology encounters the phenomenon of domination, the distorting and dissimulating character of ideology comes to the fore.[108]

Marx compares ideology negatively to a *camera obscura* in which human beings and their circumstances appear upside down.[109] Thus, a critique of ideology is not merely confined to a critique of religion, but also includes the critique of political economy in a capitalist society. The theoreticians of the Frankfurt school take science and technology to play the role of ideology. In the case of Louis Althusser (in his *Lenin and Philosophy*), Marxist science transforms itself into a partisan ideology. So Marxism functions as a system of justification for the power of the

---

107. Thomson, *Hermeneutics & the Human Sciences*, 225.
108. Ibid., 229.
109. Marx and Engels, *German Ideology*, 47.

party as the avant-garde of the working class and for the power of the ruling group within the party. For Marx, ideology is false consciousness, whereas Marxism after Marx takes ideology as expression and exercise of power and authority. At this juncture, Ricoeur attempts to liberate Marx's work from Marxism and Leninism.[110]

To promote his hermeneutical sociology, Ricoeur takes into account Karl Manheim's position regarding ideology and utopia. Manheim, in his sociology of knowledge, contends that there is a relationship between social structure and systems of thought. This refers to a structural totality of society. Knowledge is bound up in the interrelationships of history, society, and psychology. Knowledge belongs to *this* world rather than retaining a transcendental status.[111]

From this point of view comes the title of the book, *Ideology and Utopia*. By ideology Mannheim meant the total systems of thought held by society's ruling groups that obscure the real conditions and preserve the status quo. Utopian thinking is the total systems of thought created by oppressed groups that are interested in the transformation of society.

In his attempt to explain ideology, Mannheim identifies two distinct meanings: the particular and the total. The first refers to the common concept of ideology as distortion while the second refers to thought systems in a relationship between social forces and worldview. The *interests* reflected in idea systems are functions of different situations or life settings, dependent on larger spheres of age, class, and other sociological forces. Mannheim's view of a total concept of ideology[112] advances a sociological conception of epistemology, a way of understanding the relationships between historical and social structure by which knowledge is formed and judged.[113]

Ideologies are, for the most part, professed by the ruling class and denounced by under-privileged classes; utopias are generally supported by the rising classes. Ideologies look backwards, while utopias look forwards. In *Ideology and Utopia*, Manheim identifies different forms or ideal types of the utopian mentality. For example, early religious sects (such as the Anabaptists) were fixed on the establishment of a millennial kingdom on earth. The bourgeois thinking of the Enlightenment repre-

---

110. Thomson, *Hermeneutics & the Human Sciences*, 236.
111. Manheim, *Ideology and Utopia*, 292–94.
112. Ibid., 64–69.
113. Ibid., 79.

sented a utopian mentality, taking the form of a "liberal-humanitarian" ideal. The "Socialist-Communist" mode locates human freedom in the breakdown of Capitalist culture.[114]

However, Manheim's ideal types of utopian thought are content to clarify the context of ideas and their interrelations within the structure of an overall system of thought. He is not keenly aware of specifying the real, material conditions in reference to ideological and utopian visions. Manheim denounces the Weberian claim to a value-free sociology as a deceptive lure. What is at issue for Manheim is a continual readiness to recognize that every point of view is particular to a certain definite situation.[115]

For Manheim no question can be asked without presupposition. Just as conversely, no hypotheses can be formulated, and nothing can be investigated without questions. For him, the attempt to escape ideological and utopian distortions is a quest for reality. When we are aware of the limited scope of every point of view, we are on the road to search for comprehension of the whole. A total view implies both the assimilation and transcendence of the limitations of particular points of view.

Given this fact, Ricoeur regards Manheim's position as a turning point for a hermeneutic of historical understanding. Ricoeur prefers to take the long and difficult route of an epistemological reflection on the conditions of the possibility of knowledge about ideology, and in general on the conditions of the validation of explanatory discourses in the social sciences. Before any critical distance, we belong to a history, to a class, to a nation, to a culture, to one or several traditions. In accepting this belonging, we accept the very first role of ideology, as the mediating function of the image, the self-representation. Through the mediating function, we also participate in the other functions of ideology, those of dissimulation and distortion.

If objectifying knowledge is always secondary to the relation of belonging, it can nevertheless be constituted in a relative autonomy. The critical moment is fundamentally possible in virtue of the factor of distanciation, which is a part of the relations of historicity. Extending Heidegger and Gadamer's ontological hermeneutics, Ricoeur proposes his sociological hermeneutics, which contains dimensions of the critique of ideology for the sake of realism. Distanciation, dialectically opposed

---

114. Ibid., 211–47.

115. Thomson, *Hermeneutics & the Human Sciences*, 80.

to belonging, is the condition of the possibility of the critique of ideology in a work of self-understanding within the area of hermeneutics.

HERMENEUTICS OF DISCOURSE AND SOCIAL LOCATION

Ricoeur's mediation between hermeneutics and ideology critique is relevant for mediating discourse with communication. Discourse is seen in light of the dialectic of event and meaning. Discourse is realized in performance temporarily and in the present moment. Insofar as discourse is actualized as an event in dialogical performance, it is to be understood as meaning. The event is that somebody is speaking.

Regarding the dialectic of event and meaning in the performance of discourse, Ricoeur, like Habermas, utilizes illocutionary acts. In a speech act, the saying has a doing aspect related to the event. Three elements are interconnected in the performance of discourse: Saying something (the locutionary act), doing something in saying (the illocutionary act), and the effect by saying (the perlocutionary act). As long as the illocutionary act produces effects by saying, this act presents the dialectic of event and meaning. A study of language as communication comes from an internal structure of discourse, dialogue rather than a sociology of communication.[116]

Discourse as an event in dialogical performance and process makes the private experience of language a public one. The criterion of the noetic is the intention of communicability, so that the noetic is the soul of discourse as dialogue. Language is, owing to expression, exteriorization or transformation of the private life into the noetic. The dialectic of event and meaning as an internal dialectic of the meaning of discourse embraces two sides of meaning: subjective and objective.

The subjective side of meaning refers to the self-reference of the sentence, the illocutionary dimension, and the intention of recognition by the hearer. The objective side of the meaning is the utterance meaning in the sense of the propositional content. Ricoeur distinguishes the "what" of discourse from the "about what." The "what" of discourse is its sense while the "about what" is its reference. The dialectic of sense and reference articulates the notion that we bring experience to language, which is the ontological condition of reference.[117] Here, language is con-

---

116. Ricoeur, *Interpretation Theory*, 15.
117. Ibid., 21.

ceptualized in an ontological, referential sense. His strategy in the perspective of a philosophy of discourse is to release the psychologizing and existential prejudices of hermeneutics. This hermeneutics of discourse marks a shift from speaking to writing.

It is certain that Ricoeur emphasizes the nature of language as a speech event and articulates discourse as the actualization of a language in a speech event. Language as discourse refers beyond itself to the world. To the extent that the text is alienated from the author's intention and the original historical situation, it enters into the public sphere, inspiring many interpretations. Nevertheless, the world of the text is the locus of Ricoeur's hermeneutical inquiries, so that the interpretation of the world of the text is an interpretation of the self, appropriation of the narrative identity of the text.

For Ricoeur, appropriating Heidegger's analysis of *Dasein* as a primordial correlation between the self and the world, a being as a self is in the world, and the being of the self presupposes the totality of the world, namely the horizon of its care.[118] Thus, the self is not grounded within itself, but linked to the other. "There is no pure consciousness at the heart.... there is no self alone at the start; the ascription to others is just as primitive as the ascription to oneself."[119] Without ascribing one's thoughts potentially to someone else, one cannot speak meaningfully of one's thoughts and world.

Nevertheless, a hermeneutics of discourse does not remain fixed to the world of writing. Rather, it can articulate a synchronic dimension of human life in a social, cultural location. In a shift from the text to discourse, unlike Ricouer, there is a demand for analyzing power realities in the emergence of meaning and knowledge. Discourse means not only "someone says something to someone" but also demands attention to forms of power operative in the someone, the something, and the "to someone." Discourse analysis does not merely reduce meaning and knowledge to power relations, but reveals the hidden meaning and relationships of gender, class, and race as marginalized thus far in historical hermeneutics.

For instance, modern biblical research contends that the Bible is like a small library containing many different voices and divergent views rather than a unity without contradiction and constraints. The Bible is

---

118. Ricoeur, *Oneself as Another*, 310.
119. Ibid., 38.

indispensably connected with the historical character of the message and the particular conditions and times of the writers. The narrative character of the Bible brings us today into contact with whom and what it witnesses to.

As Luther states in his *Introduction to the Psalter, 1531*, in the Bible we see into the heart of all saints. The humanity of the biblical authors is actually exposed to the reader here and now. A social-critical method is a method of questioning a history, and brings into profile and contour the historical character of the texts and authors who speak. The text and the author are shaped and conditioned by the social circumstances and conflicting interests of their time. The socio–critical dimension of the Bible is of importance for the second stage of translation, understanding and interpretation, in reference to our time and different circumstances. This refers to "a prophetic dimension of Biblical interpretation" which is an indispensable part of a hermeneutics in social location.[120]

A synchronic hermeneutics in social location, which stands under the influence of hermeneutics of suspicion and critical theory, helps today's hermeneutically oriented theology to become more practical and ethical-political without ceasing to be hermeneutical. Abandoning the hermeneutical origins in an analysis of discourse exposes the study as foundationalist or relativist. At this point, it is important to defend a postfoundational hermeneutics with emphasis on God's act of speaking, saying in social location, and interpersonal discourse.[121]

With science, we interpret the world of nature. In science, language inevitably influences our understanding of both data and facts. Reality is constituted by the interaction between a text, or world, and a questioning interpreter. However, what is lost in this scientific framework is the social and historical character of all understanding through language. We find ourselves understanding in and through particular and public languages. These languages are social and historical in character. A hermeneutical understanding of language challenges instrumentalist thinking and displaces the autonomous self from its privileged status of mastery and certainty.

In a social context, Heidegger-inspired hermeneutics meets a serious challenge from a hermeneutic of "saying" over "said," and from a hermeneutic of the other over the self. In pursuing self-identity in light

120. Gollwitzer, *Introduction*, 58–59.
121. Tracy, *On Naming*, 136.

of the other, the self is summoned to responsibility by the other. Such a challenge is radical and deconstructive of an ontological hermeneutic for the sake of good, with a commitment to ethics in the face of the others. This new perspective belongs to Levinas's concept of God and philosophy which will be discussed in the next chapter.

8

A Postmodern Ethics of the Other and the Hermeneutics of Saying

LEVINAS'S METAPHYSICAL ETHIC (in association with a hermeneutic of the Infinite's Saying through the face of the other) deeply challenges Heidegger's hermeneutics of ontology and discourse project. Emmanuel Levinas (1906–1995) was born in Lithuania into a liberal Jewish family. At age seventeen he moved to Strasbourg to study, and found himself drawn to philosophy. From 1928–1929 he studied in Freiburg under Husserl and Heidegger. At Freiburg Levinas delved into Heidegger's major work *Being and Time*. In 1939 Levinas was drafted into the French army, was captured, and became a prisoner of war. Most of his family in Lithuania was murdered by the Nazis. Levinas maintained that the reality and the memory of the Holocaust always dominated his thinking.

In his early work, *From Existence to the Existents*, he analyzed the labor camp and raised issues of ethics, a need for thinking beyond ontology. Levinas's work reverses the orientation of Heidegger's thought, which aims to transcend the metaphysics of beings (existents) to Being (existence). Levinas asserts that the Good commands an exodus that transcends the limits of being. He is a post-Shoah philosopher, who paves a new way to ethically ground Western philosophical tradition and hermeneutics.

INFINITE AND ALTERITY

According to Descartes, the *cogito* ("thinking I") can give itself the sun and sky; the only thing it cannot give itself is the idea of the Infinite. The idea of Infinity is exceptional beyond human thinking. Integrating Descartes' idea of the Infinite, Levinas articulates the transcendence of the Infinite in regard to the "I." Thus "the intentionality of transcendence" lies at the heart of Levinas's ethical project.[1]

Knowledge is always an adequation between thought and that which the subject thinks. Sociality with the Other is a means to escape being as conceptualized by knowledge. The Other is not reduced to intentionality. Levinas's thought casts doubt on the Husserlian idea of intentionality.

Husserl's solution to the problem of certainty is non-Cartesian. The structures of the subjective act and of the object are correlatives, because consciousness is intentional. Intentionality takes place in the context of being in a world. This pattern is totally strange to the subject-object schema. For instance, the natural sciences posit objects without analyzing the structures of consciousness that enable them to do so. In this scientific naturalization of consciousness, consciousness becomes reified and reduced to the level of thing. This natural attitude must be abandoned in order to recover the original thought. For this task, we need to suspend our engagement with the world, which means the phenomenological reduction.

We must reduce reality from its existence to its meaning for us in the conscious act. To the effect that consciousness can have a *Wesenschau* (look into essence or eidetic intuition) of its essential nature, reality must be bracketed, phenomenologically reduced. The *epoché*, which is the bracketing of the world's existence, reduces the world's being to a kind of annihilation and thus, it locates certainty in the transcendental consciousness as such.

This consciousness lends and posits a meaning to things. This transcendental consciousness alone, which is distinguished from the world, is apodictic. Husserl seeks to ground all meaning in an absolutely indubitable foundation of absolute consciousness. The real world can have its meaning as the existing reality, which is in fact the intentional meaning-product of transcendental subjectivity.[2]

The world is not annihilated and exists as meaning in relation to consciousness. Phenomenological reduction does not posit the natural world as the world of being. Rather it reduces the world to an intended meaning (*noema*) correlate of the intentional act (*noesis*) of an absolute consciousness. Thus the putting out of action, our disconnection, and

1. Levinas, *Totality and Infinity*, 49.
2. Husserl, *Ideas*, 14.

bracketing of the natural world implies the free act of placing it "like the bracketed in the bracket, like the disconnected outside the connectional system"[3] rather than the destruction of the world.

In the reduction of the natural thesis of the world to an intentional field of meaning, there remains a new region of Being, pure consciousness with its pure correlates of consciousness, and its Pure Ego. "I" as this individual essence is the transcendental Ego. The pure correlates of consciousness are subject to the absolute pure ego. The existence of the pure ego and its personal life is necessary and plainly indubitable.[4] Through phenomenological reduction the world is placed as meaning for "me" in absolute dependence on the intentionality of consciousness.

To the degree that intentionality is characteristic of consciousness, all consciousness is consciousness of something. Intentionality is the act of bestowing a meaning. Consequently, intentionality makes the exteriority of the object disappear. Consciousness is understood as the presupposition, condition, ground, and basis for the existence of the world. However, Husserl's later turn to lifeworld is a counter proposal to the limitation of the transcendental reduction founding meaning within itself. A return to ego must be overcome by one's lived experience with the Other in the world. The world precedes consciousness, becomes the basis for all reflection on human experience.

According to Levinas, Husserl's theory of consciousness is ahistorical. Husserl's deconstruction of a naturalistic view of history is undertaken without consideration of the essential historicity of human existence. Husserlian *cogito* thinks of the infinite as something that lacks alterity. For Levinas the Other is the one whom we are not, while Husserl recognizes in the Other an alter ego, a modification of ego in general.[5] Levinas argues that relationships with alterity contrast with the principle of the same, which dominates or absorbs the other. This model of the same is knowledge. Against this trend, calling for recognition of otherness is a precondition for an ethic in the face of the Other.

In Hegelian phenomenology, self-consciousness expresses the universality of the same, which identifies itself in the alterity of objects.

---

3. Ibid., 18.
4. Ibid., 131.
5. Wyschogrod, *Emmanuel Levinas*,, 52.

Hegel states that I distinguish myself from myself. I thrust myself away from myself. But this which is distinguished is no distinction for me.[6]

Levinas takes issue with this statement of Hegel's, arguing that for Hegel the difference is not a difference, the "I," as other, is not an other. Rather, "the identification of the same is ... the concreteness of egoism"; the other would dissolve into the same, remaining the simple reverse of identity.[7] The metaphysical other that Levinas advocates for "is prior to every initiative, to all imperialism of the same."[8] The absolutely Other—this is the Other (*L'absolument Autre, c'est Autrui*)[9]—and its alterity is to transcend the immanence as conceptualized in the tradition of Western philosophy. And it establishes its transcendence in the midst of history.[10] Thus, Levinas's concept of infinity and transcendence underlines and elaborates human difference in a radical way.

Biding farewell to Parmenides, in whose tradition totality dominates, makes morality disappear, and brings war. Infinity, according to Levinas, is path toward peace on dialogue with and listening to the Other. What the Other offers as the transcendence of his/her being cannot be totalized. The face of the Other is the expression of the infinity.

A subjectivity which is grounded in the infinity of the Other speaks out against a Heideggerian metaphysic of being, the Husserlian horizon of consciousness, and Hegelian phenomenology of the Mind in which self-consciousness consumes what stands in the way and reduces all particularity and difference into the sameness of the self-knowing mind. Thus, the ontological tradition's "I" must be reversed with an Other that transcends the initiatives of being.[11]

According to Levinas, Buber's category of I–Thou denotes an interhuman relationship. This category of I–Thou denotes a relation with the feminine alterity rather than being the interlocutor of the other.[12] Buber's I–Thou philosophy is the prolegomena to his philosophy of religion. Grace is the means by which "You" encounters "me." "My" relationship with the "You" is election and electing, passive and active. Through the

6. Hegel, *The Phenomenology of Mind*, 211; see Levinas, *Totality and Infinity*, 36–37.
7. Ibid., 38.
8. Ibid., 38–39.
9. Ibid., 39.
10. Ibid., 40.
11. Ibid., 38–39. See Peperzak, *To the Other*, 131.
12. Levinas, *Totality and Infinity*, 155.

grace of the advents of the "You," the "You" helps us to have intimations of eternity. The "You" is the eternal butterfly; The "You" world does not hang together in space and time.[13] Through the dialogical relation the "Me" reaches the other as the "You," as partner and friend.

In Levinas' view, Buber's concept of the I–Thou relation retains a formal character, uniting the human being to things as much as articulating interpersonal relation. Levinas criticizes that the I–thou only accounts for a life of friendship: economy, the search for happiness, and the representational relation with things. For Levinas, this remains a disdainful spiritualism. Distancing himself from Buber, Levinas begins with the idea of the Infinity rather than the I–Thou relation.[14]

Levinas argues that knowledge is suppression of alterity. His major philosophical work, *Totality and Infinity* (1961) proposes a revolution not only in phenomenology but also with regard to the entire history of Western metaphysics. Levinas presents a critique of the whole of Western civilization, which is dominated by the spirit of Greek philosophy. Western thought and practice are marked by a striving for totalization, "destroying the radical alterity of the other."[15]

Against Western totalitarianism, Levinas maintains that the human and the divine other cannot be reduced to a totality. The priority of ontological thinking has ramifications ending up with totality and exalting power, reducing the right of the earth and the Other. Although Heidegger makes critique of dominance of technology, he exalts the pre-technological powers of "man's" possession. Although reproaching Socratic philosophy as forgetful of Being and so to tend to the notion of the subject and technological power, Heidegger still "finds in Presocratism thought as obedience to the truth of Being."[16]

However, the Other is associated with the Infinite. The category of totality summarizes the way in which the ego inhabits the world, while the Infinite names the Other's incomprehensible character. The other is, in the first place, the other human being that "I" encounter. In a later development, it also stands for God. According to Levinas, the Other expresses itself. To have the idea of infinity is an ethical relation, now that the epiphany of the face of the Other is the ethical. The infinite in

13. Biemann, *Martin Buber Reader*, 185–86.
14. Levinas, *Totality and Infinity*, 69.
15. Ibid., 35–36.
16. Ibid., 46.

the finite is produced by the idea of the face of the other. In this light, "a Desire for perfectly disinterested-goodness" presupposes a relationship as a presence before a face. My orientation toward the Other in the face establishes the relationship of conversation in which the other presents him/herself as face. The face brings expression.

Approaching the Other in dialogue is welcoming his/her expression. What I receive from the Other is the idea of infinity. The notion of face in an ethical sense precedes one's act of giving meaning, signifying the philosophical priority of the existent over Being.[17] This perspective represents a function of language prior to every unveiling of being, because the function of language is not subordinate to the consciousness; rather it conditions intentionality of consciousness.

Levinas contends that the history of philosophy can be interpreted as an attempt at universal synthesis, that is, a reduction of all experience to a totality in which consciousness embraces the world, and thus becomes absolute thought. In philosophical and theological tradition, there has been little protest against this totalization. The consequence of ontological priority is loss of Otherness.

Socrates' teaching was the primacy of the same, because nothing is received from the Other. According to Levinas, the Socratic truth rests on the essential self-sufficiency of the same, that is "its identification in ipseity, its egoism." Thus philosophy is an egology.[18] Heidegger's primacy of ontology subordinates the ethical relation with someone (an existent) to a relation with the Being of existents, the impersonal dominion of existents. According to Heidegger, in order to know an existent (*Dasein*), it is necessary to comprehend the Being of existents.

In this basic framework, freedom implies the mode of being remaining the same in the midst of the Other; knowledge of impersonal Being entails the ultimate sense of freedom. Here, an ethical justice in relationship with the other is subordinated to ontological freedom; Heideggerian ontology affirms and justifies the primacy of ontological freedom over ethical justice. The primacy of the same (the totalizing Being), which marks the direction of the whole of Western philosophy, is to neutralize the existent, maintaining oneself against the other. Such a definition of freedom ensures the autarchy of an "I."[19]

17. Ibid., 51.
18. Ibid., 44.
19. Ibid., 46. At the archaeological level, Foucault also analyzes a dimension of the Other, the unthought in relation to "thinking I" of modern man. Man and the unthought

In this light, Levinas criticizes that ontology, as the first philosophy, is a philosophy of power. The egoism of ontology is established. Heidegger criticized Socratic philosophy as already forgetful of Being and already exposed to the notion of the subject and technological power. However, Heidegger expresses his allegiance to the Presocratic concept of obedience to the truth of Being.

To the degree that ontology, a philosophy of power, does not call into question the same, it remains a philosophy of injustice; it leads to obedience to an anonymous power, to imperialist domination, and to tyranny.[20] As Levinas further argues, Heidegger's ontological *Sorge* (care for the self) for the life results in "the transmutation of the other into the same, which is the essence of enjoyment."[21]

For Levinas, the irreducible and ultimate experience of relationship does not appear in synthesis, but in the face to face of humans, in sociality, and in its moral signification. First, philosophy is an ethics. In the tradition of Western philosophy, the idea of God can be made part of a totality of being. However, the term transcendence signifies precisely the fact that one cannot think God and being together. The true union or true togetherness is not a togetherness of synthesis, but a togetherness of face to face.

ETHICS IN THE FACE OF THE OTHER

In *Totality and Infinity*, Levinas tried to ground sociality in something other than a global and synthetic concept of the society. The real must be determined from the secrecy interrupting the continuity of historical time. The pluralism of society becomes possible only starting from the secrecy.[22]

It is certain that Levinas does not intend to deduce any underestimation of reason and reason's aspiration to universality. The social, with its institutions, universal forms and laws, should result from

---

are contemporaries. According to Foucault, "the whole of modern thought is imbued with the necessity of thinking the unthought⊠of reflecting the contents of the *In-self* in the form of the *For-itself*" in the sense of Hegelian phenomenology. A necessity of thinking the unthought ends man's alienation by reconciling him with his own essence, and lifts the veil of the unconscious. See Foucault, *Order of Things*, 327.

20. Levinas, *Totality and Infinity*, 46–47.
21. Ibid., 111.
22. Ibid., 57–58.

stressing the infinity, which opens itself in the ethical relationship of person to person. A theory of the public sphere becomes meaningful only in reference to recognition and respect of the Other. An ethic of the Other gathers meaning by becoming hostage to those who are not reduced to the totalizing discourse. This refers to the issue of justice in the public sphere.

A God invisible means a God accessible in justice, because the vision of God coincides with the work of justice. In Levinas's philosophical metaphysics, the human being, as separated from God, nevertheless relates to God whose relationship does not nullify divine transcendence.[23] Politics must be able always to be checked and criticized from the ethical standpoint. This ethics would render justice to a secrecy that holds to the responsibility for the Other. Encountering another means realizing that "I" am under ethical obligation.

Levinas argues that the Other is not the incarnation of God, but by the face, the Other is the manifestation of what God is as revealed.[24] What the theological realm refers to as revelation is what Levinas calls the epiphany of the human face. The face of the Other that we encounter is transcendent, coming *extra nos*, so that it escapes all attempts to reduce and totalize it into "my" own sameness. Descartes's concept of the infinity is radicalized transcendentally and ethically by Levinas's attempt at presenting a concrete human being in a face-to-face relationship. The Other remains infinitely transcendent, infinitely foreign; his face in which his epiphany is produced appeals to "me," breaking with the world.[25]

The infinite is not grasped by the idea of the infinite because it transcends the grasp of thought. We cannot integrate the alterity of the infinite into the same. The idea of infinity is generated in the form of a relation with the face. The epiphany of the infinity occurs as a face. We respond to God's expression and revelation in the face of the Other rather than struggling with a faceless God.[26] God resists us in the Other's face; the primordial expression is: "you shall not commit murder." God paralyzes human power by the infinite resistance to murder, and gleams in the face of the Other, and in the nudity of the absolute openness of the Infinity. The epiphany of the face is resistance to murder, calling for ethi-

23. Ibid., 77.
24. Ibid., 79.
25. Ibid., 194.
26. Ibid., 197.

cal resistance. Infinity presents itself as a face in the ethical resistance, paralyzing "my" powers.[27]

In the essay "Transcendence and Height," a succinct summary of *Totality and Infinity*, Levinas argues that Western philosophical tradition is a form of a fundamental monism, reducing the plurality of beings to the unity of the Same. For the critique of Western monism, Levinas contends that the priority of the idea of the infinite is asserted over the idea of ontology.[28] For Heidegger, a human being is the shepherd of Being. All differences of beings are assimilated and transmuted into the Same. The myth of philosophy rests on the totalitarianism or imperialism of the Same.[29]

Against Husserl's concept of intentionality, Levinas argues that the relation with the Other does not have the structure of intentionality. Rather, it resists the indiscretion of intentionality, overturning the very egoism of the Same. The journey of Odyssey can be compared to the movement of consciousness, which "returns triumphantly to itself and rests upon itself."[30]

The face of the Other is the poor and destitute one. This is a surplus inadequate to intentionality, binding the Other to the idea of the Infinite. The move from transcendence to destitution characterizes Levinas's ethical solidarity with God's *massa perditionis*, recognizing the gaze of the stranger, the widow, the orphan.[31] The idea of the infinite is contrary to the perfect mastery of the object by the subject in intentionality, and is signified through the face of the Other prior to interpreted meaning.[32] Self-reflection comes into question from the Infinite. In an ethical relation with the Other, Levinas speaks of God.

Recognizing the Other is desiring the Other. Such desire for the Other is justice, which, unlike political justice, can be grounded in religion. In political law, we see reciprocal recognition toward equality while religion is Desire, "the surplus possible in a society of equals" rather than struggle for recognition. In religion, we find and incorporate humility, re-

---

27. Ibid., 199–200.
28. Levinas, *Basic Philosophical Writings*, 12.
29. Ibid., 14.
30. Ibid., 17.
31. Levinas, *Totality and Infinity*, 77.
32. Ibid., 19.

sponsibility, and sacrifice, all of which are the condition for equality.[33] In a religiously-oriented concept of ethical relation with the Other, Levinas speaks of God. Thus, Levinas argues that atheism involves disregard of the Other, while religion is constituted by a recognition of Otherness. The act of recognizing and communicating with the Other makes justice possible in a religious and ethical way.

HERMENEUTICAL DIMENSION IN ETHIC OF THE OTHER

Levinas finds in Plato the transcendence of the Good concerning being. Levinas's use of ethical language, which is beyond ontology, retrieves the meaning associated with the sense that is different from the meaning or signification in a Heideggerian sense. At this juncture, Levinas's interpretation of Plato's analogy of the cave in pursuit of truth in *Phaedrus* is different from Heidegger. To recognize the truth as the disclosure implies the horizon of the Infinite who discloses. Plato's identification of knowledge with vision in the myth of the chariot of the Phaedrus expresses that the disclosed being is relative to us. "The pure experience of the other being would have to maintain the other being καθ'αὐτό"[34]

According to Levinas, the manifestation of the καθ'αὐτό implies a being that tells itself to us independently of every position by expressing itself.[35] Human interpretation of the truth consists of attending and listening to the Infinite who expresses itself. The dynamism of the Infinite's speech act or saying constitutes a basis and subject matter of human interpretation. Like language, human experience no longer appears in isolated elements. At this juncture, Levinas contends that experience is a reading, and the understanding of meaning is an exegesis, a hermeneutic. However, meaning is not a modification affecting a content that exists outside of all language.[36]

In Heidegger, being is revealed out of the hiddenness and mystery of the unsaid. Unlike Heidegger, however, for Plato the world of meanings precedes language and culture, which express it. Meanings exist before their expression. For the modern philosophy of anti-Platonic meaning, thought and language are correlated. This forms the funda-

---

33. Ibid., 64.
34. Ibid., 65.
35. Ibid.
36. Levinas, *Basic Philosophical Writings*, 38.

mental historicity in the form of the mixed interconnection of meaning, consciousness, and language.[37] This philosophy subordinates the intellect to expression, embroiled in the network of language.

Running counter to ontological hermeneutics, Levinas proposes to find the sense beneath the meaning. Cultural meanings take on meaning in dialogue with the Other. The world and language "have lost the univocity which would authorize us to expect from them the criteria of the meaningful."[38] The bond between expression and responsibility is the ethical condition or essence of language. The language enters into discourse with the other. This function of language is prior to all disclosure of being.[39]

We cannot evade by silence the discourse that the epiphany of a face opens. The face of the destitute opens the primordial discourse. Rabbi Yochanan's saying fits: "To leave men without food is a fault that no circumstance attenuates."[40] The primordial expression precedes the circle of understanding, or the hermeneutical circle. The attestation of oneself is possible only as face, as discursive speech.[41]

In Western tradition, a philosophical journey is likened to that of Odysseus, "whose adventure in the world was only a return to his native island—a complacency in the Same, an unrecognition of the Other."[42] However, for Levinas, Abraham's journey is radically conceived as a movement of the Same toward the Other, which never returns to the Same.[43] This is a departure with no return, without entering into the Promised Land.[44]

According to Heidegger, a subject is defined by care for itself. To this concept, Levinas opposes the desire for the other. In desire the "I" is born, with insatiable compassion toward the Other, having the hunger to infinity. In a hermeneutical structure, the desire for the Other expresses itself. The Other in the face of "me" is not included in the totality of "my" expression and interpretation. The Other is the sense which primordi-

37. Ibid., 43.
38. Ibid., 47.
39. Levinas, *Totality and Infinity*, 200.
40. Ibid., 201.
41. Ibid.
42. Levinas, *Basic Philosophical Writings*, 48.
43. Ibid., 49.
44. Ibid., 50.

ally gives sense to expression. The analysis of desire is made clear by the analysis of the alterity toward desire. "The understanding of the Other is thus a hermeneutics and an exegesis,"[45] because the Other is present as a text in its context. The Other comes to us without mediation, and the phenomenon of the Other's aspiration is a face. Its manifestation is "a surplus over the inevitable paralysis of manifestation."[46]

At this point, universalizing ontology or hermeneutics is relativized for the sake of an ethical hermeneutic of the desire for Other by being placed into question in terms of the Infinite and the Other. Hermeneutical meaning is situated in the ethical realm. Language is to be envisioned out of the revelation of the Other. Divine speech comes to me through the Others. Like the lifeworld is present and pre-given to consciousness, there is only an abject meant. Being cannot fulfill meaning.

In Levinas's view, the proclaiming of something as something lies at the foundation of consciousness that he calls a *kerygma*. Subjectivity as consciousness is interpreted as the rediscovery of being on the basis of an ideal principle or *arche*. All meaning reverts to the kergmatic structure of thinking. Every phenomenon is a fragment of discourse, so that the individual can only be attained in discourse. What is kerygmatic in thought carries proximity between me and the interlocutor. The interlocutor cannot be known, and discourse arises from *a priroi* proximity. This proximity is a signification, the immediacy of human presence, implying a new ethical intentionality.

The illeity of a third person, beyond being, is not definable by the self. The illeity is in the trace of transcendence. To be in the image of God does not mean to be an icon of God but to find oneself in God's trace. Exodus 33 tells us that to go toward God is to go toward the others who stand in the trace of illeity.[47] God's saying is not reducible to rational discourse. God is withdrawn into an irreversible past, because this irreversibility is God's illeity. To the extent God appears as a trace, the trace means becoming visible through the discursive act of speech while keeping its transcendence. Insofar as the Other is in the trace of illeity, the face is in the image of God, namely the trace of illeity.

For Heidegger, language conditions thought in such a way that the language is an attitude of the Same with regard to the Other. Against

45. Ibid., 52.
46. Ibid., 53.
47. Ibid., 64.

this view, Levinas contends that language comes to me from the Other, reverberating in consciousness by putting it in question rather than enacted with a consciousness.[48] Here, there is a surplus of signification over representation. Language is rescued from the standpoint of the logical discourse, because the Other means prior to meaning bestowal, prior to all intentionality. Language as discourse undercuts a privileged status of consciousness.

Hermeneutical signification, through the primordial event of the face, makes the sign possible. The primordial essence of language is to be sought in the presentation of meaning, and meaning is the face of the Other. Thus, words are enacted already within the primordial face-to-face of language. The comprehension of the primary signification is society and obligation before being interpreted as a "consciousness of."[49]

A consideration of the life of the Other in the public sphere is a basis for Levinas's hermeneutic of saying over said, for the sake of the destitute, the margin, and the poor. Language refers to a horizon transcending the things rather than merely representing them. One cannot outline all the contexts of language, so significations are not limited to any specific realm of objects. The word "fall" has a meaning beyond the season: it can refer to status of morality and so on with equal primordiality. The essence of language illumines what is beyond the given and being as a whole. Expression is the expressive gesture and meaning enters into a preexistent cultural world.[50] Language is the language of activity and event. God's speech event opens forth from the face of the Other who wears the face of the poor, the stranger, the widow, and the orphan. But it is also the face of the master who is called to invest and justify one's freedom.[51] The human Other's infinity reveals itself as a command. Face and discourse are tied so that the face speaks.

HERMENEUTICS OF SAYING OVER THE SAID

Levinas distinguishes in discourse between the saying and the said. For him, the said (*le dit*) does not count as much as the saying (*le dire*) itself. Philosophy produces instances of the said, but every said is preceded

---

48. Levinas, *Totality and Infinity*, 204.
49. Ibid., 206.
50. Wyschogrod, *Emmanuel Levinas*, 154–55.
51. Ibid., 251.

and transcended by a saying. The said must be brought back to the saying. "The saying does not exhaust itself in apophansis."[52] Likewise, "Apophansis does not exhaust what there is in saying."[53] What is otherwise than being is stated and articulated in a discursive saying that must not be reduced to that which is said. The beyond, saying, and the Infinite become and also do not become the meaning of being.[54]

Given this fact of priority of saying over the said, Levinas conceives of the language as *Davar* in a Hebrew manner (Ps 33:9). This is to say, the unity between word and effect: Word as action and action as "speaking" action. Theology which strives for its subject matter and self-reflectively on the way to the subject matter will remain a theology of the said, rather than that of the saying. Such theology in deliberation of the Word of God contends that all the said comes to the saying, and so it attempts to define a relation of the said to the saying.

The said is the *epos* of saying, and the being has meaning through the *kerygma* of the said. However, "the signification of saying goes beyond the said."[55] The signifying-ness of saying beyond essence justifies the ontology, rather than ontology raising up the speaking subject. Levinas argues that we must go back to the saying, the hither side of the amphibology of being and entities in the said. The signification of the Other occurs in proximity, and it can be conceived of as a responsibility for the Other. The said arises in the saying, namely the hither side of ontology. The saying and the said in their correlation denote the subject-object structure.

A hermeneutical dimension arises out of this relationship, in which the manifestation of saying out of the said does not dissimulate or falsify the signifyingness proper to the said. The saying, in the form of responsibility for other, is bound to a diachrony, an irrecuperable, unrepresentable past. An analysis of proximity recognizes the responsibility as a substitution.[56]

In Levinas's hermeneutics of the saying, the written text has its goal in the saying in ethical commitment for the life of the other. Here, a care for the Other, an ethical responsibility, challenges Heidegger's concept

52. Levinas, *Basic Philosophical Writings*, 113.
53. Levinas, *Otherwise than Being*, 6.
54. Levinas, *Basic Philosophical Writings*, 125.
55. Ibid. 37.
56. Levinas, *Otherwise Than Being*, 46–47.

A Postmodern Ethics of the Other and the Hermeneutics of Saying

of the care of *Dasein*. From a theological perspective we find a parallel between Levinas and Barth. Barth's theology of the Word of God in the threefold sense articulates the priority of *Deus dixit* (God's speech) over the biblical testimony to God in Christ, in reference to preaching and the Scripture. God is free to speak to the Church through the extra-ecclesial outsiders. It is certain that Bultmann knows about the saying of God (*kerygma* as the center of salvation history). However, he seeks the goal of the kerygmatic Word of God in "faith and understanding" rather than in God's saying through the face of the other. This difference in hermeneutical perspective between Barth and Butmann will be a topic of theological hermeneutics in the next chapter.

In Levinas' sense, the saying is basically the eternal meaning of the said. The essence of language is the relation with the Other. The ethical event of sociality commands an inward discourse. Because the subject of signification is infinity that is the Other. The signification of Saying precedes a meaning-giving of the said, marking the limit of hermeneutical ontology. "Here the inexhaustible surplus of infinity overflows the actuality of consciousness."[57]

In Western tradition, the *logos* of the saying became the *logos*-principle of the worldly said, without hesitation. However, in John 1:2, the *logos* was in the beginning *pros tov theon* (in the direction of, or in the proximity of God). The *logos* is the Word of God who is in the act of Saying. The Word was in the beginning toward God so that this *logos* marks "*Jenseits*" (otherworldly) of Being.[58] Reason is defined by signification, thus signification is not defined by the impersonal structures of reason.[59]

The saying is important in that it is addressed to an interlocutor. The saying is a way of greeting the Other, submitting the consciousness to the Other. To greet the Other is already to answer for him/her. The first word of the face is the "Thou shalt not kill." However, the face of the Other is destitute, and poor. Justice at the institutional level must be held in check by the initial interpersonal relation. Levinas struggles to develop a non-ontological language in order to express the beyond of being. At this juncture, Levinas thinks in a biblical way: in favor of

---

57. Levinas, *Totality and Infinity*, 207.
58. Marquardt, *Eia*, 537–38.
59. Levinas, *Totality and Infinity*, 208.

the eschatological distance from the totality of the Being. The Infinite transcends also all transcendence bound to immanence.[60]

His second major work, *Otherwise than Being, or Beyond Essence* (1974), focused on the extreme passivity of being assigned responsibility for another person. According to Levinas, to say is to approach a neighbor who is not exhausted in "ascriptions of meaning."[61] Saying as discursive communication is a condition for all communication as exposure. Proximity and communication are accomplished in saying rather than a modality of communicative rationality. Saying approaches the Other, breaking through the *noema* involved in intentionality, in expressing itself, and in being expelled.[62]

Saying uncovers the one who speaks in the sense that one discloses oneself by neglecting one's defenses, exposing oneself to outrage, insults, and wounding. The saying signifies the passivity, and in the saying, the passivity signifies exposure in response to the Other. The saying, the most passive passivity is a disinterestedness, "an otherwise than being" turning into a "for the Other," burning for the Other. The de-posing or de-situation of the ego, which is the very modality of dis-intrestedness, has the form of a corporeal life that is devoted to expression and to giving. This denotes a self despite self, and in incarnation characterized by offering, suffering, and trauma.[63] In a Christian understanding of incarnation, Jesus Christ represents disinterestedness, devoted to the face of the poor, the alienated, and the widow: being for the Other, God's minority people, *massa perditionis*.

Heidegger taught that the history of Western thought and culture since its Greek beginnings has been an "onto-theo-logy," which is theology in the guise of subject-object ontology conceived in a representational fashion. What is truly present is not the manifest unfolding of what is. The world is the reflection, the re-presentation of God, substance, and transcendental ego. Against this onto-theo-logy, Heidegger reintroduces a thinking of the world in its coming to be, without recourse to metaphysics. He sought a language in which being can speak. In his later turn, Heidegger appeals to the end of metaphysics through the poetry of

---

60. Ibid., 486–7.
61. Levinas, *Otherwise than Being*, 48.
62. Ibid.
63. Ibid., 49–50.

thought, the yieldedness, to hearken to the epochal revelatory voice of appropriation. Here, language is the house of being.

However, Levinas resists Heidegger's turn. "Speaking, rather than 'letting be,' solicits the Other."[64] Prior to language as a poetic harkening, saying retains a radical ethical sincerity. To some extent, the saying is exhausted in things said for Western philosophy. The trace of saying obliges the responsibility for the Other, which is never assumed and binds and obeys us to a command which is never heard. Religion is this relationship of responsibility for the Other. Religion "orders me in an anarchic way, without ever becoming or being made into a presence or a disclosure of a principle."[65]

For Levinas, ethic only comes into its own with the collapse of onto-theo-logy. His ethics as the first philosophy reflects on his own experience of victimization and genocide in our enlightened, but murderous century. According to Levinas, to be is not enough. To be or not to be is not the question, because ethics occurs as an-archy, the compassion of being. Responsibility in proximity with the Other is more precious than the fact of being given.

In *Otherwise than Being*, Levinas speaks of moral responsibility as the essential, primary, and fundamental structure of subjectivity. The very node of subjectivity is knotted in ethics understood as responsibility. He understands responsibility as responsibility for the Other. There is dia-chrony before all dialogue in which the signification of the face is an order signified. Subjectivity goes to the point of substitution for the Other, becoming initially hostage. The "otherwise than being" is responsibility that is incumbent on "me" exclusively. "I" can substitute "myself" for everyone, but no one can substitute himself/herself for "me." Such is my unalienable identity of subject.

In the presence of the Other, the Infinite enters into language. In Jewish mysticism, the faithful one begins by saying to God "Thou" and finishes the prayer by saying "He." It is as if in the course of this approach of the "Thou" its transcendence into "He" supervened. Levinas calls this situation the illeity of the Infinite. Here, the same is more and more extended with regard to the other, to the point of substitution as a hostage.

---

64. Levinas, *Totality and Infinity*, 195.
65. Levinas, *Otherwise Than Being*, 168.

In the last analysis transpires "the extraordinary and diachronic reversal of the same into the other in inspiration and psyche."[66]

The way in which the Infinite manifests itself in subjectivity is called the very phenomena of inspiration. The "otherwise than being" exists for the glory of God, because the idea of the Infinite expresses the disproportion which is inspiration itself. "My passivity breaks out in saying: "Here I am!" The exteriority of the Infinite becomes "interiority" in the sincerity of the testimony.[67]

Levinas, in his "God and Philosophy," further develops his conclusion in *Otherwise than Being*. For Western philosophical tradition, transcendence is destroyed in the name of immanence. Plato's term "beyond being" (*epekeina tes ousias*) exceptionally refers to the good. Descartes's proof of the existence of God in the *Third Meditation* affirms the idea of Infinity. This transcendence assumes an ethical meaning.

Levinas disrupts the concept of philosophy by inserting a God who is infinite, a God who comes to mind. In philosophical discourse, the God of whom the Bible speaks is situated within human existence. However, Levinas contends that "the God of the Bible signifies the beyond being, transcendence."[68]

Against the transcendence of God, the history of Western philosophy has been a destruction of God's transcendence. Thus, rational, ontological theology seeks to explain the transcendence of the God of Abraham, Isaac, and Jacob within the framework of being by articulating that God exists par excellence.[69] However, the God of the Bible is not reduced to ontology.

To the extent that both being and thinking arise in consciousness, Levinas thinks of consciousness in terms of the presence, which implies the identity of the Same, the presence of being, and return to itself. It is only a forgetting of the Other, by awakening the Same from within. The incessancy of presence takes up an apperception of representation.[70]

Levinas interprets the apperception of consciousness as a unified temporal horizon, in which everything that is real is present. Representation manages to hold the past and the future as present in

66. Ibid., 146.
67. Ibid., 146–47.
68. Levinas, *Basic Philosophical Writings*, 130.
69. Ibid., 131.
70. Ibid., 133.

consciousness. In the representation, what is present is bound in immanence. Through consciousness whose extreme form is reminiscence, the universal presence, and the universal ontology, the past is only a modification of the present.

Levinas challenges this presence of representation, arguing that philosophy is the reflection that binds reality to immanence. In fact, philosophy is representation, the reactualization of presentation and immanence itself.[71] At this point, Levinas regards the experience in religious experience as located clearly within consciousness and transcendental reflection. Religious experience does not shake a philosophy of immanence. Rather, religious revelation is assimilated to philosophical disclosure. The Word of God in freedom and action can be captive to the unity of the "I think."[72]

Insofar as religious experience cannot break with presence and immanence, Levinas is suspicious of Otto's argument that one can go from some sort of experience to a correlate numinous being, in which the being to which the experience corresponds is limited by the field of consciousness. However, Levinas contends that the Infinite signifies prior to its manifestation, and thus the meaning is not reducible to the representation of presence.[73] The idea of the Infinite is proper for negation of the finite so that the "in" of infinity affects subjectivity through the putting of the Infinite into it. The negativity of the "in" of the Infinite is otherwise than being, divine comedy hollows out a desire beyond satisfaction for what is beyond being; it is "dis-interstedness, transcendence–desire for the Good."[74]

Furthermore, the correlation of being and thinking is determined as the correlation of reality and its meaning. Against this philosophical tradition, Levinas raises a question of how to talk and think about God. Paradoxically, against Heidegger's rebellion against Descartes, Levinas uses the Cartesian idea of God to break up immanent ontology. This idea is the Infinite, an idea that thinks more than it can think. The basic structure of correlation is shattered in the idea of the Infinite in which one discovers one's passivity, one's lack of control in one's own thinking.

71. Ibid., 134.
72. Ibid., 135.
73. Ibid., 138.
74. Ibid., 139.

The Infinite comes into the finite. The Infinite, its difference from the finite, cannot be posited as a correlate of the subject.[75]

The metaphysical structure of the Infinite, beyond being, is performed in relation to another person, a person with material needs. In the desire for the Infinite there is no absorption in immanence, but the reference to the other which is awakening to proximity, a responsibility for the neighbor. Transcendence is ethics and subjectivity is a responsibility for the Other, a subjection to the Other, a hostage for the Other rather than the "I think," or the unity of transcendental apperception.

The way for the Infinity in proximity of others from the standpoint of illeity is a reversal of the "thinking I." To the degree that the goodness of the Good orients itself toward the Other, and thus toward the Good, ethics is otherwise and better than being rather than a moment of ontology. In this ethical reversal of disinterestedness, God is drawn out of presence and being, thus God's transcendence is true with a dia-chronic truth and without any synthesis.[76]

Given this fact, Levinas argues that the ethical signification of transcendence and of the Infinite can be worked out beginning with the proximity of the neighbor and "my" responsibility for the other.[77] Positing subjectivity in one's responsibility for the Other, one's passivity is consumed for the Other in which one is not in opposition to the Other. Such meaning is the consuming or surmounting of a holocaust.[78] Such an example can be seen in Abraham's intercession for Sodom.

For Levinas the saying is not what is said but is the giving of "myself" in giving words to another. Levinas calls the saying the signifying, the giving of a sign. This is a performative dimension of language. Using words can allow for meanings that exceed the correlation of thinking and being. Language is not a mere doubling of thought and being, but is the way to make oneself available for the Other, for whom one is already responsible. Saying as testimony precedes all the said. As "a way of signifying prior to all experience,"[79] saying therefore leads to a vital activity in

---

75. Ibid., 138–39.
76. Ibid., 141.
77. Ibid., 141.
78. Ibid., 143.
79. Ibid., 145.

the life of responsibility: witnessing. Saying bears witness to the Other of the Infinite by awakening me in this saying.[80]

PROPHETIC DIMENSION IN THE HERMENEUTICS OF GOD'S SAYING

Western philosophy appeared as the reduction of transcendence to immanence. But ethics of the Other appears as a discourse that attends to what cannot be thought so that forgetfulness of being is challenged by forgetfulness of the other. The ethics of the other can witness and speak of the saying present when that which exceeds words happens. The transcendence of God begins in a cry of ethical revolt, in prophecy.[81] Levinas calls this mode of discourse inspiration or prophecy, but he refuses to locate it in the confines of religious experience. Prophecy is a way to testify by speaking in responsibility to others. It does not refuse the said—a presence for others in words—nor the unsaying—a reopening of the philosopher for others.

For Levinas, biblical prophetism is embedded with the assumption of responsibility for the Other, which is a way of testifying to the glory of the Infinite. There is prophetism and inspiration in the humans who answer for the Other. This responsibility prior to the Law is God's revelation. Prophecy interprets itself in concrete forms of the public sphere. To be worthy of the messianic era, one must admit that ethics has a meaning, even without the promises of the Messiah. According to Levinas, the great miracle of the Bible lies in the confluence of different literatures toward the same essential content. The pole of this confluence is the ethical, which dominates the Bible. In the reading of the Scripture, one must add to this the necessity of confrontation and dialogue which calls for a hermeneutic of ethical other. The Scriptures signify through the expression of the face of the other person. A human life cannot remain life satisfied in its equality to being. Rather it is awakened by the Other.[82]

Saying institutes the relation of ethical egalitarianism and thereby recognizes justice. Through the face of the Other, being can present itself in identity. The saying is addressed to the face which demonstrates absolute resistance to the temptation of absolute negation, or murder.

---

80. Ibid., 145.
81. Ibid., 147.
82. Levinas, *Ethics and Infinity*, 122.

An ethic is not a corollary of the vision of God, but it is itself the vision of God. The way leading to God leads to human being. The justice performed to the other gives "me" proximity to God.[83] To be seized by the Good is total submission, thus it commands obedience prior to specific commands. This responsibility prior to obedience is the an-archic which transcends all principles to be universalized.

The Other which is presented as being absolutely Other, the radical alterity does not destroy or negate "my" freedom in relation to the Other. For Levinas, "being for the Other" is not the negation of the I. Only an "I" can respond to the injunction of a face of the Other.[84] In ethical perspective, the Heideggerian *Geworfenheit*, which marks a finite freedom, is thus revealed as the irrational. The encounter with the Other, according to Sartre, threatens "my" freedom. Here "my" freedom falls under the gaze of another freedom.[85] Levinas's resistance in the name of the Other to Heidegger and Sartre finds its parallel in Barth's critical analysis of Heidegger and Sartre regarding nothing and being. We confine our analysis to Barth's view of Heidegger.[86]

Barth examines and takes issue with Heidegger's basic statement that "existence means being projected into nothing."[87] Projection into nothingness, which is based on hidden dread in Heideggerian sense, is the overcoming of the transcendence. Thus, the human being becomes "the *locum tenens*" for nothing.[88] Enquiry concerning nothing is a metaphysical question according to which Heidegger expresses the potency of nothing against existence.[89]

Recognizing Heidegger's philosophy is not atheistic, however, Barth argues that for Heidegger it is difficult to envisage a place of God that exists outside Heidegger's threefold postulate of "that which is

---

83. Levinas, *Difficile liberté*, 38.
84. Levinas, *Totality and Infinity*, 304–5.
85. Ibid., 303.
86. Barth, *Church Dogmatics* III/3: 334–38.
87. Ibid., 335.
88. Ibid., 336.

89. However, Sartre understands that human existence is conditioned by nothing. Thus, Sartre demonstrates forceful denial of the existence of God for the sake of categorical Yes of human existence. Barth states that "in Heidegger we are concerned with the premise of Sartre, in Sartre with Heidegger's conclusion." Barth, *Church Dogmatics*, III/3: 338–39.

A Postmodern Ethics of the Other and the Hermeneutics of Saying

(human) existence and nothing."[90] Heidegger considers nothing as the pseudonym concealing the Godhead from the standpoint of human being. As far as human existence is founded on nothing, Heidegger's philosophy is "a mythological theogony."[91] To the degree that nothing is the basis, criterion, and elucidation of everything, human being can only be a *locum tenens*.

In 1929 Heidegger accepted Hegelian identification of nothing with being. Later in *Letter on Humanism* in 1946[92] Heidegger introduced the truth of being, under which he brings forth an idea of affirmation of being. Here, existence as projection into nothing becomes ecstatic, namely entry into the truth of being. God is only found as a dimension of being. Heidegger's dialectic pursuing Gnosticism and mysticism is vulnerable to the danger of real nothingness in the biblical sense. Such dialectic is not capable of understanding the transcendence of the biblical God in an authentic sense. Barth argues that the biblical conception of the living God is entirely unaffected by Heidegger's mythological fabrication. In Barth's concept of nothingness against Heidegger's concept of nothing, we perceive his critique of the reality of lordless powers in socio-economic and cultural political realms.[93]

Furthermore, Barth's critique of Heidegger's ontology of totalization can be seen in his later doctrine of God's words and lights in pluralistic contour *extra muros ecclesiae*.[94] Barth's hermeneutical recognition of the difference and otherness of words and lights in the world from the perspective of God's speech act is in affinity with Levinas's hermeneutic of saying over the said. We shall have an opportunity to discuss this issue in more detail in the next chapter regarding hermeneutical subject matter between Bultmann and Barth.

At any rate, for Levinas, a hermeneutic of saying in the face of the Other is embedded with an ethic in solidarity with the poor and the needy in the public sphere who are not capable of exercising a communicative rationality and argumentation. The saying of the Infinite which challenges and transcends "my" consciousness turns "me" to understand and interpret such speech act through the face of the Others, the mar-

90. Barth, *Church Dogmatics*, III/3: 343.
91. Ibid.
92. Heidegger, *Basic Writings*, 213–65.
93. Barth, *Christian Life*, 213–33.
94. Barth, *Church Dogmatics* IV/3.1 § 69.1.

ginalized, and the voiceless. Thus, justice comes from God the Infinite through the face of the poor, the needy, and the destitute—God's minority people.

CONCLUSION: ETHICAL-DISCURSIVE CONFIGURATION FOR THEOLOGICAL HERMENEUTICS

The universal dimension of hermeneutic and its linguistic discourse is sharpened and expanded in encounter with socio-critical theory of life-world and emancipation. A conflict of interpretation accentuated social-economic factor as effecting and characterizing existential intentionality in understanding of the text. A theory of interpretation does not need to exclude totality of life in the public sphere. Rather it presupposes and integrates complexities of life in a hermeneutical circle through analysis and reconstruction. The pursuit of a reconstructed life situation within socio-economic realms traces and grounds the individual's lived experience and life meaning in a social location. Socio–critical hermeneutic moves *à la recherche de temps perdu* to decipher the life horizon of those who are marginalized and silenced in the world of the text, and it further reconstructs an emancipation project toward a social historical praxis in today's theological existence.

For example, the texts of classical English economics provide a horizon for *Marx's Critique of Political Economy*, which implies Marx's social existential exposition of the social forces and economic relation in early capitalistic society in which he lived. Marx's theory of interpretation is undertaken through the scientific-dialectical analysis and appropriation of new meaning for the sake of interpretation of life experiences of those who suffer and are buried in the downside of the universal history of the privileged. This theory of interpretation belongs to a hermeneutic of suspicion.

History is no longer conceptualized following Hegel's notion of identity of absolute knowledge that universalizes and totalizes the complicated and multiple relations between the cultural life sphere and human consciousness into the Sameness. The history is radically immanent and present in our contemporary society, normalizing and underlying the discursive practices, institutionalized complex, and religious worldview of the powerful in the past.

This considered, history as the history of effect is to be reinterpreted as the history of discrepancy, imposing domination of the powerful upon the weaker. Social actual existence and ideological expressions in the interpretation of the text must be considered and undertaken in order to rescind the metanarative of the powerful, to enhance multiple narratives of the particular and the different, and to promote human praxis for the full humanity of those who are burdened on the underside of history. This interpretative strategy becomes a corrective to revolutionary excess in Marxism as well as to its unfortunate tendency to totalize different emancipation visions and projects in scientific positivism. A hermeneutical shift from the history of the effect to the discourse in social location sharpens a radical side of the interpretation rather than rescinding the tradition as the reservoir of meaning for us.

Social critical hermeneutics uncovers and explains the existence of false consciousness by analyzing reified structures of consciousness. It does this in view of social structures of lordless powers that come into being on a socio-cultural level through reification and through colonization of our lifeworld. An interpretation in defiance of violence and injustice is undertaken to explain and to understand the genesis of innocent victims' knowledge of realty in light of social existence and competing interests. Through the mediation of the texts and documents, hermeneutical comprehension is embedded with the dialectical reconstruction of the social and actual life.

Here, language functions as the appropriation of social material reality, revealing a historical reality of class struggle imposed from above to below. A critique of ideology and a deciphering of competing interests and conflicts within society do not undermine the place of intellectual, artistic, and idealistic spheres of contribution influencing the social material life. An epistemology from the top down is communicatively related to social material reality from the bottom up.

The content of human consciousness cannot be explained by a theory of cognition, or copy in a crude sense, because the content of consciousness cannot be regarded as copying or reflecting merely a social reality existing independent of it. If human consciousness is "conscious of" in the sense of intentionality, human consciousness is also shaped and characterized by the life horizon in the social cultural realm, together with the life of the other. The text is read to elicit what its subject matter intends. An intersubjectivity between intentionality of consciousness and lifeworld finds its validity in socio-critical hermeneutic in defiance of ideology and colonization of lifeworld through discovering the language of the silenced, the deviated, and the victim.

Narrative intentionality in the Bible is conversed and articulated anew in a living way through the continuity of ongoing textual dialogue and exegesis in proclamation of the Word of God within the faith community. The community's experience of the World of God and worldly occurrences ground their point of view and narratives in the world of the text, as conversely the text projects itself as the *kerygma* of liberation through exodus and resurrection before the faith community.

Language produces, elicits, and brings forth the human being and experience. *Kerygma,* the proclamation of something as something functions as an a priori of shaping and influencing human consciousness. Consciousness is linguistically constructed consciousness, and language as signifyingness and expression is prior to intentionality of consciousness. To the extent that all meaning reverts to the kergmatic structure of interpretation, every phenomenon is discourse or a fragment of discourse. As proclamation, or *kerygma*, language is signifying. The individual can only be attained in discourse. No matter what the content of discourse, genuine speech is contact proposing a relation with the Other. The saying, the discursive act of speech, does not exhaust itself in the representational form of "apophansis-as" which does not exhaust what there is in saying. What is the otherwise than being is stated in a saying.

Given this fact of priority of saying over the said, it is certain that Levinas conceives of the language in a Hebrew manner of *Davar* (Ps 33:9). The Word of God is in action, which is "speaking," discursive action. Given this fact, theological hermeneutic strives for its subject matter in the Scripture and self-reflectively on the way to living voice of God (*viva vox evangelii*) that speaks in action through the face of the Other.

Theological hermeneutics in deliberation on the Word of God brings all of the said to the saying, and critically reexamines the said in light of the saying and the unsaid, which underlines and promotes the narratives of the silenced and voiceless in the text. The signification of the discursive saying goes beyond the said. The signifyingness of saying beyond ontology justifies human experience of God's Word in analogical-discursive way. If the signification to the other occurs in proximity, which can be conceived of as a responsibility for the Other, God comes to us as speech event. An analogical dimension of language based on similarity-in-difference speaks of God, articulating the significant place of dissimilar and different discourse of those on the margin, namely God's people of minority.

The saying and the said in their analogical-discursive correlation denote the subject–object structure in interpretation of the text in which God as the infinite horizon of the text is the one who speaks through the face of the Other. Thus, language refers to a horizon transcending things represented. Meaning is always contextual, referring to other words, and situated within the multiple horizons of language game. Like language, human experience cannot merely be reduced into the metalanguage or metanarrative in description of universal experience. If human experience of the Word of God can be a reading of meaning, an exegesis, a hermeneutic,[95] it is essential to develop a theological hermeneutic of God's discursive act assuming analogical-discursive direction, expressing transcendental-ethical relationship with the other.

When language is the language of activity and event, language fulfills its analogical-discursive medium in bearing witness to the dynamic quality of God's speech event through the face of the Other. There is no such thing as a metanarrative or language into which all different languages and particular experiences with divine reality can be translated and communicated. Languages penetrate one another laterally, revealing meaning and expression through transhistoricity under an eschatological dimension. Thorough language which signifies transhistorically and transculturally, the discourse of the Other is revealed as bearing a relationship to the absolutely Absent, the beyond from which the Other comes.

Thus, a critical function of the discursive hermeneutic can be found in a theological discourse of *parrhēsia*, which approaches God by returning to others standing in the trace of illeity. It belongs to an essential dimension of *Sprachlichkeit* of theological hermeneutic. It is fundamental to propose a theological discourse of speaking *parrhēsia* for God's sake and for God's *massa perditionis à la recherche de temps perdu* in the trace of God's freedom and transcendence in the past as well in our present.

Here, theological hermeneutic of God's speech act *extra muros ecclesiae* (extra ecclesial sphere) in Barthian fashion meets a radical ethic in the face of the Other standing in the trace of God. God who is the Subject of speaking, speaks through the face of the Other. This is

---

95. *Levinas: Basic Philosophical Writings*, 38.

always posited as the poor, the stranger, the widow, and the orphan. A metaphysical idea of the Infinite meets a living God of Israel and Jesus Christ in Judeo-Christian religion in which God's radical presence in the ugly face of Christ speaks continually through God's people of *massa perditionis* in all corners of life. According to Barth, Jesus as the partisan of the poor and his relationship to his neighbors and sympathy with them belong to his innermost being. Jesus interposes himself for them, putting himself in their place so that he makes their state and fate his own cause. "Jesus is immediately and directly affected by the existence of His fellows."[96]

For Barth, the whole of *parrhēsia* in which we live as Christians or as witness to the world is undercut by the threat of inhumanity and one's exploitation of one's neighbor. Christian discourse of *parrhēsia* resists ideologically distorted forms of inhumanity and exploitation.[97] Different from Barth, Foucault seeks to rehabilitate *parrhēsia* as a form of speech that is both resistant to the doctrinal mode and alert to the religious categories that had come to be employed politically. Against humano-centrism, Foucault retrieves a Christian form of *parrhēsia* against fascist, totalitarian life and for the sake of the silenced.[98]

A theological discourse of *parrhēsia* speaks out against the reality of inhumanity and violence in contradiction to the myth of a Heideggerian ontology of nothingness. To the extent that a theological hermeneutic of God's discursive act is allied with an ethic of the Other through the theological discourse of *parrhēsia*, ethical-discursive configuration of hermeneutic challenges and dethrones the god of philosophers. Western philosophy and rationality is accomplished by way of the God of the scholastics, which is a god adequate to reason, a god of *theologia gloraie*. This comprehended god, who complements the autonomy of *analogia entis*, is a *deus ex machina* who finds in its adventures returning home like Odysseus who is only on the way to his native island through all his peregrinations.[99]

A theological understanding of Church and *theologia crucis* in light of God's speech event finds its permanent role in becoming negativity and corrective to totalization of metanarrative of rational discourse, up-

---

96. Barth, *Church Dogmatics* , III/2: 211. See Chung, *Karl Barth*, 419–48.
97. Barth, *Church Dogmatics*, IV/2: 442.
98. Bernauer and Carette, *Michel Foucault and Theology*, 77–97.
99. Taylor, *Deconstruction*, 346.

holding *parrhēsia* for the sake of those downtrodden in different place and time. Church and society thus understood *semper reformanda* in view of the subject matter (*viva vox evangelii*) of the Scripture as well as in listening to the voice of God through the face of the Other, standing in the trace of God as transcendent illeity.

An appropriation of meaning for those devoured in the history of the privileged is to be found in a hermeneutical critical reframing of history of effect in light of history of non-effect of the underprivileged. Prejudices and pre-understanding inherited and impacted previously by socio-cultural life horizon must stand hermeneutically and social existentially under a historio-critical investigation with respect to its dominant discursive practices and episteme in the past as well in the present. This perspective will be examined in our discussion of theological hermeneutics and its analogical, socio-critical and cultural-linguistic configuration in the next chapter.

9

Interpretation of Scripture and Analogical Hermeneutics

IN THE PREVIOUS CHAPTER, we discussed a debate between hermeneutic theory and social critical theory. In the sociological-hermeneutical debate, a theory of interpretation can be reframed with a shift from a historical, diachronic horizon toward a social-synchronic location. A theory of interpretation gains its sharpened character by critically distancing itself from a tradition that presents itself as a distortion and dominion of cultural life. Furthermore, a theory of interpretation gains a pubic character when the subject matter of the text opens a projection of its horizon in front of the reader; such projection calls for multiple interpretations in the public domain rather than revealing one univocal meaning. The text as a written discourse characterizes its social critical character by integrating a sociological interest in emancipation. In a social location of interpretation, an issue of the Other is seriously raised by Levinas. When a theory of hermeneutics is uninterested in the ethical commitment to the life of the Other, it becomes an ideology of totalizing the Other into Sameness.

For Christian theology to proclaim effectively the biblical message, it must first seek to understand the Scripture and interpret the message for the Church in the public sphere. The more seriously Christian theology takes the Word of God, the more it takes on a hermeneutical character, encountering the life of the others in the public sphere. In this chapter, we shall be concerned to examining theological hermeneutics, paying attention to hermeneutical theology of Rudolf Bultmann in view of Karl Barth and Gerhard Ebeling. Then we will further deal with David Tracy's analogical imagination and Lindbeck's postliberal theology in hermeneutical perspective.

HERMENEUTICS AND THE INTERPRETATION OF SCRIPTURE

Heidegger's relationship to theology becomes obvious in Rudolf Bultmann and the so-called school of the New Hermeneutics represented by Gerhard Ebeling and Ernst Fuchs. Rudolf Bultmann (1884–1976) was a colleague of Heidegger, with whom he was closely associated during their stay at the University of Marburg in the 1920s.

Early on, Bultmann allied himself with Karl Barth, forming dialectical theology in protest of liberal theology. Liberal theology intends to incorporate the divine within the horizon of human experience and history, viewing the realization of the kingdom of God as a progress advanced within world history. For Bultmann, however, God is the subject matter of theology to the extent that God radically negates and sublimates human being. The recognition of God as "wholly other" or as crisis is the basic principle of the dialectical theology.

When the second edition of Karl Barth's *The Epistle to the Romans* appeared in 1922, Bultmann's review expressed a considerable degree of agreement. Bultmann and Barth share Wilhelm Herrmann as a common teacher who attempted to secure the independent place of religion, in other words, "the 'wholly other' of the world of faith."[1] Bultmann is well known for his radical program of demythologizing the Scriptures. The idea and the program of demythologizing originated between the years 1922 and 1928, when Bultmann was in close contact with Martin Heidegger during his Marburg stay.

Bultmann's point of departure lies in Heidegger's ontology expressed in *Being and Time*, the existentialist interpretation of human being-in-the-world. Heidegger's fundamental theory of being centers on being itself as the ground of all that is. There is an ontological difference between being itself and all that is (existents). Due to the distinctive feature of the human's peculiar mode of being, a human being, different from animal, projects him/herself in freedom and thus realizes his/her existence in the world. The human's distinctive mode of being, which consists of the transcendence of human existence, enables a human being to surpass all individual existents. A horizon of all human understating is constituted in reference to being, rather than in a metaphysical

---

1. Schmithals, *An Introduction*, 11.

concept of God. At every moment of human present existence, a human being is determined by both past and future.

For Heidegger, metaphysics (that is, onto-theo-logy) maintains the separation between the realm of the sensible-empirical and the metaphysical-supranatural realm from Plato onwards. The subject-object schema affirms this representational thinking. Only the individual existent is considered in relation to being and forgotten being itself. The history of being can thus be regarded as a history of forgetting being.

According to Bultmann, the message of the Scripture lies in its existential appeal. This appeal is clothed in a mythological form of discourse, an expression of the worldview and thinking of the times that shapes and influences the writers of Scripture. Bultmann argues that the business of theology is to penetrate this mythological shell via interpretation. In other words, it must pass through what is merely said to what is actually meant—the existential core of the text.

When Bultmann lectured on his hermeneutic of demythologizing program (entitled "The Problem of demythologizing the New Testament Proclamation")[2] to the pastors of the Confessing Church in Frankfurt (April 21, 1941), its controversial ramification was immense. Bultmann's hermeneutic of demythologizing articulates that the New Testament was written at a time when mythical thought and worldview of a three-storied structure (according to which the earth lies between heaven and the underworld) held sway. Heaven is the dwelling place of God and of angels, while the world below is hell in which Satan and his demons dwell. These supernatural powers intervene in natural occurrences and human life. All these mythological languages can be traced back from the mythology of Jewish apocalyptism and of the Gnostic myth of redemption.[3]

However, people of modern thinking in the public sphere, who are shaped by modern science, are not familiar with the ancient worldview. People who have come of age through science and technology since the enlightenment are not forced to accept *sacrificium intellectus*. Bonhoeffer's recognition of the world come of age also finds its echo in Bultmann's hermeneutical concern of how to relate and interpret the message to modern people in the public sphere.

---

2. Bultmann, *New Testament and Mythology*, 1–43.
3. Ibid., 2.

The modern worldview offers a critical standard for the exegesis of Scripture to the extent that myth is to be reinterpreted and reunderstood. The *kerygma* in the New Testament refers to God's action in Christ for human salvation. Interpretation aims at uncovering the *kerygma* rather than radically rejecting mythological language. Speaking of God as Father means speaking of God's love, God's concern for humanity, and God's action for our sake. Such language is an analogy or language of analogical imagination. The language of analogy is understood in an unmythological sense.[4]

Demythologizing is not an instrument of rationalist demystification and iconoclasm in the manner of Freud, Nietzsche, or Marx. Instead, it regards the mythical symbol as a window to the sacred. To interpret the symbol or myth is to collect its original, authentic meaning by interpreting hidden meaning in anthropological—or better—existentialist terms.[5]

For example, if the *kerygma*, or the message of God's act in Christ for salvation, is seen as the kernel, the mythological language and worldview is the husk. In Bultmann's view, the mythological eschatology of Jewish apocalypticism and Gnostic eschatology are already eliminated by St. Paul and St. John.[6]

Theological interpretation distinguishes what is said from what is meant and measures up the former by the latter. Bultmann's "what is meant" (that is, the true kernel of the Scripture) is essentially what is meant also by Heidegger's existential hermeneutics. Bultmann's interest is both philosophical and methodological in its intent. In agreement with Dilthey, Bultmann quotes Dilthey's letter to Graf York:

> All dogmas must be reduced to their universal value for every human life. They were formulated once under a historically conditioned restriction.[7]

If dogmas are seen in light of historical restriction and condition, they are the expression of human historicity. Bultmann attempts to retrieve a demythologizing dimension of the New Testament message in light of the eschatological event. God's salvation seen in Christ, which

---

4. Schmithals, *An Introduction*, 263.
5. Bultmann, *New Testament and Mythology*, 9.
6. Ibid., 18–9.
7. Ibid., 22.

has history-transforming meaning, is expressed in terms of the eschatological event. The word of proclamation calls us to believe in the death and resurrection of Christ as the eschatological event, opening us up to the possibility of understanding ourselves.[8]

KERYGMA AND THE SUBJECT MATTER OF INTERPRETATION

In *The Problem of Hermeneutics* (1950), Bultmann states that in any interpretation, one must consider first the vital existential relationship which both the author and the interpreter share with respect to the matter at hand as expressed in the text.

Schleiermacher constitutes a hermeneutical rule in a sympathetic way: putting oneself in the author's place for understanding the text. The social life of the human being in speech and understanding is formed on the basis of general human nature. Interpretation is a matter of re-production (or reconstruction) taking place in living relation to the process of literary production. The author and the interpreter constitute a commonality of universal human nature in speech and understanding. Dilthey further developed Schleiermacher's psychological interpretation with respect to life experience in a historical connection. Dilthey describes hermeneutics as "the art of understanding expressions of life fixed in writing."[9] Dilthey narrows down hermeneutics to expressions of life that are fixed in writing, that is, monuments of culture and literary documents including works of art.

As a New Testament scholar, Bultmann is concerned with the exegesis of Scripture. The New Testament contains the Word of God that is *kerygma*: "To hear the Scriptures as the Word of God means to hear them as a word which is addressed to me, as *kerygma*, as a proclamation."[10] An historico-critical investigation of the New Testament reveals that the canon is not identified unreservedly as the norm of the Word as the Word of God. Luther, with whom Bultmann was allied, demonstrates his hermeneutical approach in his preface to the Epistle of James. For Luther the true touchstone for testing the scrip-

---

8. Ibid., 39.
9. Ibid., 69.
10. Bultmann, *Jesus Christ and Mythology*, 71.

tures is to discover whether they emphasizes the prominence of Christ or not. "All Scripture sets forth Christ."[11]

In this regard, Luther argues that what does not preach Christ is not apostolic, not even if it is taught by Peter or Paul. However, what does preach Christ is apostolic, even if Judas, Annas, Pilate or Herod teaches it.

What Luther calls "emphasizing the prominence of Christ" is for Bultmann the Word, that is, God's saving event.

The exegete's task is to disclose the understanding of the Scripture with the best possible method. Heidegger's ontological hermeneutic corrects and improves the psychological method of interpretation regarding Schleiermacher and Dilthey. In all cases, the interpreter's specific interest in the text determines the course of the interpretation. This implies that interpretation is not possible without presuppositions, guided by a preunderstanding of the subject matter. The subject matter of the text, according to Dilthey, is the personal, historical life as underlined and fixed as expressions of life in the texts.[12] Bultmann accepts Dilthey's concept of a hermeneutical circle (experience-expression-interpretation) as a presupposition of understanding. Every interpretation "grows out of the context of life to which the subject matter belongs."[13]

The interpreter approaches the text with a question, asking what the text wants to communicate. Interest in the subject matter motivates interpretation and further provides a way of asking questions.[14] The text itself was not written to answer interpreters' questions. Therefore, the enquiry, the direction of the investigation, and the hermeneutic principle arise from the interest of the subject. The object of interpretation can be established by interest in history as the sphere of life in which human existence lives and moves. In this light, Bultmann affirmed the freedom of inquiry, that is, the historico-critical method. The Bible is subject to the same condition of understanding that is applied to any other books. Bultmann's combination of pre-understanding and historico-critical method prioritizes the historical condition of the interpreter.

Furthermore, Heidegger's existential analysis of history and the historicity of human existence find its influence in Bultmann's existential

11. Dillenberger, *Luther Selections*, 35–36.
12. Bultmann, *New Testament and Mythology*, 73.
13. Ibid., 74.
14. Ibid., 76.

interpretation of the Bible. The objective of interpretation can be given and guided by an interest of the interpreter in reconstructing and actualizing the continuum of past history.[15] An interest of the interpreter in history as the sphere of life provides the objective of interpretation. All texts are subjected to the interest or questioning of the inquirer, which is guided by pre-understanding. Without such a pre-understanding and a questioning constituted by it, the texts remain silent. At issue here is the critical assessment of the pre-understanding for understanding the text.[16] The present shapes and determines the past!

The understanding of history presupposes an understanding of the efficient forces that connect the individual historical phenomena. Such forces include economic needs, social exigencies, political struggles for power, human passions, ideas, and ideals. In assessing such factors, the individual historian is guided by some specific way of raising questions, some specific perspective.[17]

For instance, we cannot understand Luther's Reformation theology without understanding Roman Catholicism at his time. We cannot understand the *Communist Manifesto* of 1848 without understanding the principles of capitalism and socialism. Hence, "Historical understanding presupposes an understanding of the subject matter of history itself."[18] The historical understanding always presupposes a relation of the interpreter to the subject matter expressed in the texts. This relation is grounded in the actual life-context in which the interpreter stands.

This encounter between interpreter and history is defined as the "existential encounter."[19] Existential concern in interpretation is to hear the text anew in each new situation under critical interrogation and investigation of the text. In other words, history, in its objective content, can only be understood by a subject who is existentially moved and alive. Augustine's remarks are compelling: "Thou hast made us for thyself, and our heart is restless, until it rests in thee."[20]

According to Bultmann, there is a presupposed life-relation between the exegete and the subject matter of the text, and together with

15. Ibid., 83
16. Ibid., 84.
17. Ibid., 148–49.
18. Ibid., 149.
19. Ibid., 150.
20. Ibid., 87.

this relation a pre-understanding. This pre-understanding as an existential encounter is not a closed one, but rather it remains open. "The meaning of the text discloses itself anew in every future."[21] To support his existential interpretation without discarding the historico-critical method, Bultmann further develops his hermeneutics of demythologizing. According to him, myth talks about reality, but in an inadequate way. This way of perceiving reality is for Bultmann demythologizing or disenchantment of the world in Weber's sense.

However, against an empirical-scientific or value-free methodology, Bultmann proposes the modern understanding of history that sees reality as the reality of human beings existing in history. Human being as existence does not mean a mere presence like plants and animals, but rather a specifically human mode of being. Bultmann's interpretation of history, called existential interpretation, attempts to reinterpret mythological languages that appear more plausible to the modern reader. Since God is not an objectively ascertainable phenomenon in the world, God must be interpreted existentially. The testimony to God's creatorship and transcendence has a legitimate ground only in the existential self-understanding of human being. It is a hermeneutical method.[22]

HERMENEUTICS AND THE CRITIQUE OF SUBJECT MATTER

Bultmann's program of demythologization, which belongs to a post-critical age of faith, intends to better comprehend the text and to realize the intention of the text, which speaks of the event. The genuine hermeneutical circle is methodological in character. Here a socio-critical interest, an interest-constitutive question, finds its place in Bultmann's hermeneutical critique of subject matter.

The hermeneutical circle, which does not suppress a critical-mythological query, originates from the fact that all understanding presupposes a pre-understanding; the text's answer is—to a certain extent—shaped by the interpreter's question, while the subject matter of the text corrects the question. The hermeneutical circle is a presupposition of all historical critical understanding, which in turn moves in this circle.

---

21. Ibid., 151.
22. Ibid., 99.

As Heidegger says, "what is decisive is not to get out of the circle, but to come into it the right way."[23]

The hermeneutical circle becomes important in the critique of subject matter. For Bultmann, critique of subject matter is to distinguish between what is said and what is meant, measuring up what is said by what is meant. Such critique is a critical means for understanding the text in the light of the subject matter. The critique of subject matter which serves to clarify the matter, moves in a hermeneutical circle. Radical demythologizing for Bultmann is the parallel to the Pauline-Lutheran doctrine of justification by faith alone without the works of the law.[24]

The Scripture principle of the Reformers is, rightly understood, a hermeneutical principle. For Luther, the *res* of Scripture can remain a mystery while the grammatical sense of Scripture can be clear to anyone. This position is different from the orthodox identification of Scripture with the Word of God. The return to the theology of the Word of God resulted from a passionate wrestling with the hermeneutical problem. In this light, the various prefaces of Barth's *Romans* are also impressive testimonies to that.

As Barth argues in the preface of his second edition of *Romans*, "the critical historical people are not critical enough for me." The basic hermeneutic impulse of Barth's dialectical theology does not displace the right of the historico-critical method of research. We are aware of two different directions: the passion for the Word of God tends toward the disparagement of the hermeneutic problem, while the interest in the hermeneutic problem appears to jeopardize what is said of the Word of God.

Furthermore, Barth considers that God speaks to us in our sociopolitical sphere. Barth's delineation of the kingdom of God as theological subject matter integrates the in-breaking reality of God into our social location. To see through our social location to God's irruption is a more critical and radical approach than the historico-critical method. Thus, a social and political problem, seen in light of Barth's principle of understanding, becomes foundational for shaping and characterizing the meaning of historical criticism.[25]

---

23. Heidegger, *Being and Time*, 195.
24. Schmithals, *Introduction*, 122.
25. Chung, *Karl Barth*, 9.

Barth's *Church Dogmatics* presents an implicit answer to the hermeneutical problem. The hermeneutical problem in Barth has been taken up into the discussion of the subject matter of theology. For Bultmann, the theme of hermeneutics is the methodological vindication of a theology of the Word of God.

Like Barth, Bultmann is faithful to the theological statement that God is truly revealed in Jesus Christ, so that Christian *kerygma* enters into human life as something new and unexpected. In his existentialist interpretation, the statements of Christian confessions are not reduced to statements about the inner life of a human being. The existentialist interpretation takes into account the fact that a human being exists only in a living connection and encounter with God. Bultmann wants to clarify the objective reality of God as the reality outside the believing subject, who is indispensable for Christian faith in answering the peculiarity of human existence. Barth is basically in agreement with Bultmann regarding the objective side of God, but is working out a genuinely theological concept of reality rather than an ontological clarification.[26]

Barth brings out the unity of hermeneutics by claiming a general necessity for the hermeneutics to be dictated by the Bible. According to Barth, there is no such thing as a special biblical hermeneutics. The only valid hermeneutics has to be learned by means of the Bible as the testimony to revelation.[27] Contrary to Barth, however, Bultmann approaches the hermeneutical problem from definite standpoint of general hermeneutics. For Bultmann, the language of faith has recourse to analogies. God summons me as a person, encounters me as a friend, and commands me as a father. These expressions are a way of speaking analogically. The concept of the *analogia entis*, against which Karl Barth fought all his life, provides Bultmann with an adequate way of representing God's act, which is analogous to the human act.

Critically viewing Bultmann, Ricoeur argues that, for Heidegger, the existential description does not just concern a person but also the place. *Dasein* is "being there" or "being in the world." This aim is not for anthropological or existential humanism.[28] The meaning and the objectivity of the text, which holds the two elements of myth and *kerygma*, initiates the existential movement of appropriation of meaning. The act

---

26. Gollwitzer, *Existence of God*, 26.
27. Barth, *Church Dogmatics*, I/2, 466.
28. Ricoeur, *Conflict of Interpretations*, 399.

of God has its first transcendence in the objectivity of meaning, thus *kerygma* takes an initiative on the part of meaning, making speech a correlate of existential decision.[29] Being is coming into language. Ricoeur is convinced of Heidegger's *Letter on Humanism*. Only in the light of the essence of divinity, "whatever the word God names can be thought."[30]

Furthermore, Ricoeur advocates for an eschatological aspect in light of Christian hope and freedom, which entails a communitarian, historical, and political expression. Bultmann runs the risk of reducing the rich content of eschatology to an existential understanding.[31] In this light, Ricoeur is critical of the Greek Christologies which disguise the God of the promise, the God of Abraham, Isaac, and Jacob, by making the incarnation the temporal manifestation of eternal being and the eternal present.[32]

As far as a relationship between the proclamation of the Word of God and a cosmic manifestation of the sacred, Ricoeur transcends a limitation of Bultmann's program of demythologization. Israel's experience of the luminous is not entirely eclipsed in the religious life of Israel, despite its emphasis on the prophet's iconoclasm. The Word of God can be recorded and integrated into Israel's experience of the sacred as visible in the Wisdom writings. Experience of the mystery of the sacred is taken up into hermeneutics of the Word of God, which reemploys such language and symbolism as a support for the new language as revealed by God to the community of Israel. If Golgotha becomes a new *axis mundi* for the Christian, every new language is the reemployment of an ancient symbolism.[33]

HERMENEUTICS OF WORD-EVENT AND UNIVERSAL HISTORY

The approach developed by Bultmann and those who followed him received the name *the new hermeneutics*. According to the later Heidegger, interpretation has its focus in terms of language rather than in terms of understanding human existence. In the new hermeneutics, it is not

---

29. Ibid., 398.
30. Ibid., 400.
31. Ibid., 407.
32. Ibid., 406.
33. Wallace, *Second Naiveté*, 39.

a human being who is expressing him/herself in language; rather, it is language itself that speaks. However, Bultmann's hermeneutics focused on human existential self-understanding and analyzed the Scripture in terms of the historico-critical method.

Gerhard Ebeling turns to language itself and its relation to reality. According to Ebeling, existence is existence shaped and influenced through word and in word. Bultmann's existentialist interpretation can be developed and improved as interpretation of the text with regard to the word-event.[34] Ebeling has made the word-event the center of his hermeneutics of word-event. For Ebeling, the object of hermeneutics is the word event as such. In the realm of Biblical hermeneutics, understanding is not understanding of language, but understanding through language.[35] Language as speaking transpires in the world of what is ready-to-hand. Therefore, language is located at the center of human nature rather than a tool of an objectification of an authentic self-understanding.[36]

Like Bultmann and Barth, Ebeling regards theology as relating to the event of proclamation, namely the praxis of the kerygma of the church. Without this ecclesial praxis, theology would be blind.[37]

According to Bultmann, the structure of human existence as such is questionable, so that human being approaches the text as a questioner. Interpretation requires a relation of life to the subject matter expressed in the text. What guides the interpretation depends on the interest behind interpretation—pre-understanding. The most fundamental interest which can guide an interpretation is the interest in history as the sphere of life. Human existence acquires and develops its possibilities in history. In history, which is an expression of the possibilities of human existence, we come to a knowledge of our own possibilities.

At issue in interpretation of the New Testament is for Bultmann to examine the understanding of human existence expressed therein. Bultmann's basic question—*what does it mean to speak of God* (1925)—is fundamental to his existentialist interpretation of Christian discourse about God. Here, talk about God becomes possible as talk about ourselves. The New Testament is relevant only as a possibility of understanding human existence regarding authenticity or inauthenticity.

34. Ebeling, *Word and Faith*, 331.
35. Ibid., 318.
36. Robinson et al., *New Frontiers*.
37. Ebeling, *Theology and Proclamation*, 20.

Bultumann's concept of the kerygma's addressing to the human existence is integrated by Ebeling to develop his theological hermeneutics. The linguistic event of revelation in listening to the Word of God provides theology its proper object. This occurrence includes Bultmann's proper concern of existential interest.

For Ebeling, the Word of God is not any special, supernatural Word, but simply the finally valid Word in a true and proper sense. The Word discloses understanding in the act of discourse or as a verbal event. So, the theological hermeneutic is defined as the theory of the Word of God. To the degree that the word-event unlocks understanding, the basic structure of the Word is not a statement in the sense of information, but the message in the sense of communication, which discloses human existence. The objectifying statement has a derivative mode of understanding and language. For Ebeling, the true nature of the word and language as the communication of existence and the word which opens up existence is the promise. Ebeling sees the true nature of word and language in general as fulfilled in the gospel as the *promissio Dei*.

Given this fact, Ebeling attempts to integrate the transmission of the Word of God as the history of effects in light of the word-event which took place in the gospel of Jesus Christ. Therefore, Ebeling transcends Bultmann's existential hermeneutic in terms of the word-event in the concept of the Word of God by including the process of tradition. The Word of God is interpreted as a history of effect extending linguistically the history of Jesus, while the Word of God is interpreted as the truth of word and language in general in the event of communication and promise. The true meaning of language as the communication which unlocks existence makes authentic existence possible.[38]

For Ebeling, speaking about God means speaking about the all-determining reality as conceived of as present and active in every event. Similarly we see such a parallel in Barth's theology of irregularity of the Word of God associated with the word of reconciliation. However, Pannenberg asks how God's reality active in language can turn human language into the Word of God. Pannenberg argues that there is in Ebeling's hermeneutical theology still an element of positivity because of

---

38. For the critical analysis of the relationship between Bultmann and Ebeling, see Pannenberg, *Theology and the Philosophy of Science*, 169–77.

his focus on a revelatory authority. Against Ebeling, Pannenberg argues that the revelatory authority must be rationally proven.[39]

Attached to the rational verification of the revelation, however, Pannenberg does not consider a linguistic-discursive character of analogy as a language event in connection to God who is the infinite horizon of all-determining reality. The Christian concept of revelation does not depend on human rational verification. In hermeneutical perspective, Jüngel makes a contribution toward theological analogy by refining Ebeling's theology of the word-event and overcoming the limitation of Pannenberg's attempt to integrate the Word of God into the totalizing metaphysical framework of universal history. A hermeneutical theology of analogy begins with God's particular history in the gospel of Jesus Christ which is analogous talk about God as all-determining reality.[40]

Pannenberg's concept of universal history in a Hegelian fashion justifies and upholds a theological metanarrarive which reduces and totalizes all particular and different expressions of human possibilities in different history and contexts into a pan-eschatological vision of prolepsis. The analogical character of language—similarity in difference—is left behind for the sake of the progressive movement of universal history, which sidesteps those historically on the margins.

Pannenberg's position is induced by Gadamer's hermeneutic. Thus, he affirms that the task of interpretation is an attempt to fuse the horizons of the author and the interpreter. Such a horizon presupposes the totality of history as its ultimate frame of reference.[41]

For his concept of universal history as the totality of history, Pannenberg accepts Dilthey's concept of experienced meaning in the historical life context. According to Pannenberg, this meaning is accessible only in the anticipation of a future which has not yet appeared. Here, the idea of God as the all-determining reality in universal history places the hermeneutical concern within historical confines rather than coming together.[42] Furthermore, Pannenberg shares his view with Moltmann's project of anticipation and making present of the end of all things for the deliverance of all things.[43]

39. Ibid., 281–82.
40. Jüngel, *God as the Mystery*, 261–98.
41. Pannenberg, *Theology and the Philosophy of Science*, 284.
42. Ibid.
43. Ibid., 285.

ANALOGICAL-NEGATIVE HERMENEUTICS

Bultmann's analogical imagination regarding God's personal relationship with us finds its echo in David Tracy's theology of analogical imagination. On the other hand, Barth's critique of liberal theology in the second edition of *Romans* (in which Barth utilizes the Kierkegaardian principle as a counter proposal to the Cartesian and Hegelian modernist concept of human reason and experience) offers an impulse to Lindbeck for a cultural-linguistic study of religion. Analogical hermeneutics and the postliberal framework, while moving in different directions, present themselves as different ways of reframing the relevance of religion for the public sphere.

David Tracy, an important Catholic theologian, represents a hermeneutic of analogical imagination for Christian systematic theology. In introducing systematic theology as hermeneutical, he calls for a systematic theology as interpretation in contrast to authoritarian, dogmatist, and fundamentalist theologies, all of which are ideologies or mere repetitions.

For the hermeneutical project of Christian theology, Tracy rejects two poles: an autonomous self, free from the influence of history, tradition, and language, and a dogmatist approach for the sake of heteronymous obedience to the tradition itself. The word "hermeneutical" is defined by Tracy as a description that denotes a realized experience of understanding in conversation. All reflections in which the subject matter determines the questioning have a properly hermeneutical character. This hermeneutical model admits "the ground of real finitude and radical historicity in all hermeneutical understanding."[44]

Interpretation of the text for Tracy is taken as realities-in-process, which demands the interaction of genuine conversation to actualize the questions of the interpreter and response of the text. In other words, it implies the identity-in-difference in the process of an ever new and ongoing interpretation. The fusion of horizon takes place when the reader allows one's present horizon to be vexed, provoked, and challenged by the claim of the text itself.[45] Like Gadamer, Tracy gives the classic text "an excess of meaning."[46] Thus, every interpretation, as a mediation of past

---

44. Tracy, *Analogical Imagination*, 103.

45. Ibid., 105.

46. Ibid., 102.

and present and a translation, is carried on within the effective history of a tradition for retrieval of its strange and familiar meanings.[47] However, a hermeneutical retrieval of meaning in the sense of appropriation is juxtaposed with a critical distanciation of the ideologically distorted system of language. When Tracy proposes Gadamer's concept of conversation, it is certain that, for Tracy, an ideology-critical function comes from an understanding of language through language.[48]

In the process of conversation between the text and the reader, the real meaning of a text may be uncovered by deciphering the mind of the author, the social circumstances, the lifeworld of the text, or the reception of the text by its original addresses.[49] Nonetheless, Tracy argues for "the need for the controls of historical criticism, social scientific methods or ideology critique for all our classics"[50] in favor of the dialectic of an authentically critical understanding. Hence, the subject matter (for instance, "*kerygma*" in Bultmann's sense) becomes a question for the interpreter. Furthermore, Tracy accepts Ricoeur's interpretation theory as offering an important corrective to the Heidegger-Gadamer tradition. In all discourses, the said (the noematic, ideal meaning) is distanced from the saying (the noetic and temporal event of discourse). Rather than being imposed from outside of history or of the text, a critical distanciation is essential to any expression or interpretation.

For a Christian analogical imagination, Tracy finds analogical and dialectical languages as the principal candidates. A language of analogy is defined as a language of ordered relationships that articulates similarity-in-difference and produces some harmony to the several analogues constituting the whole of reality. In Christian systematics, the primary focal meaning is the event of Jesus Christ, proving itself as the primary analogue for the interpretation of the whole of God's reality. When the Christ event is acknowledged as the radical mystery of the self-manifestation of God, incarnation calls for us to consider negation in the interpretation of reality in view of God's mystery. In Tracy's concept of analogy, a negative aspect in talk about God's event comes to the fore, so that it is articulated as principles of intensification, negating any slackening of the sense of radical mystery.

47. Ibid., 99.
48. Ibid., 101.
49. Ibid., 105.
50. Ibid., 106.

In the theological use of analogies, the *via eminentiae* becomes possible only on the condition that the *via negationis* is upheld. The ultimate incomprehensibility of God's event provides the focal meaning for developing analogies-in-difference.[51] Furthermore, any analogical concepts emerge from dialectical relationship between critical reflection and real participation in God's radical event so that analogy never loses the intensive power of the negative. When this negative power is lost, analogical language of similarities-in-difference becomes degenerated into a mere likeness.[52]

Aristotle's dictum is attractive for him: "to spot the similar in the dissimilar is the mark of poetic genius."[53] A participatory act in the originating event and self-distanciation from the event, in terms of the self-constituting demands of critical reflection, is at the heart of an analogical imagination that offers the profound similarities-in-difference in all reality. Here, Ricoeur's dictum gains a sharpened contour: "The symbol has given rise to thought but thought now returns reflectively to the symbol expressing the event."[54]

When thought returns reflectively and critically to the symbol, a critical method should be allowed for an existentialist deciphering of the symbol. When analogical imagination loses the sense for the negative, the Christian cataphatic concept of grace becomes "cheap grace" (Bonhoeffer). Tracy's theological task is to express in the reflective form of negative dialectics when the proclaimed word reveals God's grace to Christian faith. The negative dialectic, which is inherent to the subject matter of the proclaimed word, constitutes the dialectic of theological language. This is reminiscent of Barth's dialectical theology of crisis, because the Word of Jesus Christ discloses the reality of the infinite, qualitative distinction between God and self-justifying self. "Let God be God" becomes the watchword of the theology of the Word of God.[55]

In Barth's study of Anselm and in his *Church Dogmatics* he articulates a theological language of the analogy of faith and grace. Barth's concentration on God's revealed Word in Jesus Christ includes a constitutive dialectical component within its analogical form. His positive language

---

51. Ibid., 409.
52. Ibid., 410.
53. Ibid.
54. Ibid., 411.
55. Ibid., 415.

of analogy of grace or *analogia relationis* heads toward a universalism in which his dialectical analogical language focuses on the event of Jesus Christ. Like Tracy, the essence of God is not comprehended *per analogiam*. Rather God's action in self-communication in Jesus Christ offers a ground for a functional similarity in biblical designations of God in an analogical, personal manner.

For Bultmann, the language of *kerygma* can be positively conceptualized in analogical-personal terms, while recognizing God's transcendence. Tracy appreciates that Bultmann articulates a genuinely theological, analogical-dialectical language. Bultmann's hermeneutic correlates the reality of God and the reality of the human in existentially meaningful terms.[56]

At least, Barth's language of analogy offers an insight into human life in a particular social location rather than remaining in the personal-existential realm. From early on, Barth's language of analogy, which finds its concrete political expression in the "Tambach lecture" (1919), has a connection with his later political-analogical theology in "The Christian Community and the Civil Community" (1946). For Barth, the line and direction of Christian judgments, purposes and ideals in socio–political affairs is undertaken concerning the parabolic capacities and needs of political organizations in view of the coming kingdom of God.[57] The public political sphere, which stands in support of democracy and "the greatest measure of social justice," can serve as an analogy or a parable in the service of the Kingdom of God.[58]

Different from Barth's theology of analogy, Tracy's project of hermeneutics is to develop a Christian theology of analogical imagination based on Gadamer, Ricoeur, and (to some degree) Habermas, in view of the reality of pluralism in the public sphere. Tracy steers and navigates a breathtaking journey between the Scylla of foundationalism (based on a modernist concept of rationality) and the Charybdis of postmodern relativism (based on anti-subjectivism). The merit of hermeneutics is that it takes the historical context with full seriousness, thus abandoning foundationalism without becoming a prisoner of anti-subjectivism. In this light, it is necessary to consider his concept of analogy and dialectic in terms of similarities-in-difference.

56. Ibid., 418.
57. Green, *Kark Barth*, 280.
58. Ibid., 284.

Furthermore, influenced by Habermas, Tracy argues for the necessity of shifting from text toward discourse, from historical and diachronic emphasis toward social location. The historical consciousness can become cultural and economic as well as social and political, as seen in the case of political theology, liberation theology, and feminist theology. In hermeneutical terms, the meaning of historical consciousness and historicity has two overarching consequences. First, is the widespread recovery of practical philosophies (for instance, the Aristotelian concept of *phronesis* or the Hegelian and Marxist concept of praxis). Second, is post-Heideggerian and post-Gadamerian hermeneutics. The use of critical theory in view of Habermas and also the development of a hermeneutic of suspicion in view of Ricoeur locate Tracy's hermeneutics of analogy in socio-critical terms, or in the public sphere.

Political, liberation, and feminist theologies have clearly demonstrated our problem with history (the tradition) and in history (our present social, economic, political, and ecclesial situation). This hermeneutic in social location, applies the hermeneutic of suspicion to all human realms including: ideology, dominion, gender, race, and class issues in all theological interpretation and all hermeneutics. It demonstrates not merely correction, but advocates for the transformation of reality by way of praxis.

Nevertheless, in Tracy's language of analogical imagination similarity-in-difference does not fully articulate an interplay between analogy and discourse in a social cultural location in light of the power-knowledge nexus. If a hermeneutic of existence in a diachronical sense shifts toward a hermeneutic of suspicion or an ideology critique in a synchronic sense, should not an analogical imagination of similarity-in-difference be explored in a socio-political and cultural lifeworld where God breaks into the public sphere for the sake of those who are burdened and alienated economically, politically and culturally? If Jesus utilizes secular and dissimilar discourse of *massa perditionis*, a hermeneutic of analogical imagination should take into account the discursive form and practice of those historically and socially on the margin. To what extent does the analogical imagination retain the unique narrative of Christian discourse on the God of Israel and the father of Jesus Christ in a society of religious pluralism? In this regard, it is important to deal with postliberal theology and its interpretive dimension in a socio-cultural and linguistic perspective.

POSTLIBERAL THEOLOGY AND WORLD OF TEXTUALITY

Lindbeck moves away from Tracy, finding a problem in post-Enlightenment or liberal times to the degree that religious doctrines have been understood as non-discursive symbols of inner feelings, attitudes, or existential orientations.[59] Lindbeck calls this approach the experiential-expressivist conception of doctrine. Experiential-expressivism portrays ecclesial teaching as a function of the historicity of human expression or inner feeling, which is inclined to a subjectivist orientation (in view of Schleiermacher, Troeltsch, and Bultmann).

In the experiential-expressive framework, Christian doctrine remains a non-informative and non-discursive symbol of human experience. If one follows a logic of experiential-expressivism in an interfaith context, every religious experience would fundamentally remain the same. As an exaggerated example, a Buddhist might have the same faith as a Christian, even though they would express it in different ways.[60] This critique is indirectly aimed at David Tracy, when Tracy argues for his concept of a godhead above god in the Christian mystical sense and an analogical imagination in engagement with an inter-religious dialogue.

Lindbeck's postliberal or cultural-linguistic framework of doctrine insists that doctrine should function as a communally authoritative rule of discourse, attitude, and action rather than as expressive symbols or truth claims.[61] Like culture, religion resembles language in its correlative forms of life; thus, doctrine functions as a normative grammar. Thus, doctrines in a cultural-linguistic framework offer a stable and yet flexible identity in light of the Word of God.

At this point, there is an influence of Wittgenstein on Lindbeck. In the *Tractatus Logico-Philosophicus* (1921), Wittgenstein states that language pictures the world.[62] In his famous conclusion he argues that what "we cannot speak about we must pass over in silence."[63] Later on he changed his view that language has a single purpose to state facts. Wittgenstein, in his *Philosophical Investigations*, argues that language as elementary expression abides with grammar: "Essence is expressed by

---

59 Lindbeck, *Nature of Doctrine*, 16.
60. Ibid.,17.
61. Ibid.,18.
62. Wittgenstein, *Tractatus Logico*, 39.
63. Ibid.,151.

grammar."[64] The grammar of terms is embedded in everyday language. Every word has a meaning correlated with the word. Language is inseparable from activities, for instance, in commanding, greeting, asking, etc. Participating in these activities, we learn our native language. In fact, we learn both forms of words and forms of life. The whole of language and the activities weave into one another. The speaking of language is part of activity, that is, a form of life. For Wittgenstein, theology is the grammar of the word "God." "God loves me" is a matter of dogma, which shapes Christian identity in a particular-grammatical way of life. Christian and Buddhists think differently to the extent that they use different grammar of language in a different life context.[65]

Thus, Wittgenstein advocates for viewing context itself as a network of interrelated and mutually constitutive meanings that shape the meaning of discourse. A truth claim is shaped by the vast complexity of circumstances that life offers and it also influences life.

His concept of language game implies that each use of language transpires within a separate system with its own rule, similar to playing a game. To the extent that each use of language constitutes a separate language game, the various games has little to do with one another.[66] Wittgenstein's insight into language games contradicts Descartes's principle of *cogito* existing apart from a social context. As a language game is correlated with a form of life, so a culture has cognitive (epistemological) and behavioral (influencing factor of human experience) dimensions, as well.[67] The concept of truth as correspondence with reality, in other others, a picturing of reality is abandoned. Instead, the truth is characterized as an internal function of language dependent on its context, namely, the language game. Insofar as any sentence has multiple meanings in diverse contexts in which it is used, we cannot claim for the final truth in any ultimate sense. In fact, language is a social construct, and its meaning is acquired in social interaction.

Human experience is shaped and constituted in a cultural and linguistic location. Given this fact, Paul Tillich's famous dictum—religion is the substance of culture, and culture is the form of religion—can be better situated, according to Lindbeck, in the following way: religion is the

64. Wittgenstein, *Philosophical Investigations*, 371.
65. Brenner, *Wittgenstein's*, 150.
66. Wittgenstein, *Philosophical Investigations*, 32.
67. Lindbeck, *Nature of Doctrine*, 33.

ultimate exterior of culture, shaping and constructing the experiential matrix, which achieves, in turn, significant cultural life.

Allied with Barth's critique of liberal theology and Wittgenstein's insight, Lindbeck characterizes his position as non-foundational or post-liberal in the sense of overcoming the foundationalism of philosophical Enlightenment. The holistic world of Christian doctrine and practice as language–games poses a meaningful frame of reference for the believer's experience, not vice versa. Lindbeck accords interpretive priority to the normativeness of doctrinal tradition and also to the understanding of the Scripture in connection with the ecclesial community.

If the Christian doctrine Is "given" in an ecclesial-linguistic episteme, how do Christians criticize the tradition of the ecclesial community regarding its fatal mistakes and failures in the past against people of other cultures? It is certain that Lindbeck is open to the possibility that people of different religions and cultures may have an incommensurable concept of truth, experience, and categorical adequacy of "God."[68] Nonetheless, a Christian understanding of the public feature of religion is not to be conceptualized as expressive and evocative symbolization or externalization of human internal or existential experience.[69] For instance, Lindbeck rejects the notion that Meister Eckhart's and Shankara's descriptions of mystical union are likely to imply the same experience. Lindbeck stands in contrast to sentiments claiming that Buddhists know more about contemplation, while Christians know more about social action, and thus perhaps they can learn from each other in the spirit of complementarity. Against this expressive-experiential route, Lindbeck illustrates that the agonies of Grunewald's *Crucifixion* cannot be imaginable from an image of goodness on Buddhist soil.[70]

However, Lindbeck does not go far enough. For example, an image of goodness, compassion, and beauty of the lotus on Buddhist soil cannot be adequately understood without a connection to the Buddhist expression of the serious painful agonies inherent in the reality of human-cosmic suffering (*dukkha*). Rather, the crucifixion in light of the Lotus (symbolic flower of enlightenment) can become a corrective to the Western theological imagery of forensic atonement or the sacrificial language of violence and crusade, which has been a part of ecclesial

68. Ibid., 49.
69. Ibid., 21.
70. Ibid., 84.

doctrine. Religious discourse or interfaith dialogue is not reduced to the different world of language games. Furthermore, religion—at least for Wittgenstein—is not the same as religious doctrine. Religion is a spirit that can pervade all language games.[71]

For Lindbeck, a cultural-linguistic approach may allow a strong case for an interreligious dialogue.[72] Lindbeck rejects the idea that all religions share a core experience of God. To suggest otherwise benefits no one. This does not exclude a theological-doctrinal rationale for commitment to interreligious discussion and cooperation.[73] However, should not a post-liberal, non-experiential theology recognize the different as different to the extent that a cultural linguistic episteme involves a self-critique of the power-knowledge configuration regarding an ecclesially distorted language of doctrine?

At any rate, Lindbeck understands theological faithfulness as intratextuality. This refers to a commitment to the authority of the Biblical text and its validated understanding in the doctrinal decision and interpretation. Lindbeck's famous statement reads: "it is the text, so to speak, which absorbs the world, rather than the world the text."[74] Intratextuality is compatible with a cultural-linguistic approach, while an extratextual method is compatible with a propositional or experiential-expressive approach.

Therefore, Lindbeck's attempt is to re-describe reality within the scriptural framework rather than translating Scripture into extrascriptural categories. Clifford Geertz's understanding of the ethnographer's work as "thick description" offers Lindbeck a good analogy for deciphering a thick description of the lifeworld of the ecclesial community. What makes theology intratextual is that it explicates religion from within in the stronger sense; in other words, it describes everything from inside, as interpreted by the "religious shaped second-order concepts."[75]

Just as a history of effect presupposes human understanding and existence, intratextuality—the explication of religion from within—blocks human mimetic creativity in an interpretive-critical engagement with ecclesial communal language of doctrine. Like the anthropologist, the

71. Brenner, *Wittgenstein's*, 151.
72. Lindbeck, *Nature of Doctrine*, 53.
73. Ibid., 54.
74. Ibid., 118.
75. Ibid., 115.

theologian must offer a close, detailed description of scriptural meaning and coherence, wisdom, and fulfillment, which individuals, society, and history can find within the Biblical narrative world. A hermeneutical approach runs the risk of locking the ethnographer's analysis from "the informal logic of actual life." With recourse to Geertz, Lindbeck argues that culture or religion is not a power, something to which social events or institutions are attributed. Rather it is a context, "something within which they can be intelligibly—that is, thickly—described."[76]

The task in the study of religion and culture is to undertake a thick description of the context without a place of subject. A language, culture, or religion is employed to give meaning to a new domain of human thought. To make a thick description possible, a theologian needs to explicate a multiplicity of complex conceptual structures that are at once strange, irregular, and implicit. He/she is not to generalize across cases but to generalize within them. Such description is literally intratextual rather than metaphorical.

According to Lindbeck, culture's radical pluralism actually enters the method of theology, and it is employed as a medium for translating the gospel to the world, whether existential, phenomenological, or hermeneutical. The pluralism permeates and results in that translation in terms of extrabiblical categories, content, and meaning by substituting Christian unique narrative. For Lindbeck, rationality or foundationalism, as it actually functions, is only context-specific.

However, Lindbeck seems to ignore that historical-linguistic tradition also conditions human existence and understanding. At issue for Lindbeck is the application of the rules of the doctrinal tradition to the ever-changing circumstances of life, culture, and history. Postliberal theology is skillful in demonstrating the text's capacity to absorb the world in the sense of application, particularity in view of the culture of pluralism. For him, a scriptural lifeworld and narrative is able to absorb the multiple horizons of the universe.[77]

Along the line of Reformation theology, Lindbeck contends that the theological task is an exegetical description of the Christian web of belief systems, self-understood as scriptural narrative. The Reformers resisted allegorizing interpretation and put the greater emphasis on intratextual-

---

76. Ibid.
77. Ibid., 117.

ity (*scriptura sui ipsius interpres*), highlighting the importance of proclamation. Scripture was interpreted by its use: the *viva vox evangelii*.[78]

At this juncture, Lindbeck rejects Ebeling's hermeneutics of the Word of God, for the sake of literal and intratextual meaning and its application to the modern world.[79] Ebeling takes Luther's insistence on the *verbum externum* seriously for the process of human proclamation of God in human words. Every talk of God is worldly, humane, and secular talk, which Lindbeck appears not to have considered sufficiently in his construction of a cultural-linguistic study of religion in reference to the public sphere.

Perhaps Ebeling's limitation stems from his basic thesis that "God comes to expression as event."[80] This thesis has its ground in the word–event implying a universal human potentiality constitutive of the essence of language. Although Ebeling states that the word-event takes place in the gospel, he is careful to clarify the special revealing event of Jesus Christ in reference to Yahweh's speaking to Israel in promise of it. In a linguistic event through which one speaks the gospel to another and opens a future, the Word in a Biblical context always refers to the Word of the Speaker, God's saying in action. God speaks and uses humanity for God's speaking.[81]

At any rate, for Lindbeck, meaning is not what the text reveals and discloses in front of the text for those who have extraneous metaphysical, historical, or experiential interests.[82] Meaning has to be that which the text says in terms of communal and ecclesial language for which the text is an instantiation.

Against a cultural-linguistic framework of religion, however, God's Word happens and illuminates human existence in an ongoing way, involved in human social existence. The divine speech opens up and brings human existence to understand and to encounter the reality of divine speech to the world. This is an indispensable aspect of Luther's discovery of the Word of God: a post-foundational and an irregular side of God's

---

78. Ibid., 118–19.

79. Ibid., 119.

80. Ebeling, *Word and Faith*, 325.

81. For a critique of Ebeling in light of *verbum Dei loquentis*. See Gollwitzer, *The Existence of God*, 179.

82. Ibid., 120.

saying, which stands over that which is literally and intratexually written and said.

However, Lindbeck is skeptical of human experience in interaction with God's historical action. For him "the grammar of religion, like that of language, cannot be explicated or learned by analysis of experience, but only by practice."[83] Christian theology begins by hearing and testing what the Word of God has been and is proclaimed to be in the churchly sphere. Given this fact, Karl Barth, in his exegetical emphasis on narrative, appears to be a theological mentor of intratextual postliberal theology in the fashion of a cultural-linguistic concept of religion and a regulative view of doctrine.[84]

Unlike Lindbeck, however, Barth's theology of the Word of God is deeply embedded in the centrality of Jesus Christ, who is the primary understanding of the Word of God. The Word of revelation occupies the higher position as compared to a written, narrative form of the Word of God and its proclaimed form within the ecclesial sphere. Jesus Christ as the Lord of the Church and the Lord of the world is free to speak to us through the churchly and scriptural narrative tradition and also through extrabiblical narratives or worldly occurrences.[85]

The latter side refers to Barth's irregular and post-foundational (in the sense of post-ecclesial) dimension coming out of God's Word, which is always in action to speak freely to the world. In the doctrine of reconciliation in *Church Dogmatics* 4/3.1 § 69 (which esamines the extraecclesial words and lights of God) Barth fully develops his theology of the Word of God in a particular, inclusive, and universal sense in light of God's reconciliation with the world. God may speak to us in a completely different manner in the reconciled world. Listening to this extrabiblical voice of God, the church remains humble and open before the mystery and freedom of God. For Barth, human language and imagination can serve as analogies to God's mystery as *ratio veritatis*. In this light, human language or hermeneutics is accepted as *misterium verbi divinis* rather than being rejected. This aspect is a flaw in Lindbeck's project of postliberal theology, although it is, nonetheless, an important contribution to ecumenical ecclesiology in a postmodern era.

83. Lindbeck, *Nature of Doctrine*, 129.
84. Ibid., 135.
85. Barth, *Church Dogmatics* I/1.

10

Christian Mission and the Interpretation of the Gospel in the Presence of the Other

Levinas contends that the Other must be closer to God than oneself. The Other's priority is given in relation to oneself, in which the face of the Other is the source of ethic for oneself as well as the medium through which God, the Infinite, speaks to "me." Levinas's hermeneutic of God's saying over against the said marks a new development in the theory of interpretation in a more public and ethical sense, listening to God's voice from the face of the Other. Similarly, Barth's theology of God's Word considers a dialectical relationship between the regularity of divine speech and its irregularity in an analogical configuration. A theology of God's Word expresses a hermeneutical dimension in which the divine speech event precedes and transcends ontological discourse and interpretation.

When God speaks to the Christian Church, listening to God's "saying" leads Christian existence to a humble attitude and a spiritual poverty before God's mystery and freedom at work in the lifeworld of religious outsiders. This hermeneutical listening is connected with ethical justice that respects the Other, doing so in an interfaith and intercultural context, where it is important to take seriously the wisdom and experience of religious Others.

This chapter will investigate cross-culturally the Christian encounter with the Chinese people during both the seventh century of the Tang dynasty and the sixteenth century of Ming dynasty. Christianity in the Tang period came from Persia, and its missionary head was Alouben. He was a monk and most probably a bishop, who took the inroad to Chinese culture which flourished amidst three co-existing religions: Daoism, Confucianism, and Buddhism. In the intercultural encounter and cross-fertilization, a Christian interpretation of the gospel is woven into a multi-religious tapestry of non-Christian belief systems, languages, and ethical codes.

On the other hand, the seventeenth century Jesuit missionary Matteo Ricci entered Ming dynasty China embarking on a mission of accommodation or inculturation in finding similarity-in-difference between Christianity and Confucianism.

These two cases offer examples for seeing the Christian mission in terms of interpretation of the gospel in the presence of Others. If interpretation takes into account the socio-cultural and religious language of people of other faiths, otherness and difference among people in indigenous cultures is appreciated. Thus a different understanding of the Christian discourse and message is promoted and respected. A Christian mission constitutes an indispensable communicative bridge to the Other, engaging in a social cultural life of people of other faiths in a multi-religious society.

INSCRIPTION TEXT IN THE "NESTORIAN" TABLET

The Stone Sutra stele in the Forest of Stone Steles Museum, Xi'an reads: "The luminous Religion from Roman Empire becomes popular in China."[1] James Legge translated the full title as *The Eulogistic Verses on the Stone Monument (Commemorating) the Diffusion of the Illustrious Religion in the Middle Kingdom with Prefatory Notices*.[2]

During the Ming dynasty in China, construction workers, in the course of excavation, digged a grave in the countryside near Xi'an in Shaanxi Province and happened to discover a huge stone stele buried deep in the earth. Although the exact date of discovery is unclear, scholars generally date the discovery between the years 1623 and 1625. The monument is engraved on dark gray limestone, standing about eight feet high, over three feet wide, and about a foot thick. The tablet has been part of the collection of ancient stone inscription in the Beilin, or forest of stones in Xi'an.

The inscription in the stone stele is entitled "Monument of the Spread of the Jing Religion of Da Qin in China." Surprisingly enough, it

---

1. Li, *Study of the History*. See Palmer, *Jesus Sutras*.

2. Legge, *Nestorian Monument*.. Wylie translates the full title of inscription of the Nestorian Monument as "Tablet Eulogizing the Propagation of the Illustrious Religion in China, With a Preface; Composed by King-Tsing, A Priest of the Syrian Church." See Inscription of the Nestorian Monument, vol. XXIII.

reported the arrival in 635 CE of a new religion to China. (The inscription dates to 781.) A formal delegation of Christians arrived in Xi'an, most likely from Persia, traveling along the Silk Road. The Silk Road facilitated trade between China, Central Asia, and beyond including the Roman Orient. Caravans from the Silk Road brought traders and jugglers, monks and pilgrims, carpets, food and animals from far away Persia, Armenia, Byzantium and Central Asia to China. Many towns on the Silk Road became the meeting places for people along from many different religions: Christians, Buddhists, Manicheans, Zoroastrians, and later Muslims.[3]

The stone tablet now stands in the Beilin Museum in Xi'an (ancient Chang'an). The upper part depicts a cross entwined with dragons. Other carvings on this section include a Maltese cross emerging from a lotus flower, depicted among a cloud and two branches. The lower part of the tablet is the inscription containing 1,756 Chinese characters and some seventy Syriac words. On the narrow sides of the stone are an additional 70 lines in Chinese and Syriac.

HISTORICAL BACKGROUND OF "NESTORIAN" CHURCH

The stone tablet, which is also called the "Nestorian" Tablet of Xi'anfu, is an indication of Nestorian Christian activities in the Tang period. The term "Nestorian" implies certain prejudices, which may not reflect the reality of Christianity as practiced in Tang China. The text merely documents the existence of East Assyrian Christian activity and understanding in Tang China.[4]

In order to avoid the "Nestorian" misnomer, some historical background about the Nestorian Church (called Chaldean Syrian Christianity) in reference to the Assyrian Church of the East is in order. Nestorius was the patriarch of Constantinople (428–431) who came into conflict with Cyril of Alexandria, the patriarch of Alexandria. John Nestorius was neither an Assyrian, nor did he know Syriac language. He was a native of Antioch and Patriarch of Constantinople. As a disciple of Theodorus of Mopsuestia, he was ordained as a presbyter at Antioch, and followed the traditions of the Antiochian school. Nestorius took issue with the term

---

3. Li, *A Study of the History*, 77–78. Against this positive view of Christianity in pre-Tang dynasty, see Gillman and Klimkeit, *Christians in Asia*, 265–67.

4. Wickeri, "Stone Is a Mirror," in 19–46.

theotokos, or "mother of God," an idea supported by the Alexandrian school. "Call ye not Mary, mother of God," said Nestorius, for she was but human and God cannot be born of a human being.[5]

At the Council of Ephesus in 431, Cyril successfully accused Nestorius of heresy for teaching the division of Christ into two natures: the eternal *logos* and the separate human, Jesus, son of Mary. (This was exclusively a Western Church controversy at the time, and the Syrian Church had no involvement in it.) The Assyrian Church of the East was established in Edessa, a small kingdom between the Roman and Parthean Empires in the first century of the Christian era. Mar Mary, who was sent to Persia by the fellow workers in Edessa, began to organize the Church in the second century. The teaching of the four gospels in Aramaic in the Church in Edessa spread to the Persian Empire.

From about 280 CE Mar Papa organized this Church. The metropolitan seat of Seleucia became the headquarters (now known as Salman Park, thirty miles from Baghdad). Mar Aprim the Assyrian represented the Church at the first ecumenical council at Nicea in 325. He is recognized by the Roman Catholic Church as a doctor of the Universal Church.

Resulting from the persecution of Nestorius' followers, many Christians fled from the officially Christian Roman Empire and found refuge among the followers of the Church of the East. The headquarters of the Church, Selucia-Ctesphon, was at a strategic place on both banks of the River Tigris, which was the center of travel between Europe and Asia. By the middle of the sixth century, the Church had spread into Egypt, Syria, Arabia, Mesopotamia, Persia, India, Ceylon, China, and Mongolia. This Church had great missionaries who widely covered Asia. They spread the gospel all across the vast Asian continent, at great personal cost, often including martyrdom. The Assyrian Church missionaries included bishops, priests, monks, and deacons. Here, the work of the missionary became a blessing to the nations, far from demonstrating Christian sense of superiority over and exclusion of wisdom and belief system of non-Christian people.

The Church of the East uses the Aramaic Bible "Peshitta" as its text. "Peshitta" comes down from Biblical times, unchanged and unrevised. Its doctrine of the Holy Trinity conforms with that of the Council of Nicea, at which it was represented. The Church professes Jesus Christ Our Lord

---

5. Holm, *The Nestorian Monument*, 36.

and God in two natures; namely, divine and human in one person of the Son of God. These two natures are united eternally and inseparably. However, it rejects the term *theotokos* or "Mother of God" used for the Blessed Virgin, holding that the term has no scriptural authority, and that consequently it is prone to misunderstanding and error.

The Church of the East regarded Nestorius as an adherent of the orthodox faith in regards to the two natures of Christ and to the rejection of the appellation "Mother of God." His excommunication at Ephesus, then—according to the Church, would compare to the excommunication of the Apostles in the Western Church. However, the Apostolic Catholic Assyrian Church of the East to this day is commonly known to Western Christianity as the "Nestorian" Church. This misnomer has led many to think that Nestorius established Church, and that it received its teaching from his followers.

It is recorded on the stele. During the rule of the Accomplished Emperor Taizong (627–649 CE), there was a man of the highest virtue called Alouben in the country of Da Qin. Guided by the azure clouds, he carried with him the true Scriptures. In the ninth year of the period Zhenguan (635 CE) he arrived at Chang'an.[6]

After reading the text, a local magistrate in Xi'an figured out that it described the same religion that Western Jesuit missionaries in Beijing spread. Soon thereafter, a copy was taken to a friend in Hangzhou, Li Zhizao, a Jesuit-Christian scholar. A rubbing of the Stone was sent to the Jesuits, who discovered in it a brief history of the Christian message. The first translation into Latin was made by a Jesuit priest in 1625. A copy was also sent to Alvarez Semedo, the Jesuit Procurator of the Provinces of China and Japan. It then spread to Europe.[7]

However, as the news of the discovery of the tablet spread out, several Western scholars called its authenticity into question. The French philosopher Voltaire even denounced this slab of stone as a Jesuit forgery. Chinese anti-Catholic activists challenged that this tablet was Catholic forgery for the propaganda of the Christian religion. However, we cannot doubt that China established a long history of good relations with

---

6. Li, *Study of the History*, 90. For the different translation of the text see Moffett, *A History of Christianity*, 1. 291. Moffet's translation is borrowed from a Japanese scholar Saeki's translation. See Saeki, *Nestorian Documents and Relics*.

7. Gillman and Klimkeit, *Christians in Asia*, 271.

Persia even before the Tang dynasty. These two countries exchanged ambassadors between 627 and 649.

According to *Tang huiyao* (The Notabilia of the Tang Dynasty published in the Song dynasty, 961 CE), the origin and presence of the Da Qin Monastery is reported. The evidence of the first Christian missionaries who came from the East Syrian Church is hard to dispute. The Church existed for over two hundred years, namely from the seventh to the ninth century. Undergoing persecution, it saw a time of restoration later in the Mongol Yuan period.[8]

CHRISTIAN INTERACTION WITH CHINESE RELIGIONS

The first section of the inscription explains Christian doctrines such as the creation of man and the universe, the fall of man, the incarnation, salvation, Baptism, and ascension. It concludes with a eulogistic section, and then, there is a listing of about seventy-five names of bishops, monks, and presbyters in Syriac and Chinese on the bottom as well as on the sides.

In the line of VI of the inscription, we read biblical witness to the incarnation: Our triune divided God's entity, and Mishihe, the honored one of the Jing Religion hides His true Majesty and was born to be a man. A virgin brought forth the Holy one in Da Qin. Persians saw its splendor and came with tribute.[9]

Although James Legge (1815–1897) finds no indication of the gospel in the inscription,[10] it is certain that the text includes East Syrian missionaries' self-understanding of Christian doctrine in theological, existential, and intercultural way in interaction with Chinese culture and religions in Tang dynasty. Alouben's Christianity in the seventh century was called the Religion of Light, or religion of reverence of Heaven.

The text in line IV of the inscription discusses the life and work of monks of the luminous religion: Christ's ministers of the luminous religion bear the seal of the cross, keeping their beards and shaving their crowns. They hold the water of baptism as initiation to their religion to

---

8. There is a debate regarding whether Christianity in the period of Yuan dynasty is inherited from the Christianity in the earlier period. For the study of Christianity under the period of Yuan China, ibid., 285–98.

9. Li, *Study of the History*, 112. For Wylie's different translation Wylie, *Inscription of the Nestorian Monument*, 36.

10. Legge, *Nestorian Monument*, 54–55.

cleanse and purify all superficial appearance and the neophytes. They have no inward affection of their own. They worship facing east to hasten the faithful believers on the road to life and glory. They do not keep male or female slaves. They do not amass goods and wealth, displaying devotion and generosity to Chinese communities. "Purification is made perfect by seclusion and meditation; Self-restraint grows strong by silence and watching."[11] Seven times a day there is ritual praise, praying for the great protection or benefit of the living and the dead. On the seventh day, there is a public service, washing the heart to restore purity. These statements clearly indicate that it was a monastic type of Christianity in Tang China.

The inscription remains an object of scientific research and also the subject matter of interpretation inviting the interpreters to the lifeworld of Chinese Christians in the Tang dynasty. Additionally, the existence and the development of the East Syrian Church in China were further confirmed by the discovery of several Chinese Christian manuscripts in one of the caves in Dunhuang, China, in the early twentieth century. The famous "Manuscripts Cave" was used as a manuscript–storage room in the first half of the tenth century. Near the end of the nineteenth century, Wang Yuanlu, a Daoist monk discovered this cave at Dunhuang. A secretary library indicates that the cave had been sealed around 1005. Most of the scrolls in the cave room were Buddhist, Confucian, and Daoist. Cave 17 contained an enormous library of important manuscripts including Christian and Manichean writings in Chinese and central Asian languages.

Along with these scrolls, there were other scrolls telling of Jesus the Messiah. These scrolls, written in Chinese, were Christian books calling themselves the sacred book of Jesus the Messiah or "Jesus Sutra."[12] The "The Jesus Messiah Sutra, " or "Jesus Sutras" are the sacred literatures of the Christian Church of China of the Tang and early Sung dynasties from the early seventh to the eleventh century.

The stone tablet discovered near Xi'an is a monument in commemoration of the diffusion of the Da Qin Religion and erected in honor of the Syrian priest Yisi. A eulogy for Yisi, the Christian dignitary who is likely honored for the stele, follows. His Persian name was Yazdbozid (or Jazedbuzid). He is described as a highly decorated court official and

11. Gillman and Klimkeit, *Christians in Asia*, 273.
12. Ibid., 275–76.

general in the Chinese army of the three emperors, but also as a priest and rural bishop of Khumdan: Yisi is the one who "expended his acquisition in deeds of benevolence" and his "science surpassed that of the three dynasties." He is "a man of harmonious nature and loving to do good, hearing the Way [Dao] and diligently practicing it."[13]

He came from the city of Rajagriha and served in the Emperor Suzong's palace, was appointed assistant to Duke Guo Ziyi, the famous general, and helped to suppress a rebellion. Despite holding such a high position, Yisi behaved as an ordinary person and made donations to charity work and for the renovation of church buildings: The hungry are fed; the cold are clothed; the sick are cured and restored to health; the dead are buried and laid to rest in their graves.[14] "Every year he gathered the monks of the surrounding monasteries together; acting reverently, serving precisely, he provided everything for fifth days."[15]

Yisi is such a purest and most self-denying *Dasuo*, whose goodness was never heard of. *Dasuo*, as compared to the Persian word "*tars ā*[set macron over a]" (fearer of God), implies Christian rather than *Tarsa* as the transcription of the Sanskrit term *dasarhas* means Buddhist.[16] Yisi was mentioned as "the Imperially-conferred-purple-gown priest, titular Great Statesman of the Banqueting-house," He was associated Secondary Military Commissioner for the Northern Region, and Examination-palace Overseer.[17] Yishi is praised as the priest who distributed wealth in deeds of benevolence and did not accumulate treasure for his private use in keeping with the discipline of the illustrious religion. His charitable activity and excellence was never head of even among the most pure and self-denying of the Buddhists.[18]

According to the inscription (line XV–XVI), the great emperor Gaozong (650–683) supported monasteries of the Jing religion (Christianity) and built them in every province. He held Aluoben in esteem, and raised him to the Lord-king of the Great law for the whole

---

13. Ibid., 271.

14. The Inscription, line XXV–XXVI; Li, *Study of the History*, 96. See Moffett, *History of Christianity*, 300.

15. Gillman and Klimkeit, *Christians in Asia*, 272.

16. Li, *A Study of the History*, 29. I am less convinced of Wylie's interpretation of Yisi as a Buddhist priest. Wylie, *Inscription of the Nestorian Monument*, 40.

17. Wylie, *Inscription of the Nestorian Monument*, 40.

18. Ibid.

country. In the seventh month of the year 638 the imperial proclamation was issued. "The Greatly-virtuous Olopun (Aluoben), of the kingdom of Syria" established instruction "in accordance with the object of benefiting the people at large." Having examined the principle of this religion, the emperor deemed the Western religion to be beneficial to all creatures and advantageous to humankind.[19]

The Jing religion spread through all provinces and monasteries filled in a hundred cities. Families in China were richly blessed by this religion. According to the Inscription text, the Jing religion spread in Taizong's time (638) and reached its climax during the time of Tang Gaozong (650–683).[20] Gaozong honored Aluoben as the great spiritual lord and guardian of the country: The State became enriched, every city was full of churches, and the royal family enjoyed blessing and happiness.[21]

According to line XVI–XVII of the Inscription text, the Buddhists took advantage of the strength and made their voices heard in the capital of the Eastern Zhou in the year of Shengli (698–699). When the emperor died in 683, the days of persecution began under the Buddhist Empress Wu, who set up a new dynasty (690–705), changed the name of dynasty Tang to Zhou. The Empress became a follower and a defender of Buddhism. The Buddhists hailed her as an embodiment of Messiah Buddha, the Maitreya. The Christian churches in China were invaded and sacked.[22]

When Empress Wu retired in 705, the Church began to recover. The Emperor Tang Xuanzong, who took office in 712, supported the restoration effort. In lines XVII and XVIII of inscription, we read that "Xuanzong, the emperor of the Perfect Way," visited the blessed temple and rebuilt an altar. The sacred stone, thrown down for a time, was again replaced. In 744, a second missionary team from Persia, under the leadership of Chi-ho, arrive at Xi'an. The emperor ordered the monks Luohan, Pulun, and seven other missionaries, with Chi-ho of great virtue, to practice meritorious virtue and perform a thanksgiving liturgy in the Hsing-ch'ing Palace.[23]

19. Ibid. 37–38.
20. Moffett, *History of Christianity*, 292.
21. Wylie, *Inscription of the Nestorian Monument*, 38.
22. Moffett, *History of Christianity*, 294–95.
23. Gillman and Klimkeit, *Christians in Asia*, 274.

Receiving support from the next two emperors Daizong (reign 762–780) and Dezong (reign 780–805), the "Nestorian" Tablet was erected in the year 781 during the period of Dezong. However, the religious persecution under Emperor Wuzong in 845 reflected the Da Qin religion until the Mongol period. The mission of the Da Qin religion experienced a time of stability, growth, and then disappearance from 635 to 980. The Christian church became extinct from 781 to 980.[24] The most severe religious persecution against the foreign religions declined severely but returned by Confucians between 840 and 846. At the time Buddhism was in severe disarray, though under the Mongol Yuan dynasty it would regain prominence.

It is certain that Buddhism had wider influence in Tang dynasty than Da Qin Christianity. Da Qin Christianity was limited by infrequent contact with the local Chinese people at a grassroots level. Rather it existed mainly in the form of monasticism and depended on the government's support. In comparison to Buddhism, the influence of Da Qin religion was limited in Chinese culture and society.

In 1260, Kublai Khan, a grandson of Genghis Khan, became Great Khan. Four years later, he relocated his capital from Mongolia to Beijing in northern China, and in 1271 he adopted a Chinese dynastic name, the Yuan. Kublai Khan had decided to become the emperor of China and start a new dynasty. The Yuan was the shortest lived of the major dynasties from the time that Kublai occupied Beijing in 1264 to the fall of the dynasty in 1368. Kublai Khan allowed Nestorian Christians and Roman Catholics to set up missions, as well as Tibetan lamas, Muslims, and Hindus.[25]

CHRISTIANITY AND INCULTURATION IN THE "SACRED TEXTS OF DA QIN RELIGION"

The Dunhuang texts were discovered and then published between 1907 and 1949. The discovery of the "Manuscripts Cave" took place in Sir Aurel Stein's international archaeological research in the area of Dunhuang. During his archaeological expedition in Chinese Gansu province (from 1907 to 1908) many ancient Chinese manuscripts were discovered from the Jin (265–420 CE) to the Northern Song dynasties

---

24. Moffett, *History of Christianity in Asia*, 302.
25. Gillman and Klimkeit, *Christians in Asia*, 287–97.

(960–1127). Among the Dunhuang texts, seven ancient Da Qin texts in the Tang period were preserved.

Zunjing (*Honored Persons and Sacred Books*), one of the Da Qin texts, records that Da Qin religion possesses five hundred and thirty sacred books as written on Pattra Sutras (*beiye fanyin*). Aluoben presented the doctrine of religions. Fang Xuanling and Wei Zheng requested these books to be translated. Later Jing Jing, the great virtuous one of this religion, was summoned to translate thirty of them. The rest of books were not translated and preserved on Pattra leaves.[26]

One of the texts is the *Book of Jesus, the Messiah* (*Xuting Mishisuo jing*). The term *jing* denotes a sacred text, and in the Buddhist context, it means *sutra*. The Bible is also translated as the holy sacred *jing*. Three other texts are entitled *jing*: *Zunjing* (*Honored Persons and Sacred Books*), *Zhi xuan anle jing* (*Book on the Mysterious Peace and Joy*), and *Xuanyuan zhi benjing* (*Book on Declaring the Origin of the Jing Religion of Da Qin*).[27]

Two texts were categorized as Aluoben's: *On the One-God* (*Yishen lun*) and the *Book of Jesus, the Messiah* (*Xuting Mishisuo jing*). Aluoben was the leader of the mission journey in 635.[28] According to the inscription (line XII–XIII), he brought scriptures and images to the Emperor, who allowed the scriptures to be translated for the imperial library. After carefully investigating the translations, the Emperor issued an edict in 638, accepting the teachings as helpful and profitable to all.

Alouben's teachings were "mysteriously spiritual, and of silent operation" and covering all of most important things in human life. The language of his teaching is free from perplexing expressions.[29] The *Book of Jesus, the Messiah* is likely the first doctrine of Da Qin religion presented to the Emperor Taizong. In the middle part of the text, the au-

---

26. *Honored Persons and Sacred Books* (*Zunjing*), line 20–22; Li, *A Study of the History*, 187.

27. Li, *A Study of the History*, 87.

28. The oldest of the texts is the *Book of Jesus, the Messiah*, purchased in 1922 by Dr. Takakusu. Prof. Saeki dates the text between 635 and 638. This text is declared as the first Nestorian text ever composed by Aluoben in China. A second manuscript contains three other early writings attributed to Aluoben. All four of the documents were published in 1931 by the Kyoto Institute of the Oriental Culture Academy with an introduction by Prof. Haneda, and dated to 641 CE. See Saeki, *The Nestorian Documents and Relics*.

29. Moffett, *History of Christianity*, 293.

thor reveals the book's purpose: the one who serves the Lord of Heaven wrote this text in order to explain the basic teaching and doctrines of his religion.[30]

According to Chinese sources, Jing Jing was a Persian monk called Adam, a bishop and missionary scholar. His father was regarded as Yisi for whom the tablet was erected. Jing Jing composed and inscribed the text on the "Nestorian" Tablet. In line II of the inscription, his identity is inscribed: "Handed down by Jing Jing, a monk of the Da Qin Monastery" and then in Syriac "Adam, Presbyter and Chorepiscopos, and Papas of Chinistan (China)."

Jing Jing reportedly had worked with the famous Buddhist missionary Prajna (who reached the Chinese capital in 782 from India) on translating the *Satparamita Sutra* (Sutra on the seven perfections [of a Bodhisattva]). Jing Jing was highly knowledgeable about Chinese language and literature; even Buddhist missionaries asked for help in translating their own sacred texts into Chinese. This interfaith collaboration marks the importance of encounter between Buddhists and Christians for translation and interpretation of the sacred texts.[31]

In addition to the inscription text, scholars believe Jing Jing also wrote the other two texts, *Gloria in Excelsis Deo* and *Book on Mysterious Peace and Joy*. Although the *Book Declaring the Origin of Origins and Praise to the Transfiguration of the Great Holy One* was not written by Jing Jing's hand, these writings are combined with his texts in collections.

From *Gloria in Excelsis Deo* we read a beautiful liturgical hymn:

> Great Holy-One Who art adored by all, Messiah Thou,
> We praise Thy gracious Father for His ocean-store of love.
> Great Holy-One Who dost proceed from Him, the Holy Ghost,
> We know Thy will shall here be done, all human thought above.[32]

In *Book on Declaring the Origin of the Jing Religion of Da Qin*, the second fragment ends with *Book on Declaring the Beginning Reaching the Origin of Jing Religion of Da Qin*. The second fragment appropriates some phrases from chapter sixty-two of Laozi's *Dao de jing*. Toward the end of the text (line 20), the terms *Dao* and *Logos* are used interchange-

---

30. Ibid., 301.

31. Ibid., 301–2; Against positive interfaith relationship of cooperation between Buddhists and Christians, see Gillman and Klimkeit, *Christians in Asian*, 282.

32. Foster, *Church of the T'ang*, 137.

ably. "Believing in the Dao/Logos can cast out all demons. It can give life and longevity."[33]

INTERPRETATION AND INCULTURATION IN ALUOBEN'S TEXTS

The inscription (line VI) demonstrates a Trinitarian understanding of the incarnation. The *Book of Jesus, the Messiah* witnesses to Jesus's birth, life, and death. *On the One-God* contains the Easter story, including the Passion of Christ, as well as the resurrection, the Christian mission, the ascension and Pentecost.[34]

The *Book of Jesus, the Messiah* translates Jesus as Yishu and Messiah as Mishihe. This book does not necessarily identify Jesus as the Honored One, but rather as the means for the people to see the Honored One. The text compares the heavenly Lord with the wind, calling the Holy Spirit the "cool wind." In the inscription (line VII) we read that Christians "institute the washing of the law by water and the wind/the Spirit." The Hebrew word *ruach* means "breath," and the pure wind is a Greek idea. In Chinese, cool wind connotes calm, pacifying, and refers to the great comforter.[35]

The heavenly Lord includes "all the Buddhas" who "toured around all the famous places in the world in admiration."[36] Buddhas are those whom the heavenly Lord has received, who receive the teaching of the heavenly Lord, and who were first sent by the Lord. "All the Buddhas as well as the Kinnaras and the Superintending Devas and Arhans can see the Lord of Heaven."[37]

The *Book of Jesus, the Messiah* uses the Buddhist terms *Fo* (meaning Buddha/Buddhist) to refer to God, *Fo ming* for God's name and *Fo fa* for God's law. Here, all beings are close to the knowledge of *Fo*, because the heavenly Lord made human figures to be devoted to worship. Here,

---

33. Li, *Study of the History*, 122.

34. On the One Heaven Part I, The Sermon of the Lord of the Universe, line 90–95, line 95–100, line 100–105, line 110–15, line 120–25; Li, *A Study of the History*, 175–77.

35. *On the One-God*, we perceive that the name God is translated as *Shen* which denotes spiritual Being. In Dunhuang documents the term *Tianzun*, the heavenly respected which refers to God while *Tianzun* is Buddha for Buddhists or the celestial beings for Daoists.

36. *Book of Jesus, the Messiah*, line 10–15; Li, *Study of the History*, 146.

37. *Book of Jesus, the Messiah*, line 75–80; Moffett, *History of Christianity*, 310.

Buddhist theory of karma is integrated to the point where the seed of cause had been originally planted in the previous life.[38]

Furthermore, fear of God in the Decalogue equates with the Confucian ethic of obedience to the emperor and filial piety: First, serve the heavenly Lord, second, serve the Emperor, and finally serve one's parents.[39] Aluoben's texts appropriate many Buddhist and Daoist terms and ideas. Interestingly enough, a Confucian ethic, "look for the best in others and correct what is worst in yourself" (an ugly stone in the mountain is to be made a way of correcting your worst thing), is intertwined with the Christian ethic: "Otherwise it is as if you were trying to take a speck of dust out of someone else's eye while all the time you had a great beam of wood in your own."[40]

In the *Book on Mysterious Peace and Joy* we find Daoist terms like emptiness and non-doing. Buddhism, which came to China earlier than Christianity, had an enormous influence on Chinese literature. Jing Jing worked with a Buddhist monk called Prajna to translate the scriptures of Da Qin religion. It is possible that Jing Jing adopted some terminologies that Buddhism had already developed in interaction with Confucianism and Daoism. For instance, no desire, no action, no merits, and no demonstration are raised as four principles to attain peace and joy that Jesus taught.[41]

This understanding of Jesus as the *Honored One's* Messiah does not explicitly coincide with the Greek idea of *homoousious*. "Mishihe was not God." "He did not cling to his equality with God."[42] Such translation finds a consonance within a Daoist concept of the transcendence of Dao, which is revealed and operated through *de* (virtue or yang) and *qi* (life breath or yin).[43] The Holy Spirit is depicted as the Pure Wind, which brought the enlightenment to the disciples.

---

38. *Book of Jesus, the Messiah*, line 40–45; Li, *Study of the History*, 148.

39. *Book of Jesus, the Messiah*, line 65–70; Li, *Study of the History*, 150.

40. Palmer, *Jesus Sutra*, 61. Unlike Palmer's positive interpretation, Li Tang translates the statement in different way: "Do not look at others' sins. Because you have no righteousness, so you want others to be perfect." On the One Heaven Part I, line 20–25. Li, *Study of the History*, 171.

41. *Book on Mysterious Peace and Joy*, line 50–55; Li, *Study of the History*, 191.

42. *On the One Heaven Part I, The Sermon of the Lord of the Universe*, line 62–63, line 60–65; Ibid., 174.

43. Ibid., 63.

Nevertheless, we cannot ignore that these same doctrines do accurately express statements of Christian doctrine. For example, the *Book of Jesus, Messiah* states that the Messiah offered his body to the evil-doers. For the sake of all beings he was sent to this world and died on their behalf.[44] The documents also affirm the doctrine of Jesus's conception by the power of the Holy Spirit and the virgin birth.[45]

On the One-God states that the visible and the invisible were all created by this One-God.[46] The text presents the resurrection, ascension, and Pentecost in a biblically orthodox way. Jesus came to the world. For our sins, he died freely. His body was resurrected in three days. By the power of the heavenly Lord, He ascended into heaven. This world is the world of the glory of Mishihe. All will be resurrected.[47]

The core message in the texts agrees with the gospels as we know them. It is certain the texts use Daoist or Buddhist terms to enunciate Christian teaching. There is a tendency to emphasize oneness of God and the work of the Spirit in relation to Jesus Christ. Jesus's life is portrayed in an inseparable connection with the Holy Spirit, "the action of the World-Honored One's qi."[48] Even the sacred Spirit took a body and became the Messiah.

On the One-God applies the Buddhist theory of five *skhandas* to the Christian understanding of human being. In Buddhism, a human body has no soul. Instead, it is composed of five elements: *Rupa* (the material element of the body), *Vedanta* (feelings), *Samjina* (illusion or image), *Samskara* (will), and *Vijnana* (consciousness). Similarly, the text states that "Soul and Spirit were made of five components."[49] There is a priority of the body over the soul, because the soul depends on the body. The soul is the guest while the body is the master. The five elements of the body and the soul are in one.[50]

A Daoist influence in discussion of the power of God is also clear. The power of God "accomplishes everything naturally by itself" that is, the way of Dao in course of *tzu yan* (nature). God the Creator formed

---

44. *Book of Jesus, the Messiah*, line 160–165; Li, *Study of the History*, 156.
45. *Book of Jesus, the Messiah*, line115–120; Li, *Study of the History*, 153.
46. *On the One-God*, line 1–5; Li, *Study of the History*, 157.
47. *On the One-God*, line 125–130; Li, *Study of the History*, 177.
48. Li, *Study of the History*, 66.
49. *On the One-God*, line 20–25; Li, *Study of the History*, 161.
50. *On the One-God*, line 45–50, line 50–55; Li, *Study of the History*, 164.

the five components and works through what is of itself and self so.[51] The Inscription text in the Tablet and Aluoben's texts *Book of Jesus, the Messiah,* and *On the One-God* (including Jing Jing's texts) can be regarded as Chinese Christian classics that express the East Syrian interaction with culture, language, and people in Tang China.

REVIEW AND APPRECIATION

In light of what has been described, we perceive that the inscription text in the Tablet and Dunhuang texts appropriate the adoption of certain Chinese ways of thinking, language, belief systems, and religious worldviews as a means of effective communication.

In 618 CE, the Tang Dynasty began. The second Emperor, Li Shimin ruled from 627 until 650, and encountered the first official Christian mission to China in 635. He declared a policy of religious tolerance. Confucianism, Daoism, and Buddhism received the same weight. He reintroduced the Confucian idea of a bureaucracy, scholarship, and magistrate civil examination. Daoism had a special place in the Tang dynasty, because the royal family of Tang and the Daoist saint Laozi shared the same family name "Li."

Daoism and Confucianism were the indigenous belief systems in China. Laozi, believed to be a contemporary of Confucius (Kong Fuzi), developed a different understanding of Dao than Confucius. Laozi was concerned with perceiving the Dao's manifestation through *de* and *qi* in light of the unvarying and permanent Dao, while Confucius centered on the revealed manifestation of Dao at a social, ethical level. For Laozi, the Dao that one can teach and explore is not the same as the unvarying and permanent Dao. Nonetheless, we can talk of Dao through its self-manifestation through *de* (virtue) and *qi* (spirit of breath).[52]

The second founder of Daoism, Zhuangzi, expresses through his dream of the butterfly a Daoist desire to transcend the limitations of Confucian ethical morality, for the sake of the wholeness of life in unity with the Dao. He dreamt that he was a butterfly, flitting around and enjoying bliss, forgetting himself as Zhuangzi. After waking up, he asked himself: was he dreaming that he was a butterfly or was he a butterfly who was dreaming it was Zhuangzi?

---

51. *On the One-God,* line 30–35; Li, *Study of the History,* 162.
52. *Laozi,* Ch.1.

This dream experience refers to the life of change. Life is in flux, not fixed. The interplay of *yin* and *yang* is a great challenge to hierarchically established Confucianism. Confucian rationality based on interpersonal communication and respect is not certain, and the Chinese society that built on that rationality became considerably deteriorated, excluding people with different views and orientations. Rationality became institutionalized and ossified, instrumentalized in the service of the people in power. The power system in a society is justified by a knowledge system. Rationality without consideration of the Other and a subjectification without recognizing difference, met serious resistance in Daoist-inspired revolts.

Daoist-inspired revolts in certain provinces mocked, attacked, and denied the institutionalized system and the social political ideology of Confucianism, calling for the transformation of the Confucianism-based political principle of the empire. Aware of this situation, the Emperor Taizong supported the Daoists, claiming that he was a direct descendent of Laozi, while developing the Confucian hierarchy.

Buddhism, like Christianity, was classified in China as a foreign religion. The early form of Buddhism in China was Theravada, which found a limited appeal among the ordinary people. Later, Mahayana Buddhism entered China, becoming a dominant religion by the time of the Tang dynasty. The central figures in Mahayana Buddhism are the Bodhisattvas who are deeply concerned and compassionate for the life of the masses. The compassionate Bodhisattva's worldview is expressed in Santidieva. It is this compassion that also underlines the *Lotus Sutra*, one of the most popular of all Buddhist sutras in China from the fourth century to today.

In the *Book of Jesus, the Messiah* we see that the Buddhist issues of karma and reincarnation are fully integrated into the life, death, and redemption of Jesus Christ. The Holy Spirit is portrayed as the Spirit of compassion for all life. The human soul has five *skandas* (form, perception, consciousness, action, and knowledge). A Christian understanding of the immortality of the soul is also transformed by the Buddhist concept of no-soul, because the soul can only exist owing to the five *skandas*. Without the five *skandas*, there is no soul. The soul is the guest of the body. The Buddhist influence on Christian anthropology of embodiment in the Chinese context undermines the Greek influence on Western Christians' concept of the immortal soul.

Furthermore, the Daoist concept of *qi* (life breath) creates the body and soul, and a Christian understanding of God is reinterpreted in light of a natural way of Dao. The wisdom and power of God is without origin, it is changeless and immutable. This is naturally so. Dao, like a natural watercourse, is connected with Dao as the great Void, as well as the fullness.

God, like the permanent Dao, is without origin, but God is naturally so. The sacred Spirit is everywhere, existing in non-action, being in beinglessness and is beyond touch. The Daoist idea of non-action—action without attachment—embraces the mysterious freedom of the Spirit. Because the Spirit is everywhere, creation is like no beginning and no end. Creation out of nothing comes from the Spirit, which is uncreated and is the essence of all existence.

Jesus is portrayed as the Messiah orbited by the Buddha's and *arahts*. God is like the wind, and all great teachers such as the Buddhas are moved by this wind. The power of God's sacred Spirit can grant longevity and lead to immortality, the idea in consonance with the Daoist concept of longevity and immortality of the body.

The sacred Spirit's power of God works in everybody and brings all to fullness. God's grace is bestowed in Buddha nature. Here, the Buddhist core concept of Buddha nature is juxtaposed with the Christian idea of God's grace, from which a Christian religion in universal compassion and love would emerge. Buddhist core messages such as compassion, Buddha nature, karma, and reincarnation are integrated in the description of Jesus as the Bodhisattva, launching the raft of salvation and compassion, freeing people of the karma and bringing them back to the original nature. God gives the first people the original nature of goodness. "Man originally came from the God of goodness. Man had originally a good cause."[53] This original nature can be seen in the biblical idea of the image of God. It is certain that the text does not ignore sinful condition tempted by the evil.

The authors in the Dunhuang texts demonstrate a remarkable depth of understanding of Chinese culture, language, and religions. An interpretation of God and the Trinity in these texts enriches and enlarges the Greek horizon of Christianity in terms of fusing the Christian belief system into Chinese multi-religious horizons. Recognizing the divinity of Jesus through virgin birth, the text affirms the priority and

---

53. *On the One-God*, line 105–110; Li, *A Study of the History*, 167.

transcendence of God the Father, to the degree that Jesus did not cling to his equality with God.[54] Such a Christology seems to have a parallel with St. Paul's theology of Israel in light of the mystery and freedom of God (Romans 11).

Alouben's mission and ministry marked the first Christian mission in co-existence with people of other faiths, appropriating the wisdom of Chinese religions for the sake of East Syrian missional interaction with Chinese culture, while keeping Christian identity and uniqueness in confession of Jesus Christ as the Messiah in the presence of the Holy Spirit of the One God. Chinese Christianity in the Tang dynasty remains a source and an example of inculturation when Christians are engaged with the intercultural issue of the Christian message in different places and times to promote the gospel in the presence of the Others.

INTERPRETATION AND SELF-CULTIVATION: MATTEO RICCI AND ZHU XI

Matteo Ricci, born in Macerata on October 16, 1552, arrived in the capital of China in 1601. He is referred as the "wise man from the West."[55] In Ricci's time in China, the Ming dynasty (1368–1644) tolerated three religions: Confucianism, Buddhism, and Daoism. The term Neo-Confucianism, a Western coinage, refers to the later development of Confucianism. Interpreting the worldview of the *Book of Changes*, Neo-Confucians attempted to renew Confucian doctrine in a changed situation in which they found themselves in a competitive rivalry with Daoism and Buddhism.

Although Ricci had a good command of the Chinese language and of Confucian culture, he felt uncomfortable about a cosmological–metaphysical worldview of Neo-Confucianism. Rather, his interest was to retrieve the original meaning of Confucianism represented by Confucius (551–479 BCE) and Mencius (ca. 372–289 BCE). For this task, he undertook a strategy of articulating more consonance between Roman Catholicism and Confucianism regarding God and the Lord of Heaven (*T'ian*).

---

54. *On the One Heaven Part I*, line 62–63; Li, *Study of the History*, 174, footnote 152.

55. Cronin, *Wise Man*.

Ricci's masterpiece, *The True Meaning of the Lord of Heaven*, was written to uphold his basic approach: appropriating Confucius and Mencius as mentors for his Christian mission of inculturation. Ricci's preference for these two entails his mission strategy to combat Neo-Confucian scholars under the Daoist-Buddhist influence, asking them to return to the original form of Confucianism. As such Confucianism would become a genuine religious-ethical partner with Western Christianity in commonly witnessing to God or Heaven.

Central to the Confucian Way is the principle of the harmonious oneness of Heaven and humanity. The way of humanity is essentially the way of moral life. In human terms, the Way is called humaneness and righteousness. Therefore, Confucians establish education and self-cultivation as the center of the human way. Confucius writes in his biography.

> At fifteen I set my heart upon learning. At thirty, I had planted my feet firm upon the ground. At forty, I no longer suffered from perplexities. At fifty, I knew what the biddings of Heaven were. At sixty, I heard them with docile ear. At seventy, I could follow the dictates of my own heart; for what I desired no longer overstepped the boundaries of right.[56]

Confucius is concerned with seeking personal advancement for the sake of realizing his principle in his social and political life. The moral and political requirements of Confucianism are crystallized as Three Guiding Principles and Five Constant Regulations on which Confucian society and government are established. Among the three principles, the first one is the subordination of a subject or minister to his/her ruler, which is followed by that of a son to his father and of a wife to her husband. The five regulations are actually five Confucian virtues: humaneness (*Ren*), righteousness, ritual/propriety, wisdom and faithfulness, which are believed to be as constant and unchanging as natural laws.

Ren can be understood in terms of the four words, *k'o-chi fu-li*, taken from *Analects* 12:1. *K'o-chi* refers to self-conquest and goes on to explain *fu-li*, the restoration of propriety or ritual law, as the recovery of Confucius' own kind of propriety. This is what applies to noble people and commoners alike: *Ren*, conquest of self and return to propriety. Confucius was troubled by political irregularities. Some of his concerns

---

56. Waley, *Analects* 2:4.

were about the discrepancy between names and reality, between language and action, and between rights and duties. The beginning of the collapse of ritual/propriety was when names were violated (such as father-son, king-servant, and husband-wife). This would bring about social disorder and political chaos. This theory refers to a Confucian concept of rectifying names. This idea was actualized in a political context by Mencius.

According to Mencius, Confucius' concept of the moral life must be developed in reference to Mencius' idea of the nascent moral sprouts, which are part of human nature. The person is by nature good, and evil comes with the formation of bad habits. There are four beginnings (dispositions) in the human heart. All people have a human nature, which cannot bear to see the suffering of Others. This is reflected in the four dispositions: feeling of commiseration for others (beginning of *Ren*), feeling of shame and dislike of anything dishonorable (beginning of righteousness), feeling of modesty and yielding (beginning of propriety), and a sense of right and wrong (beginning of wisdom). Human four beginnings are manifested in the organization of society and constitute the human ethical relationships in the society.[57] Thus, people are the most important element. The sovereign is the least. In his development, Mencius extends the Confucian idea of self-cultivation and rectification of the names to the public sphere of government and society.

Mencius' concept of the beginning of virtue is embedded with his idea of self-cultivation. Since all human beings have the four sprouts within themselves, it is vital to attend to the task of self-cultivation. Through this, one accumulates righteousness and develops oneself into a full and realizable moral person. This is a self-cultivation in a gradual sense accumulating the righteousness and virtues and running into a full course of blossoming into sagehood. In this gradual process of growth, one gains greater and greater moral strength, which is called "flood like qi." This is the greatest and most unyielding of energies that grow within a person practicing a way of self-cultivation. As they grow, the energy of *qi* grows flooding and blossoming, filling up the space between Heaven and earth.[58]

Regarding a Confucian teaching of human nature and self-cultivation, Ricci, in the *True meaning of the Lord of Heaven*, grounds the Confucian principles of the Five Human Relationships and the three

---

57. Fung, *History of Chinese Philosophy*, 1, 121.
58. Ivanhoe, *Ethics*, 92.

guiding Bonds in terms of the Supremely Honored One, the first Father and creator of all. Ricci argues that *Shang-di* (Sovereign on High) in Confucianism denotes this God of Christianity. According to Ricci, the Confucian teaching of the Great Ultimate includes sincerity, the subject of self-cultivation so that this teaching is closer to a Christian moral teaching.

In a Neo-Confucian context, Zho Dunyi (1017–1073) attempted to integrate the Daoist concept of Non-Being and the Buddhist idea of voidness or emptiness into the Confucian idea of the Great Ultimate. In his framework, the Great Ultimate becomes ultimateless, or empty. All things emerge and are differentiated from the Great Ultimate. However, in Ricci's view, a Neo-Confucian development seems to be close to the teaching of Buddhism and Daoism.[59] Criticizing that Neo-Confucianism is no less than the teaching of Buddhism and Daoism, Ricci retrieved the teaching of Mencius to justify his own position.

As already mentioned, according to Mencius, humanness and righteousness are essential ingredients of true humanity. Humanness is rooted within the human mind/heart. Based on the four beginnings (dispositions) in the human heart, one should be cultivated like a shoot. One grows up, full of expressed virtue, to become like a beautiful blossoming tree. Mencius' theory of humanity and innate goodness provides Ricci with a springboard to promote the Catholic teaching of human nature and meritorious virtue.

Equating Christian love with Confucian humanity, Ricci appropriates the Confucian way of the virtuous life through self-cultivation toward the perfection of sagehood in the Catholic sense. The Lord of Heaven bestows a grace, instructing people in a moral way, strengthening faith. To articulate the place of the Catholic God within the Confucian framework, Ricci also criticizes Zhu Xi's explanation of the Great Ultimate in terms of the *Li* (Principle) of heaven and earth. In Ricci's view, Zhu Xi, influenced by Zho Dunyi, obscured the personal character of the Sovereign on High.

Be that as it may, Neo-Confucians' philosophy of *Li* is more complicated than Ricci expected. It is not easily to define nor is it superficial or unwise for Ricci to identify *Li* as reason. Within the Neo-Confucian tradition, Zhu Xi's philosophy of Principle marks a creative development of Confucian self-cultivation in reference to Confucius and Mencius.

59. Ricci, *True Meaning*, 113.

Furthermore, he offers an important insight into an art of reading which is replete with implications for a philosophical hermeneutic.

ZHU XI AND THE ART OF INTERPRETATION

It is instructive to consider Zhu Xi's position about self-cultivation and his art of interpretation. Zhu Xi (1130–1200) is the preeminent scholar and first rate analytic and systematic thinker during the Song Dynasty in China (960–1279). He is, along with Confucius and Mencius, regarded as a figure who had a profound influence on East Asian culture. His philosophy implies a new development in Confucian philosophy. His elaboration of a systematic metaphysics is based on his reading of the Four Books as influenced by the advanced ideas and concepts represented by the Neo-Confucian thinkers in the Northern Sung.[60]

Zhu Xi's program of learning and interpretation, in which the concept of *ko wu*, or "apprehending the principle in things" plays a central role, is connected with his idea of self-cultivation in reference to the philosophy of the Principle. Zhu felt a crisis in academic learning in his time. Inspired by Confucius in the *Analects,* Zhu distinguished between learning for self-cultivation and learning for the sake of others (i.e. winning secular acclaim and privilege). According to Zhu, learning for the sake of others is ironically motivated by the Confucian-based civil service examination, which promises the rewards for success, official status, power, and wealth. The desire for worldly success deviated students from the real purpose of learning. They study and learn only for the sake of the civil service examination.[61]

For his idea of learning, Zhu revived the White Deer Hollow academy with which he was associated during his lifetime. His items of the Five Teachings are worth quoting: "Affection between parent and child; Righteousness between ruler and subject; Differentiation between husband and wife; Precedence between elder and younger; Trust between friends."[62]

Zhu advocates for a profound learning and understanding of the Confucian truth. Here is Zhu's contribution for hermeneutical theory (to use his own term, *tu-shu fa*). His art of reading instructs his students

---

60. Zhu edited and commented on the great Neo-Confucian masters in the Northern Sung and compiled an anthology. See Chan, *Reflections on Things,* 110–11.

61. Gardner, *Chu His Learning,* 17.

62. Ibid., 29.

to know how to read more effectively for attaining the true meaning of the great Way of the sages in the past. According to Zhu, the students have to experience the texts personally by making them their own:

> Generally speaking, in reading we must first become intimately familiar with the text so that its words seem to come from our own mouths. We should then continue to reflect on it so that its ideas seem to come from our own minds. Only then can there be real understanding.[63]

The genuine understanding of the Way becomes approachable when texts are read according to the proper order. For reading the Four Books, Zhu recommends the following order: the *Great Learning*, the *Analects*, the *Book of Mencius*, and finally the *Doctrine of Mean*. In Zhu's opinion, the *Great Learning* sets the pattern of the Confucian Way in a precise order. The *Analects* establishes its foundation, the *Book of Mencius* observes its development, and finally the *Doctrine of Mean* discovers the mystery of the ancients.

In his hermeneutic of intimate familiarity, Zhu put a priority on the lifeworld of the text over the reader's own prejudice. Effective reading is dependent on a willingness to be suspicious of the reader's own biases. Casting aside all preconceived and misguided ideas, the reader strives for the meaning of the text. Here, the commentaries on the text are regarded as the slave while the classical texts are the master.[64]

An intimate familiarity with the text is an approach to the text without disturbed mind and impediment, settling the mind like still water or a clear mirror. A reading in a quiet setting is the art of meditation immersed in the text. Nonetheless, this meditative approach does not discard the reader's critical and analytical thinking, but rather, fully appreciates it. This art of reading can be compared to a spiritual reading or a sacred reading in a Christian fashion.

In order to learning the classics, one needs a disposition of reverence, which is a central part of Zhu Xi's self-cultivation. Reverence means keeping a sense of caution and vigilance, reverently attentive to, and in contact with the Heaven, the text, and others. According to Mencius, reverence means preserving the mind. In *Analects* 13:19, "in private life, courteous; in public life, diligent; in relationships, loyal." Along this line,

63. Ibid., 43.
64. Ibid., 47.

Zhu Xi keeps the reverence of Heaven as the Principle of Heaven and removes human selfish desires. The practicing of self-cultivation is defined as collecting together or recollection (in a sense of spirituality, it implies a condition for the interior life.)[65]

The Confucian explanation of subduing one's self and recovering the virtue of propriety (*k'o-chi fu-li*, *Analects* 12:1) is integrated into Zhu Xi's spiritual art of interpretation in terms of the investigation of things with reverence and extension of knowledge. Through the practice of reverence, the investigation of things, which lies in the extension of knowledge, a sudden enlightenment breaks through at the end of a lifelong pilgrimage.

According to Zhu, all things in the universe possess the Principle that is manifested in particular and different ways. Principle underlies everything and every affair in the cosmos. In human being, this Principle is identical with the human nature endowed at birth. In every person, Principle is morally good, constituting the four cardinal virtues: benevolence, righteousness, propriety, and wisdom as Mencius earlier established.[66] However, every person is also born with an endowment of psychophysical stuff, which gives every person his/her peculiar form and characteristics. The human being lives with the capacity of being fully moral, yet finding oneself in a predicament, falling short of moral perfection.

According to Zhu, the mind embraces human nature and the emotions so that the mind becomes a field of tension in the process of self-cultivation. If the Principle is not overwhelmed by emotions or selfish desires, the mind would be in a state of equilibrium. To be present and balanced, the mind has to be made *ching*, a state undistracted by anything else. The person who practices a state of *ching* possesses a capable mind of apprehending the principle in things (*ko wu*).

The effort to probe the principle to the point of complete apprehension is the crucial step in Zhu' program of self-cultivation and interpretation of the Principle. Since the Principle in external things and the Principle in human being are interconnected, apprehending Principle either in things or in oneself is, in fact, self-realization.[67] As Zhu Xi states,

65. Ching, *Religious Thought*, 124.
66. Fung, *History of Chinese Philosophy*, II, 558.
67. Ibid., 561.

after exerting himself in this way for a long time, he will suddenly find himself possessed of a wide and far-reaching penetration. The qualities of all things, internal and external, subtle and coarse, will all then be apprehended, and the mind, in its entire substance and in its relation to things, will become completely manifest. This is called the investigation of things; this is called the perfection of knowledge.[68]

Zhu's art of reading and understanding (*tu-shu fa*) is the way to apprehend Principle and to realize oneself engaged meditatively and analytically in the text. Now an encounter between the lifeworld of text and that of the reader takes place, since for Zhu Xi, we seek moral principle not merely from the text, but realize it in ourselves. We have to discover for ourselves what the text explained. Through the text, we find such principle in our own life. The principle of the text that the reader seeks, finds its meaning and realization in the mind of the reader. Experiencing intimate familiarity with the text means experiencing the self, which is transformed in the process of encounter and confluence with the text. This refers to a spiritual enlightenment in which the text has an effective power in transforming the reader. While experiencing this, the reader realizes and fulfills self-principle in existence.

Reading for Zhu is a method of self-cultivation in engagement with an investigation of things in the world out there. The world of the text out there is realized and fulfilled in one's experience of it within one's life horizon rather than merely waiting to be discovered methodically. His art of learning and understanding is a lifelong process to become an enlightened sage.

Zhu's concept of self-cultivation articulates the way of developing the mind to the utmost and knowing one's nature and knowing. The investigation of things consists of the extension of knowledge. In the process of self-cultivation, the Truth appears in a spiritual journey beyond a subject/object distinction. This is like polishing a mirror or rescuing a Pearl from impure water. Hermeneutically speaking, the Truth of the heavenly Principle is hidden, yet it reveals itself through reverence and the extension of knowledge. It is significant to investigate the truth of things at hand to extend knowledge of ontological truth.

For Zhu Xi, the Heavenly Principle is like the pearl lying in muddy water. All one's efforts must be concentrated toward acquiring this real-

---

68. Legge, *Chinese Classics* 1, 365–66.

ization through the exercise of reverence and the extension of knowledge.[69] The Supreme Ultimate, while present and immanent within all things, "is not cut up into pieces. It is merely like the moon reflecting itself in ten thousand streams."[70] The relationship between the Principle and each concrete object can be explained by his metaphor: "the moon reflecting itself in ten thousand streams."

The moon in the streams means that the stream throws back the image of the moon. It refers to a mirror relation in an analogical sense. The mirror image is analogically connected with the actual sight of the moon through the ontological investigation of things and the extension of knowledge. In this mirror-appearance, Dao (*Li*) reveals and manifests itself for us. The revelation of the Truth does not contradict a methodological aspect of interpretation in the investigation of worldly affairs. Analogical reflection in a mirror retains the mode of imaginative thinking and is not fixed, but rather, open toward the emergence of Dao itself which implies an eschatological enlightenment of the truth of Dao.

Truth and method are not disconnected from each other. But in the process of meditative and analytical thinking, the Truth reveals itself. Nonetheless, the Truth is not a prisoner of an iron cage of human experience or language, but remains an inspiration in a lifelong process of self-cultivation. At this juncture, it is significant to compare Zhi Xi's metaphor of the moon reflecting in the streams to Gadamer's speculative metaphor of the castle in the lake. If for Gadamer the mirror relation is linguistically structured and oriented based on the universal function of language, Zhu Xi's hermeneutics is of analogical-meditative character.[71]

Ricci's approach to Confucianism was to find a consonance between the Confucian reverence of the Heaven and the Catholic concept of God in a personal sense, taking up a common ethical virtue. Ricci arranged humanity, righteousness, decorum, and wisdom as subsequent to the capacity to reason, while in Neo-Confucianism, *Li*, the Principle, is called *hsing* (nature) in human beings and *ming* (mandate of Heaven, destiny) in Heaven. Ricci is anxious to locate the Catholic God in Confucian ethics by assimilating Confucian thinking into a Catholic framework.

---

69. Fung, *History of Chinese Philosophy*, II, 561.
70. Ibid., 541.
71. Gadamer, *Truth and Method*, 466.

Thus, he failed to consider a religious dimension of the Neo-Confucian concept of *Li* and its hermeneutical implication for Christianity.[72]

A Neo-Confucian concept of *Li* and the art of interpretation mark a new field of Christian-Confucian dialogue and renewal, calling for improving limitation of Ricci's legacy. Christian mission is not an accomplished fact, but a field being renewed constantly in terms of the interpretation of the gospel in order to share it with people of other cultures. Through the process of interpretation in the presence of Others, God may speak in a different manner and awaken the Christian church to the mystery of God. Here Christian mission becomes humble and self-renewing, free of its prejudices and mistakes in the past.

---

72. Ching, *Religious Thought*, 351.

Excursus

Wang Yangming and the Investigation of Things in an Ontological Context

IN THE PREVIOUS CHAPTER, we dealt with Matteo Ricci's critique of Zhu Xi and with Zhu Xi's creative development of Mencius with respect to self-cultivation and the art of interpretation. Zhu Xi's hermeneutics of investigation ("pilgrimatics of self-cultivation")[1] demonstrates a theory of interpretation regarding a dialectical revealing of the Heavenly Principle, Dao, in connection with human methodological, empirical investigation of things of the world.

Mencius's hermeneutics, which exerted an impact on Zhu Xi, also has its place in the intellectual development of Wang Yang-ming (1472–1529), a pivotal scholar of the Ming Dynasty (1368–1644). In a spiritual struggle with Zhu Xi's theory of the investigation of things, Wang came to expound his theory of attainment of innate, intuitive knowledge (*liang zhi*) in an existential manner.

Wang seriously studied Zhu Xi's doctrine of the investigation of things. One day Wang decided to investigate the principles of bamboo, because according to Zhu Xi, principles are inherent in things. Sitting in front of bamboo trees and trying to investigate their principles, Wang failed at investigating and exploring the principle of worldly affairs and then became ill. This bitter experience led Wang to turn away from the philosophy of Zhu Xi and led him to Daoism and Buddhism.[2] Finally, in 1508, when Wang was thirty-seven, he suddenly understood the Confucian doctrine of the investigation of things and the extension of knowledge. He built a small house in Yang-ming-tung on the Hui-chi Mountain and called himself Yang-ming Tzu (or philosopher of Yang-

---

1. Huang, *Mencius Hermeneutics*, 185.
2. Fung, *History of Chinese Philosophy*, II. 596–97.

ming). Wang's influence in the development of Confucian scholarship is diverse and complex within the Chinese tradition of thought. This excursus focuses on Wang's contribution to the theory of interpretation in reference to Zhu Xi rather than to a historical study of his thought.

It is instructive to compare the difference between Zhu Xi and Wang. Zhu Xi's teaching about comprehending the principles in things or affairs is limited in its elaboration of human consciousness in reference to historical and social location. His art of interpretation in pursuit of a metaphysical principle in the public realm was challenged and renewed by Wang's different interpretation of investigation of things in light of *liang zhi*, which is grounded in human life in the past and the present. A conflict of interpretation within Confucian tradition demonstrates a creative reception of and a critical engagement with the tradition of Confucian teaching and it proposes a new way of interpretation of the Confucian texts and authoritative commentaries.

For Zhu Xi the principle underlines and lies beneath every aspect of reality in the universe. All things contain within them the principle of the universe. For Zhu Xi nature (*hsing*) is Principle, while human being possesses an intellectual faculty or consciousness, which is the mind. Our mind holds within itself the Supreme Ultimate in its entirety, but not the actual concrete things that are governed by the Principle.

The concept of the Principle, which is alien to Confucius or Mencius, provides a metaphysical basis for clarifying patterns and principles for grounding and clarifying things and events. The Confucian fundamentals (such as righteousness, rites, benevolence, and filial piety) are specific and particular expressions of the Principle. Nonetheless, the Principle, according to Zhu Xi, is transcendental apart from human life and context as grounded in an existential horizon and as conditioned by a social historical sphere.

Placing the investigation of things ahead of the sincerity of the mind or will, Zhu argues for further investigation until we reach the limit. After exerting oneself in this way of pilgrimage, following the limit of the thing, one will eventually achieve a comprehensive and far-reaching enlightenment of the Principle inherent in the things of the world. A dialectics of enlightenment consists of the rational, empirical mastery of external things in light of the Principle, although the Principle is not merely reduced to human empirical method. For instance, the principle of filial piety exists in parents, so moral cultivation begins with reverence of the parents.

In a similar manner to Zhu Xi, Wang first contends that every particular is a part of a single universal body of the principle while affirming specific and particular phenomena in the relationship with the Principle. Taking a step further than Zhu Xi, however, Wang identifies the Heavenly Principle with the mind in itself, which is the original, pure, and morally perfect mind. The mind is co-extensive with the universe, constituting the life horizon of human being. All things are actually present and accumulated within the human mind. There is nothing outside the mind. The mind in itself is called pure knowing or intuitive knowledge (*liang zhi*). Like Buddha nature, pure knowing or intuitive knowledge is inherent, shared, and possessed by all human beings. The human mind is obscured by selfish human desires, while the mind in itself is the complete and perfect original state of the mind.

For instance, Zhu Xi's principle of filial piety would be absurd if it were disengaged from the action of the mind. Mind and Principle are one. "If there is no mind of filial piety, there will be no principle of filial piety." Wang agrees that Zhu Xi also taught that human object of learning is mind and principles. Although the mind is the master of the body, it controls all principles in the world. And although principles are distributed throughout the ten thousand things, they are not outside one's mind.[3]

Nonetheless, Wang argues that Zhu Xi's view is inclined to divide the mind from the Principle. Zhu's view has inevitably opened the way that the mind and principles are two separate things.[4]

Given this fact, Wang's concept of the mind in itself is different from Mencius's theory of four beginnings to the extent that Wang conceives of the mind in itself, or the moral heart and mind, as a perfect and fully-informed endowment, completely granted at birth and remaining constant throughout one's life. Self-cultivation, in Wang's view, lies in the elimination the obstacle of selfish desires and superficial understanding rather than implying gradual nourishment and progress.

According to Mencius, innate abilities (*liang neng*) are differentiated from innate knowledge (*liang zhi*). It is essential that one develop the four moral sprouts to their mature and proper state in its full form.

3. Chan, *Instructions for Practical Living*, sec. 133.94.
4. Ibid.

The four sprouts are only the beginnings of virtue. To be virtuous, these sprouts have to be protected, nurtured, and developed in order to become the effect of becoming fully virtuous. While so doing, human nature blossoms into sagehood. Thus, the importance of self-cultivation is grounded in developmental progress. Mencius's flood like *qi*, which is moral strength, grows with a person who practices the Way.

However, Wang argues that *liang zhi*, already possessed by the human being, extends to the situation at hand. Wang's concept of pure knowing (*liang zhi*), which is already and fully formed moral virtue, articulates a spontaneous manifestation of the Heavenly Principle to the degree that it is not obscured by interference from selfish desires and superficial opinion. The four beginnings in Mencius's framework are simply the external manifestations of this pure or intuitive knowledge.[5] There is a parallel between the Buddhist teaching of original nature and Wang's concept of innate knowledge. Nonetheless, because of his practical orientation and public responsibility, Wang was not blind to the error and limitation of Buddhism. As he contends, "Being attached to the non-distinction of good and evil, the Buddhists neglect everything and therefore are incapable of governing the world."[6]

Rather than merely subscribing to a Buddhist principle of non-attachment, Wang's philosophy of elimination or deconstruction allows the mind in itself to shine forth positively on the world of things. Pure knowing, like unconsciousness, is hidden below a sea of selfish consciousness and desires. The hermeneutics of the human subject in Wang's view can be traced back to a deeper horizon of ground of being which constitutes human consciousness and the actual course of life. To acquire innate knowledge as the ground of being, Wang calls for the elimination and deconstruction of the superficial phenomenon of human understanding and moral life toward action as the completion of knowledge. Wang's hermeneutics of elimination aims at a movement to return for the original substance of theory and praxis.[7]

In *Ch'uan His Lu* (*Instructions for Practical Living*), Wang engages Mencius's concept of "*Chin Hsin*" (full realization of mind-heart). According to Wang, "*Chin Hsin*" means knowing nature (*hsing*), while Wang identifies *hsing* as mind-heart's body. Thus, there exists no *li* (prin-

5. Fung, *History of Chinese Philosophy*, II. 601.
6. Chan, *Instructions for Practical Living*, Sec. 101. 64; see secs.162, 236, and 270.
7. Ibid., sec.5.10.

ciple) outside of *hsin* (mind–heart). In the light of "the principle of the unity of knowledge and action," Wang contends that Zhu Xi wrongly interpreted the doctrine of the investigation of things, because Zhu Xi identified the higher attainments of exerting one's mind to the utmost and knowing one's nature one-sidedly and inadequately with the investigation of things and the extension of knowledge.[8]

In Wang's view, the word "thing" (*wu*) in the phrase "the investigation of things" is equivalent to the word event or affair (*shih*), and both thing and event refer to the mind. From the mind emanates the will whose original substance is knowledge. When the will is directed toward seeing, hearing, speaking, and acting, each of these is a "thing." For instance, when one is directed toward serving one's ruler, serving one's ruler is a "thing." An intentionality of the mind is not separated from the object of the mind. Therefore, Wang argues that there are neither principles nor things outside the mind. The substance of the mind pervades the past and the present and exists without beginning or end.

Wang's concept of enlarging and filling out (*kuo er chong*), which originated from Mencius, transforms Zhu Xi's doctrine of the extension of knowledge in ways that the principles of all events and everything are not outside the human mind. Fully realizing one's nature and knowing the Heavenly Principle does not go beyond the extension of pure knowing (*liang zhi*). Wang argues for the extension of one's pure knowledge at the place where Zhu Xi contends that one seeks for principles by investigating things and events outside. Wang's ontology both challenges and replaces Zu Xi's epistemology. An epistemology of moral self-cultivation is existentially based and deepened in Wang's ontological interpretation of the investigation of things in the *Great Learning*.

According to Zu Xi's interpretation of *ge wu*, *ge* means to reach (*zhi*), while *wu* means affairs (*shih*). In other words, *ge wu* means fully comprehending (*qiong*) while *wu* means something close to principles (*Li*). Thus *ge wu* is to fully comprehend the principles of every affair. Against Zhu Xi's interpretation, Wang defines *wu* (things or affairs) as the locus of one's attention. It is certain that for Wang the extension of knowledge consists in the investigation of things. The word "things" (*wu*) must be interpreted as affairs (*shih*). The activity of the mind is called thought. Things (*wu*) are the objects toward which thought is intentionally directed. For instance, when our thought is intended and directed

---

8. Ibid., sec. 6.13.

toward serving our parents, the serving of our parents is then one of these "things."

Things or affairs imply the life context of the human being with others in the public realms constituting and influencing one's thoughts and intentionality in regards to the objects and events in the world as well as human internal consciousness and imagination. Principles of things or affairs are not existentially discovered by Zhu Xi's empirical investigation. Thus, Wang demands an ontological apprehension of the principles in actual life, which is a rectification of human thoughts. Wang interprets *ge* (in the phrase *ge wu*, "investigation of things") to mean *cheng* (rectifying). Here, Wang integrates Mencius's teaching that "a great man rectified the ruler's mind."[9] This means "eliminat[ing] what is incorrect in the mind so as to preserve the correctness of its original substance."[10] Wang develops his concept of the investigation of things in terms of the unity of elimination and rectification for the sake of the restoration of a state of rectitude. That is, the principle of the unity between knowledge and action.

Eliminating or deconstructing superficial thoughts and methodologies can lead to an understanding of things or affairs. This refers to a dialectical movement of rectification from what is obscured by selfish, superficial, and unenlightened desire toward what underlines and lays bare human consciousness and empirical investigation. The essence of the human mind, namely pure knowing, like a mirror, reflects the life situation at hand, constituting the beginning of action. Action is the completion of knowledge. True perception relates to the greater context of the Way, the action of the Way. This position refers to Wang's essential teaching of the unity of knowledge and action (*zhi xing he yi*). When *liang zhi*, a genuine understanding of the thing, begins, such understanding or knowledge leads to deed. In the context of *liang zhi*, knowledge and praxis are one and the same.

An analysis of things goes to inquire about being in the world of things in taking care of things in association with praxis. Wang's concept of mind unfolds from within, intertwining with past, present, and future, and articulating the character of projecting praxis in taking care of the others and in recognition of their life horizon.

9. Ibid., sec. 6.15.
10. Ibid., sec. 7.15.

Liang zhi is thus embedded in the actual events of one's own life. Human understanding or investigation of things in the world is out of the question when conceived of apart from one's life connection within the world. Praxis-leading knowledge comes from the ontological apprehension of a deeper meaning of the horizon of human life in the public sphere. Thus, a dialectical unity of theory and praxis finds its locus in an ontological sense, existentially and socially engaged in actual life in the world. This existentially-socially engaged hermeneutics transcends the limitation of a methodological investigation by Zhu Xi, waiting for the manifestation of metaphysics of the Heavenly Principle. When disengaged from the historical-social situation and location of daily life, a methodological investigation of things fails to comprehend the unity of theory and praxis in human engagement with the actual life of the public sphere.

Wang's art of interpretation of the classic texts takes on a more radical form than Zhu Xi's. Insofar as a method of self-cultivation and theory of interpretation begins with eliminating or deconstructing the obscuring selfish, superficial consciousness, and representational desire, *liang zhi* operates without interference. A return to nature's original state calls for a commitment of faith to praxis in the public realm. Once one is committed to the thought of doing good by paying attention to the operation of *liang zhi*, it is like planting a tree. The enlightenment takes place in a flash of insight.

Wang interprets anew Mencius's concept of four sprouts as indications (or clues) of the underlying innate, unconscious lifeworld. To the extent that the light of *liang zhi* shines like the sun behind the clouds, the truth connects concretely with human life within the world. Such enlightenment, existentially and socially engaged, has less to do with looking to the illuminating sun waiting outside the cave of human mind. The past, the present, and the future fuse within the human experience of the existential and public lifeworld through which *liang zhi* operates.

Given this fact, *liang zhi* is not confined to the Confucian classics or to Confucius and Mencius's teaching. The dynamic speech–act of Dao, *liang zhi*, is appreciated more than the said: the written text. According to Wang's critical engagement with Confucius, Confucius' contribution lies in his edition and interpretation of classics, by eliminating the complicated and confused words for the sake of seeking meaning. The core of the Confucian written tradition is to be understood as a way of eliminating or deconstructing the complex world of the text for the sake of reconstructing the meaning in a deeper sense, while still preserving a limited core of essential writings.

A critical-reflective attitude toward the text is appreciated in favor of the subject matter of dynamic action of *liang zhi*. The subject matter invites a critical reflective engagement with the text. Through this process, the subject matter is interpreted differently than in the classics and the interpreter is transformed through such an ontological encounter with the subject matter in the present horizon.

To the degree that the subject matter in the classics is the operation of *liang zhi*, the classics are records of the operation of *liang zhi* in the past. The classics preserve traces of *liang zhi* by becoming histories of *liang zhi* in action and presence. Therefore, the classics have a qualified authority to the extent that the *liang zhi* in the texts speaks to or corresponds to one's own *liang zhi* grounded in one's contemporary life context. "If in the course of learning, I understand what is fundamental, all the Six Classics are my footnotes."[11]

As traces of *liang zhi* in their past, the sages (or the authors) encounter, enlarge, and transform the horizon of one's own *liang zhi* in their social cultural location. Dao, as *liang zhi*, guides one's understanding, interpretation, and action through the mediation of the life of the sages and the classics which are not identical with *liang zhi* as such. The classics and the sages are not the focus of self-cultivation and interpretation, but the *liang zhi* in the past history and its presence in one's own present location is the subject matter of self-cultivation and interpretation of the truth. "Truth and method" (Gadamer) are embedded with the dynamic presence of Dao in action within our own particular life context and experience.

In this light, Wang made extensive comments on Mencius's *Great Learning*, and *Doctrine of Mean*. The approach of his art of interpretation in these classics is to look for the subject matter of the text, *liang zhi*, as the ultimate arbiter rather than providing a thorough and comprehensive commentary on the classical texts in a traditional manner. Wang's eliminating hermeneutics of the subject matter, seeking the original face of *liang zhi* leads to his critique of the texts as well as of traditional hierarchical authority, while articulating equality of people in the actual course of daily life. Going deeper in the sense of elimination pairs with

11. Ivanhoe, *Ethics*, 124.

coming back to the public sphere of people's life in which *liang zhi* is also dynamically present.

This implies a shift of interpretation and self-cultivation from the written text toward the real lives of those ordinary people in the public sphere as shaped, conditioned, and connected by the actual world of things or affairs. In light of subject matter of *liang zhi*, people's life experiences and horizons in the world of things or affairs are fully integrated into Wang's hermeneutics of elimination and engagement.

Extending intuitive knowledge in Wang's perspective implies expanding one's horizon and lifeworld in an encounter and interaction with tradition and classic texts, and in connection with people in the world of things or affairs. The act of Dao in dynamic saying interacts with critical reason to search for the subject matter of the truth. It embraces and mediates discourse in public, social location and textuality in the classic tradition. In this regard, interpretation of the Dao is carried out in connection with life horizon of the others, articulating a practical dimension of interpretation.

This is Wang's contribution to the art of interpretation and self-cultivation as distinct from Zhu Xi's. Unfortunately, Ricci's engagement of Confucianism at his time was not an adequate intellectual struggle with the historical development of Confucianism as connected with the reality of actual life in China. The legacy of Ricci should not be found in the past. Rather, its meaning must be interculturally reframed for the present and must interact with the tradition of Confucian hermeneutics from which Ricci left off.

Conclusion

Odysseus, Abraham, and Laozi

The intercultural reframing of religion, interpretation, and the public sphere as pursued and discussed in this book offered analysis of and arguments for connecting the spiritual life with the socially embodied life. This study of intercultural theory of interpretation and religion in the public sphere looked both theologically and philosophically at the Platonic concept of soul's supremacy over the body in terms of the biblical message of bodily resurrection and its relevance to the economic and material life. It also analyzed the debate about the process of Western civilization's disenchantment of the world and the resultant iron cage (Max Weber). Then it is connected with Habermas's project of emancipation of lifeworld from colonizing power of state, economy, and mass media in a sociological public sphere and Foucault's genealogy of power and knowledge in postmodern perspective.

A critical theory of communicative rationality is guided by an interest in emancipation and uncovers communicatively distorted language. It intends to overcome a reified development of instrumental rationality. In proposing a civil society based on deliberate democracy and discourse ethics, a critical theory of communication is directed against a social system steered by money, administrative power of the state, and mass media, which are colonizing the lifeworld. In considering a critical theory of the lifeworld, however, we cannot ignore a sociological genealogy that analyzes and reframes the power-knowledge interplay within a given society. If a communicative ethic ignores an analysis of the discourse of those who are marginalized, deviated, unfit, and unsaid, it tends to become a grand narrative which universalizes all particularities and differences into a communicative idealism.

According to Levinas, God the Infinite is not to be rationalized or demythologized. Rather, the Infinite must be actualized as a prophetic desire for God through an ethical radicalism toward Others. God beyond philosophy is an inspiration for the prophetic testimony of God's Word, which is reflected in the face of the Others. A postfoundational hermeneutic of God's "saying" over the "said" takes into account a synchronic analysis of power and knowledge to promote a discourse of *parrhēsia* and to mobilize solidarity with God's minority in the public sphere. In this regard, a theory of interpretation and socio-critical theory are dynamically mediated and interdisciplinary reframed for engagement with lifeworld of the public sphere.

A diachronic hermeneutic of the history of effect which emphasizes belongingness to the cultural and linguistic tradition can be challenged and renewed by a sociological-synchronic analysis of human life grounded in social location. Furthermore, a lifeworld of non-Christian religions becomes an opportunity for the Christian religion to develop its horizon in more pluralistic, multicultural perspective, while offering a corrective to a Western Christianity that stands unilaterally under the influence of a Western metaphysic and culture. Theological hermeneutics of divine speech event in analogical-discursive configuration as pursued in this book attempts to actualize and deepen the irregularity of God's speech through textual world as well as in extrabiblical narrative. In this light, Christian mission following in the footsteps of Christ for God's reign in the world is examined and discussed in terms of relating Christian mission in China to the interpretation of Christian narrative in the presence of religious outsiders.

This book's conclusion necessarily remains fragmentary because the interdisciplinary tension and complexity of engaging religious tradition, interpretation theory, and the public sphere in a cross-cultural context resist systematization. In concluding remarks, let us consider three people—Odysseus, Abraham, and Laozi—as models for our major metaphors, cave and butterfly.

1. Those engaged with the *Dialectics of Enlightenment* find Homer's *Odyssey* to be of particular interest. In the *Odyssey* Homer enacts the dialectic of enlightenment. In this interpretation, the Homeric world possesses a bourgeois Enlightenment element. For Horkheimer and Adorno the *Odyssey* narrates the progress of human subjectivity and

culture in the face of enlightened reason. Here, Odysseus is depicted as "a prototype of the bourgeois individual."[1]

Horkheimer and Adorno attempt to analyze how the struggle for self-preservation and autonomy connects with sacrifice, renunciation, and autonomy in the life voyage of Odysseus. The central character in the epics exemplifies a struggle for liberation from myth and nature: the self-positing, autonomous subject, and the bourgeois individual. In his voyage from Troy to Ithaca, enlightenment (in opposition to myth) is represented in the surviving individual ego, which struggles with a multifarious fate. In Odysseus's adventures, the magical power and world of gods or demons lose their mighty powers for the sake of his self-preservation and the return to his homeland.[2]

For example, the beautiful goddess Circe, the temptations of the Sirens or the Lotus, and the cattle of Hyperion challenges his potential autonomy. For his survival, however, Odysseus must come to the point of a "denial of nature in man for the sake of domination over non-human nature and over other men."[3] This denial for self-preservation is shown as "the nucleus of all civilizing rationality," that is, the "germ-cell" of the bourgeois individual proliferating mythic irrationality.

Odysseus, as such a prototype, survives and wins only by demystifying himself and the powers he encounters. His deception is the prototype of his cunning nature, which is thus elevated to self-consciousness.[4] Given this fact, the means are elevated as an end "which under late capitalism is tantamount to open insanity."[5] Odysseus, then, stands as a model of totalitarian capitalism's irrationalism. Consequently, the history of civilization is the history of renunciation, deception, and manipulation for self-preservation, representing a society gaining mastery over itself in expiation.

In the society characterized by holocaust, mass violence, and genocide, imitation for the mastery of the other enters into the service of domination to the extent that a human being is anthropomorphized for a human being. Through rational calculation, the human being masters nature. In the journey from Troy to Ithaca, the gods are mastered. Thus,

1. Horkheimer and Adorno, *Dialectic of Enlightenment*, 43.
2. Ibid., 46–47.
3. Ibid., 54.
4. Ibid., 50.
5. Ibid., 54.

they "are overthrown by the very system by which they are honored."[6] Through reason, wit, and a cunning mind, Odysseus advances his interest and pursues his goal. "The possibility of failure becomes the postulate of a moral excuse for profit. From the standpoint of the developed exchange society and its individuals, the adventures of Odysseus are an exact representation of the risks which mark out the road to success."[7]

In the legend of the Sirens, the self is lost once the song of pleasure is heard. The Sirens are a temptation threatening the "I." Aware of the danger that lies ahead, Odysseus commands his men to plug their ears with wax. Passing the Sirens, Odysseus instructs the men to tie him to a mast so he can hear the song without falling prey to its temptation. Although Odysseus indulges in the beauty of the song as a passive listener, the Sirens' voices become art, a mere object of contemplation. "In primitive bourgeois history it [the quality of the Sirens] is neutralized to become merely the wishful longing of the passer-by."[8]

By imitating nature, he learns to adapt to it. In learning to imitate, Odysseus learns renunciation. His enlightenment comes into the service of domination and deception. Deception is a mode of exchange in which the contract is fulfilled, yet the other party is deceived. According to Weber, surpluses are causally exchanged, but the principal source of supply is self-production.[9]

The authors of *Dialectic of Enlightenment* view Odysseus's behavior from an economic perspective. Irrational reason finds its echo in cunning minds standing for the assimilation of bourgeois reason to unreason. Odysseus, the wily solitary, is *homo oeconomicus*, like Robinson Crusoe. Both Odysseus and Crusoe embody the principle of a capitalist economy,[10] living by the original constitutive principal of civil society. Deception is the mark of their rationality, using those they met as tools or mere things.[11] In the encounter with the Cyclops Polyphemus (the giant with one enormous eye), Odysseus uses trickery to seemingly befriend the giant, telling him his name is "No-man." This trick ensures his survival.

6. Ibid., 49.
7. Ibid., 61–62.
8. Ibid., 59.
9. Ibid., 61.
10. Ibid.
11. Ibid., 62.

Odysseus's ultimate return to his wife, Penelope, denotes a return to the pleasures of a fixed order of life and property. Under the pressure of civilization, women are forced to adopt a "civilized" position as woman, defaming the sex. As a representative of nature, woman in bourgeois society reflects the pure lie for domination, becoming the enigmatic image of irresistibility and powerlessness.[12]

The Odysseus-like homecoming is a return to a life of self-identity in distanciation from myth and nature. For this life of self-identity, all different particulars are deceived and defeated. Rationality in Western civilization juxtaposes the enlightening role of reason with calculation, trickery, and exchange or self-preservation. In turn, it alienates the Other by subordinating them to the self-identity of reason. In this life journey, as described in the *Odyssey*, it is difficult to recognize the Other for the sake of co-existence.

The Odysseus of self-identification through the totalizing existents for his survival and interest finds its locus in Heidegger's care for one's being-in-the world. Care is a characteristic of human life for its own sake. This too is reflected in Greek mythology. Once "Care" was crossing a river when she took a piece of clay and began to shape it. As she pondered what to make with it, Jupiter came by. "Care" asked him to give it spirit. This he gladly did, but when asked to grant the name, Jupiter forbade it. While "Care" and Jupiter were arguing, Earth arose and wanted her name to be conferred upon the clay creature. When they asked Saturn to be the judge, Saturn's decision was: "Since you, Jupiter, have given its spirit, you receive that spirit at death; and since 'Care' first shaped this creature, she shall possess it as long as it lives. And because there is a dispute among you as to its name, let it be called 'homo,' for it is made out of humus (earth)."[13]

In a Western understanding of human being, care has a priority regarding the spirit and body. Being-in-the-world for its lifetime is dominated by care and this being is left to Saturn (time). In this fable, a Western understanding of the essence of human being is envisaged by its temporal sojourn in the world to come back to his ontological authenticity with anxious effort as well as with carefulness and dedication. The human project of understanding of the world is an accomplishment of

---

12. Ibid., 72.
13. Heidegger, *Being and Time*, 184.

care. Hermeneutics of the care for life is oriented toward self-realization rather than life in promotion of the Others in the public sphere.

Hegel's dialectics of mutual recognition can correct the Odyssean-Heideggerian prototype or the care of being-in-the-world. Recognizing the importance of labor and interaction in the social, public sphere, Hegel develops and renews a dialectic of enlightenment toward a dialectic of recognition for progress, freedom, and liberation through social praxis and labor. Nonetheless, nature becomes reified and instrumentalized through human labor. Finally the reified nature threatens human life in a progressed civilization. As far as a dialectical negativity and intersubjective recognition of the Other remains corrective to a totalizing system of Hegel's absolute knowledge, a dialectic of enlightenment entails a potential for an immanent critique of instrumentalized and reified reason and its civilization.

2. Levinas once characterized Odysseus as a prototype of the Western philosophy of Sameness and self-identity. Rather than Odysseus, he advocates for Abraham as the prototype of life for the Other. Abraham is the cardinal example of Judaism, Christianity, and Islam. In Abraham's journey, we read that Ishmael, the first circumcised, enters into Abraham's blessing. In Genesis 12, there is a comprehensive blessing for the descendents of Abraham. In addition to Isaac, Ishmael is also a participant in Abraham's promise of blessing. The dimension of the promise of blessing is valid for all the people of the world. We are aware of the God's sympathy in Genesis for Hagar and Ishmael. The God who elects Israel is also an advocate for Ishmael and Hagar. Likewise, all nations also participate in the history of the blessing of this covenant through Jesus Christ.

The Bible then goes on to speak in a more surprising way. We think particularly of the encounter between Abraham and Melchizedek, the "king of justice" from Jerusalem. For Jews, like Christians and Muslims, it is surprising and extraordinary that Abraham is blessed by Melchizedek (Gen 14).

This thinking from the perspective of the Other and the fascination with the wealth and beauty of the Other is a part of Abraham's experience of the irregular grace of God. Listening to the strange, unexpected voice of God from the Others—Ishmael, Hagar, Melchizedek, and so on—characterizes Abraham's life journey of discipleship and *diakonia* in a humble and open attitude before the mystery of God. This irregular, unexpected, and even provocative perspective in Abraham's life, unlike that of Odysseus, proposes an ethic of living and thinking with respect to Others in our multi-faith context. Abraham's journey is different from that of the hero of the Greek myth, Odysseus. Unlike the Odysseus myth, in which he comes back to Ithaca, Abraham leaves his homeland forever in order to travel to a still unknown land in wholehearted trust in the promise of God. Upon his return, Odysseus is exactly the same as he was when he left Ithaca. All particulars and differences are deceived, humiliated, and alienated by his instrumental reason for self-preservation.

However, Abraham's life of journey and expulsion represents the realism of daily and concrete living in recognition of the Other. Christian theology is a theology of journey and traveling, with full trust in the promise of God, into the foreign and different world of other people, a world where God waits to bless us. In view of God's blessing of Abraham through Melchizedek, God's Saying can be heard in the figure of the Other. This line of thought in the biblical narrative has been unsaid and suppressed for the sake of a christomonism in which the Jewish character of Jesus is undermined and buried by the Greek metaphysical language of God.

As F.-W. Marquardt articulates regarding the affinity between Jesus Christ and Abraham, "we can hardly in its importance overesteem the fact that in the New Testament, the Jesus proclamation and the understanding of Christian faith is brought into connection with Abraham's faith and history."[14] Jesus's message is placed in the sign of Abraham's promise that embraces the Jews, the Muslims, and all others.

God as Saying is not captive to Greek metaphysics. Rather it breaks through it, widening its horizon for a much larger horizon in the world of people and religions. God as the place (*topos*) of the world is the One who loves, renews, and participates in worldly affairs for the sake of the victims, the marginal, and the unfit while keeping God's freedom over the world. God is the horizon of the world, challenging and transforming it toward God's kingdom. In our global world characterized both by peace as well as violence among religions, God challenges the iron cage of today's Empire civilization. The reality of the lordless powers in the public sphere is demythologized.

A Christian theology of the public sphere is a critical reflection of God's grace in Christ and God's companion to the Others in light

---

14. Marquardt, *Von Elend und Heimsuchung*, 280.

of God's speech event. A human being, a political animal, is also an interpreting animal with a mimetic capacity and desire. Human reason is invited to join God's lifeworld, which works through the Word and the Spirit, to take sides with God's life in protest of the ideological weapon of death under dominion, violence, and sacrifice of the Others.

3. According to the authors of *Dialectic of Enlightenment,* a lotus flower—a symbol of idle life and bliss—contradicts a life of conscious self-preservation, and lotus-eater is detached from the advantages of rationally planned civilization of food and meal. In an encounter with Lotus-eaters, people who have eaten the lotus sink into a harmonious relationship with their environment. However, for adherents of the rationale of self-preservation, this idyll is impermissible because the happiness offered by the lotus is mere illusion, the absence of the awareness of misfortune.[15] The Lotus, which is an Eastern food in India and China, is attached to the idle life; thus, eating flowers symbolizes the promise of a state that assures "the reproduction of life is independent of conscious self-preservation and the bliss of the fully contented is detached from the advantages of rationally planned nutrition."[16]

Laozi is a prototype of harmony with nature. Unlike Laozi, Confucius's ethic can be articulated in the following way: I co-exist therefore I am (*ren*). However, this interpersonal ethic of coexistence is structured in a hierarchical way through the rectification of names. Confucian rationality begins by taking issue with the discrepancy between name and reality. When the name does not correspond to reality, disorder occurs in all corners of life. Rectifying the name in accordance with reality, Confucian rationality is satisfied with a representational aspect of human life in terms of self-cultivation. Nature is suppressed. A harmonious life with the spontaneity of nature yields to self-cultivation and preservation in the communitarian sphere (family, organization, society, and state).

However, Laozi points in a different direction. The Dao of heaven is ineffable rather than conceptualized by a Confucian ethic of humanness and righteousness. A Dao that can be discussed is not the permanent Dao. In a Christian fashion, it implies that "I will be that I will be." Dao is an origin and source of life, a forwarding reality in the interplay of *de*

---

15. Horkheimer and Adorno, *Dialectic of Enlightenment*, 63.
16. Ibid., 64.

(virtue) and *qi* (life breath). The Dao is what happens in self (*tzu-jan*). The Dao does nothing, but nothing is left undone. It loves and nourishes all things but does not control it. This life companion will emerge of itself, without external compulsion. *De*, unlike the Confucian concept of *de* (humanity, righteousness, and rationality), is the realization or expression of the Dao in an actual, harmonious living. Laozi's picture of the ideal person is articulated in that when establishing something great, one is willing not to abide in one's achievement, retreating from what is done. This is an ethic of action without attachment. All social values are based on prejudices: reason vs. unreason, history vs. myth, ethics vs. nature, goodness vs. evil, and the sane vs. the mad.

In an analysis of madness and civilization, Foucault once argued that reason needs to learn from the non-reason of Nietzsche, Van Gogh, or Artaud. Through Nietzsche's madness, his thought opened out to the modern world. Nietzsche's last cry—declaring himself both Christ and Dionysus—"is not on the border of reason and unreason, but finally realized and immediately vanishing, of a reconciliation of the 'shepherds of Arcady and the fishermen of Tiberias.'"[17]

How is such an advocacy possible in Laozi's way? Laozi argues for a spirituality of mutual life in which the dialectic of enlightenment faces a dialectic of nature (*tzu-yan*), what is of and through itself. In light of spontaneous simplicity, those who are suppressed in the universal history of reason are rehabilitated. Femininity, nature, unreason, spontaneity, and childlike simplicity find their place herein.

According to Laozi, a dialectic of enlightenment follows Dao's path or direction, its standard is the spontaneity. Dao, which is the first principle of all things, cannot itself be a thing. The Dao which is to be said or objectified is not the permanent Dao. *De* (*logos*: reason) is Dao's dwelling in objects, so that individual objects obtain *de* from Dao. The ability to know about Dao's action of spontaneity through *de* and *qi* is called enlightenment (*ming*).

> All things . . . return to their root. This return to their root is called quiescence, which is called submission to Fate. Submission to Fate is called the Invariable. To know this Invariable is called enlightenment.[18]

---

17. Foucault, *Madness and Civilization*, 287.
18. *Laozi*, ch. 16.

Our body is the site of enlightenment; "know thyself" must be transformed to "take care of your body" ensouled and engaged with the Others. Anyone who knows the Dao's Invariable is tolerant, liberal, and generous toward things. Being tolerant, one is without prejudice. Without prejudice, one is comprehensive. Being comprehensive, one is vast. Being vast, one is of Dao. Practicing enlightenment in following Dao is to help and support creatures in need.[19]

Care or anxious effort in pursuit of self-identity or sameness is sharply rejected in light of Dao as the Way. A relationship between truth and being is not characterized by historicity or temporality, but by following the Way of non-discrimination. A practicing of enlightenment grounds Laozi's ethic of interdependence of the opposites (mutual arising). A logic of contradiction of two opposites, for instance, being and non-being, difficulty and easy, high and low, is to be seen in light of a logic of their growing out of one another in a harmonious way.

> It is because everyone under Heaven recognizes beauty as beauty, that the idea of ugliness exists. And equally if everyone recognized virtue (goodness) as virtue (goodness), this would merely create fresh conceptions of wickedness.[20]

Therefore, the sage relies on and practices actionless activity. Actionless life in option for what is soft and weak denotes Laozi's dialectic of a companion of life against a companion of death.[21]

Like Abraham, Laozi's life journey ends in a form of disappearance, never returning to his home. To the degree that Abraham never returned to his home, it characterizes his identity for the Others under the power of God. Laozi's disappearance from his country is believed to be a meeting with the Other: historical Buddha for mutual sharing of wisdom. This legend characterizes a spirit of mutual life in companionship with the foreign religion of Buddhism. Laozi is a prototype for practicing a dialectic of enlightenment in coexistence with the Other in mutually sharing and learning.

Neo-Confucian hermeneutics of "investigation of things and extension of knowledge" is partly influenced by a spirit of Daoist-Buddhist co-existence. Dao is revealed as Nature and Way through the pilgrim-

---

19. Ibid., ch. 27.
20. Ibid., ch. 2.
21. Ibid., ch. 76.

age of self-cultivation in harmonious life with the Others. Language is not adequate to express Dao ahead of us while being present in our life. Language is also conditioned and distorted in an historical, interpersonal, and cultural context like human being-in-the-world. Language analogically mirrors the moon (the truth) reflecting in and recognizing the streams of interpretation of it. No one monopolizes the truth, impartiality, and compassion of Dao.

How does language articulate Zhuangzi's dream of the butterfly? Zhuangzi's dream of the butterfly radicalizes Laozi's philosophy for the sake of transcending the language of consciousness. In Zhuangzi's view, one is thought and viewed at a place where one does not belong. One's existence remains partial and incomplete without connection to the life horizon of the Other which shapes and characterizes one's harmonious life with him/her. Before belonging to the world, I belonged to the Way in the embrace of *yin* and *yang*. This is a postfoundational resistance in East Asian sense for the sake of the Other, the different, and the deviated, to the principle of a dialectic of enlightenment as depicted in the life journey of Odysseus which is characterized by self-care and temporality. The happiness offered by the lotus is more than illusion because harmony in a genuine sense comes from mutual interdependence in the embrace of the different rather than an instrumentalization of the different to the sameness of one's consciousness.

In the civilization of the third millennium Odysseus, Abraham, and Laozi represent different lifeworlds in a non-connected way. An intercultural reframing of reason (Odysseus), faith (Abraham), and life of harmony (Laozi) in view of the interpretation of religion and truth in the public sphere remains open to the future, rather than implying a closed systematization. It is in the service of this vision that this work is offered.

Bibliography

Ackrill. J. L., editor. *A New Aristotle Reader*. Princeton, NJ: Princeton University Press, 1987.

Adorno, Theodor W. *Negative Dialectics*. Translated by E. B. Ashton. New York: Seabury, 1973.

Auerbach, Erich. *Mimesis: The Representation of Reality in Western Literature*. 1953. Reprint, Princeton, NJ: Princeton University Press, 2003.

Augustine. *The City of God*. Edited and translated by Marcus Dods. New York: Hafner, 1948.

———. *The Confessions of St. Augustine*. Translated by John K. Ryan. Garden City, NJ: Image, 1960.

———. *The Immortality of the Soul*. Translated by Ludwig Schopp. New York: Fathers of the Church, 1947

Barth, Karl. *The Christian Life, Church Dogmatics IV.4 Lecture Fragments*. Translated by Geoffrey W. Bromiley. Grand Rapids: Eerdmans, 1981.

———. *Church Dogmatics* I/2., III/2.3., IV/2. Edited and translated by Geoffrey W. Bromiley and T. F. Torrance. First paperback edition. Edinburgh: T. & T. Clark, 2004.

Bendix, Richard. *Max Weber: An Intellectual Portrait*. Berkeley: University of California Press, 1977.

Bernauer, James, and Jeremy, Carrette, editors. *Michel Foucault and Theology: The Politics of Religious Experience*. Hampshire, UK: Ashgate, 2004.

Bevans, Stephen B., and Roger P. Schroeder. *Constants in Context: A Theology of Mission for Today*. Maryknoll, NY: Orbis, 2004.

Bonhoeffer, Dietrich. *Gesammelte Schriften*. Munich: Kaiser, 1960.

———. *Letters & Papers from Prison*. Edited by Eberhard Bethge. Translated by Reginald H. Fuller et al. New York: Macmillan, 1971.

Bosch, David J. *Transforming Mission: Paradigm Shifts in Theology of Mission*. Maryknoll, NY: Orbis, 2004.

Brenner, William H. *Wittgenstein's Philosophical Investigations*. Albany: SUNY, 1999.

Buber, Martin. *The Martin Buber Reader: Essential Writings*. Edited and translated by Asher D. Biemann. New York: Macmillan, 2002.

Bultmann, Rudolf. *Jesus Christ and Mythology*. New York: Scribner, 1958.

———. *New Testament and Mythology and Other Basic Writings*. Edited and translated by Schubert M. Ogden. Philadelphia: Fortress, 1989.

Calhoun, Craig, editor. *Habermas and the Public Sphere*. Cambridge, MA: MIT Press, 1992.

Chan, Wing-tsit, translator. *Instructions for Practical Living and Other Neo-Confucian Writings by Wang Yang-Ming*. New York: Columbia University Press, 1963.

———, translator. *Reflections on Things at Hand: The Neo-Confucian Anthology.* Compiled by Zhu Xi and Lü Tsu-Ch'ien. New York: Columbia University Press, 1967.

Ching, Julia. *The Religious Thought of Chu His.* Oxford: Oxford University Press, 2000.

Chung, Paul S. *Christian Mission and A Diakonia of Reconciliation: A Global Reframing of Justification and Justice.* Minneapolis: Lutheran University Press, 2008.

———. *Constructing Irregular Theology: Bamboo and Minjung in East Asian Perspective.* Leiden: Brill, 2009.

———. *Karl Barth: God's Word in Action.* Eugene, OR: Cascade, 2008.

Confucius, *The Analects.* Translated by Arthur Waley. Beijing: Hunan People's Publishing House, 1999.

Cronin, Vicent. *The Wise Man from the West.* Glasgow: Collins, 1961.

De Las Casas, Bartolomé. *The Devastation of the Indies: A Brief Account.* Translated by Herma Briffault. Baltimore: Johns Hopkins University Press, 1992.

Diamond, Irene, and Lee Quinby, editors. *Feminism & Foucault: Reflections on Resistance.* Boston: Northeastern University Press, 1988.

Dillenberger, John, editor. *Marin Luther, Selections from His Writings.* Gaden City: Anchor, 1961.

Dreyfus, Hubert L., and Paul Rabinow. *Michel Foucault: Beyond Structuralism and Hermeneutics.* Chicago: University of Chicago Press, 1983.

Duchrow, Ulrich and Franz J. Hinkelammert. *Property for People, not for Profit: Alternatives to the Global Tyranny of Capital.* New York: Zed, 2004.

Duchrow, Ulrich. *Alternatives to Global Capitalism: Drawn from Biblical History Designed for Political Action.* Heidelberg: International Kairos, 1998.

Ebeling, Gerhard. *Luther: An Introduction to His Thought.* Translated by R. A. Wilson. Minneapolis: Fortress, 2007.

———. *Theology and Proclamation: Dialogue with Bultmann.* Translated by John Riches. London: Harper Collins, 1966.

———. *Word and Faith.* Translated by James W. Leitch. Philadelphia: Fortress, 1963.

Foucault, Michel. *The Archaeology of Knowledge.* Translated by A. M. Sheridan Smith. New York: Harper Colophon, 1972.

———. *Discipline & Punish: The Birth of the Prison.* Translated by Alan Sheridan. New York: Vintage, 1995.

———. *Fearless Speech.* Los Angles: Semiotexte, 2001.

———. *Herculine Barbin: Being the Recently Discovered Memoirs of a Nineteenth-Century French Hermaphrodite.* Translated by Richard McDougall. New York: Pantheon, 1980.

———. *The Hermeneutics of the Subject: Lectures at the Collège de France 1981–1982.* Edited by Frédéric Gros, English edited by Arnold I. Davidson. Translated by Graham Burchell. New York: Picador, 2005.

———. *The History of Sexuality I: An Introduction.* Translated by Robert Hurley. New York: Vintage, 1990.

———. *Madness and Civilization: A History of Insanity in the Age of Reason.* Translated by Richard Howard. New York: Vintage, 1988.

———. *The Order of Things: An Archaeology of the Human Sciences.* New York: Vintage, 1973.

Foster, John. *The Church of the T'ang Dynasty.* London: SPCK, 1939.

Frettloeh, L., and Jan-Dirk Doehling, editors. *Die Welt als Ort Gottes—Gott als Ort der Welt: Friedrich Wilhelm Marquardts theologische Utopie im Gespräch*. Munich: Kaiser, 2001.

Fung, Yu-lan. *A History of Chinese Philosophy*, I. Translated by Derk Bodde. Princeton: Princeton University Press, 1983.

———. *A History of Chinese Philosophy*, II. Translated by Derk Bodde. Princeton: Princeton University Press, 1953.

Gadamer, H.-G. *Truth and Method*. 2nd ed. Revised, edited, and translated by Joel Weinsheimer and Donald G. Marshall. New York, London: Continuum, 2004.

Gatti, Maria Luisa. "Plotinus: The Platonic Tradition and the Foundation of Neoplatonism." In *The Cambridge Companion to Plotinus*, edited by Lloyd P. Gerson, 10–37. Cambridge: Cambridge University Press, 1996.

Gerth, H. H., and C. Wright Mills, editors. *From Max Weber: Essays in Sociology*. New York: Oxford University Press, 1974.

Gerson, Lloyd P., editor. *The Cambridge Companion to Plotinus*. Cambridge: Cambridge University Press, 1996.

Gillman, Ian, and Hans-Joachim Klimkeit. *Christians in Asia before 1500*. Ann Arbor: University of Michigan Press, 1999.

Girad, René. *Things Hidden Since the Foundation of the World*. Translated by Stephen Bann and Michael Metteer. Stanford: Stanford University Press, 1978.

Gollwitzer, Helmut. *The Existence of God As Confessed by Faith*. Translated by James W. Leitch. London: SCM, 1965.

———. *An Introduction to Protestant Theology*. Translated by David Cairns. Philadelphia: Westminster, 1978.

Gordon, Colin, editor. *Power/Knowledge: Selected Interviews & Other Writings 1972–1977 by Michel Foucault*. New York: Pantheon, 1977.

Gradner, Daniel K, translator. *Chu His Learning to Be a Sage: Selections from the Conversations of Master Chu, Arranged Topically*. Berkeley: University of California Press, 1990.

Green, Clifford, editor. *Karl Barth: Theologian of Freedom*. Minneapolis: Fortress, 1991.

Habermas, Jürgen. *Between Facts and Norms: Contributions to a Discourse Theory of Law and Democracy*. Translated by W. Rehg. Cambridge, MA: MIT Press, 1996.

———. *Justification and Application: Remarks on Discourse Ethics*. Translated by Ciaran P. Cronin. Cambridge, MA: MIT Press, 1993.

———. *Knowledge and Human Interests*. Translated by J. J. Shapiro. Boston: Beacon, 1971.

———. *Legitimation Crisis*. Translated by Thomas McCarthy. Boston: Beacon, 1975.

———. *On the Logic of the Social Sciences*. Translated by S. Weber Nicholsen and J. Stark. Cambridge, MA: MIT Press, 1991.

———. *The Structural Transformation of the Public Sphere*. Translated by Thomas Burger Cambridge, MA: MIT Press, 1989.

———. *The Theory of Communicative Action, I: Reason and The Rationalization of Society*. Translated by Thomas McCarthy. Boston: Boston, 1984.

———. *The Theory of Communicative Action, II: Lifeworld and System: A Critique of Functionalist Reason*. Translated by Thomas McCarthy. Boston: Beacon, 1992.

———. *Theory and Practice*. Translated by John Viertel. Boston: Beacon, 1973.

Hegel, G. W. F. *The Phenomenology of Mind*. 2nd ed. Translated by J. B. Baille. New York: Macmillan, 1955.

Heidegger, Martin. *Basic Writings*. Revised and expanded. Edited by David Farrel Krell. New York: HarperCollins, 1993.

———. *Being and Time*. Translated by Joan Stambaugh. New York: SUNY Press, 1996.

———. *Nietzsche, I*. Translated by David Farrel Krell. San Francisco: Harper & Row, 1979.

———. *Pathmarks*. Translated by Thomas Sheehan. Edited by William McNeill. Cambridge: Cambridge University Press, 1998.

Hick, John, and Brian Hebblethwaite, editors. *Christianity and Other Religions*. Philadelphia: Fortress, 1980.

Hinkelammert, Franz J. *The Ideological Weapons of Death: A Theological Critique of Capitalism*. Translated by Philip Berryman. Maryknoll, NY: Orbis, 1981.

Holm, Frits V. *The Nestorian Monument: An Ancient Record of Christianity in China*. Edited by Paul Carus. Chicago: Open Court, 1909.

Horkheimer, Max, and Theodor W. Adorno. *Dialectic of Enlightenment*. Translated by J. Cumming. New York: Herder & Herder, 1972.

Horkheimer, Max. *Critical Theory: Selected Essays*. Translated by M. O'Connell et al. New York: Seabury, 1972.

———. *Eclipse of Reason*. New York: Seabury, 1974.

———. *Die Sehnsucht nach dem Ganz Anderen*. Hamburg: Furche, 1975.

Huang, Junjie. *Mencius Hermeneutics: A History of Interpretation in China*. New Brunswick, NJ: Transaction, 2001.

Huntington, Samuel. *The Clash of Civilizations and the Making of World Order*. New York: Simon & Schuster, 1996.

Husserl, Edmund. *Ideas: General Introduction to Pure Phenomenology*. Translated by W. R. Boyce Gibson. New York: Collier, 1962.

Ivanhoe, Philip J. *Ethics in the Confucian Tradition: The Thought of Mengzi and Wang Yangming*, 2nd ed. Indianapolis: Hackett, 2002.

Iwand, Hans J. *Luthers Theologie*. 5 vols. Edited by Helmut Gollwitzer et al. Munich: Kaiser, 1983.

———. *The Righteousness of Faith according to Luther*. Edited by Virgil F. Thompson. Translated by Randi H. Lundell. Eugene, OR: Wipf & Stock, 2008.

Jüngel, Eberhard. *God as the Mystery of the World: On the Foundation of the Theology of the Crucified One in the Dispute between Theism and Atheism*. Translated by Darrell L. Guder. Grand Rapids: Eerdmans, 1983.

Kirwan, Christopher, translator. *Aristotle's Metaphysics*. Oxford: Clarendon, 1971.

Kojève, Alexander. *Introduction to the Reading of Hegel: Lectures on the Phenomenology of Spirit*. Translated by James H. Nichols Jr. Edited by Allan Bloom. Ithaca, NY: Cornell University Press, 1991.

Kolb, Robert, and Timothy J. Wengert, editors. *The Book of Concord: The Confessions of the Evangelical Lutheran Church*. Minneapolis: Fortress, 2000.

Knitter, Paul F. *No Other Name? A Critical Survey of Christian Attitudes Toward the World Religions*. Maryknoll, NY: Orbis, 1996.

Legge, James. *The Nestorian Monument of Hsi-an Fu in Shen-Hsi, China Relating to the Diffusion of Christianity in China in the Seventh and Eighth Centuries*. London: Trübner, 1888.

Legge, James, translator. *The Chinese Classics 1*. Oxford: Clarendon, 1893.

Levenson, Jon D. *The Death and Resurrection of the Beloved Son: The Transformation of Child Sacrifice in Judaism and Christianity*. New Haven: Yale University Press, 1993.

Levinas, Emmanuel. *Basic Philosophical Writings*. Edited by Adriaan T. Peperzak, Simon Critchley, and Robert Bernasconi. Bloomington: Indiana University Press, 1996.

———. *Difficile liberté: Essais sur le judaïsme*. Paris: Albin Michel, 1976.

———. *Otherwise than Being or Beyond Essence*. Translated by Alphonso Lingis. Pittsburgh: Duquesne University Press, 1998.

———. *Totality and Infinity: An Essay on Exteriority*. Translated by Alphonso Lingis. Pittsburgh: Duquesne University Press, 2007.

Lindbeck, George A. *The Nature of Doctrine: Religion and Theology in a Postliberal Age*. Louisville: Westminster John Knox, 1984.

Louth, Andrew. *The Origins of The Christian Mystical Tradition: From Plato to Denys*. Oxford: Clarendon, 1983.

Lukacs, Georges. *History and Class Consciousness: Studies in Marxist Dialectics*. Translated by R. Livingstone. Cambridge: MIT Press, 1971.

———. *Der Junge Hegel: über die Beziehungen von Dialektik und Ökonomie*. 2. Frankfurt am Main: Shurkamp, 1973.

———. *Zur Ontologie des gesellschaftlichen Seins: Die ontologischen Grundprinzipien von Marx*. Neuwied and Darmstadt: Hermann Luchterhand, 1972.

Lull, Timothy F, editor. *Martin Luther's Basic Theological Writings*. Minneapolis: Fortress, 1989.

Luther, Martin. "An die Pfarrherren, wider den Wucher zu predigen." In *D. Martin Luthers Werke*, 51:331–424. Weimar: German Böhlaus Nachfolger, 1914 (=WA).

———. "How Christian Should Regard Moses." In *Martin Luther's Basic Theological Writings*, edited by Timothy F. Lull, 135–48. Minneapolis: Fortress, 1989.

———. "The Large Catechism (1529)." In *The Book of Concord: The Confessions of the Evangelical Lutheran Church*, edited by Robert Kolb and Timothy J. Wengert, 377–480. Minneapolis: Fortress, 2000.

———. "Prefaces to the Old Testament (1545, 1523)." In *Martin Luther's Basic Theological Writings*, edited by Timothy F. Lull, 118–34. Minneapolis: Fortress, 1989.

———. "The Smalcald Articles" (1537). In *The Book of Concord: The Confessions of the Evangelical Lutheran Church*, edited by Robert Kolb and Timothy J. Wengert, 295–329. Minneapolis: Fortress, 2000.

Lyotard, Jean-François. *The Postmodern Condition: A Report on Knowledge*. Translated by Geoff Bennington and Brian Massumi. Minneapolis: University of Minnesota Press, 1984.

Manheim, Karl. *Ideology and Utopia: An Introduction to the Sociology of Knowledge*. Translated by Louis Wirth and Edward Shils. New York: Harvest, 1936.

Marquardt, F.-W. *Eia, wärn Wir da—eine theologische Utopie*. Munich/Gütersloh: Kaiser, 1997.

———. "Gott oder Mammon aber: Theologie und Ökonomie bei Martin Luther." In *Einwürfe*, edited by F.-W. Marquardt, Dieter Schellong, and Michael Weinrich, 176–216. Munich: Kaiser, 1983.

———. *Die Juden im Römerbrief*. Zurich: TVZ, 1971.

———. *Theologie und Sozialismus: Das Beispiel Karl Barths*. Munich: Kaiser, 1972.

———. *Von Elend und Heimsuchung der Theologie: Prolegomena zur Dogmatik*. Munich: Kaiser, 1988.

Marx, Karl. *Capital*. Vol.1. Translated by Samuel Moore and Edward Aveling. New York: Modern Library, 1906.

———. *Early Writings*. Translated by T. B. Bottomore. New York: McGraw-Hill, 1964.

———. *Karl Marx Selected Writings*. Edited by David McLellan. Oxford: Oxford University Press, 1988.

Marx, Karl, and Friedrich Engels. *The German Ideology*. Edited by C. J. Arthur. London: Lawrence and Wishart, 1970.

Meyers, Ched. *Binding the Strong Man: A Political Reading of Mark's Story of Jesus*. Maryknoll, NY: Orbis, 1988.

Moffett, Samuel H. *A History of Christianity in Asia*. Vol. 1, *Beginnings to 1500*. Maryknoll, NY: Orbis, 2001.

Moltmann, Jürgen. *The Crucified God: The Cross of Christ as The Foundation and Criticism of Christian Theology*. Translated by R. A. Wilson and John Bowden. Minneapolis: Fortress, 1993.

———. *God for a Secular Society: The Public Relevance of Theology*. Translated by Margaret Kohl. Minneapolis: Fortress, 1999.

Mueller-Vollmer, Kurt, editor. *The Hermeneutics Reader: Texts of the German Tradition from the Enlightenment to the Present*. New York: Continuum, 1985.

Nietzsche, Friedrich. *The Will to Power*. Edited by W. Kaufmann. New York: Vintage, 1968.

Palmer, Martin. *The Jesus Sutras: Rediscovering the Lost Scrolls of Taoist Christianity*. New York: Ballantine, 2001.

Palmer, Richard. *Hermeneutics*. Evanston, IL: Northwestern University Press, 1969.

Pannenberg, Wolfhart. *Systematic Theology*. Vol. 1. Translated by Geoffrey W. Bromiley. Grand Rapids: Eerdmans, 1991.

———. *Theology and The Philosophy of Science*. Translated by Francis McDonagh Philadelphia: Westminster, 1976.

Peperzak, Adriaan. *To the Other: An Introduction to the Philosophy of Emmanuel Levinas*. West Lafayette: Indiana University Press, 1993.

Plato. *The Republic*. Translated by Desmond Lee. New York: Penguin, 1987.

Plotinus. *The Enneads*. Translated by Stephen MacKenna. London: Penguin, 1991.

Rabinow, Paul, and Nikolas Rose, editors. *The Essential Foucault: Selections from Essential Works of Foucault, 1954–1984*. New York: New Press, 2003.

Ricci, Matteo. *The True Meaning of the Lord of Heaven (T'ien-chu Shih-i)*. Translated by Douglas Lancashire and Peter Hu Kuo-chen. Edited by Edward J. Malatesta. St. Louis: Institute of Jesuit Sources, 1985.

Ricoeur, Paul. *Interpretation Theory: Discourse and the Surplus of Meaning*. Forth Worth: Texas Christian University Press, 1976.

———. *Oneself as Another*. Translated by Kathleen Blamey. Chicago: University of Chicago Press, 1992.

———. *Time and Narrative*. Vol. I. Translated by Kathleen McLaughlin and David Pellauer. Chicago: University of Chicago Press, 1983.

Rieth, Ricardo. *"Habsucht" bei Martin Luther: Ökonomisches und theologisches Denken, Tradition und soziale Wirklichkeit im Zeitalter der Reformation*. Weimar: Böhlau, 1996.

Rifkin, Jeremy. *The Age of Access: The New Culture of Hypercapitalism, Where All of Life is a Paid-for Experience*. New York: Putnam, 2000.

Bibliography

Rist, John M. *Augustine: Ancient Thought Baptized.* Cambridge: Cambridge University Press, 1994.

Robinson, James M. et al, editors. *New Frontiers in Theology: Discussions among Continental and American Theologians.* Vol. II, *The New Hermeneutic.* New York: Harper & Row, 1964.

Rongpei, Wang, translator. *Zhuangzi, I.* Hunan, Beijing: Hunan People's Publishing House, 1999.

Rumscheidt, Martin H, editor. *Fragments Grave and Gay.* London: Collins, 1971.

Saeki, Yoshiro P. *The Nestorian Documents and Relics in China.* 2nd ed. Tokyo: Maruzen, 1951.

Sanneh, Lamin. *Whose Religion is Christianity? The Gospel beyond the West.* Grand Rapids: Eerdmans, 2003.

Schmithals, Walter. *An Introduction to the Theology of Rudolf Bultmann.* Translated by John Bowden. Minneapolis: Augsburg, 1968.

Schroeder, Frederic M. "Plotinus and Language." In *The Cambridge Companion to Plotinus,* edited by Lloyd P. Gerson, 336–55. Cambridge: Cambridge University Press, 1996.

Stendahl, Krister. *Paul among Jews and Gentiles.* Philadelphia: Fortress, 1976.

Tang, Li. *A Study of the History of Nestorian Christianity in China and Its Literature in Chinese.* Frankfurt: Lang, 2002.

Taylor, Mark C., editor. *Deconstruction in Context.* Chicago: University of Chicago Press, 1986.

Thompson, John, and David Held, editors. *Habermas: Critical Debates.* London: Macmillan, 1982.

Thomson, John B., editor and translator. *Hermeneutics & the Human Sciences.* Cambridge: Cambridge University Press, 1981.

Tiedemann, Rolf, editor. *Minima Moralia.* In *Gesammelte Schriften,* Vol. 4. Frankfurt: Suhrkamp, 1996.

Tracy, David. *The Analogical Imagination: Christian Theology and the Culture of Pluralism.* New York: Crossroad, 2000.

———. *On Naming the Present: God, Hermeneutics, and Church.* Maryknoll, NY: Orbis, 1994.

Troeltsch, Ernst. *The Absoluteness of Christianity and the History of Religions.* Translated by David Reid. Louisville: Westminster John Knox, 1971.

———. *Protestantism and Progress: The Significance of Protestantism for the Rise of the Modern World.* Translated by W. Montgomery. Boston: Beacon, 1958.

———. *The Social Teaching of the Christian Churches.* Vol. 2. Translated by Olive Wyon. Louisville: Westminster John Knox, 1992.

Waley, Arthur, translator. *Laozi.* Hunan, Beijing: Hunan People's Publishing House, 1999.

Wallace, Mark I. *The Second Naiveté: Barth, Ricoeur, and the New Yale Theology.* Macon, GA: Mercer University Press, 1995.

Weber, Max. *Economy and Society.* Vol. 1. Edited by G. Roth and C. Wittich. New York: Bedminster, 1968.

———. *The Methodology of the Social Sciences.* Edited and translated by Edward A. Shils and Henry A. Finch. Glencoe, NY: Free Press, 1949.

———. *The Protestant Ethics and the Spirit of Capitalism.* Translated by Talcott Parsons. New York: Dover, 1958.

———. *Weber: Selections in Translation*. Edited by W. G. Runciman. Translated by Eric Matthews. Cambridge: Cambridge University Press, 1978. .

Welton, Don, editor. *The Essential Husserl: Basic Writings in Transcendental Phenomenology*. Bloomington: Indiana University Press, 1999.

Wickeri, Phillip L. "The Stone Is a Mirror: Interpreting the Xi'an Christian Monument and Its Implications for Theology and the Study of Christianity in Asia." *QUEST* 3:2 (2004) 19–46.

Wittgenstein, Ludwig. *Philosophical Investigations*. Translated by G. E. M. Anscombe. Oxford: Blackwell, 1953.

———. *Tractatus Logico-Philosophicus*. Translated by D. F. Pears and B. F. McGuinness. London: Routledge & Kegan Paul, 1961.

Wyschogrod, Edith. *Emmanuel Levinas: The Problem of Ethical Metaphysics*. New York: Fordham University Press, 2000.

Zion Bokser, Ben, translator. *The Talmud Selected Writings*. Mahwah: Paulist, 1989.

Index

Adorno, Th., x. 70, 78–81, 85, 108, 169, 256, 276, 277
Alētheia, 4–6
Alouben, 243, 246, 248, 253, 256
Analects, 257, 260
Analogia entis, 210, 221
Analogia relationis, 229
Anamnesis, 11
Anselm, 228
Anthropologia crucis, 57
Aquedah, 29, 30
Aquinas, Thomas, 15
Aristotle, xi, 4, 6, 10–14, 140, 148, 172, 228
Armor Dei, 55
Assumptio carnis, 34
Augustine, 15–21, 55
Axis mundi, 222

Barth, K., xii, xvi, 27, 42, 43, 76, 204, 205, 212, 213, 220, 221, 223, 228, 229, 233, 237
Bio-power, 123, 124, 128, 130
Bonhoeffer, D., 36, 39, 47, 214, 228
Bultmann, R., xvi, 213–19, 221–24, 226, 227, 229

Conformitas crucis, 23
Confucius, 256, 257, 260, 272, 282

Dao de jing, 249
Davar, 196, 208
Descartes, R., 113, 183, 190, 201
Deum justificare, 36, 47
Deus absconditus, 3
Deus dixit, 197

Deus ex machina, 210
Deus revelatus, 3
Dilthey, W., 133–38, 142, 150–52, 163, 165, 166, 171, 173, 174, 215–17
Dukkha, 233
Durkheim, E., 95

Ebeling, G., xvi–xvii, 212, 223–25, 236
Entelechy, 11, 12
Epoché, 151, 152, 155, 163, 164, 184
Eschaton, 51
Extra muros ecclesiae, 205, 209

Fetishism, 29, 43, 71, 72
Feuerbach, 19
Fons vitae, 22
Foucault, M., xiii, xv, xvi, 40, 102, 103, 105–8, 110–13, 122, 124–26, 128, 129, 130–32, 275
Freud, S., 119, 163, 215
Fruitio Dei, 19, 23

Gadamer, H.-G., xiv, xvi, 3, 5, 13, 14, 96, 112, 116, 133, 137, 146–63, 167–71, 173, 174, 178, 226, 227, 229, 273
Geertz, C., 234, 235
Genealogy, 113–18, 122, 127, 128, 129
Gollwitzer, H., 27

Habermas, J., xv, xvi, 67, 71, 72, 84–91, 93–102, 133, 135, 136, 162, 163–73, 229, 230, 275

295

Hegel, G. F., x, xiv, 12, 78–80, 82, 86–89, 116, 148–52, 154–58, 161, 186, 206, 280
Heidegger, M., xiii, 3–5, 19, 106, 107, 117, 133, 136–46, 148, 149, 152–56, 165–67, 169, 178, 180–83, 187–89, 191–94, 196, 198, 199, 201, 204, 205, 213, 214, 217, 220–22, 227, 279
Hinkelammert, F., 43,72
Homo oeconomicus, 278
Homo religious, xi, xii
Homoousious, 159, 251
Horkheimer, Max, x, xvi, 67, 70, 78–85, 133, 169, 276, 277
Husserl, E., xiv, 136, 140, 152, 155, 158, 163–65, 183–85, 191
Hypostases, 8

Iwand, H. J., 36

Kant, I., xiv, 79, 81, 110, 134, 135, 147
Kerygma, xii, 194, 196,197, 208, 215, 216, 221, 222,227

Laozi, xvii, 253, 254, 275–85
Lebenswelt, xiii, 151
Legge, J., 243
Levinas, E., xiii, xvi, 182, 183, 185–205, 238, 275, 280
Lindbeck, G., xvi, xvii, 212, 231–37
Lukacs, G., xvi, 67, 70–74, 78, 79, 83, 133, 169
Luther, M., xv, 27, 36, 44–47, 53, 67, 69, 112, 181, 216, 217, 236

Makom, 27, 28, 32
Manheim, K., 177,178
Marquardt, F.-W., 26–28, 281
Marx, K., 41, 43, 44, 47, 68, 71–74, 76, 79, 80, 84, 87–90, 97, 98, 119, 120, 162, 163, 175–77, 206

Massa perditionis, xii, xiii, 37, 40, 198, 210, 230
Mencius, 256, 258, 259, 266–69, 271, 273
Metanoia, 45, 101
Methesis, 11
Mimesis, 4, 13
Ministerium verbi divinis, 237
Minjung, 23, 37, 57, 62
Moltmann, 20–24, 53, 225

Nestorian, xvii, 239–42, 247
Nietzsche, F., 80, 82, 103, 113–17, 120, 153, 163, 215, 283

Odysseus, xvii, 210, 275–85

Pannenberg, W., 224, 225
Panopticon, 108, 109
Paranesis, 42, 47
Parrhēsia, 130, 131, 133, 209, 210, 276
Pathos, 13
Perichoresis, 49
Poesis, 13, 172
Plato, ix, xi, 1–8, 10, 14, 148, 192
Plotinus, 7–10, 16–18
Phronesis, 230

Reification, xvi, 71–74, 78, 84, 95
Ren, 257, 282
Ricci, M., 256, 258, 259, 264, 265, 274
Ricoeur, P., xvi, 133, 165–68, 171–75, 177, 179, 180, 221, 222, 227–29
Ruach, 250

Sanctorum communio, 56
Sapientia experimentalis, 22
Schleiermacher, F., 19, 25, 148, 216, 217
Shang-di, 259
Shekhinah, 27

Simul peccator et justus, 56
Spes naturalis, 51

Theologia crucis, xv, 24, 32–34, 48, 52, 53, 57–59, 61, 65, 210
Theologia providentia, 33
Theologia publica, 21
Theologia viatorum, 58, 65
Theologia vitae, 48, 52, 57, 61
Theosis, 23
Theotokos, 241, 242
Thick description, 235
Tillich, P., 232
Tracy, D., xvii, 212, 226–31
Troeltsch, E., 19, 24–26
Tzu yan, 252, 283

Unio mystica, 8, 9, 23

Via aeterna, 50, 55
Via eminentiae, 228
Via negationis, 228
Viva vox evangelii, 208, 211, 236

Wittgenstein, L., 90, 91, 231, 232
Wang Yangming, xvii, 266–74
Weber, Max, xvi, 67–71, 73, 75–78, 81, 83, 89, 90, 94, 98, 105, 106, 108, 112, 127, 133, 174, 176, 219, 275, 278

Yada, 22, 54

Zhuangzi, ix, 253, 285
Zhu Xi, xvii, 259–64, 266–68, 270, 271, 274